HERALDRY DECORATION AND FLORAL FORMS

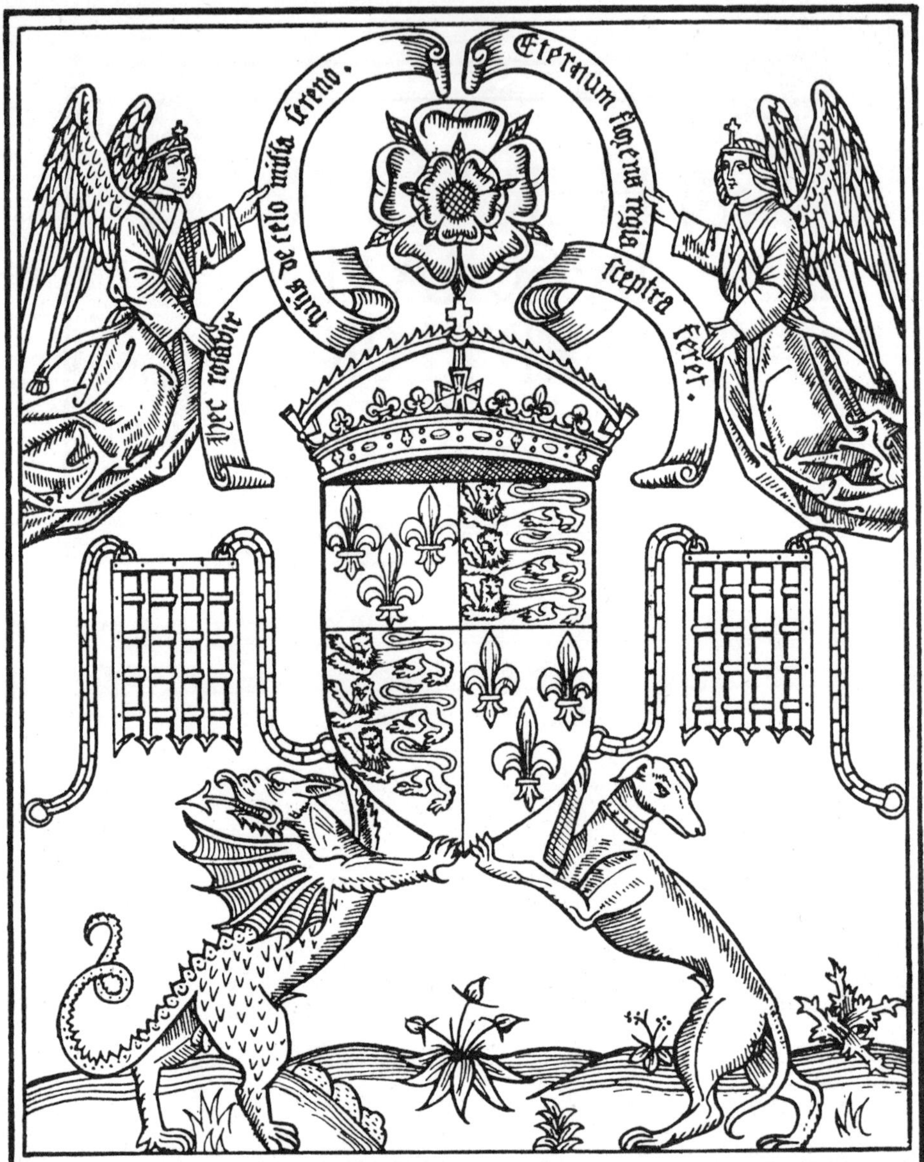

Frontispiece to "England & Wales Parliament" ~ printed in 1543

HERALDRY DECORATION AND FLORAL FORMS

BY HERBERT COLE
WITH DRAWINGS BY
THE AUTHOR

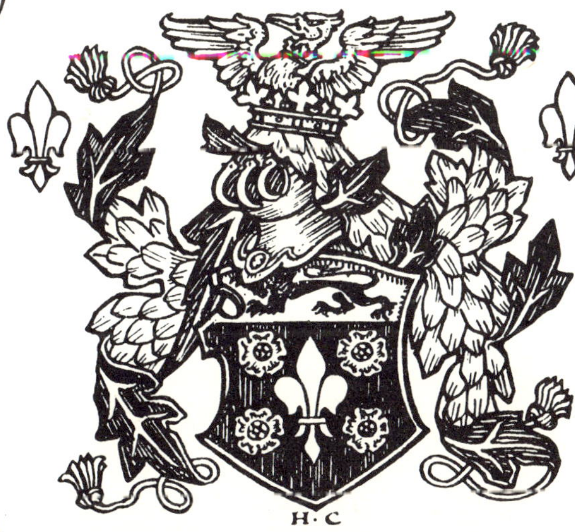

BRACKEN BOOKS
LONDON

This edition published 1988 by Bracken Books
a division of Bestseller Publications Ltd
Princess House, 50 Eastcastle Street
London W1N 7AP, England

ISBN 1 85170 182 6

Printed in the U.S.A.

HERALDRY

HERALDRY
AND ITS USE IN DECORATION

CHAPTER I

HERALDRY! The word is like the sound of a trumpet. It calls up visions of pageantry and state or the pomp and circumstance of mediæval war with blaze of colour and decoration on shield and banner. No wonder that the subject has retained its fascination for the antiquary and the artist, and though to-day it has somewhat changed its function, and though we see it to a large extent in a debased form, it is still of immense interest.

Decorators and designers of nearly every kind are certain at some time or other to come in contact with heraldic decoration or design, and though these chapters are not intended for a technical treatise, the specimens in the illustrations will no doubt lead some of my readers to dive deeper into this historically and artistically interesting subject.

To a large extent the study of heraldry is like learning a language, which, in one sense, it is. It was veritably a method of "picture-writing" which had a definite use in a time when the reading of the written word was not a subject of general education, but a comparatively rare accomplishment.

The old writers on heraldry, enthusiasts in their speciality, went to great pains to prove the antiquity of the art, and no doubt instances can be brought to show that warriors of very remote times placed on their shields or banners symbols and badges by which they were known to their followers or their enemies.

Such were the Roman Eagle and the Raven of the Danes, who raided our coasts in Saxon days. Harold's men fought round the "Dragon" standard of Wessex at the Battle of Hastings, and even the tribes of ancient Israel were grouped under banners which represented the four cardinal points, north, south, east and west, the devices being taken from the Zodiacal signs.

But heraldry, as we know it, only became fully developed about the end of the twelfth and beginning of the thirteenth century. At any rate, it became thoroughly systematised in the reign of Henry III., A.D. 1216–72, and it was the advent of complete body armour which acted as the cause of its development.

When the knight, or leader, was sheathed *cap-à-pie* in chain or plate mail, it became necessary for him to wear on helmet or shield a distinguishing sign by which his men could recognise him and so follow his lead into battle.

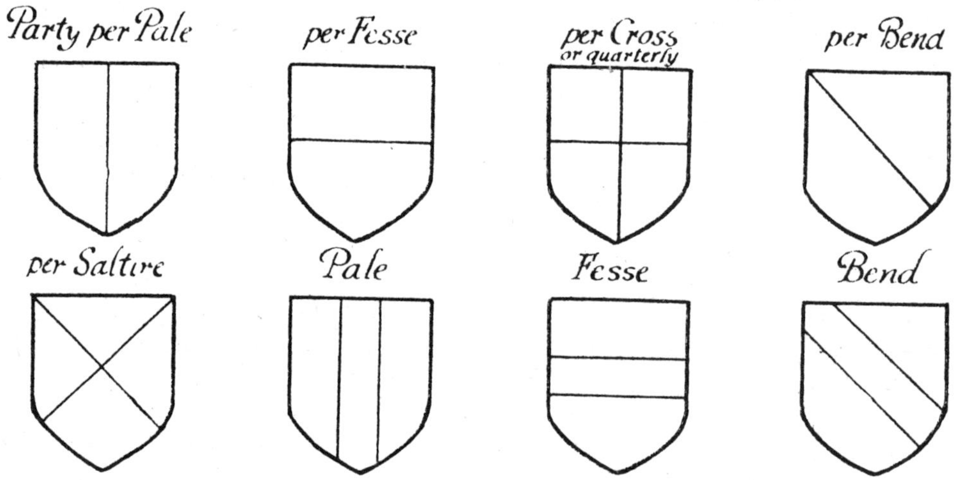

Partition lines

From this it will be easily seen how the granting and bearing of some special device for deeds of bravery or skill in arms arose, and how such favours bestowed by the monarch acted as incentives to heroic rivalry.

A secondary kind of heraldry was designed for the use of retainers and men-at-arms, consisting of badges and cognisances showing to which house or family they belonged.

These devices were generally sewn or embroidered on the sleeve or other portion of their garments, and the fashion survives to this day. The Tudor Rose worked on the coats of the Yeomen of the Guard and Beefeaters of the Tower of London may be mentioned as one existing example of this ancient custom. Other instances will

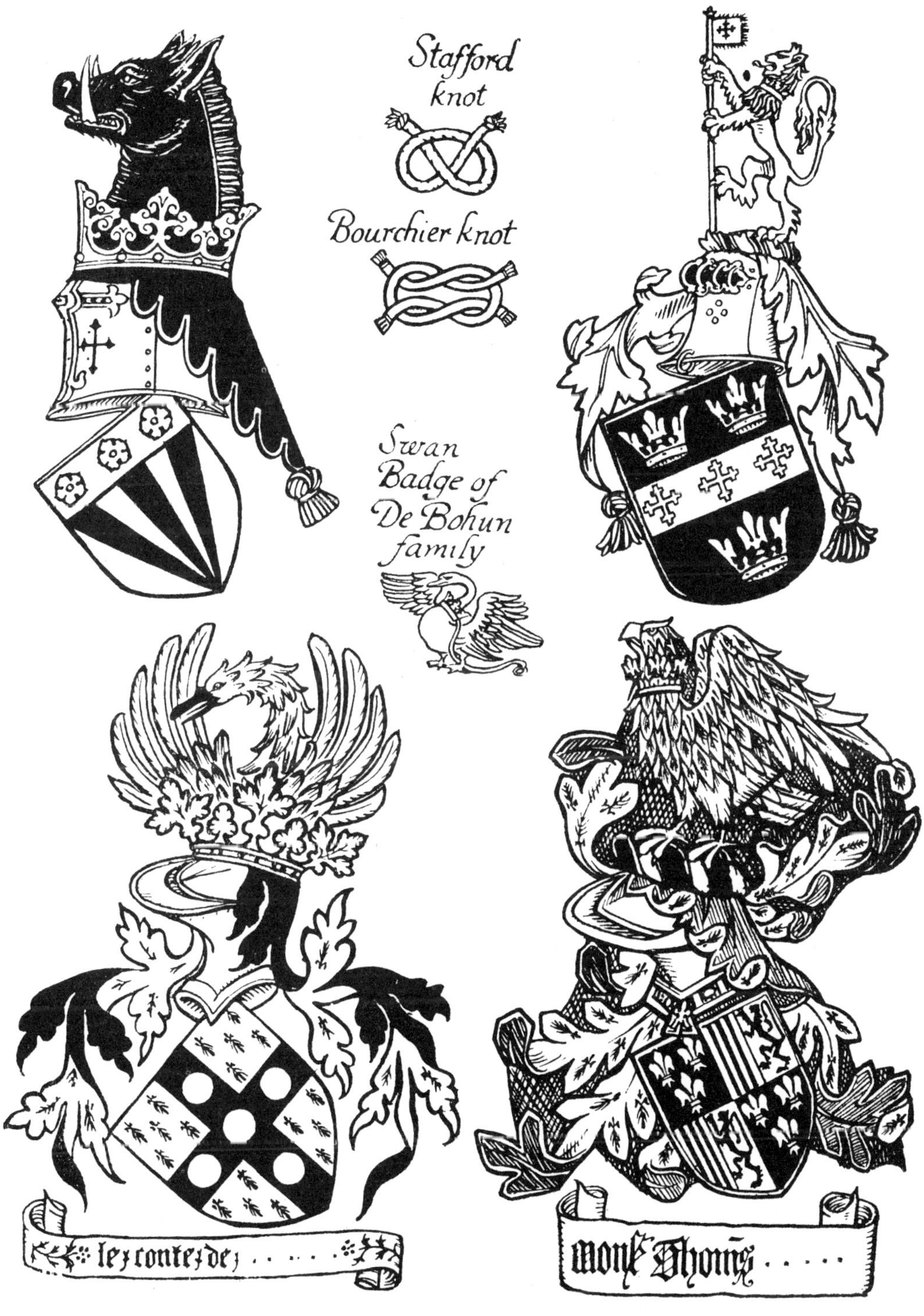

Achievements of Arms

FURS

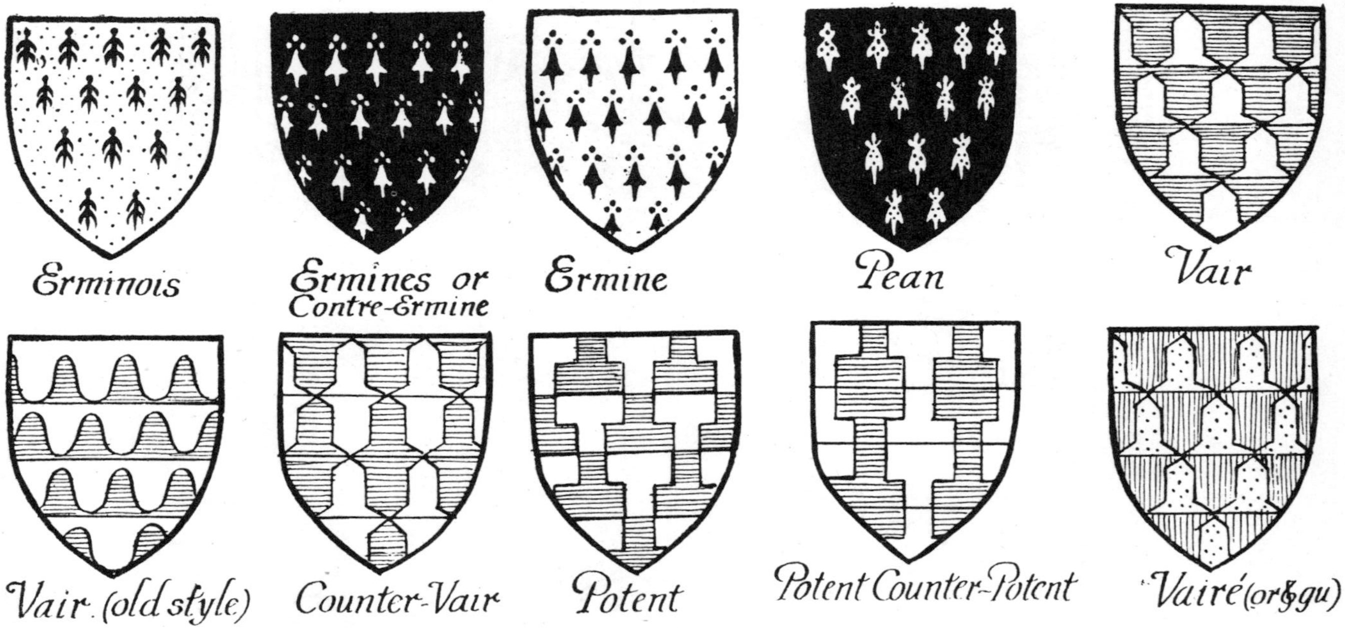

DIVIDING & BORDER LINES

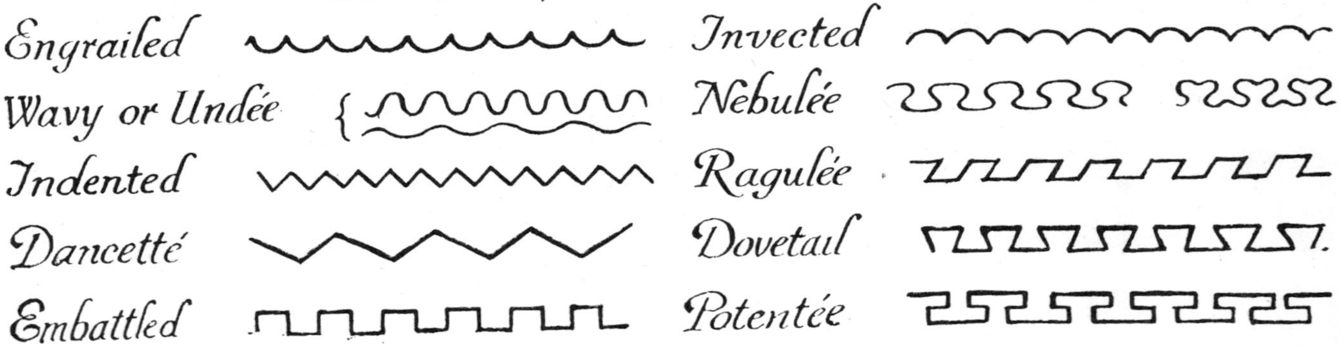

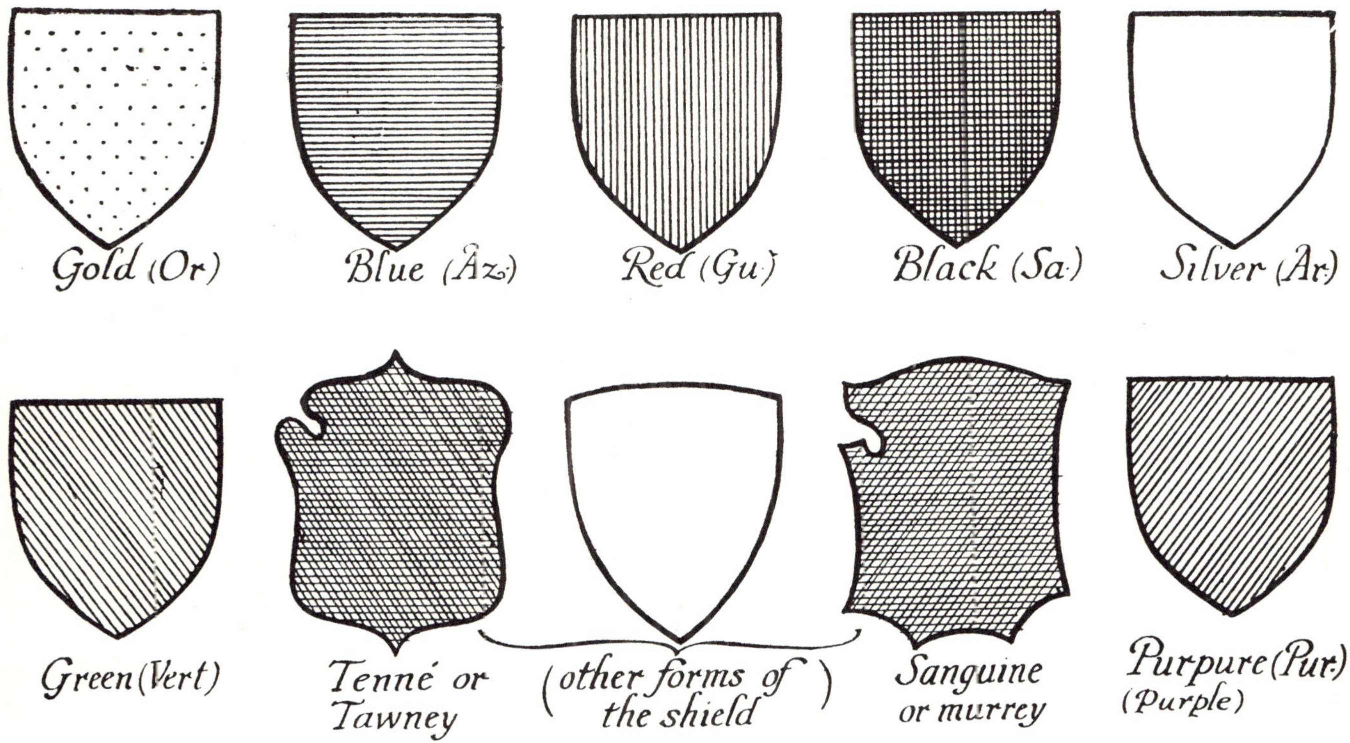

Metals:- Or & Argent : Colours:- Azure, Gules, Sable, Vert, Purpure, (Tenné & Sanguine seldom used.)

TINCTURES

also be readily brought to mind, such as the Prince of Wales's Feathers, the Stafford Knot, the Bear and ragged staff, or the White Hart of Richard II.

We still have the remnants of this system surviving in the names of the inns and hostelries so commonly seen and known throughout the kingdom—The Red Lion, the Rose and Crown, the Chequers,

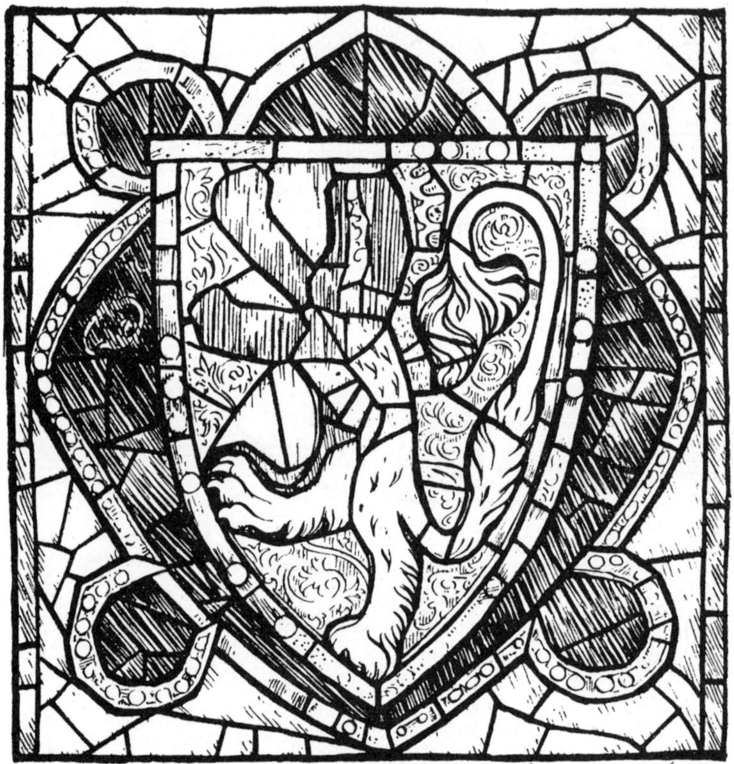

Heraldic glass - York Minster - 13th or early 14th cent.y

the White Hart, the King's Arms, and many another. Almost every country village possesses an inn whose signboard reflects the glory and importance of some local family of distinction, and the list of arms and badges in this connection could be extended indefinitely.

Cities, corporations, guilds and mercantile bodies also had their coats of arms. Seals and coins were and are to this day stamped or engraved with heraldic designs, so there still exists the necessity for a right knowledge of the subject.

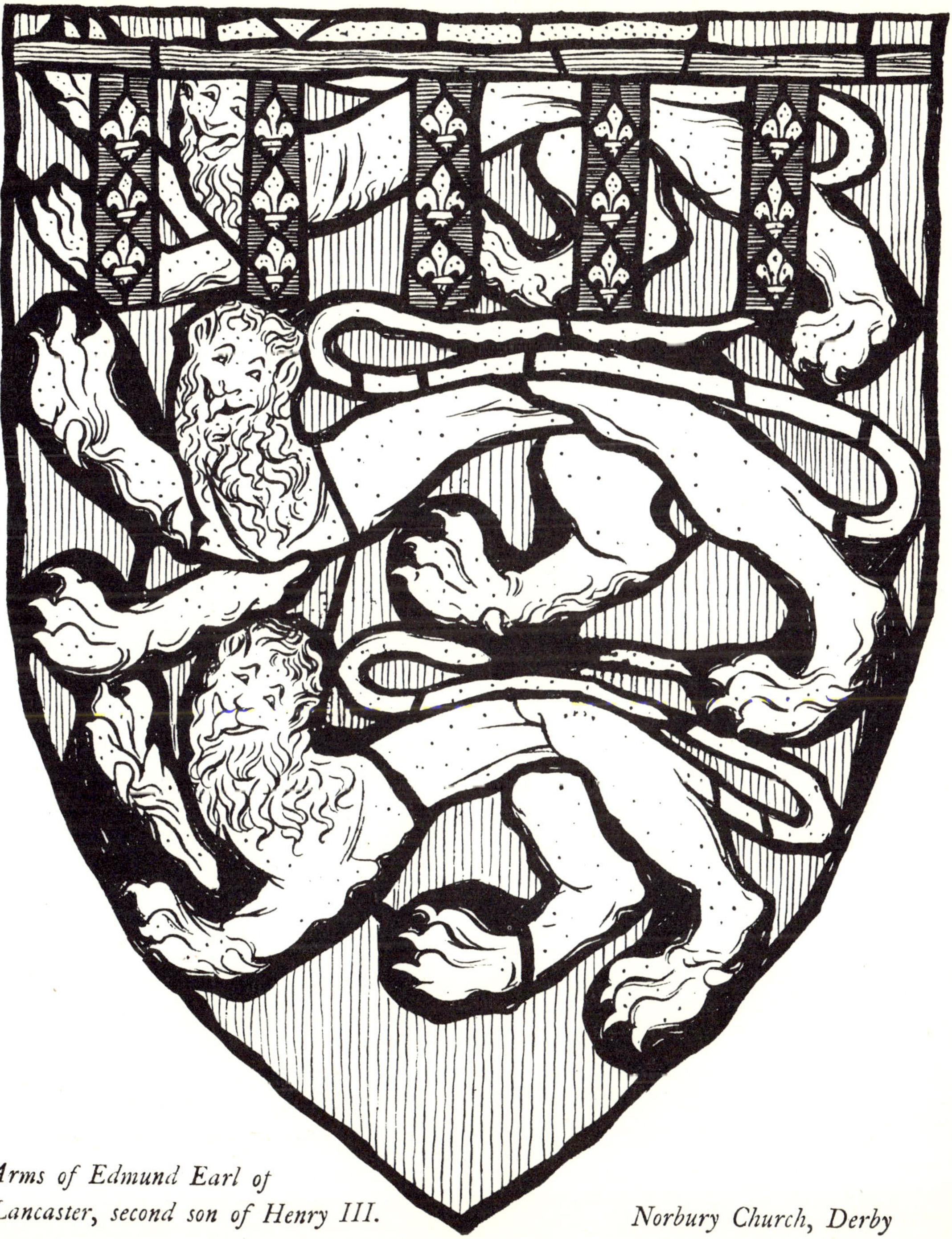

Arms of Edmund Earl of Lancaster, second son of Henry III. *Norbury Church, Derby*

Viewed from the artistic side, it must be admitted that on the whole modern heraldry is still suffering from a period of decadence from which it has not entirely recovered, though great efforts have been made by a few artists and experts to replace it on a more rational basis and to infuse it once more with those true principles of suitability of purpose and rightness of application which should govern good design of all kinds.

To explain my meaning more clearly, let us look back for a moment to the palmy days of the art. When it reached its fullest rational development, it was nothing more than a symbolical language artistically expressed by deliberate conventions of design. In the best period the signs and symbols employed received their forms through a logical process of thought and intention. For instance, a truly heraldic lion of the best phase of heraldry is not a *naturalistic* beast at all. His body is *purposely* attenuated, his claws, tongue and tail purposely *exaggerated,* for the reason that he was thus more easily recognised at a distance, on the field of battle, as a symbol of lion-like strength, courage and ferocity than a close copy by a realistic painter would have been. And in the most admirable period of heraldry, say from Henry III. to Henry VII., we have these essential principles expressed by the mediæval heralds in a manner never since excelled. Indeed, the spontaneity of design and the ease with which they adapted the forms to the given spaces, the skill with which they wielded the brush or graving-tool, remind one irresistibly of the wonderful ability displayed by the Japanese brush draughtsmen, whose work we all admire so much for its beauty and dexterity.

With the rise of purely pictorial art the decay set in.

The herald began to imitate the picture painter, and forgot that his duty was to appeal to the eye by expressive symbols, designed to serve a special purpose, and to-day, with some conspicuous exceptions, the zoological instead of the heraldic type of animal prevails.

The birds and beasts of heraldry have been the subject of skits and jests innumerable, but caricature often emphasises the real truth underlying the thing satirised, and I hope I have given a sufficient and satisfactory reason for the conventions of true heraldic design.

Let us therefore expend our study and admiration upon those examples which best carry out the principles of the art. For my part, I shall endeavour in the illustrations to choose the best types for your emulation and to show that heraldry is by no means a dead art, and though we need not seek to become experts, a slight knowledge of the general principles upon which the art is founded will be of great use towards a clear understanding and the prevention of mistakes.

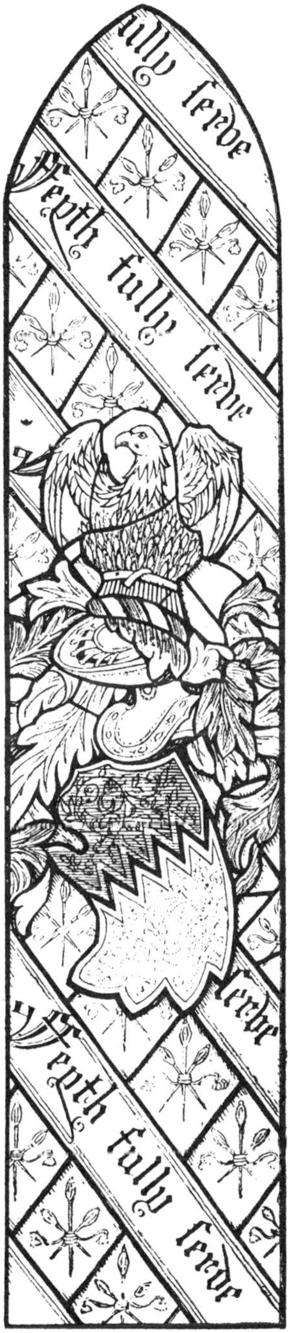

The shield or escutcheon is, of course, the first element, and the base upon which heraldic design is built up, the usual form being so common that it is generally known as "shield shape." But this shape may be varied according to the exigencies of design. The actual form of the shield in battle and tournament changed from time to time, and the heralds followed the fashions besides using their fancy a little now and then. Sometimes, especially as the art grew, the shield assumed a square or oblong plan, but generally had curved sides more or less pronounced.

Another device, called the crest, was worn on the knight's helmet. This was generally in addition to and different from that of the shield. His mantling, *i.e.* the veil of cloth, linen, or silk which hung from his helmet over his shoulders, also became more ornamental as time went on. Embroidered linings, scalloped and foliated edges, patterned badges were added, and a band or coronet secured it immediately beneath the crest. Some say it originated as a protection from the heat of the sun beating on the metal headpiece. Another explanation is that it represents the mantle or cloak of the knight, cut and jagged in battle, and again that it came from the "*contoise,*" a favour or scarf worn in honour of a lady.

However, the grouped composition of shield, helm, crest, and mantling is known as an

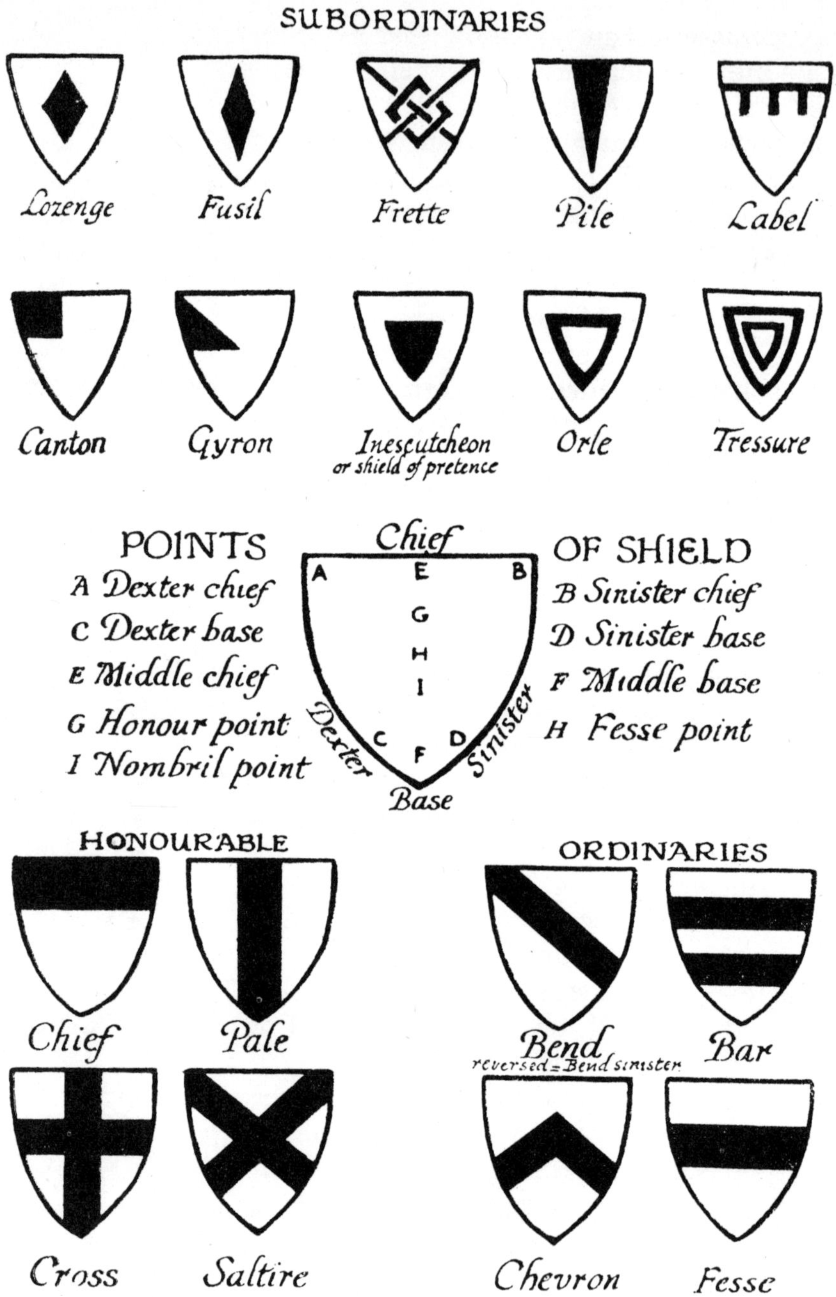
SUBORDINARIES
Lozenge
Fusil
Frette
Pile
Label
Canton
Gyron
Inescutcheon or shield of pretence
Orle
Tressure
POINTS OF SHIELD
A Dexter chief
C Dexter base
E Middle chief
G Honour point
I Nombril point
Chief
A
E
B
G
H
I
C
F
D
Dexter
Sinister
Base
B Sinister chief
D Sinister base
F Middle base
H Fesse point
HONOURABLE ORDINARIES
Chief
Pale
Bend reversed = Bend sinister
Bar
Cross
Saltire
Chevron
Fesse

"achievement of arms"—the word "hatchment" being a corruption of this term.

The diagrams shown in this chapter represent the method used in text-books of indicating the colours by dots and lines. They are only used in black-and-white heraldic drawings; when colour is available they are unnecessary.

The illustrations of achievements of arms are imaginary specimens, but they are derived from old heraldic sources of the best periods. They show that it is neither necessary to draw the mantling like the curly cabbage-leaf stuff so often seen in later work nor to imitate the mechanical repetition of details. Good heraldic designers are now going back to the early work for inspiration.

The lions in the splendid piece of heraldic glass from Norbury Church show the freehand quality enjoyed by the old designers, and the example from York Minster, maimed by restoration though it is, gives us an animal form admirably adapted in design to the shape of the shield.

The panel from Ockwells Manor is one of a lovely series of heraldic windows of the best time. Its colour is mainly blue and gold. I have not employed the "line and dot" method throughout, as it introduces a mechanical and inartistic quality into drawings and the diagrams are chiefly given as aids when books of reference are consulted.

CHAPTER II

THE object of these brief notes on heraldry is two-fold: firstly, to give some examples of heraldic decoration which shall be useful and interesting to the decorator; and, secondly, to supplement these with some diagrams which will help my readers to understand the general principles which govern heraldic design. It is impossible in the space at my disposal to enter fully into all the intricacies of the subject, but I hope to touch on the most important points.

Owing perhaps to a lack of knowledge, heraldic drawing in our time has become too rigid, too stiff, and mechanical. In the days when it was really a living art the craftsmen "wrote it down," so to speak; each one rendering it with the individuality of his own hand. They knew the rules and were therefore not afraid of making mistakes. Consequently their designs have a freedom and spontaneity which arose from close familiarity with their subject. Nowadays a designer having a piece of heraldry to put in his work scarce knows how to begin, or even in copying or enlarging is hampered by the fear of doing something wrong. Moreover, wrong things are very often done when heraldry is employed owing to ignorance of a few simple principles; for it will encourage many to know that a very little study will enable anyone to learn how to avoid mistakes, how to find the meaning of almost any term used in the art, and, above all, to know really good heraldic work when met with.

But before I enter into any description of the illustrations let me give a brief explanation of the diagrams. I shall have to beg you to refer to those in the first chapter in order to commence with clearness.

The ground or surface of the shield, whether of metal, fur, or colour, is called the "*field,*" and anything placed upon it is called a "*charge.*" Certain rules have been made from the beginning of the art with regard to the combination of these elements, the most important of which is that metal must never be placed upon metal, nor colour upon colour. For example, a red cross or other device could be placed upon a gold, silver or fur ground, but not on a black, green or blue ground. Similarly, a gold lion could not be placed upon a silver shield, or *vice versâ*.

The field of the escutcheon or shield contains nine points used by heralds for placing and reference; a glance at the diagram will explain them. (See page 10.) The most useful facts to remember in this respect are that the top of the shield is called the "*chief*," the lower part the "*base*," the middle the "*fesse point*," and the right and left sides the "*dexter*" and "*sinister*" respectively. But it is necessary to

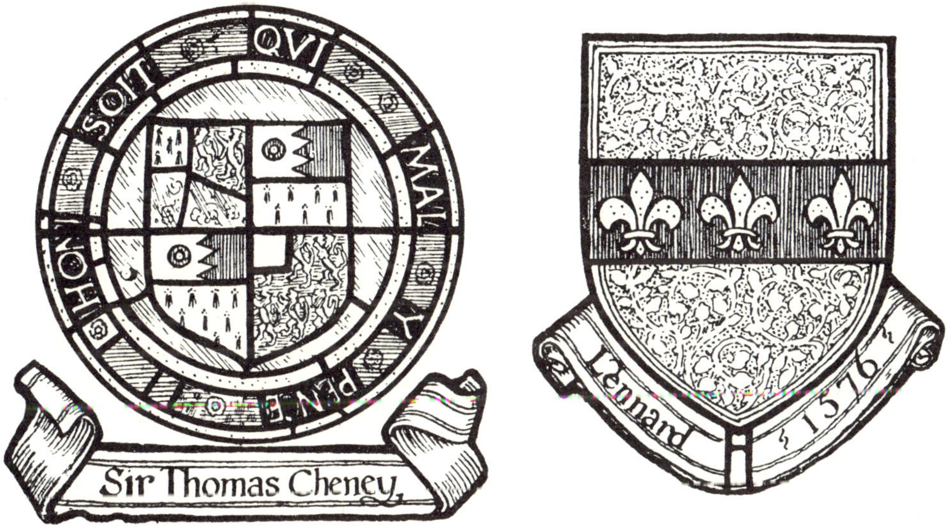

Old heraldic glass from Brasted Church, Kent—15*th and* 16*th century*

add that the words "right" and "left" mean the right and left side of the warrior when the shield is held in front of himself.

Again I must refer you to Chapter I. for examples of partition lines and dividing and border lines. When a shield is divided vertically down the centre it is called "*party*," or parted, "*per pale*"; when divided horizontally across the centre, "*party per fesse*." The other terms explain themselves, or at any rate will do so as we come to other common and general features in heraldry. The dividing and border lines should be carefully examined as they occur frequently both in partitioning the shield and in the edges of charges.

Charges consist of three groups, Honourable Ordinaries, Subordinaries, and common Charges. The first are composed of right lines, and are the simplest result of the divisions of the field. They are known as: chief, pale, bend, bend sinister, fesse, bar, cross, saltire and chevron—nine in all. Eight are given in the diagrams, the bend sinister merely being the bend reversed in direction across the shield.

Here it may be mentioned that modern heralds have made rigid laws that the "chief" or the "fesse" must be exactly one-third of the shield, the bar one-fifth, etc. The old craftsmen did not use a mechanical exactness in this matter, they took it for granted that their proportions would be understood; and such was, of course, the case, their clients being familiar with the language.

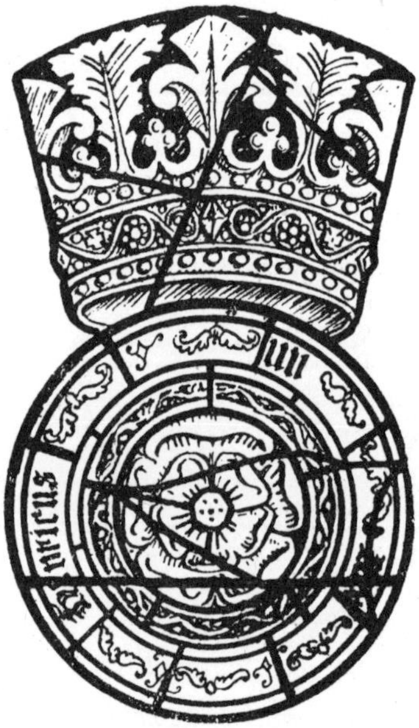

Old heraldic glass from Brasted Church, Kent 14th century

Some of the Ordinaries have two diminutives which follow a definite rule. For instance, a stripe half the width of the pale is called a "pallet" and one-half the width of the pallet is called the "endorse." Half a bend in width is a "bendlet," half the width of the latter a "cost" or "cotice." Half width of the form called chevron is a "chevronel." The remaining forms can be looked up in any heraldic glossary by those who desire to know them. The Subordinaries are, like the Honourable Ordinaries, of ancient use, but, not being formed out of the simplest main divisions of the shield, were not considered quite so important. There are about sixteen of them, and of these I have selected ten as specimens with which to supplement the illustrations. Both these and the Ordinaries can be varied by the decoration of engrailed, dove-tailed, or any of the other lines of like character shown in the diagrams. Also other charges can be superimposed upon them. We shall see examples which contain these features now that we begin to examine our specimens. In the second shield of the old glass from Brasted Church on page 13 we have a fesse gules (red) placed upon a gold field, and on the fesse

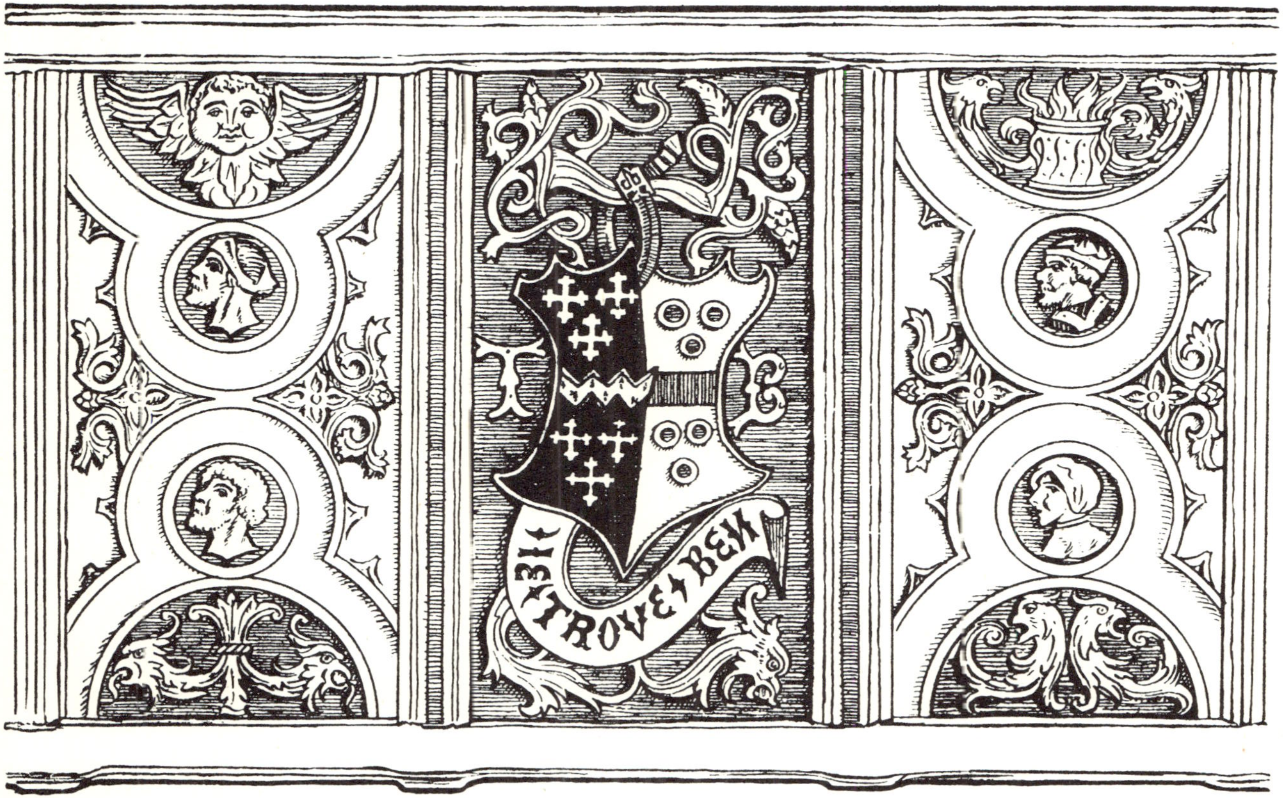

Oak panelling, carved painted & gilt. Arms of Sir Thos. Barnardiston & his wife Anne Lucas 16th c.

are three golden fleurs-de-lis. Here I may draw attention to what appears a contradiction of something before stated. It was given above as a rule that anything placed upon a shield was termed a "charge." It will be observed that the shield of Lennard just noticed is covered with a floral patterning. This is not a charge or heraldic device but is termed "diapering," and it is a specimen of the manner in which the old heralds decorated, for embellishment only, what would otherwise have remained a plain surface. A slight acquaintance with heraldic work enables one to distinguish this surface decoration from anything which has an armorial significance.

The painted oak panelling on page 15 contains two shields in one arranged side by side. This is called "impaling" and the reason will be seen on referring to the diagrams of partition lines. The central charges are a *fesse* in each case, but one is indented, the other plain. The small crosses, again crossed at their ends, are termed "*crosses crosslet,*" singly "*cross crosslet.*" The rings on the other side of the shield are called "*annulets.*" The tincture lines given in this piece will enable the reader to visualise the colouring. On the first half the field is *sable* (black), crosses *argent* (silver), fesse *ermine,* indented, with red border. The second half has a field *argent,* a fesse *gules* (red), and annulets *or* (gold), their centres being *azure* (blue), otherwise they would transgress the heraldic law against metal on metal. The background of the panels is a soft grey blue, the ornamental foliage and grotesques are gilded, the motto red, while the circular bands and ground of the side panels are cream colour with gilt edges. Altogether it makes a rich and effective piece of decoration, both heraldically and otherwise. Also it may be noted in passing that heraldic colours need not be crude and violent in tone, the red need not be vermilion, nor the green raw emerald. So long as the tinctures can be distinctly understood a convenient latitude is allowable in order that the shield and its charges may be brought into harmony with the surrounding colour scheme. This was generally present in the minds of the old craftsmen, but it is too often neglected in our day. The panel in walnut from the old French chimney-piece has the charges of the shield obliterated, a distressing misfortune, as it is a most beautiful example of helm, crest and mantling. It forms part of the same chimney-piece from which the two illustrations of vine foliage are taken in Chapters VIII. and IX. of Floral Forms,

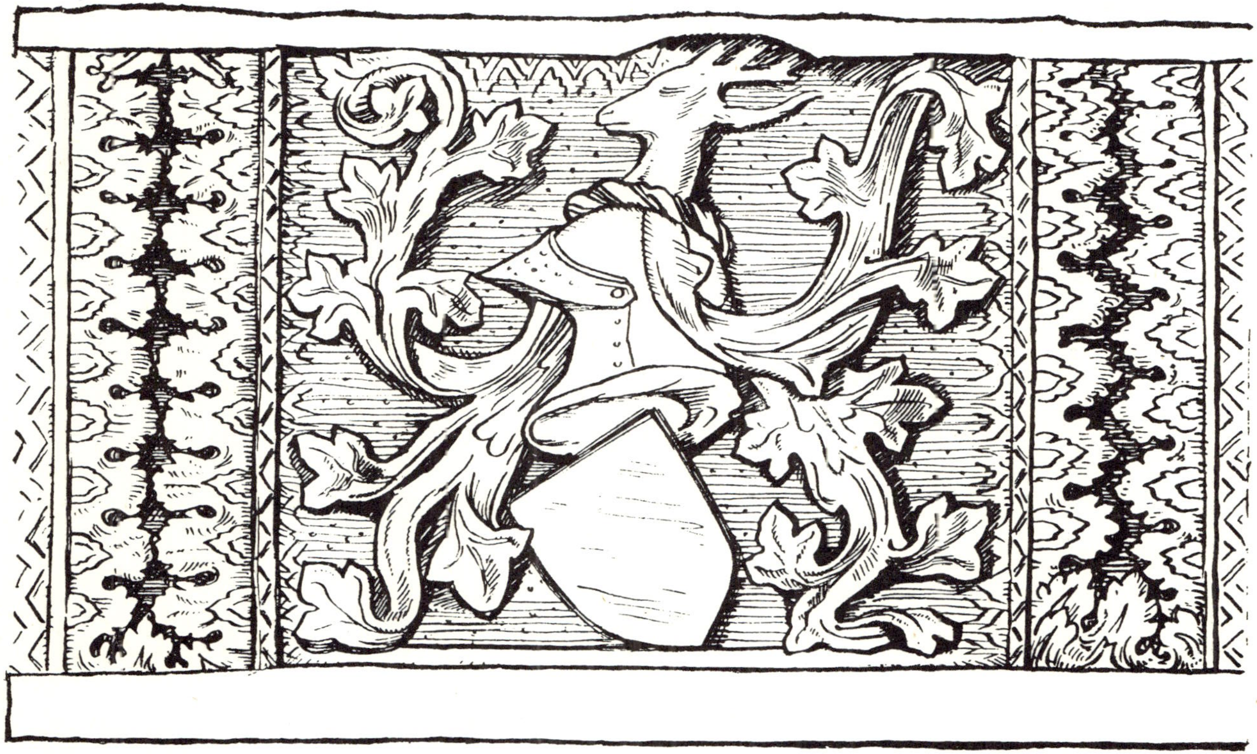

Centre panel from chimney-piece, carved walnut—French, first half 16th century

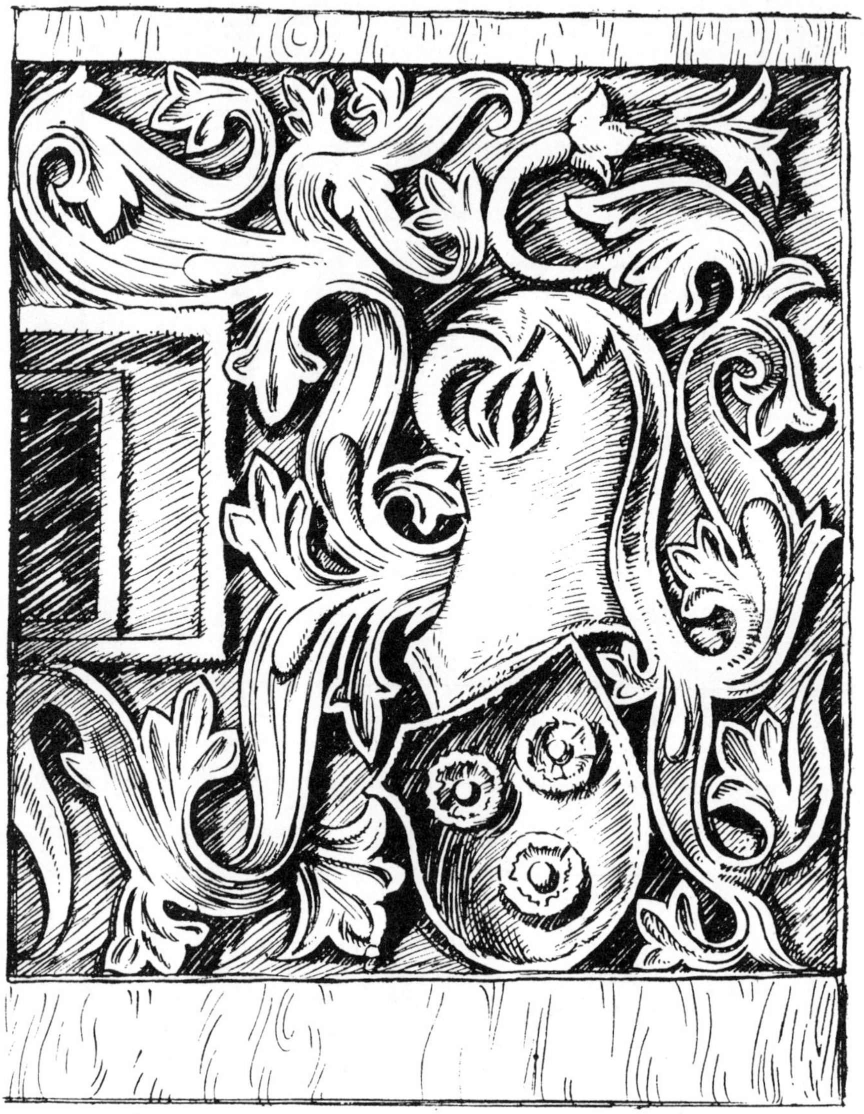

Carved oak cupboard panel ~ German ~15th century

though this centre panel is flanked by two quaint figure subjects, and the vine ornaments come at the ends. The German cupboard panel is a fine armorial space-filling and a vigorous piece of wood-carving to boot.

In the way of heraldic composition the French door-plate would be hard to beat. It contains the crown, sceptre and arms of Henry II. of France with his monogram interlaced with that of his mistress, Diane de Poictiers. This will be seen behind the "dolphin" handle—two D's back to back with the centre bar of the H connecting them. The bows and arrows and the beautiful badge of three intertwined crescents refer to the lady's name, Diana, the moon goddess. Notice the refined proportions in the slightly varied sizes of crown, wreath, handle, and cartouche containing the crescent badge; also the contrast of high and low relief, curved and straight lines, plain and bossy surfaces. Surely no one could pass its beauties by unmoved. Another beautiful crown, and an excellent piece of the glass-painter's craft, is that of Henry IV., "Harry of Bolingbroke, Lancaster and Derby," and in the roundel below his crown the red rose of Lancaster will be found (p. 14). Another very charming heraldic grouping is the pulpit panel of Abbot Jean de la Jaille. The shield is quartered, *i.e.*, divided across the centre by a vertical and a horizontal line. In the first quarter is a lion passant between four escallop shells, three in chief, one in base, these latter being, like the cross, a charge much used by crusaders and pilgrims to the Holy Land. It will be remembered that the escallop shell, staff and bottle formed the pilgrim's travelling outfit, the shell being held out when begging for alms. The second quarter is *barry* or *barrully* of ten, charged with a bend; the third

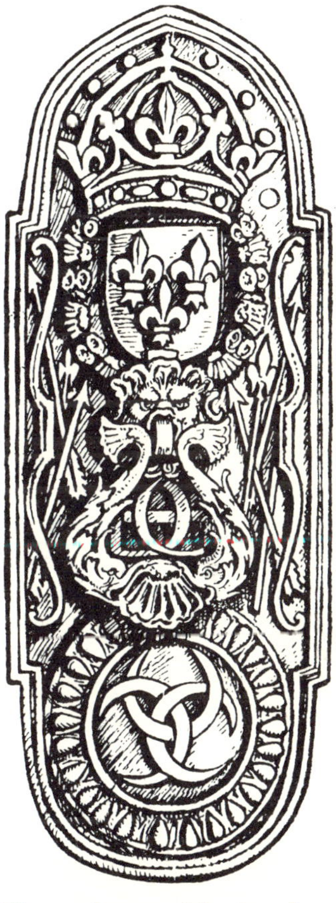

Door-plate, with knocker-handle, in gilt iron
French, middle 16*th century*

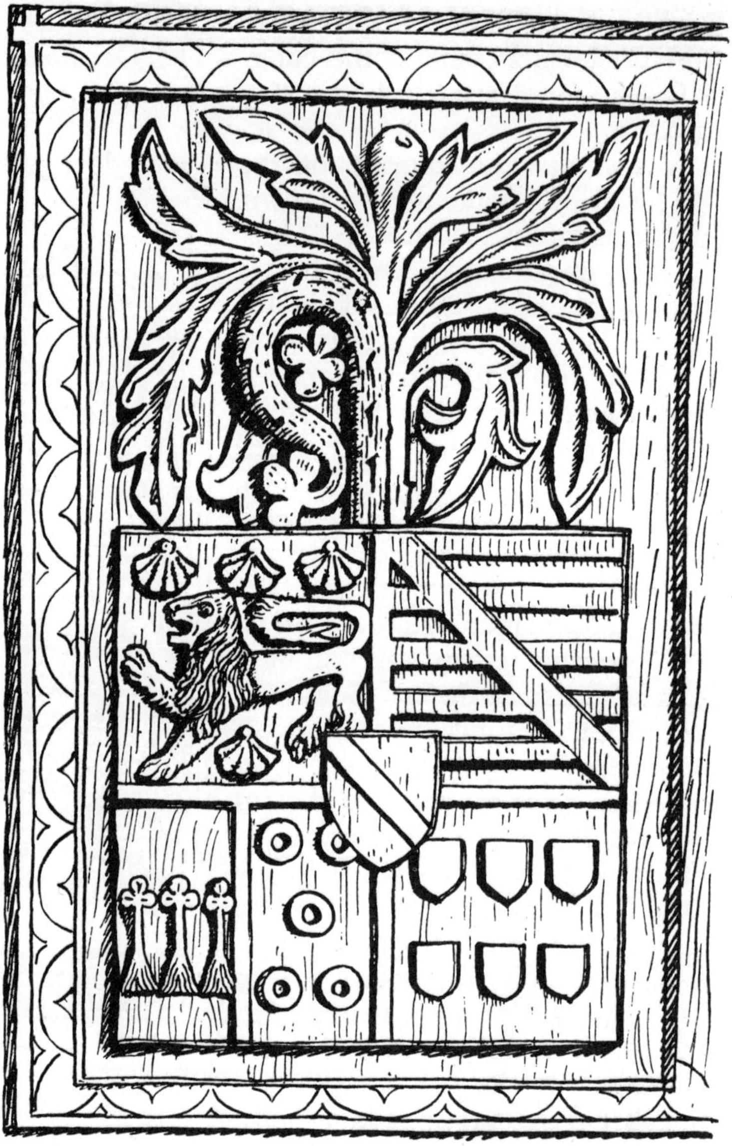

Panel from an oak pulpit ~ Arms of Abbot Jean de la Jaille ~ Cistercian Abbey of Chalocé 1486

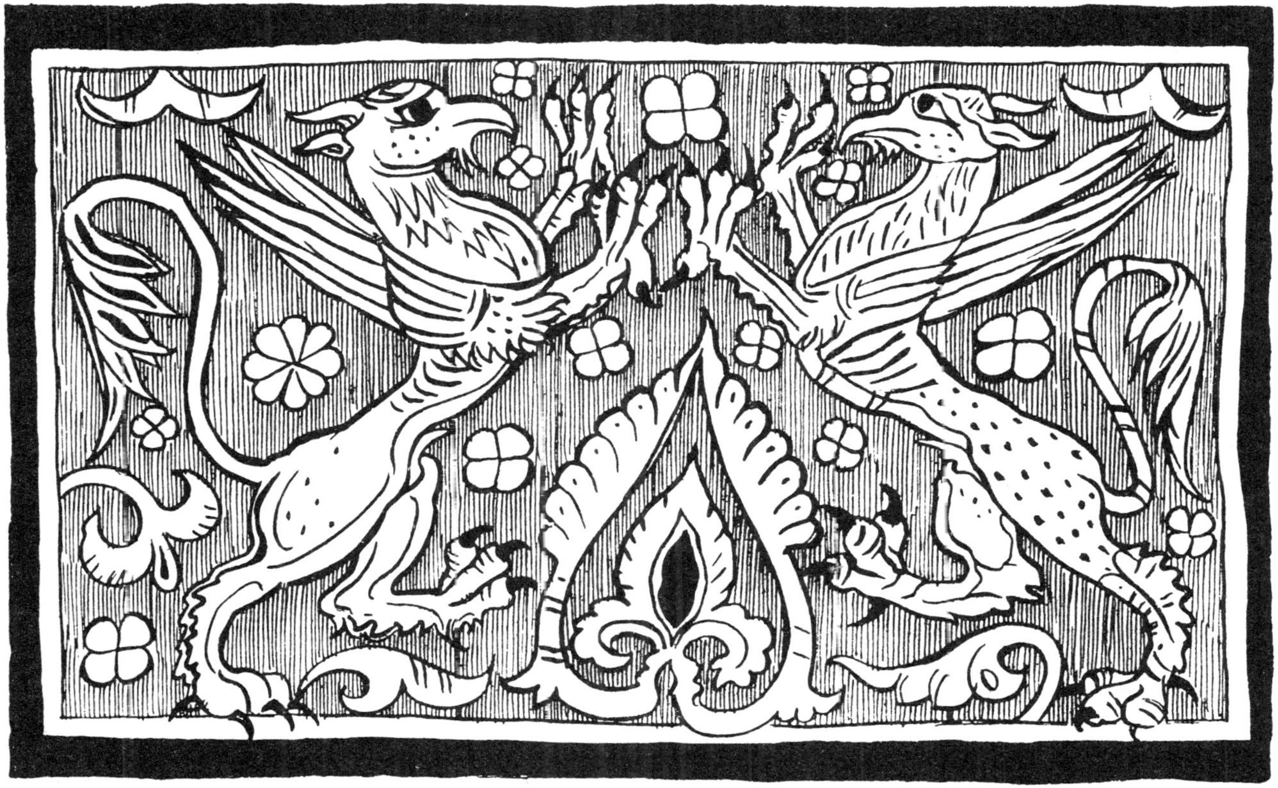

Painted heraldic panel ~ Hispano-Moresque ~ 15th centy.

quarter, three ermine spots impaling with five annulets; and the last quarter is charged with six escutcheons.

The small shield in the centre charged with a bend is called a "*Shield of pretence,*" and in this as in many other instances in heraldry we are brought up against an interesting word-derivation. To "pretend" is really to hold something forward or in front of another thing. We now use the word with something of a hypocritical significance, though we readily recall the "Young Pretender"—one who put forward a claim to the throne. A shield of pretence is therefore generally borne by one who has claims or pretensions to titles or estates—by the husband of an heiress, for instance. Many are the words borrowed from heraldry by writers and poets to give colour and picturesqueness in description, and forceful and magnificently expressive effects are sometimes suggested by the blazonry of a shield.

The foliage growing out of the crook and the bud or fruit sprouting at the top may have reference to the abbot's name—the word *jaillir* in French meaning to burst out, to gush out, or to spring. This sort of punning heraldry was very common in mediæval times and there will be more to say about it later on.

The shield, it will be noticed, is square, which is quite a legitimate liberty to take should the circumstances of decorative design demand it. The panel is not painted, so the heraldic colours cannot in this case be described, but the abbot's crosier and the foliated ornament complete a very beautiful and fascinating decoration.

There only remains the piece of Hispano-Moresque work to bring this chapter to a close. It is a good example of painted heraldry and its splendid griffins so full of nervous line would make a couple of fine supporters to any shield where their presence might be stated in the blazoning. They are dull white with black outline on a red ground, the ornaments which accompany them being a tint of brownish gold.

CHAPTER III

HAD these chapters been intended solely as a treatise on heraldry, I should have confined the illustrations to English examples only for the reason that English heraldry remained simpler, more logical and less fantastic than that of Continental nations.

It is true that much of the work found abroad is very rich and elaborate, but it became complicated at an earlier date than did the science in England. Shields were split up into numerous quarterings and the basic principles of intelligible blazoning began to be overlaid by a desire for display.

Therefore English heraldry is simpler to understand in addition to the fact that it more nearly concerns us as a branch of our own history and national art.

Seeing, however, that our subject is heraldry as used in decoration, we should be debarring ourselves from many fine specimens of heraldic ornament were we to limit our survey to our own country. There is much to learn also in the matter of treatment and fresh outlook from some of the foreign examples, though in some cases their faults are pitfalls of danger to the unwary.

I have drawn examples, therefore, from all sources where heraldry has been effectively and beautifully treated as decoration or in conjunction with decorative schemes.

In the drawing from the French coffer front we have an ingenious piece of heraldic design. The motive is the *fleur-de-lis* from the shield of France. Not only is the form itself presented on the shield in company with a splendid crown, but it is echoed in the details, and the main lines of the decoration are formed from it. Above the shorter of the two panels is a black iron lock-plate with foliated corners, but now in a fragmentary condition, and while regretting that this fine Gothic design has been so ruthlessly handled, one wonders if it was the same Vandal who tore the *fleur-de-lis* from the shield and wreaked his vengeance on the lock-plate also. But we must be thankful for what is left, and if the reader will imagine the continuation of the remaining panels across

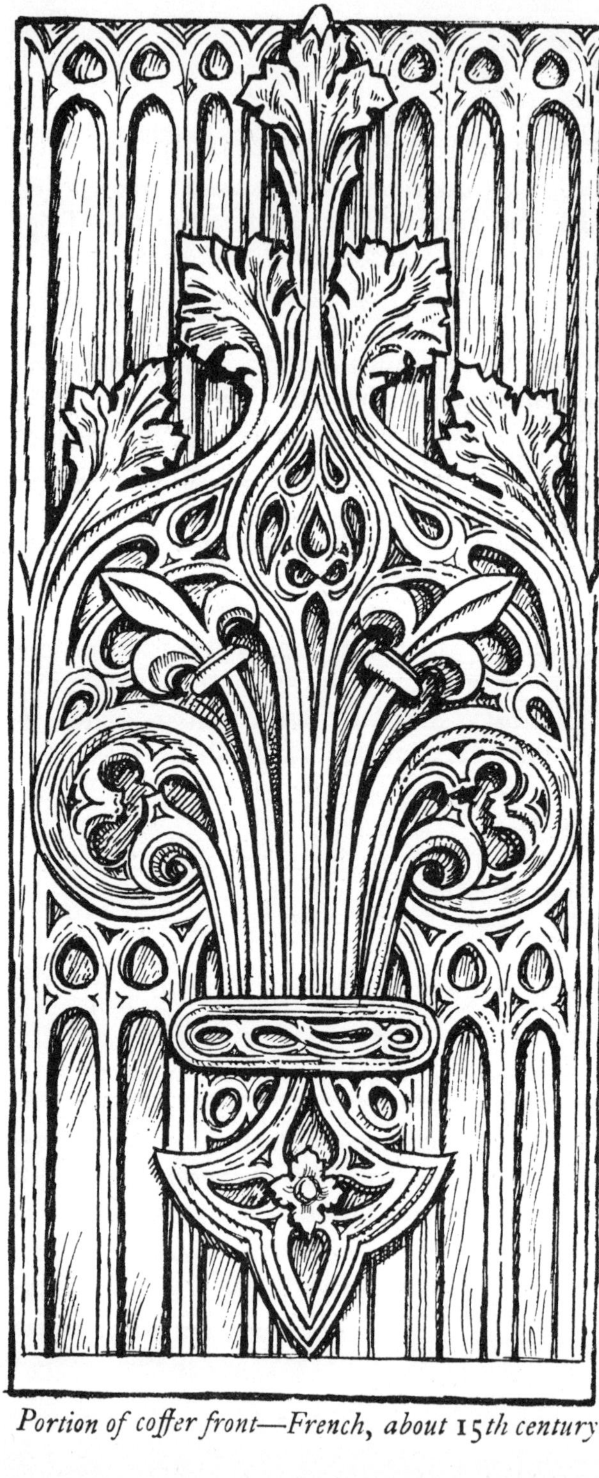

Portion of coffer front—French, about 15*th century*

the front of the coffer, he will realise what richness of effect the heraldic forms and close Gothic panelling combine to present. This piece is supplemented by some explanatory diagrams which are both heraldically and historically interesting. Edward III. laid claim through his descent to the throne of France, and having proceeded to make good the same by invading that country and making himself master of a considerable portion of it, he added, A.D. 1340, the royal arms of France to his own by changing the shield of England as it stood (three golden lions *passant guardant* on a red field) to a shield divided into four quarters, France (golden *fleur-de-lis* on a blue field) in the first and fourth and England in the second and third. It will be noticed that in his shield the number of *fleurs-de-lis* is greater than that in the shield of Henry IV., where there are but three. In the first instance the flowers are powdered or sown over the field like seeds strewn on the ground, called for this reason "*semée*" of *fleurs-de-lis,* the word in French meaning "seed-sown." About 1365 Charles V. of France reduced the thickly-strewn flowers to the number of three, and Henry IV. followed suit in those quarters of England's shield which still represented the claim of the English monarch to the French throne. James I. altered the arrangement of the shield by bringing in the arms of Scotland and Ireland, but it was not till 1801 that the *fleurs-de-lis* of France were removed from the royal arms.

The first shield of France, *semée* of *fleurs-de-lis,* is therefore referred to in heraldry as "France ancient," and the later one with only three flowers as "France modern," but it must be noted that it has no connection with the modern French Republic, but was the shield of the

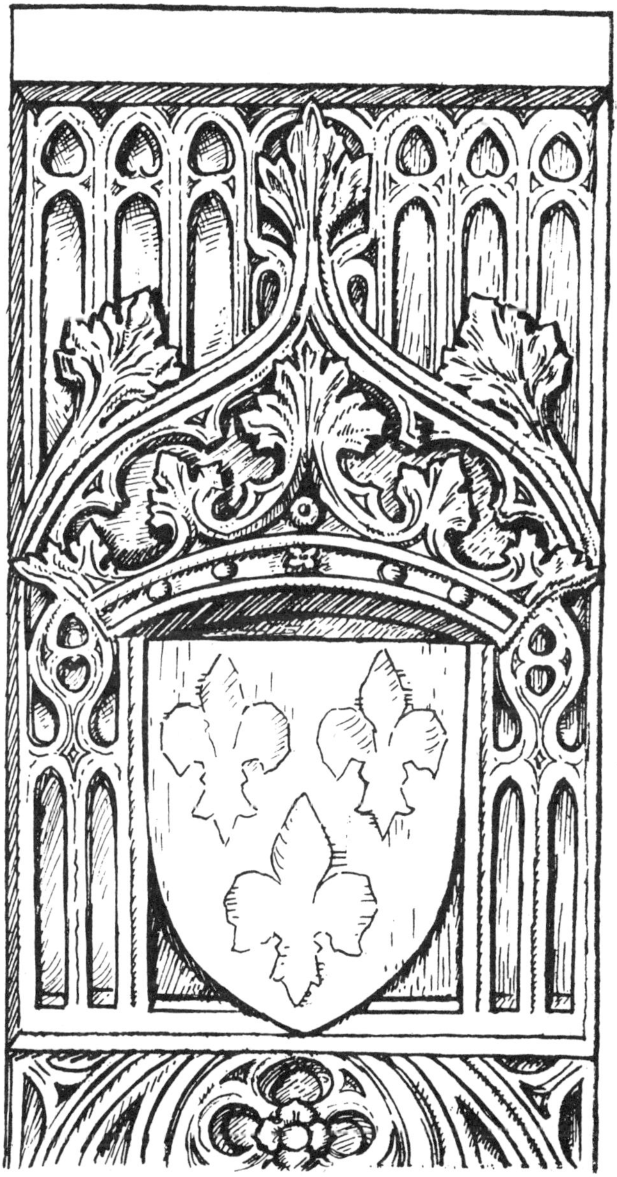

Portion of coffer front in carved walnut, showing ornament of heraldic design—French, about 15th century

Portion of coffer front—French, about 15th century

Bourbon Kings of France. The *fleur-de-lis* is a beautiful form in itself, and many were the varieties of treatment bestowed on it by the old heralds and craftsmen. In looking at old specimens of work in which it occurs, the student will notice how "freehand" the heraldic drawing was in those days; the flowers were not mechanically repeated, but each one "drawn afresh," thus giving a variety of expression and interest all over the shield.[1]

Its use will be noticed also in the carved wood column, also of French workmanship, in combination with other heraldic details, such as ermine spots, rosettes, mullets (star shapes), and escallop shell, a splendid example of rich heraldic decoration.

The mantel-pieces from Tattersall Castle are well known to heralds and antiquarians as beautiful examples of heraldry combined with figure and floral ornament. Indeed, one could not pick better examples of the differing

France "ancient" borne up to 1365

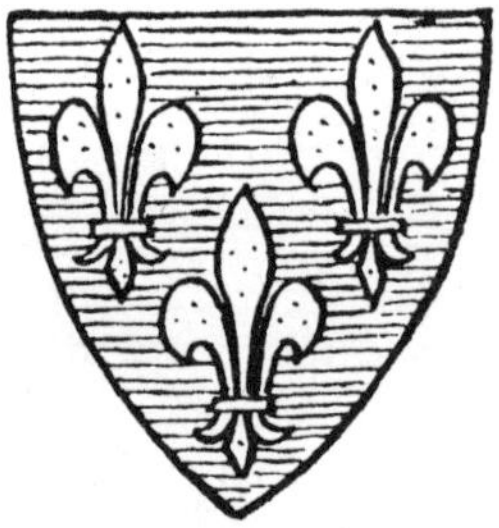

France "modern" borne after 1365.

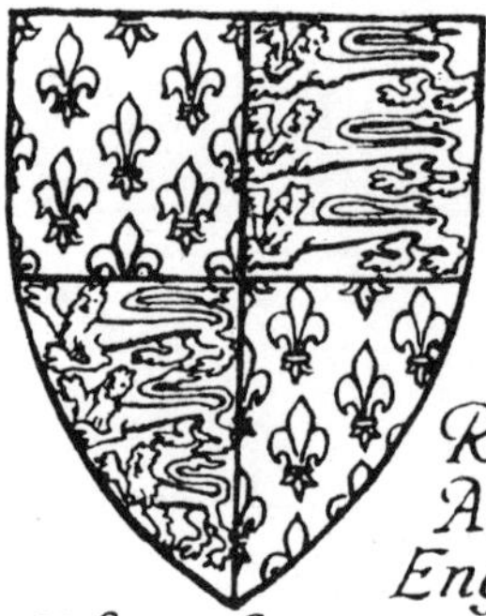

Edward III (1340) to Henry IV

Royal Arms of England

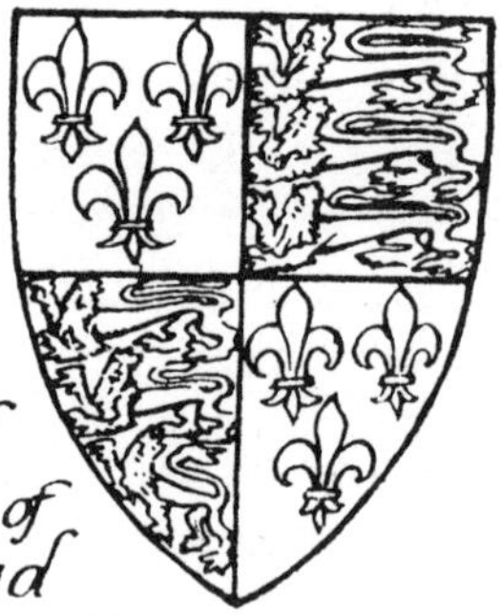

from Henry IV to Elizabeth 1603.

[1] Further examples of the *fleur-de-lis* will be found in Chapter XI. of Floral Forms, pp. 222 *et seq.*

values or reciprocal values and contrasts lent to each other by floral ornament and heraldic design in combination. Each acts as an effective foil to the other. Tattersall Castle was built by Ralph, Lord Cromwell, about 1433-55, and among the armorial decorations of the mantel-pieces will be noticed a treasurer's purse, beautifully displayed among finely designed plant forms. The motto "*Nay le droit*" is carved in Gothic lettering in these panels, but this being old French, I am at a loss to translate the word "*Nay,*" spelt in one or two places "*Naye.*" While on the subject of old French, we can also look at the two printers' devices of nearly the same date. On the shield of Michel Lenoir an incomplete monogram serves as an armorial charge. Though not an orthodox example of blazonry, the whole design is heraldically conceived, in fact, very finely so, and it will be noticed that we have here again an instance of that punning heraldry referred to in our last chapter. "*Noir*" signifying "black" in French. the designer has forced his meaning upon us by the vigorous dabs of black dispersed throughout the design as intentional accents of the owner's name. The negro crest, the negress supporters, the lettering and the field of the escutcheon are all black. The monogram is "*M. le*" only and the background is left to supply the missing word "*noir.*" The other device is more strictly armorial—the fine griffins, the beautifully drawn rose tree on which the shield hangs, the richly spotted texture of the background, the single note of black in the chevron which carries the colour of the surrounding motto into the interior, and the little ornaments of the border which "counter-change" or borrow and pay back interest in the centre, all show the skilled hand of the accomplished decorator.

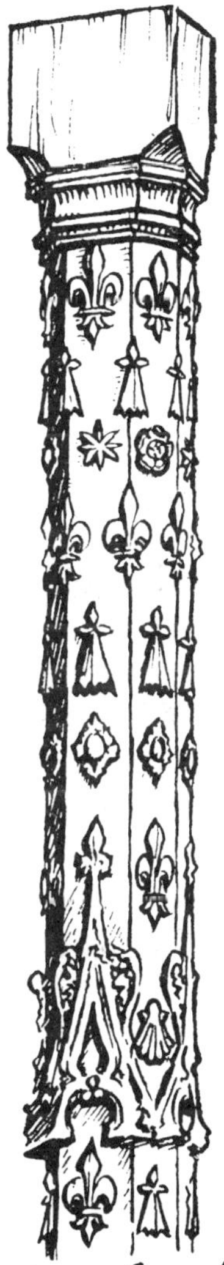
Carved wood column ~ French c.1500.

The motto "*A l'aventure tout vient à point qui peut attendre*" is the equivalent of our proverb, "Everything comes to him who waits." When I get into old French I am out of my depth as I have already confessed, but I really think this

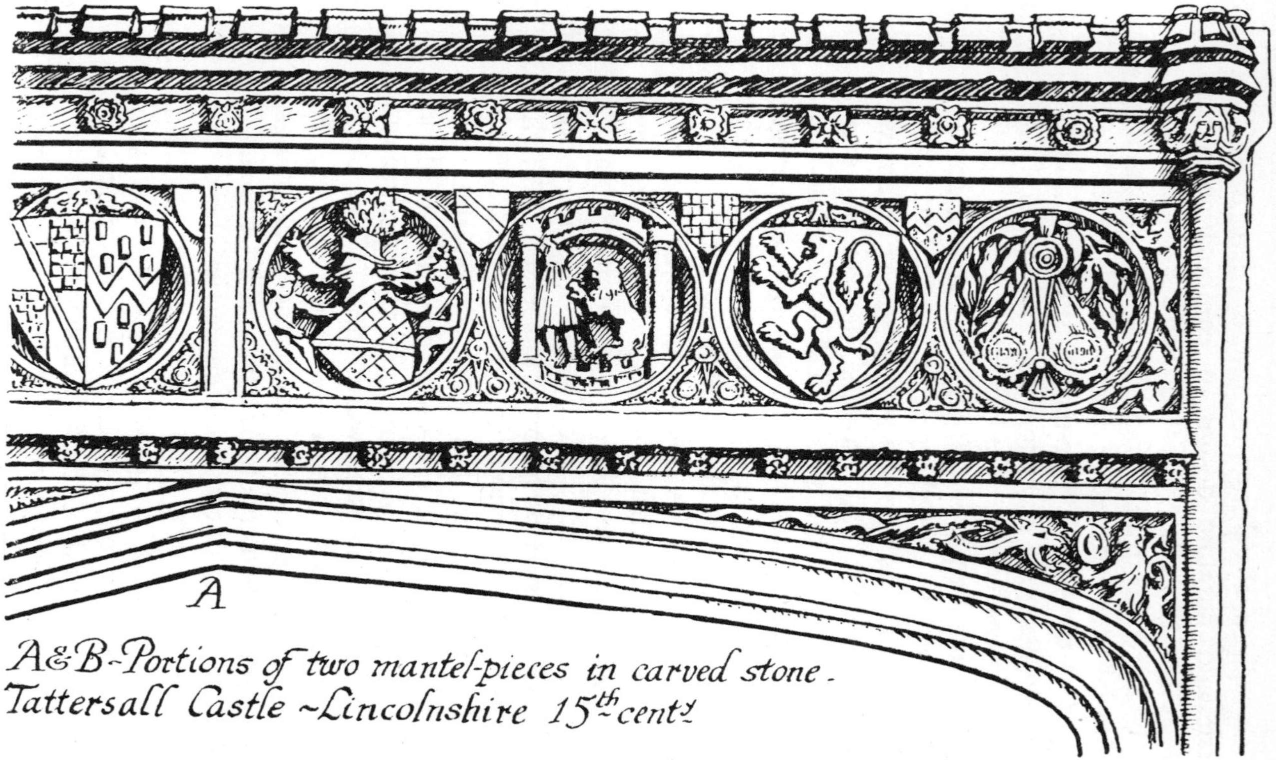

A & B - Portions of two mantel-pieces in carved stone -
Tattersall Castle ~ Lincolnshire 15th cent.

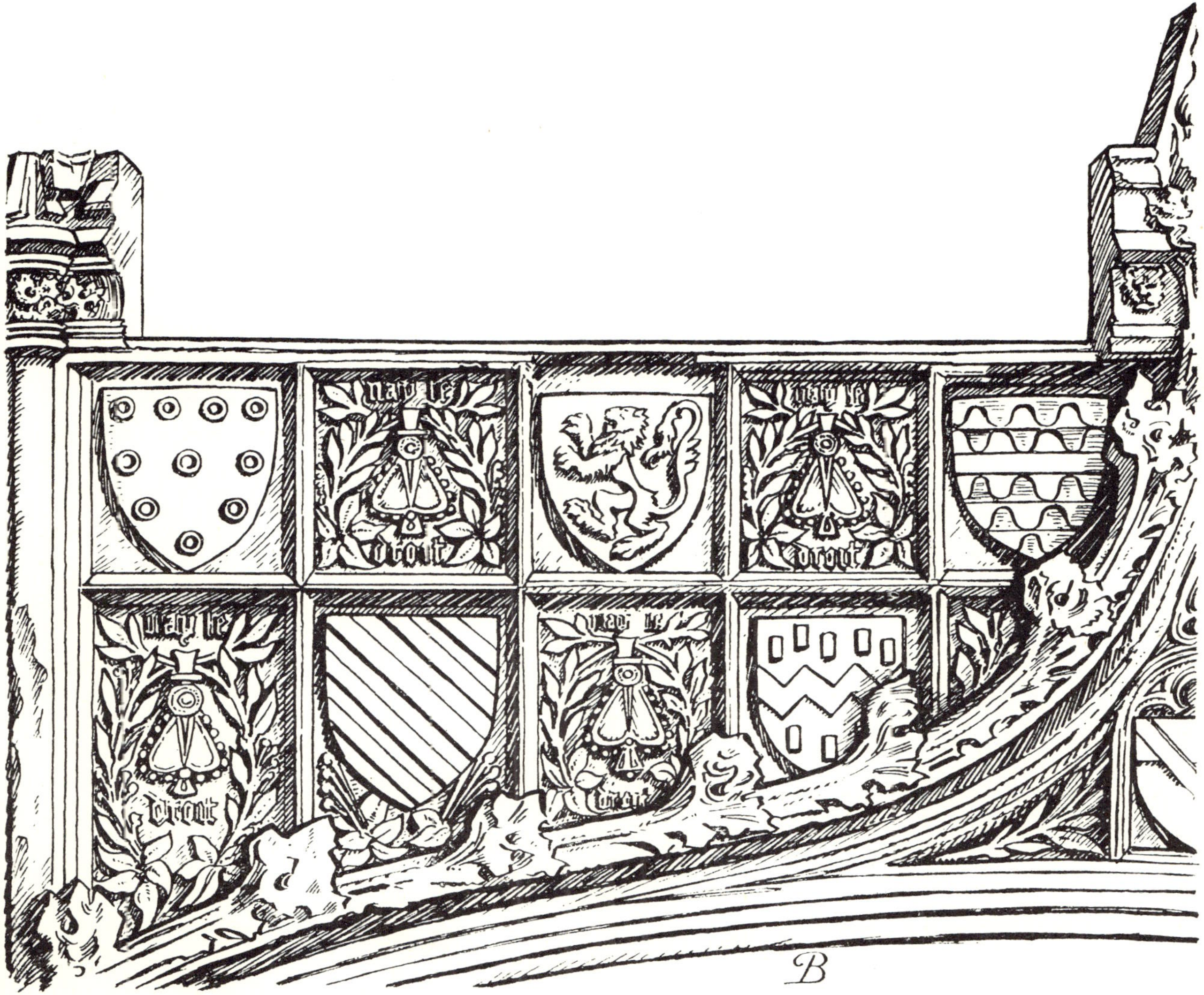

B

time the engraver misspelt the words "*à point*" and "*attendre*," probably through engraving the letters backwards, which, of course, was necessary on the block, or perhaps because spelling in those days was left very much to the whim, capacity, or taste of the individual.

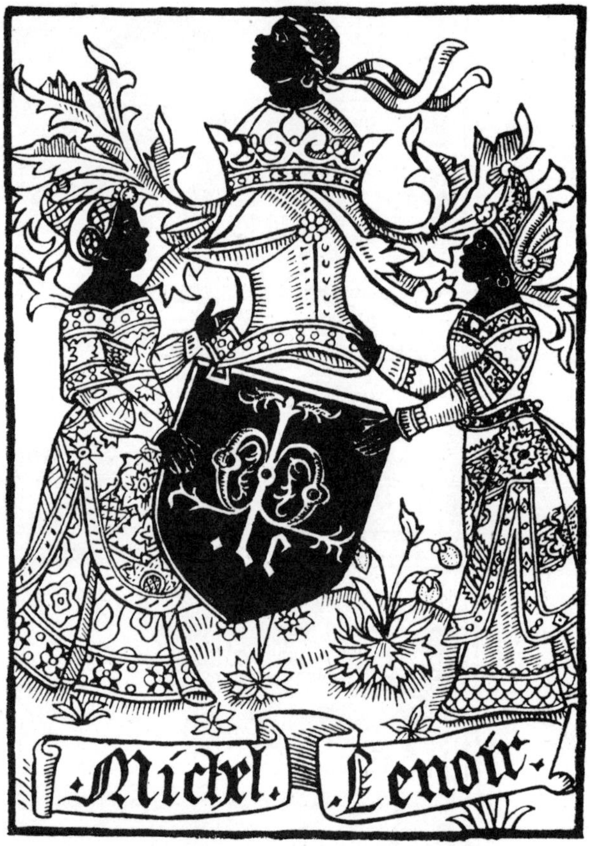

Printer's device—French, late 15th century

When we think that these two beautiful designs are merely what we should now call trade-marks, it fills us with wonder that every common thing in those days seemed to be the object of artistic care and attention. These designs were used as imprints or colophons for the title-pages or end-papers of books.

In the brass salver of German workmanship, dated 1539, we have another piece of good foreign heraldic ornament. Not strictly symmetrical, but balanced with satisfying proportion and variety of details, its life and freshness, its vital line and enjoyment in performance, hand down to us of a later day the pleasure felt in his work by a craftsman of three and a half centuries ago —a human document which can be clearly read and enjoyed by those of another time.

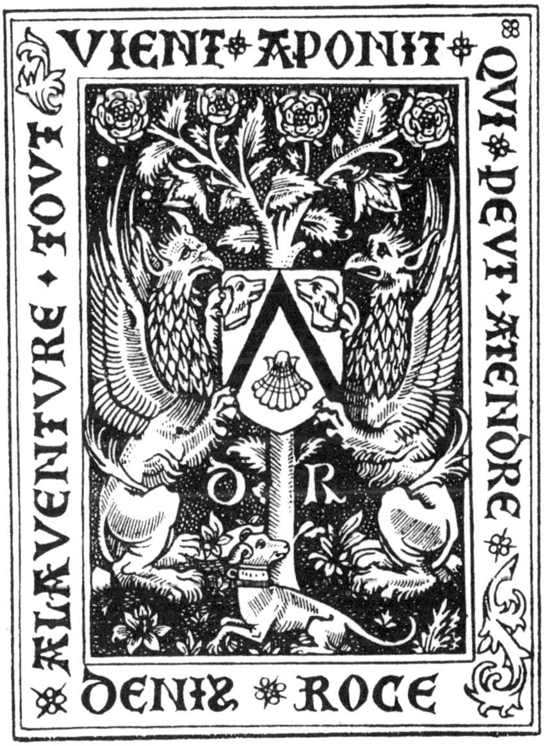

Printer's device—French, late 15*th century*

A few diagrams are added for the use of those who are interested in heraldry for its own sake. The roundels of metal or colour shown on p. 33 occur frequently in coats of arms. The colours and metals can be distinguished by the tincture lines. The one called "fountain" is composed of alternate blue and white wavy bands. The two metal roundels are always represented flat, the coloured ones often shaded in a globular form. Fountains were sometimes called "Sykes"— Bezant is so named from a gold coin of Byzantium, with which no

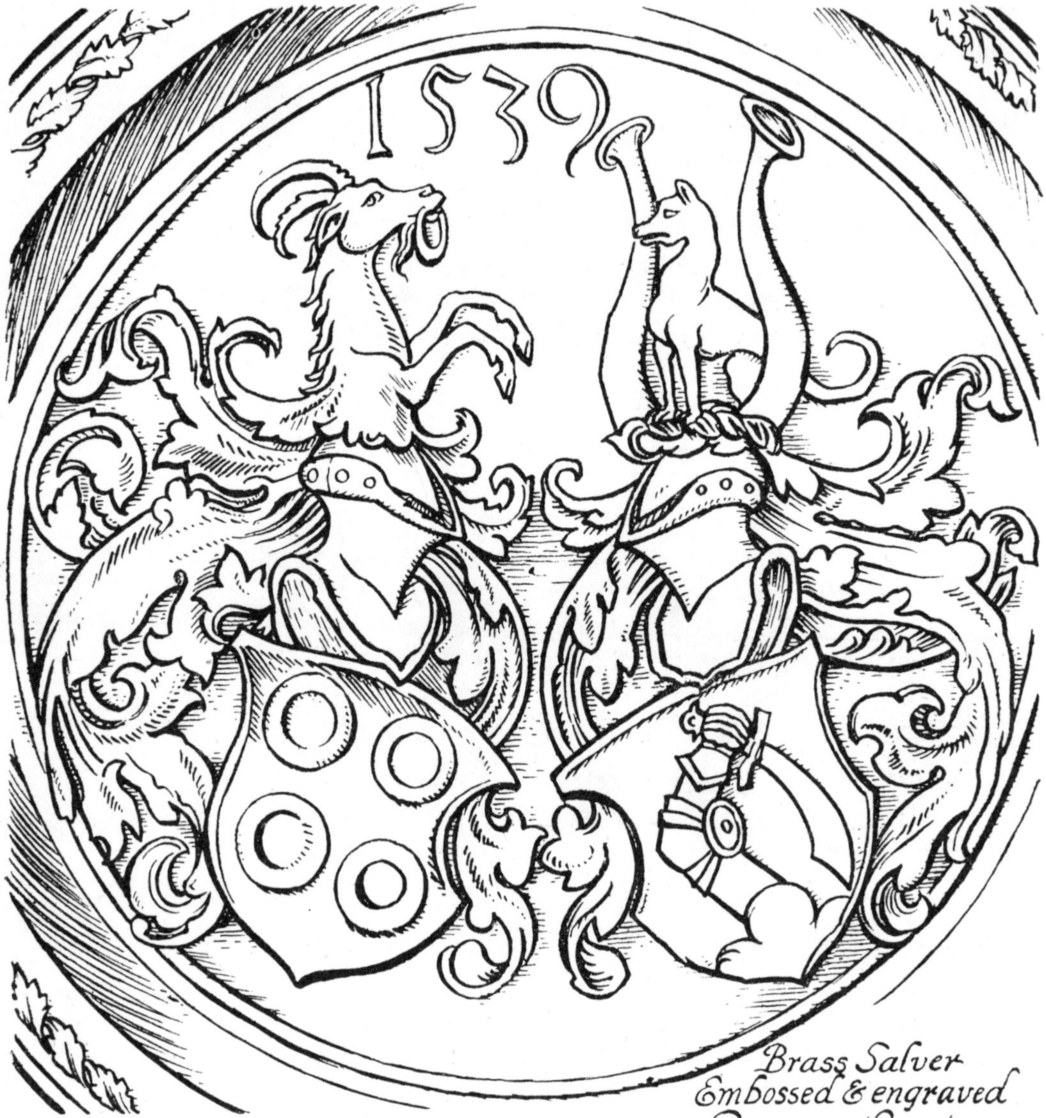

Brass Salver
Embossed & engraved
German ~ 16 centy.

doubt the Crusaders became acquainted. Bold is he who would assert himself on the philological derivation of surnames, but, to make a guess "*à l'aventure*," may not some of the names which survive to this day be of heraldic significance? Fountain, Cross, Sykes, Barry, Barralet (barrulet), Talbot (a sort of hunting dog used in crests and charges), Besant, Griffin and others may remain as names of the bearers of such devices, though their claims to the possession of arms may have been lost long ago.

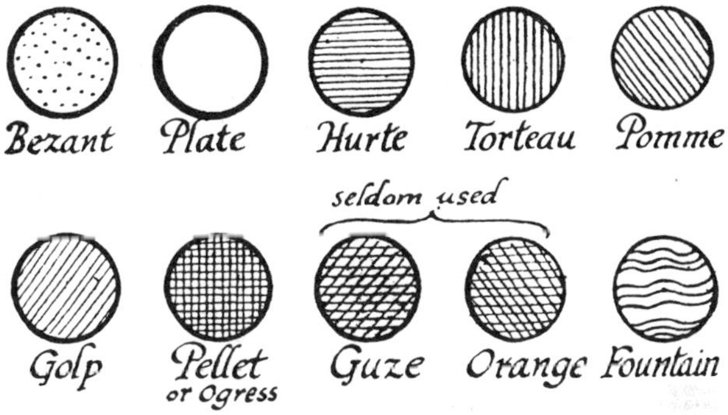

ROUNDELS

The cross raguly or *ragulée* and the bend engrailed show how the usual plain charges are sometimes varied by the ornamental lines given in Chapter I., p. 4. It must be remembered, however, that

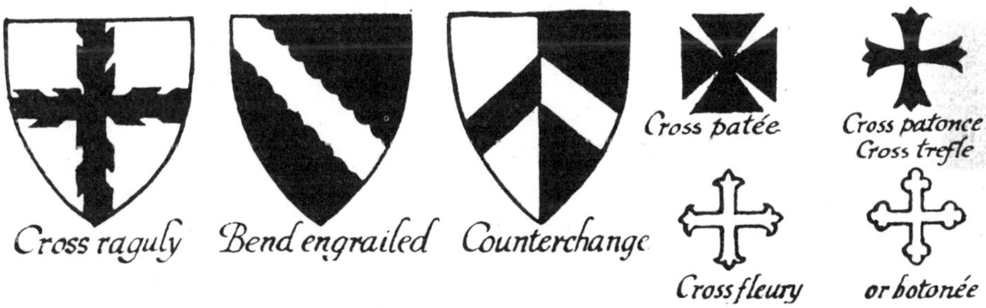

these additions are an essential part of heraldic language and must only be used when stated. "Counter-change" is described as a reciprocal exchange of metal for colour, or *vice versa*, either in the same composition or the same charge.

There are in heraldry many forms of the cross, and a few diagrams are here given of some frequently recurring shapes.

CHAPTER IV

IT has been shown both by reference to history and to examples that heraldry was essentially a Gothic art; that is to say, its best period corresponded to that of the finest Gothic architecture and to that high average of mediæval craftsmanship for which those times are justly famous. The Renaissance did nothing to improve the art of heraldry, and, speaking generally, a decline is noticeable after the new style, the re-birth of classical forms, obtained a footing in our country.

The Renaissance, with its increased knowledge of figure and animal, and other natural forms, introduced a more imitative treatment, which acted to the detriment of that forceful style of heraldic symbolism which the Gothic craftsmen had developed in their draughtsmanship.

Yet it would be unfair to the Renaissance artists to say no heraldic work of merit was produced by them. The sculptured arms of Cardinal Wolsey, from Hampton Court Palace, are a case in point. The design is rich and beautiful, the skill of execution superb, and the architectural setting altogether admirable. Harmony of line is accompanied by most interesting variety of massing and perfect finish. It was probably the work of some highly-skilled Italian artist, brought over by the great Cardinal, to assist in the decoration of his luxurious palace, in the same way that Torrigiano was employed in the previous reign by Henry VII., whose tomb, wrought by that fierce Italian, is still to be seen in Westminster Abbey—another fine piece of Renaissance sculpture with heraldic detail. It will be noticed that the Cardinal's hat takes the place of a helmet, for, with the arms of ecclesiastics, an abbot's, bishop's or archbishop's mitre is generally used to surmount the shield. This, however, is not invariably the case. On seals and other objects the armorial bearings of churchmen are sometimes displayed with the warrior's helm in place of the mitre, and in a few rare instances a combination of both has been found.

Returning to Gothic work for the moment, the piece of German heraldic sculpture from the monument of Count Johan Adelman retains much of the old spirit, in spite of the somewhat late period

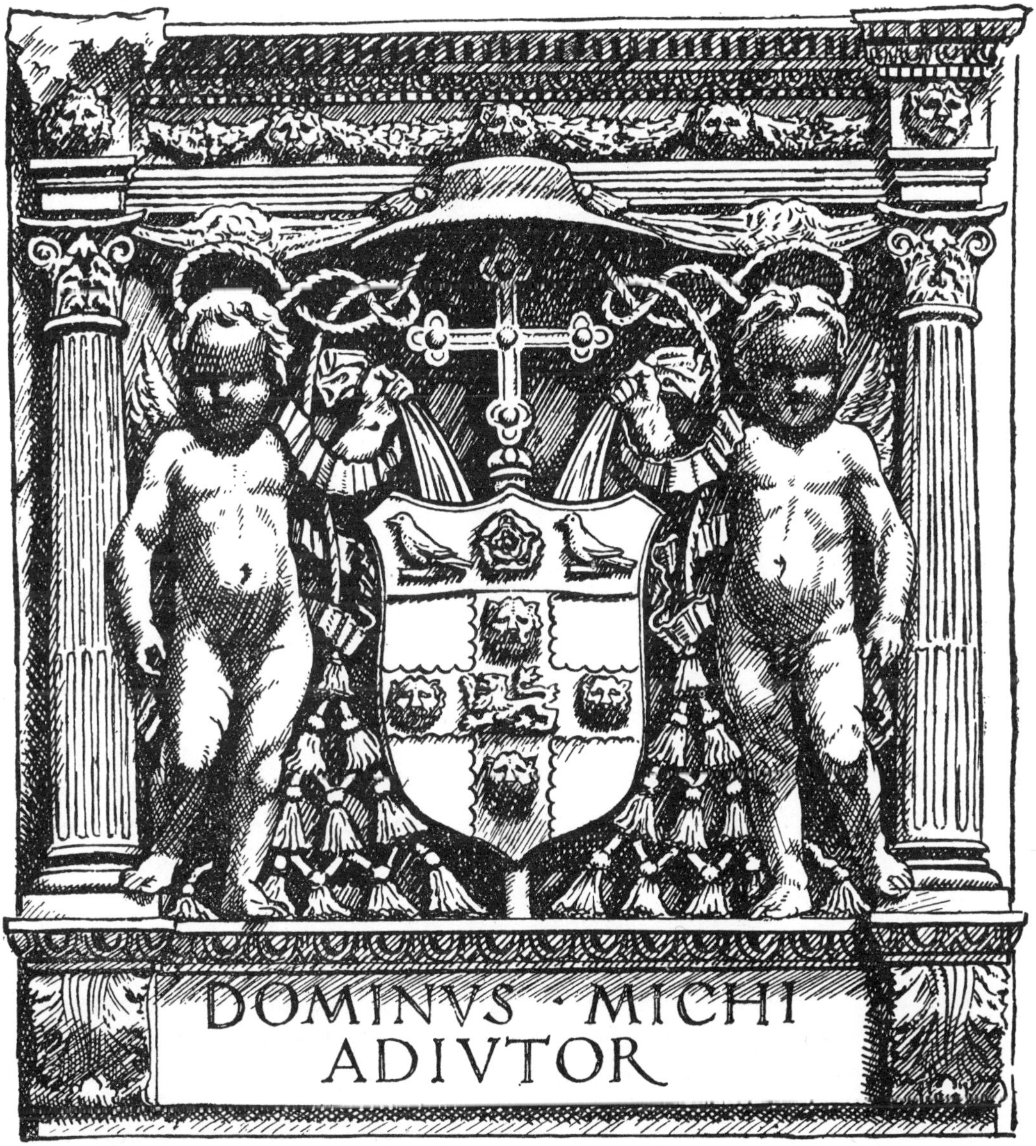

rms of Cardinal Wolsey ~ Carved stone - Hampton Court Palace ~

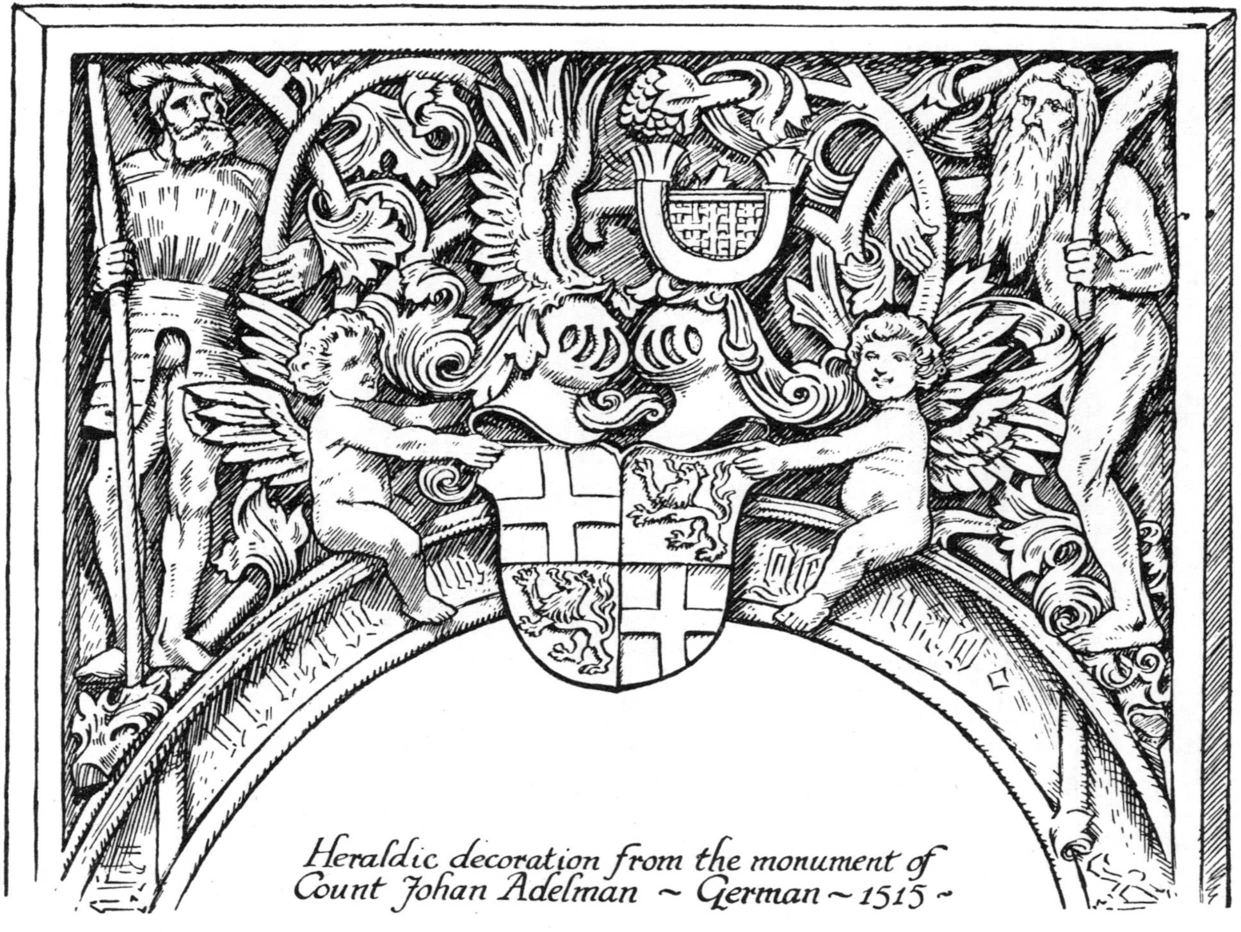

Heraldic decoration from the monument of
Count Johan Adelman ~ German ~ 1515 ~

of its execution. There is a child-like inconsequence of design about it which pleases by its unfettered, though somewhat wayward invention. The ornament, if a little crude, is vigorous, in fact, the whole

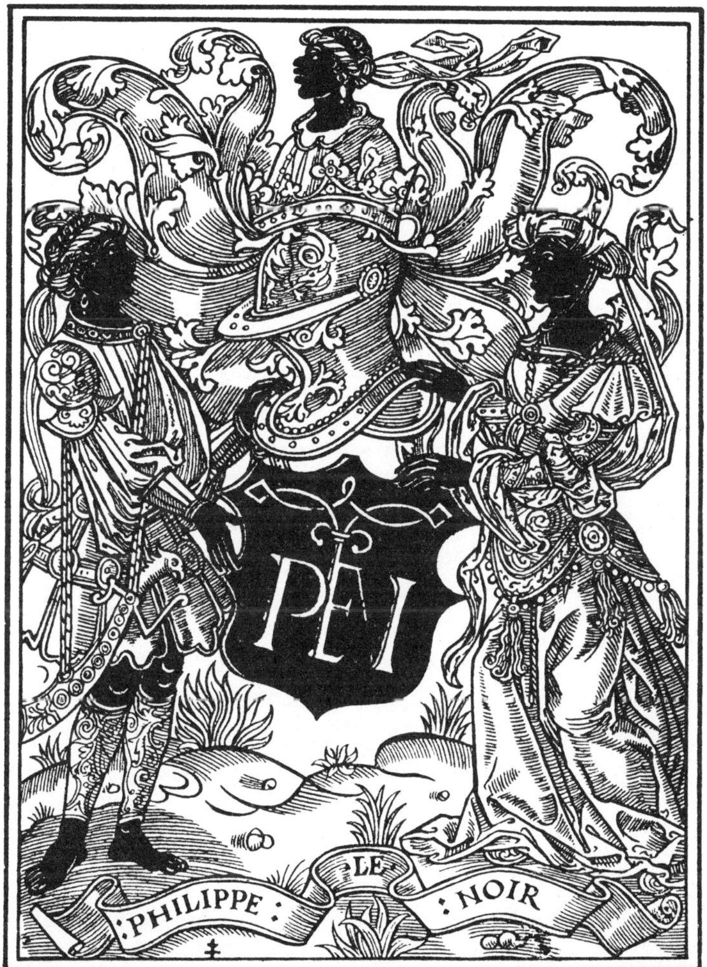

Printer's Device ~ French - about 1530 ~

composition is strong and masculine in quality. The shield, helms and crests, are typically German, and the cheerful cherubim who act as supporters are more remarkable for physical development than for ascetic spirituality; this, however, does not detract from their value as highly decorative adjuncts to the general effect. [Cupids, amorini, *putti*, as the Italians call them, and winged angels in flowing draperies, were of common use in the heraldry of old times, as "*unauthorised*" supporters, so to speak. Usually the real supporters of a shield were a part of the blazonry of a coat of arms, and could only be used by the legal possessors of the same; but the use of a cherub, cupid or angel, was common and carried no heraldic meaning with it. Like diapering on shield surfaces, they formed merely an ornamental feature. Not so, however, was the case with lions, stags, griffins, dragons, and other animals or birds, real and fabulous; they, as supporters of the shield, formed part of the particular owner's coat-armour. On the dexter side of this German monument a sort of *lanzknecht* figure is shown, and on the sinister side a savage man. The latter type occurs frequently in heraldry, both ancient and modern, often wreathed round head and loins with oak leaves. Supporters probably arose in the first place from decorative necessity—an achievement of arms placed in a circular seal, for instance, seems to call for some support at each side of the shield, and it is likely that some animal or bird in the charges was repeated on the outside dexter and sinister spaces to serve this purpose, and afterwards became inseparable from the complete group of armorial bearings.

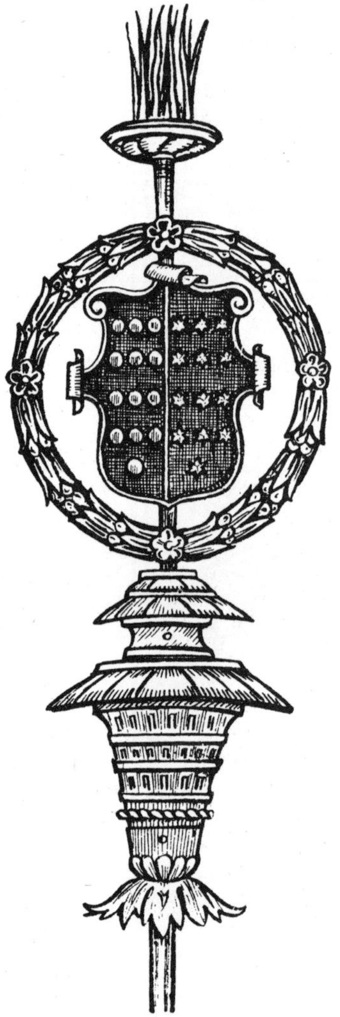

Portion of ironwork screen—Spanish, early 16th century

In the book-mark of Philippe Le Noir we have another example of fanciful heraldry, so splendid in design, so rich in decoration, and so finely drawn, that it was impossible to omit its inclusion. The same play upon words is employed by Philippe Le Noir as appeared in the device of his father, Michel, given as an illustration in our last chapter. The latter design retained largely the old Gothic spirit, while the son's device is permeated with Renaissance influence, but both are fine specimens of heraldic drawing and design, though not strictly orthodox heraldry.

The piece of Spanish ironwork from a screen in some church or

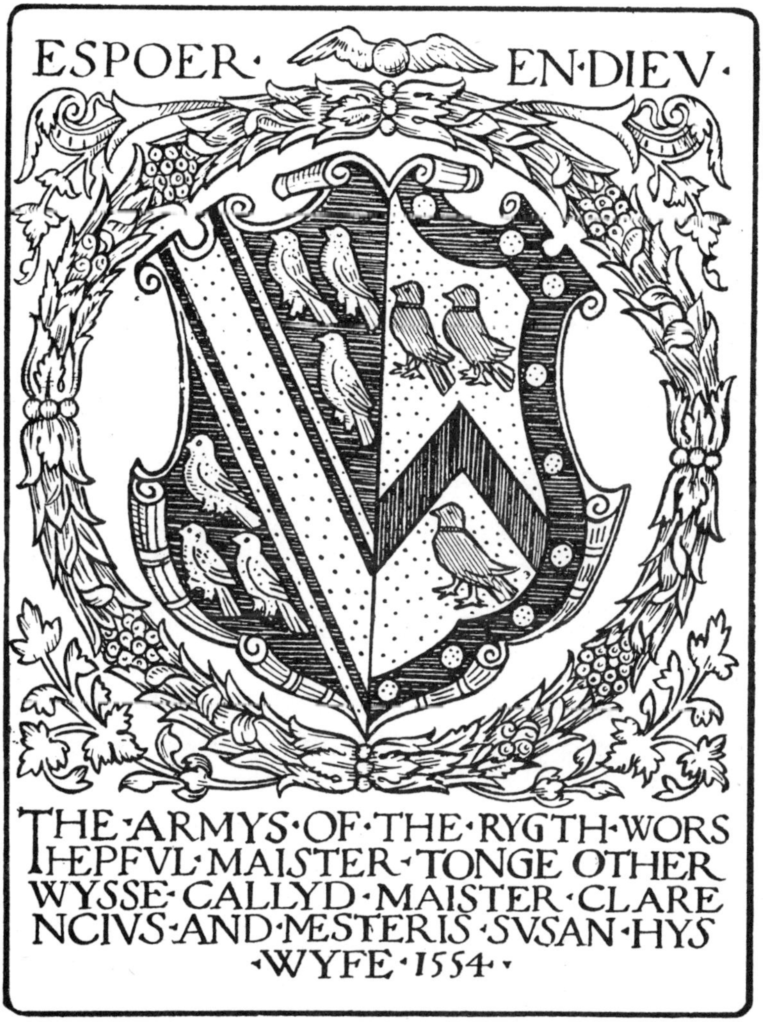

public building, also belongs to the Renaissance, and gives us a pleasing method of emphasising the presence of a shield, when helm and mantling are not used, by surrounding it with a decorative wreath. The same kind of embellishment is resorted to in the English copper plate, engraved and enamelled here. This is only a small object, about eight inches by six, but it makes up in line and colour for what it lacks in dimensions. On a gilt ground the lines of wreath and lettering are engraved, and then blacked in. The colour spaces in the shield, and its charges, are hollowed out, and then filled with coloured enamels. Again we have a man's coat of arms *impaling* with that of his wife. The bend "cotised," that is, accompanied by narrow bands on each side called "cotises," diminutives of the bend, and six martlets *or* (gold) are placed upon a dark blue field (*azure*). On the other side, the field is gold, the bordure, blue with gold plates (*bezants*), the birds, probably popinjays, are green (*vert*), and the chevron red (*gules*). The martlet was a fabulous bird without feet, but an age which implicitly accepted dragons and griffins would not boggle at a bird endowed with the capacity of perpetual flight. One old writer on heraldry after describing the size and fearsomeness of dragons, and their ability to snatch and carry off man, horse and armour, all at one handful, goes on to say that he knows it to be true as he possesses the paw of one of them, but he expresses doubts upon other matters, "because he has no proof of them."

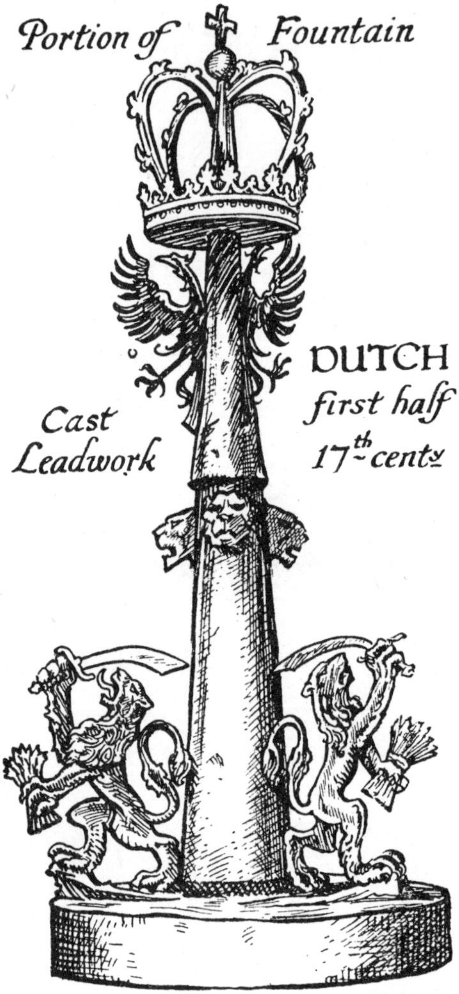

The scrolls and edge-lines of the shield are engraved and blacked in like the wreath. The effect of gold with coloured enamels and black line decoration, is very strong and rich, and it is this method which was used for those splendid heraldic decorations, the Stall-plates of the Knights of the Garter in St. George's Chapel, Windsor. Reproductions of these have been published full size in portfolio

Portion of ceiling - Sizergh Castle - Westmoreland - latter half 16th cent^{y}.

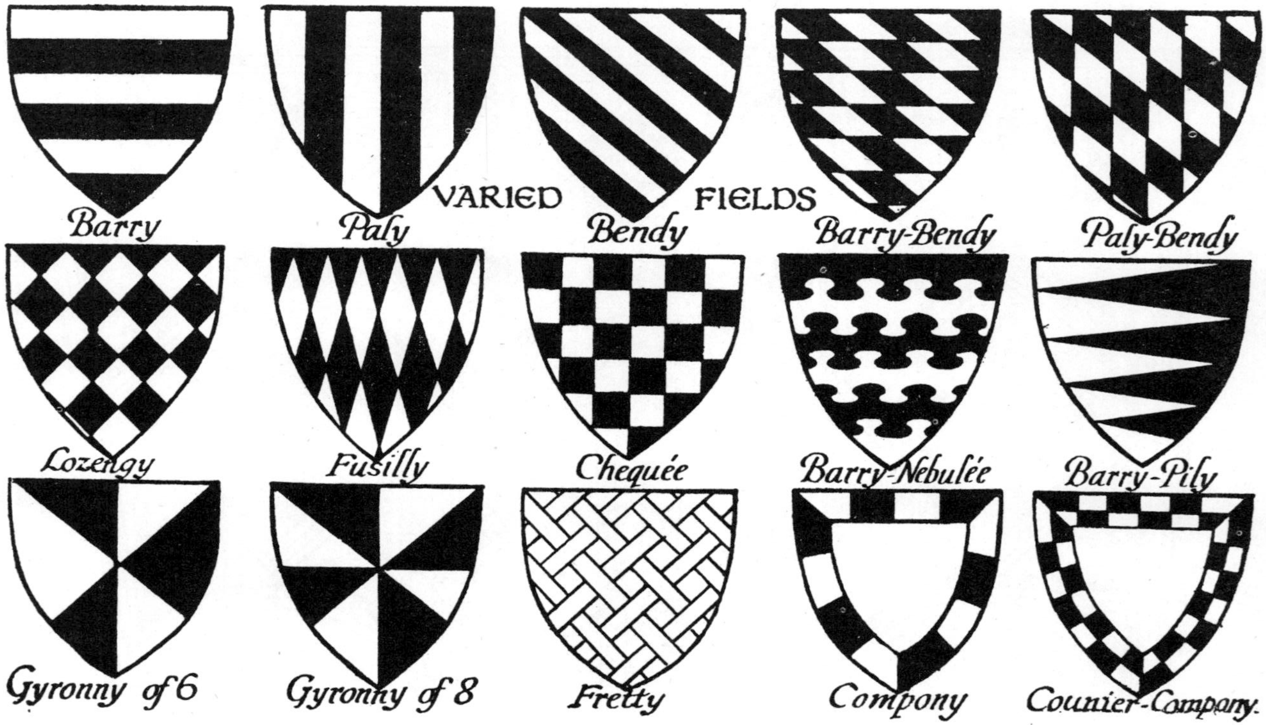
VARIED FIELDS
Barry
Paly
Bendy
Barry-Bendy
Paly-Bendy
Lozengy
Fusilly
Chequée
Barry-Nebulée
Barry-Pily
Gyronny of 6
Gyronny of 8
Fretty
Compony
Counier-Company.

form, by the late Sir W. St. John Hope, a well-known authority, and any reader who can see this in a reference library should not fail to do so if interested in heraldry. The plates will be a revelation of the artistic power possessed by the English craftsman of the Middle Ages. Modern heralds have revived this method of enamelling armorial designs on metal, with excellent results. Before leaving this example, I should like to point out the value which lettering gives to a design. The motto in old French, "Espoer en Dieu," and that on Cardinal Wolsey's arms, in ornate Latin, may be translated—"Hope in God" and "The Lord my helper," respectively. Both these compositions are made more interesting by the lettering of their inscriptions.

The Dutch fountain, and plaster ceiling from Sizergh Castle, are good examples of the use of arms and badges in accordance with their respective purposes. Leadwork is very suitable for outside use in heraldry, as it does not corrode, but takes soft and beautiful tints in the open air.

Some diagrams of varied fields are also given in this chapter, as they are frequently used as a basis for armorial charges. It should be understood that they may be of any two alternate metals or colours, and the method followed in blazonry is to mention the upper or dexter colour or metal first; for example, *barry of eight, argent and sable; paly of six, or and azure.*

The tinctures of these varied fields are meant to be on the same plane or level, therefore no shading or modelling should be brought into them.

In sculptured heraldry the case is different, and relief has to be used in order to obtain contrast.

Charges can be placed upon these fields, as upon plain fields of one metal or colour.

Company, called also Gobony, and Counter-company, can be used on charges as well as in borders.

The numerous Inns scattered over the country, called "the Chequers," are said to derive their name from the "chequy" shield of the once powerful family of De Warrenne. These varied fields, by play of colour and contrast, are a great source of beauty, and lend to heraldry much of that charm which appeals to the amateur or the expert.

CHAPTER V

FOR those who think heraldic drawing easy, there is a surprise in store. In fact, till we come to try it, we do not realise how very difficult it is, and a few trials will vastly increase our admiration of the work of the old heralds and designers. Their skill in drawing and resource in design were the results of long practice and training. The seemingly child-like simplicity of those conventional birds and animals which fill the shield so happily was not acquired all at once. It reflects a process of refinement in thought and a stripping of non-essentials in design only to be found in things which perfectly fit their purpose. In this chapter, therefore, I have given some useful diagrams of the various poses of the heraldic lion, and some skeleton lines showing the way to plan the forms of birds or animals on the shield. Some such manner of spacing should be practised till the eye and hand work together. A remarkable characteristic of the best period was the vigour and vitality which the designers threw into their animal forms—conventional though they were. The lions snarl and stretch their claws, ferocity being the motive power which tightens their sinews; the manes bristle, and ears are pricked erect and forward in a truly feline position. Eagles, with piercing eye, stiffened feather and hooked beak and talon, look the birds of prey they really are.

To such qualities as these, a subtle sculpturesque beauty is added in the example of a lion *rampant* from the effigy of Sir Thomas Cawne in Ightham Church, Kent.

It is a double-tailed specimen (an heraldic, not a natural variety, of course) called in the language of blazonry, *queue fourchée, i.e.*, fork-tailed. This beautiful lion is carved in low relief on the surcoat of the knight, and though a pen-drawing cannot give the quality of the original in a medium so entirely different, enough is here to show how exquisitely the old heralds designed their forms and with what care they worked their details. Each little ermine spot is lovingly carved and finished. This example is in an excellent state of preservation. The only part incomplete is represented by dotted lines, but this is the portion which falls under the hand of the knight, which rests upon his breast. There are other poses of the lion besides those represented in the diagrams which accompany this chapter, but they

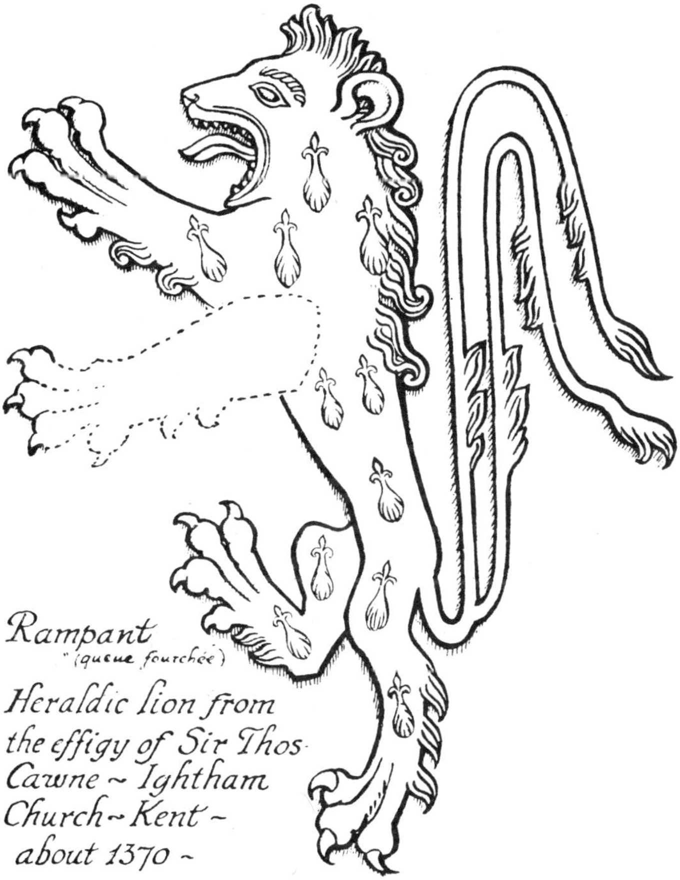

Rampant
(queue fourchée)
Heraldic lion from the effigy of Sir Thos Cawne ~ Ightham Church ~ Kent ~ about 1370 ~

are only slightly varied in detail and can easily be understood by verbal description.

Passant means walking along with the head forward, facing the dexter side of the shield—the right paw raised.

Passant guardant is the same position, but with head fronting the spectator. This is the pose of the lions in the Royal shield of England.

Passant reguardant has the head looking round backwards over the shoulder.

Rampant is springing up in a fighting attitude as shown in the example from Ightham Church. The lion of Scotland seen on the Royal Standard and coins of to-day is in this position.

If the lion is *rampant,* but with the face turned frontwards or looking back over the shoulder, it must be blazoned as *rampant-guardant* or *rampant-reguardant* accordingly.

The old heralds held the rampant position to be the natural one of the lion, therefore it is generally understood that the rampant attitude is meant when lions are mentioned on a shield unless otherwise specified.

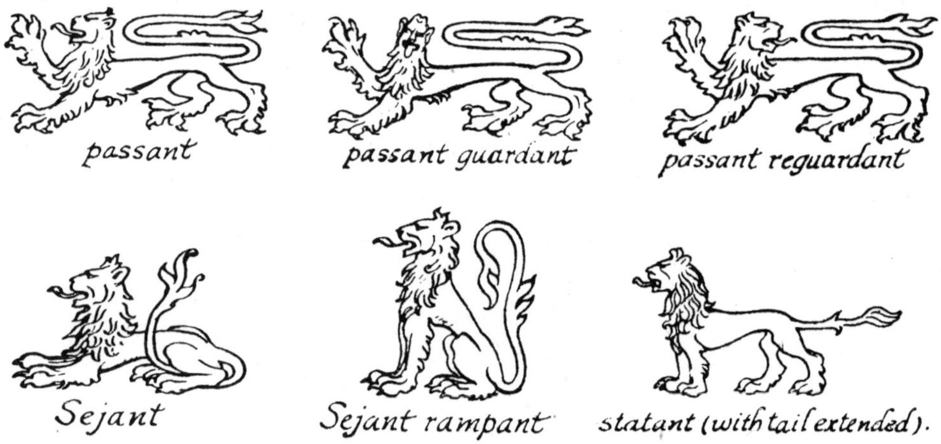

Various poses of the lion in heraldry

Salient or leaping means that the lion stands erect on the two hind legs with fore-paws and tail elevated.

Statant means simply standing on all four legs but the head may be *guardant* or *reguardant.* If no turn of the head is mentioned, it is taken for granted that the head is in profile facing forwards to the dexter side. A lion *statant* is shown with drooping tail unless the tail is mentioned as "extended."

The lion *statant guardant* above the crown forms the Royal crest, and is represented in the arms of princes in former times with the tail drooping, but it seems fashionable now to curl the tail over the back like that of the lions on the shield. This pose is seen on the coin to which it gives its name, the "Lion" shilling. It appears also in the seal of Humphrey, Duke of Gloucester, on p. 53.

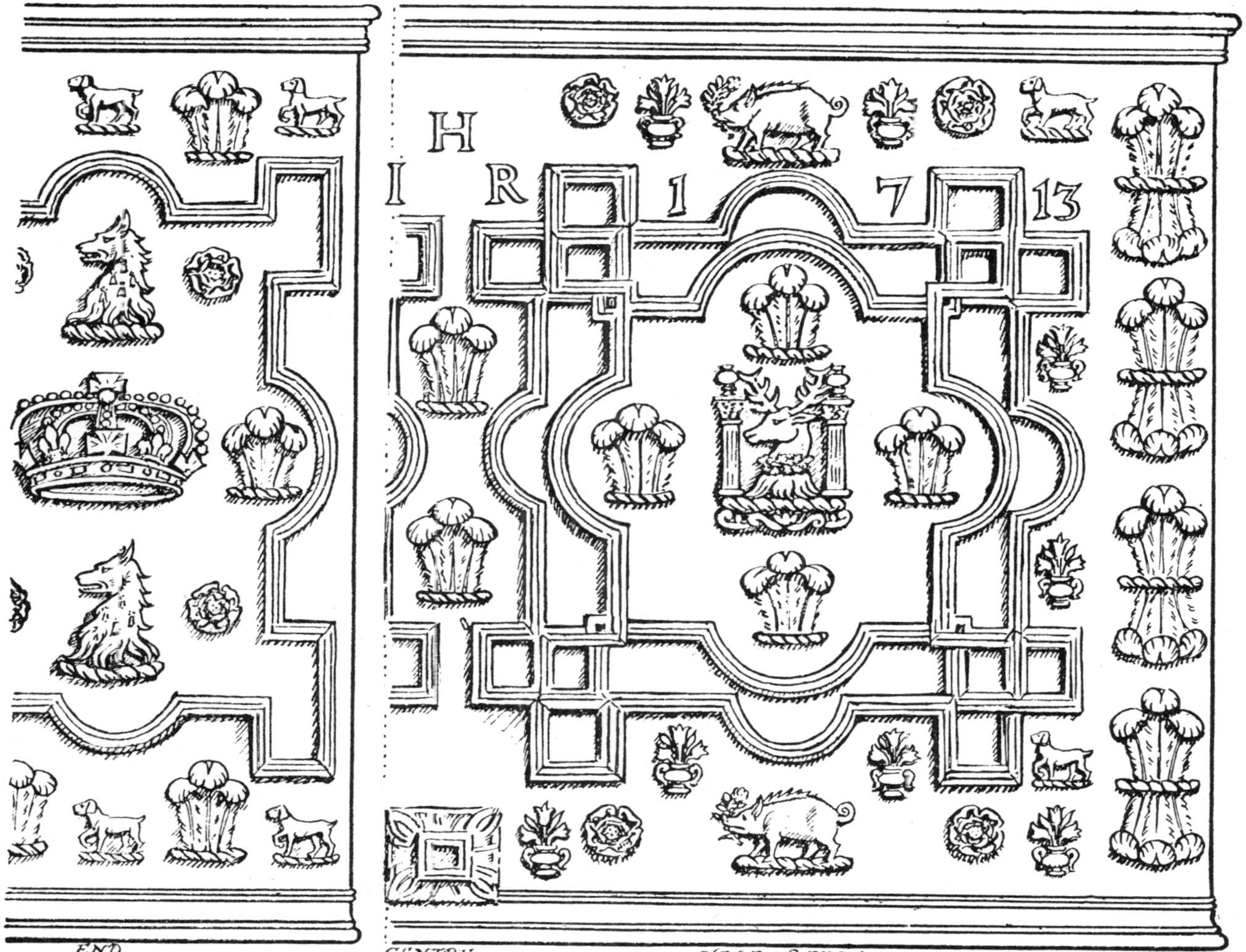

END CENTRE HALF of FRONT

CAST LEAD CISTERN with heraldic crests and badges ~ ENGLISH ~ 18th cent.

Couchant or *Dormant* is lying down or asleep, the head resting on the forepaws, which are extended on the ground.

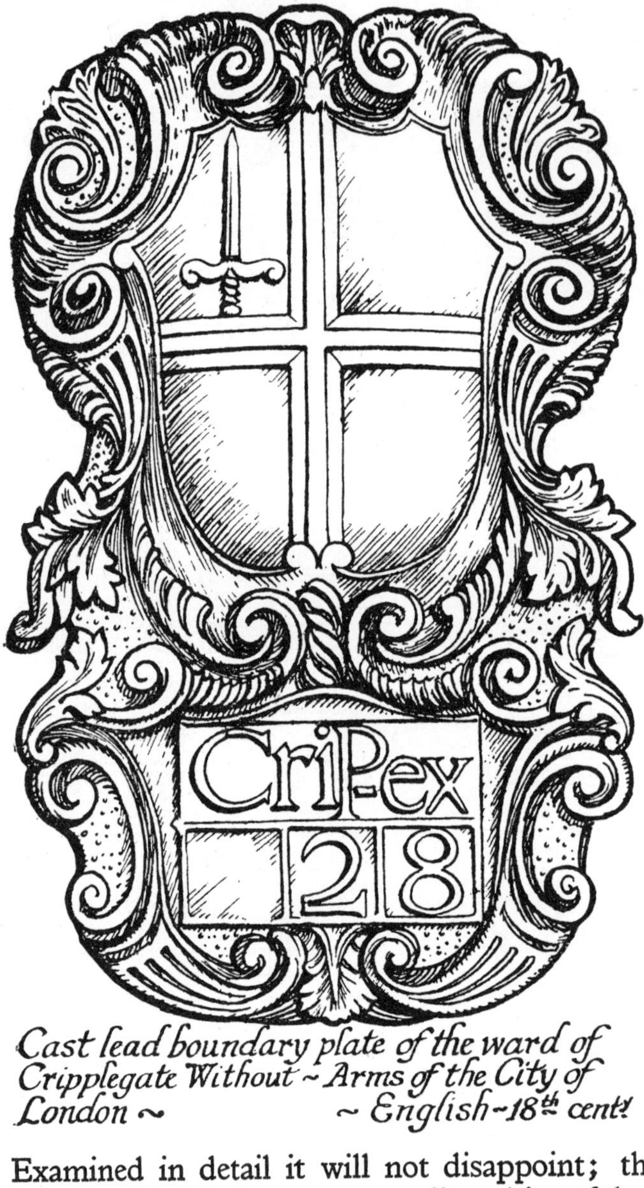

Cast lead boundary plate of the ward of Cripplegate Without ~ Arms of the City of London ~ ~ English ~ 18th centy

The lions of England up to the year 1400 or thereabouts were often called leopards—in the old blazonry, "*lupards,*" "leoparts," or "lybbardes," but now an heraldic animal of lion-like form is only called a leopard if spotted with characteristic markings. The ermine spots on the lion from the effigy of Sir Thomas Cawne, given here in the illustrations do not make him into a leopard. He is a lion "*ermine*" just as he would be a lion "*gules*" if coloured red.

The cast lead cistern, though late in date, is a very admirable piece of work and shows us what effective decoration can be obtained by tastefully distributing a few interesting forms over a surface. Examined in detail it will not disappoint; the boar, the talbot, the wolf and stag crests are excellent bits of heraldic animal drawing. When an animal's head is represented with a ragged edge as if torn off, it is blazoned as "*erased*"; when cut off straight it is said to be "*couped*."

The cartouche was a late development of the shield and was much used in monuments of the seventeenth and eighteenth centuries. A good example is shown in the boundary plate of Cripplegate Without, *i.e.*, the portion of the ward which was outside or "without," not "within" the City wall. It reflects a civic pride and a public interest which happily is now being revived by our municipal bodies. Why should not even a street sign be made beautiful by a little care as that it should become ugly by neglect of forethought?

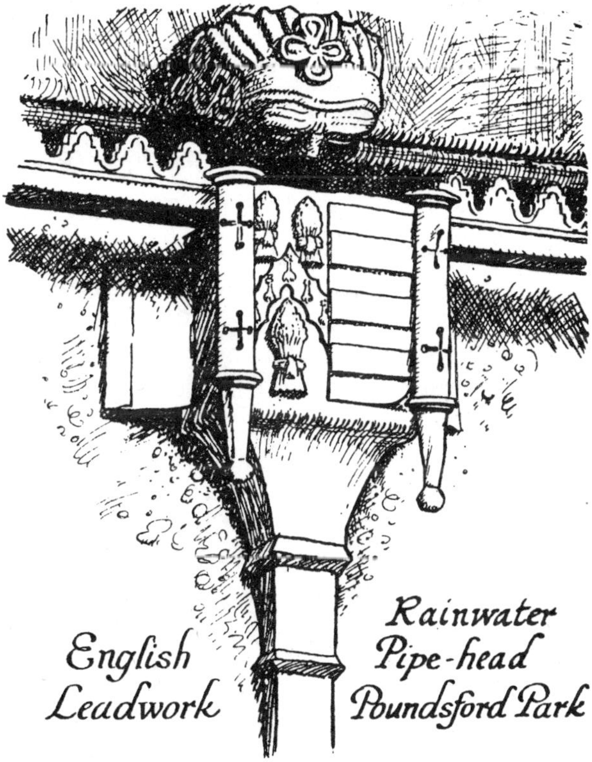

English Leadwork

Rainwater Pipe-head Poundsford Park

The rain-water pipe-heads on pp. 49 and 50 are very beautiful examples of the lead-worker's art. In the one from Poundsford Park the dexter half of the shield would be described as "a chevron engrailed ermine between three garbs." A sheaf of grain in heraldry is called a "garb," and if not otherwise specified a wheatsheaf is understood. The boars' heads in the lead work from Haddon Hall are, it will be noticed, *erased*, and having a collar round the neck they are said to be *gorged*—from the French word "*gorge*"—meaning neck or throat. Seeing that French was the language spoken at the English Court for two or three centuries after the Norman Conquest, and that heraldry developed to perfect expression during this period, it is no wonder that heraldic blazonry abounds in terms of French origin.

The remaining piece of leadwork from Bolton Hall, though

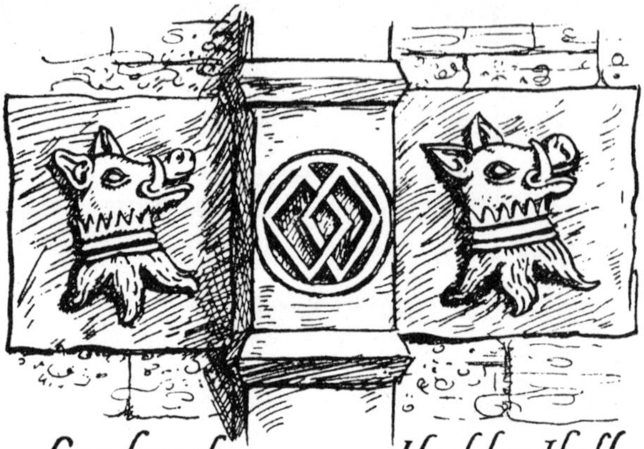

Leadwork Haddon Hall

somewhat over-elaborate, is a very rich piece of decoration, and the cartouche containing the shield of arms is well placed and sustained as the principal centre of interest in the composition.

The swan and griffin crests, which fill the circles from panels on an old organ-harpsichord, are given here as fine examples of the heraldic painter's skill. They are both very deftly touched in with the brush—a grey white on a green ground, *argent* and *vert*, outlined in black, while beak, claws and tongue are in red (*gules*). They are full of vitality in pose and vigorous in drawing and modelling. The little sketch underneath shows the position they occupy in the painted panels, which decorate the old organ-case. In other panels shields of arms occur, but these two crests are more interesting for our purpose. This curious old instrument is now in South Kensington Museum.

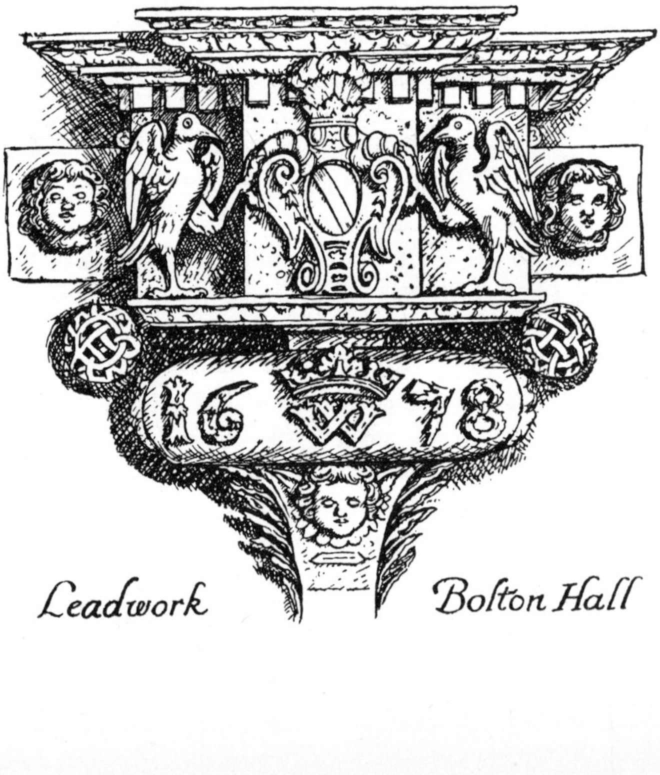

Leadwork Bolston Hall

The chiselled iron knocker of French workmanship on page 52 is a good piece of Renaissance heraldry. The treatment of the floral form on the dexter half of the shield is very choice and tasteful. The three *fusils conjoined in fesse* on

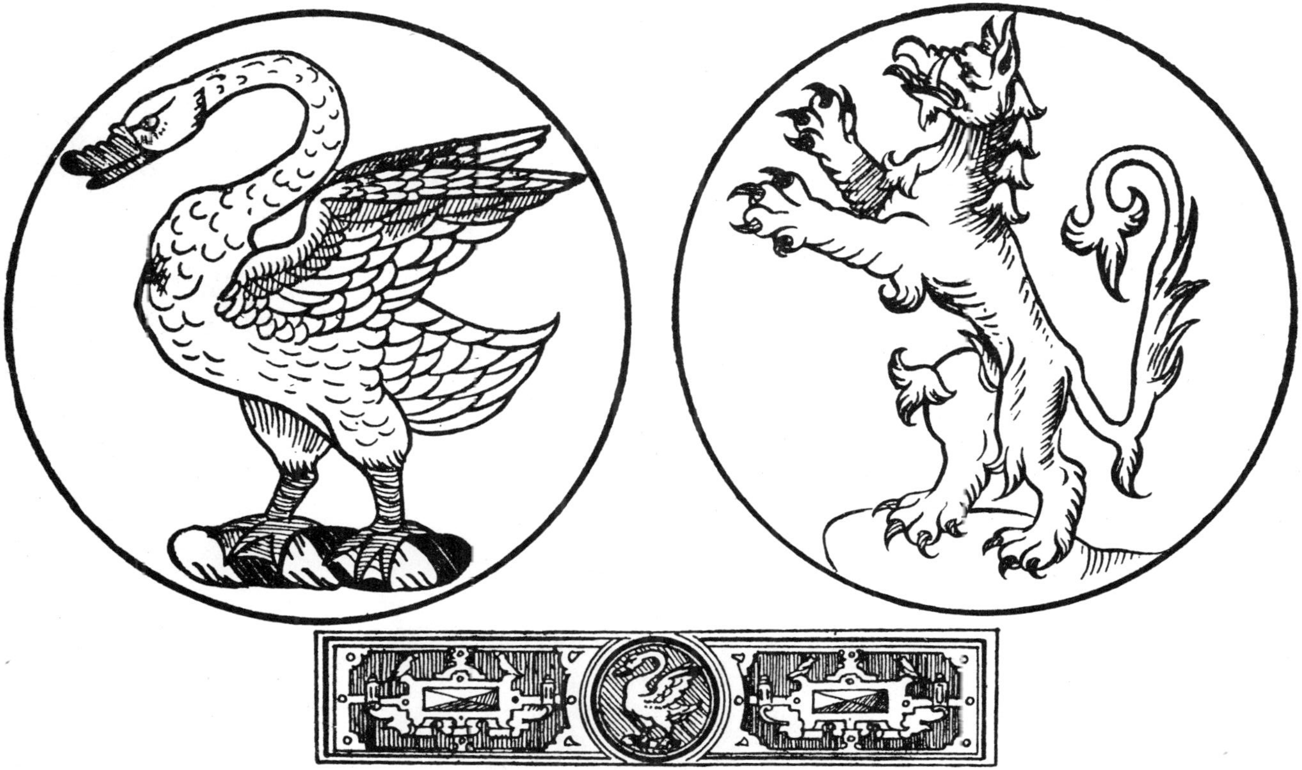

Two crests from painted panels on case of organ harpsichord. *Ightham Mote, Kent,* 1579

the sinister half are charged with *crosses crosslet fitchée*, a description used when the cross is pointed spike-fashion at the lower end.

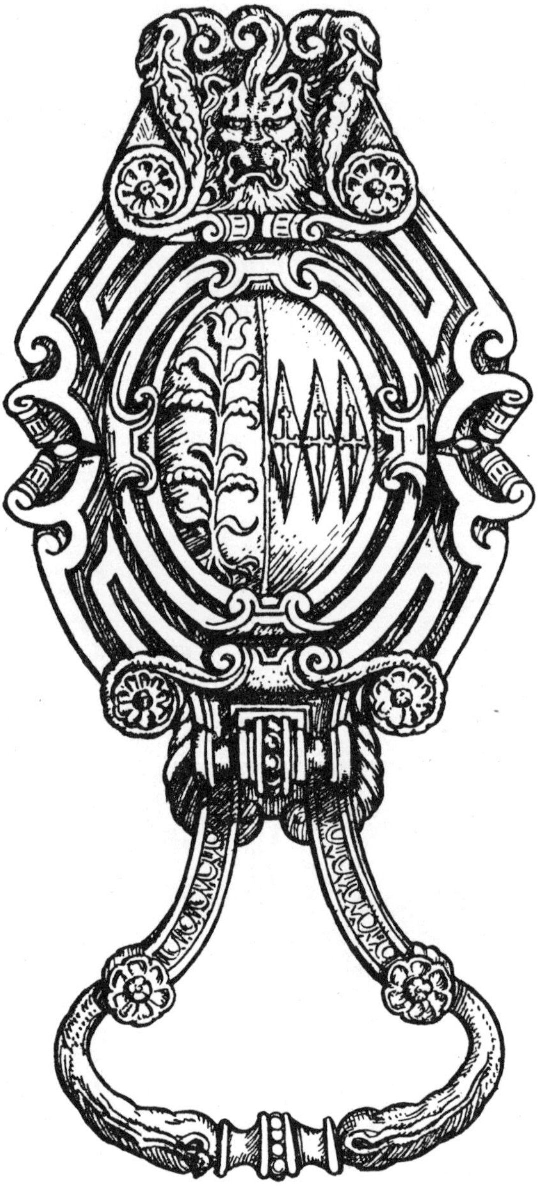

Chiselled iron knocker—French, middle 16th century

Some of the most wonderful art of the old heralds is to be found on the seals used by the kings, princes, nobles, knights, ecclesiastics, and great ladies for stamping their decrees, title-deeds, letters, or other documents in the flourishing days of heraldry.

They are indeed most exquisite little sculptures and on close examination will be found to be full of invention, play of fancy and that sense of enjoyable workmanship which counts for so much if a work of art is to interest another person as well as its maker.

Look at the variety of design in helm, mantling and floral embellishment in these beautiful objects. The delight in animal form can be seen in the bird, lion, boar's head and graceful antelope supporters in the seals of Turbock, Warbleton and Humphrey, Duke of Gloucester. Notice the jolly little unicorn whisking his tail gleefully while he lowers his head, and for the time being depresses his weapon in sympathy with the Gothic artist's difficulties of circular space-filling.

In two cases it will be noticed that a hat surmounts the helm instead of a wreath to support the crest. This is a *chapeau* or *Cap*

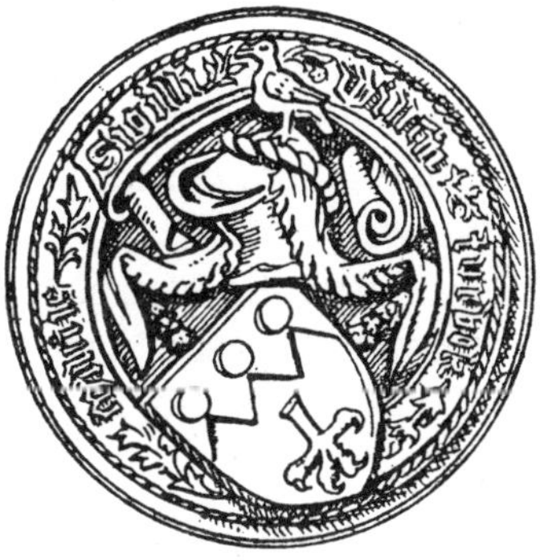

Wm - Turbock - 1480

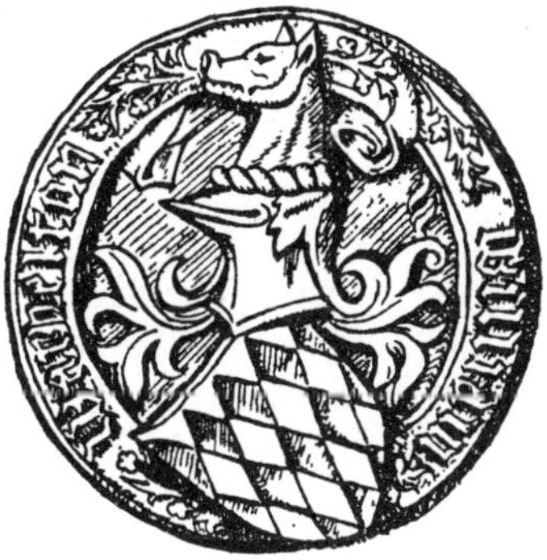

Wm - Warbleton - 1451 -

of Maintenance, generally of crimson velvet with turned-up border of ermine, most frequently used in ancient times by princes, royal dukes and others of high rank.

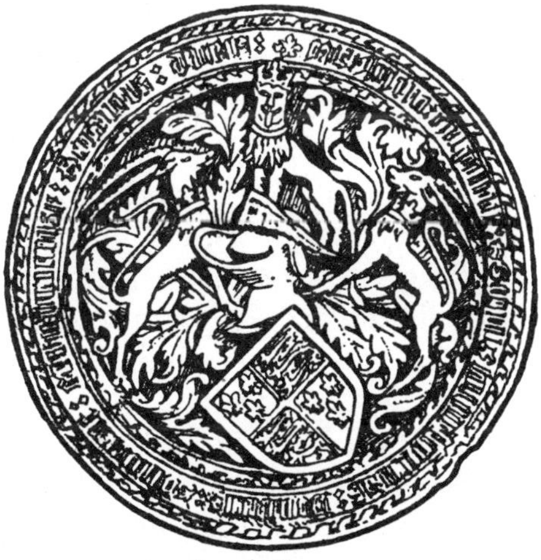

Humphrey
Duke of Gloucester
1439

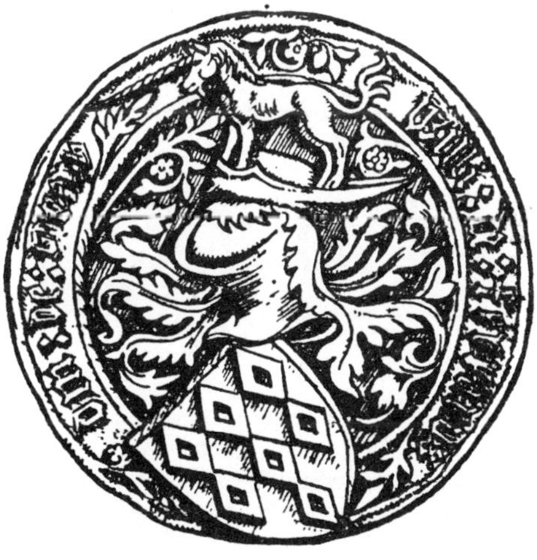

William Ferrars
1444

How skilfully the old craftsmen who made these charming little reliefs have used a band of rich old English lettering to bind and enclose their heraldic compositions!

I owe my readers an apology before closing this chapter for the indistinctness of one or two of the inscriptions, but as seals are small objects ranging from one and a quarter to two and a half inches in diameter or thereabouts, the difficulty of deciphering a closely packed motto in Gothic lettering, viewed partially upside down, added to my very limited Latinity, will excuse my inability to render the exact meaning of the words. The only alternative was a "fake" approaching the effect of the band of lettering as near as possible under the circumstances. For this deception I crave your indulgence, but in all other respects I have tried to render the detail with the closest accuracy.

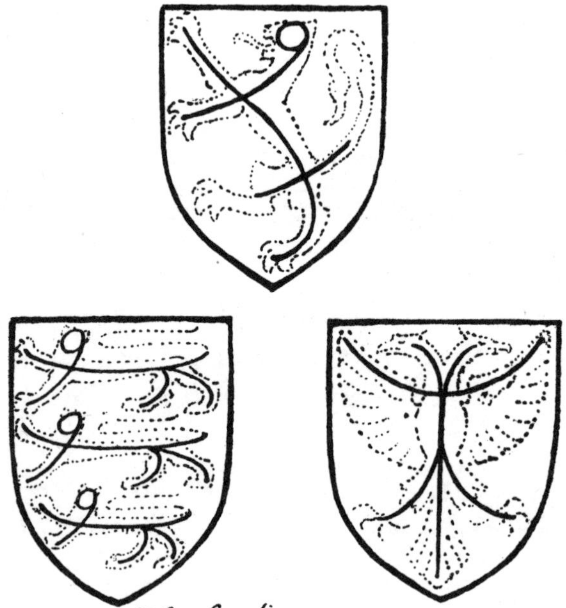

Method of spacing animal forms on shield

CHAPTER VI

IT is always pleasant to the artist or the antiquary to come across a piece of work which is out of the beaten track. Freshness and a different point of view count for so much in artistic matters. Such a specimen is the shrine of St. Simeon made at Zara, Dalmatia, by an Italian artist in 1380. About Hungarian work in general there is a national flavour of quite a distinct character, and the Italian artist seems to have absorbed some of it. There is a new treatment in the achievement of arms, and an unexpected daring and variety in the design of the rich foliage which surrounds it, that possesses a great charm. Take it to pieces and criticise it as you will, it may violate many accepted canons of design in the process, but in the end you are drawn to admire it and to waive aside your objections in favour of the whole effect. This gable-end of the shrine is only a portion of a long box capable of holding the body of a man, and the recumbent effigy of the Saint (if such it can be called, as it lies sideways on the lid) is sculptured in high relief. The sides are covered with rich decoration like that on the end here shown, and on the front a panel of rich Gothic lettering brings another element of beauty into the scheme. Vine foliage is largely used as a bordering frame for the figure subjects, which represent scenes in the life of the saint. The quaint panel in the illustration is full of human interest. The ship is in dire distress, reminding one of a passage in Matthew Arnold's poem, *The Strayed Reveller,* where:

> The cowering merchants, in long robes
> Sit pale beside their wealth.

But in this case the passengers have gone a stage further, and it will be observed that part of their worldly gear has been thrown overboard, while one of the mariners is depicted in the act of continuing the process. A merchant with his robe to his face is evidently in despair, others call upon help Divine, while one of more practical temperament assists the sailor-boy in lowering the sail, notwith-

SHRINE - said to contain the body of Saint Simeon ~ The original of silver-gilt is in the Church of St Simeon at Zara, Dalmatia. Italian ~ 1380.

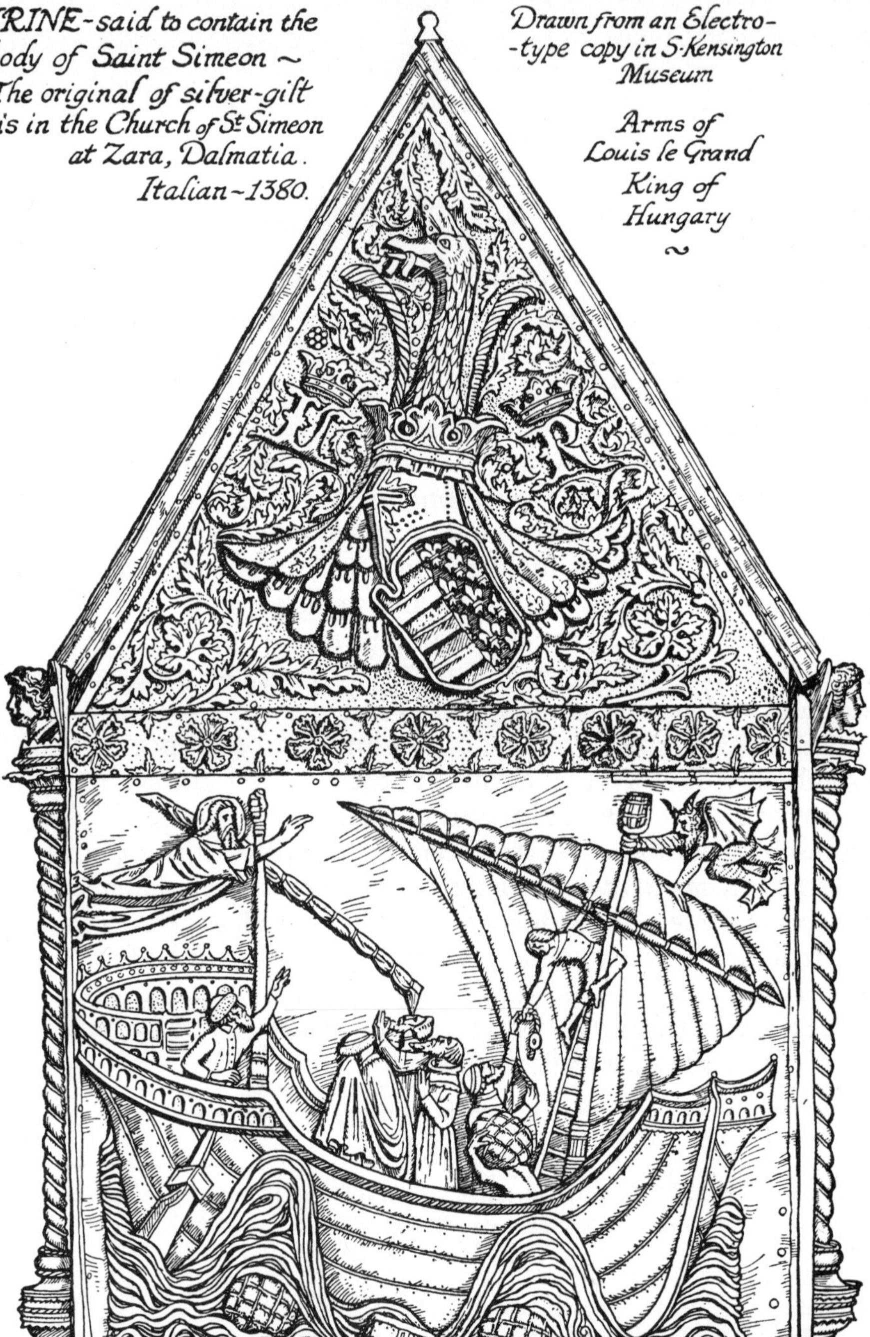

Drawn from an Electro-type copy in S. Kensington Museum

Arms of Louis le Grand King of Hungary ~

standing the machinations of the demon aloft who is doing his devilmost to send the crew and cargo to perdition. There is a fine impression of heaving stormy ocean in the design and modelling of the waves and we can imagine the spellbound interest of pilgrims gazing with serious and simple mind on these histories in pictorial form, though we are often apt to forget that in those days books were rare and reading an accomplishment possessed only by the few.

The story was the main motive with these old Gothic artists. Their appeal was direct, and they presented the facts to their audience in the simplest possible way. At the same time they were, consciously or unconsciously, masters of decorative effect and understood how to obtain the greatest amount of richness from their material.

The Reliquary made of silver in the form of a box is also a good piece of the metalworker's art from the same part of Europe, and is similar in its style to St. Simeon's shrine. The plates and borders seem to be rivetted on to the box, and whether the odd pieces are repairs or belong to the original design it is impossible to say. The strip in the centre has much more of the character of Renaissance work than the other parts, which leads one to think it is a later addition. The old craftsman, however, occasionally started off on a new motive in design without any apparent rhyme or reason, and though sometimes puzzling and irritating, these eccentricities are often fascinating and full of suggestion to the modern designer. The double-headed eagle is a fine specimen of heraldic bird drawing, full of those qualities of character we expect to find in the monarch of birds of prey, for the eagle in heraldry holds the same rank among birds as the lion does among animals. In the position shown here he is said to be *displayed*. Birds other than birds of prey in a like pose are said to be *disclosed*.

The two heraldic badges shown on page 59 are somewhat unusual examples of their kind. Separated by centuries in point of time the method of obtaining the effect is the same. Champlevé enamel means, that the spaces on the metal intended to be filled with colour are dug out. The literal translation may be given as *field-removed*. After the work has been taken thus far the next stage is to apply the enamel which consists of various mineral products in powder form fused on to the metal foundation by firing in a kiln. Thus metallic surface can be combined with jewel-like effects of colour, while great durability

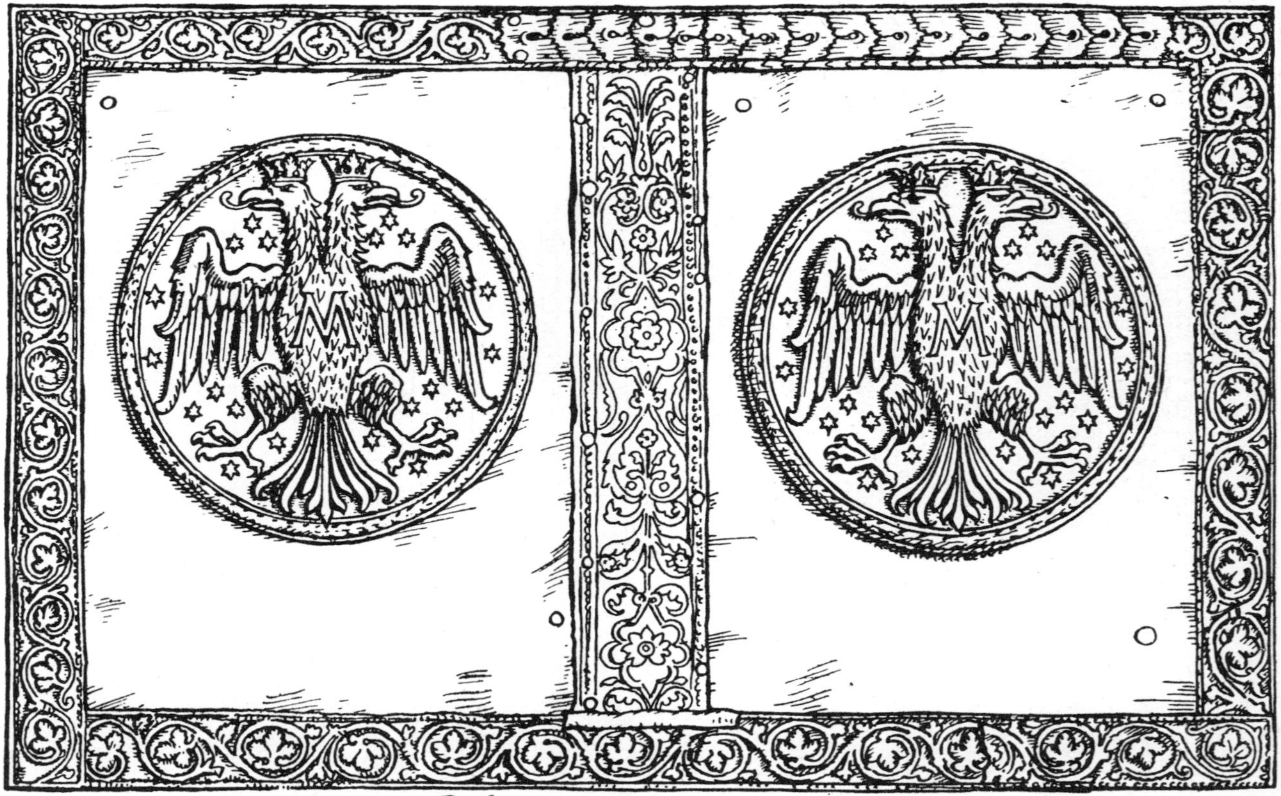

Reliquary in the form of a box
Silver, parcel-gilt – Zara,
Dalmatia, 15th cent.

is secured at the same time. Another method is to build up the partitions between the coloured enamels by fastening thin strips of copper together like walls for the outlines of the design. This is the *cloisonné* method which means "partitioned," and thus arrives at a similar result. Limoges in France was so celebrated in mediæval times for enamelling that its name has become almost inseparable from the art. In our specimen the lizards, which, with so much beauty of line twine themselves so obligingly round one another in the border, are inlaid with lines and scales of turquoise blue. The lion in the centre is *rampant* on a dull red ground and the segmental spaces which surround the shield are of a light slaty blue with metal lines of ornament.

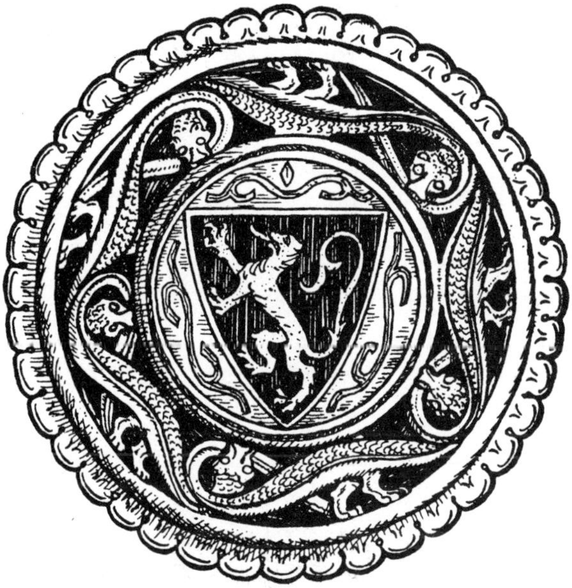

Badge—Limoges champlevé enamel. French, 13th century

The same method is followed in the badge of Charles II., but the colours are bolder and stronger. The enamel inside the crown is a deep terracotta red, while that surrounding the bust and between the floral forms is of ultramarine blue, except one or two small touches of red, and the

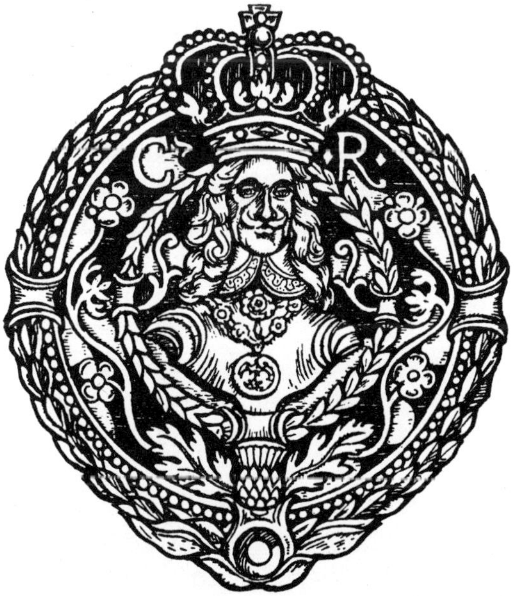

Badge—Cast brass and champlevé enamel. Charles II., late 17th century

remaining spaces are of white enamel, the latter giving great value and brilliancy to the red and blue. With the bright gold tones of the metal the combination makes a beautiful and striking effect.

The monogram of James II., on p. 112, is also of enamelled metal, the colour in this instance being blue only.

These objects were used largely by retainers and dependents, who carried the arms or distinguishing sign of king, baron or family as a mark of recognition. In some cases they are fitted with brooch-pins for fastening to a garment, saddle-cloth, or such-like trappings.

In the carved oak panel of John Schönroide we have another example of a prelate's coat of arms enhanced in beauty by the lettering

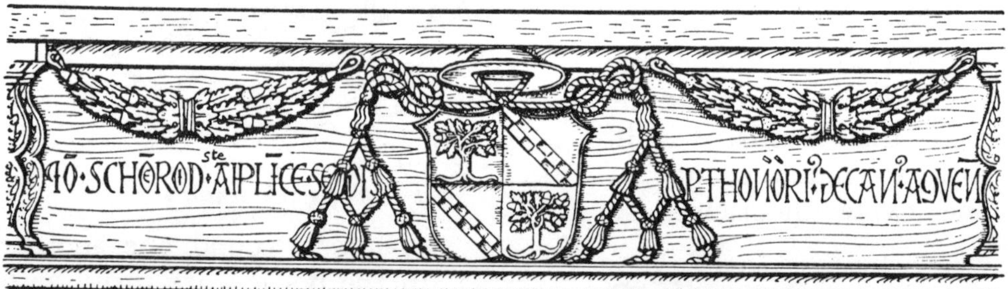

Oak chimney front ~ Arms of John Schönroide - Protonotary of the Holy Apostolic See ~ Dean of Aix-la-Chapelle ~ dated 1538.

of an inscription. They are indeed very beautiful letters, well drawn and proportioned, and admirably adapted in shape to the method of execution—they are incised, not carved in relief. The quaint little oak tree on the shield is a very decorative form and the idea of echoing it in the festoon is happy and appropriate.

The Spanish silver salver of repoussé work is both heraldically and decoratively interesting and it may be compared with the German example on p. 62. The Spanish piece retains the old Gothic feeling for plant life, but the German work has come under the influence of the Renaissance.

The great Hans Holbein, incomparable limner of the human face, made many designs of this kind for gold and silversmith's work and though they are very fine they are mostly adorned with this somewhat characterless foliage. There is more virility about the plant work on the Spanish plate if less of graceful polish than that of its German

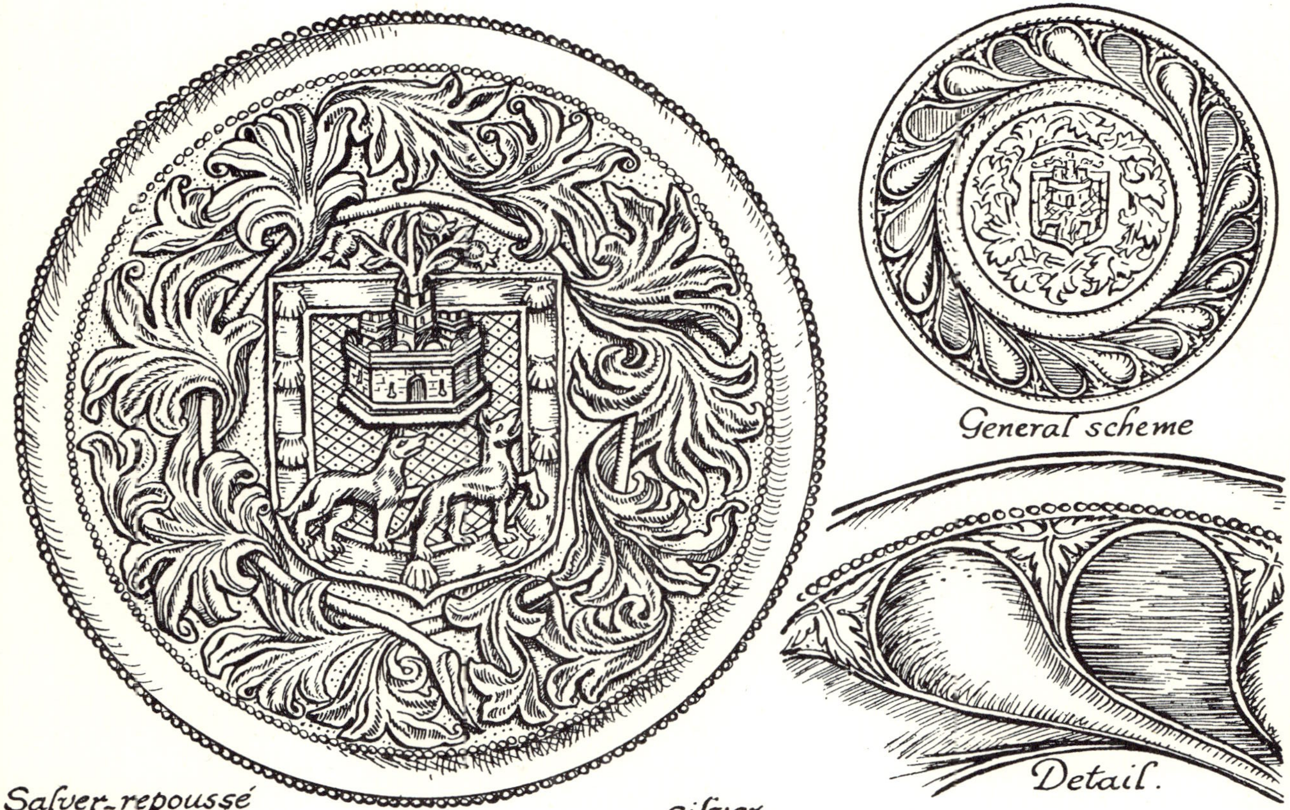

General scheme

Detail.

Salver-repoussé
Spanish
c. 1480

silver

rival. On both, however, the heraldic portions are well treated, the arms of Luneburg being made more striking by the addition of a little enamel in black and red, which makes an agreeable harmony with the tones of silver and gilt. A tazza is a shallow dish with a

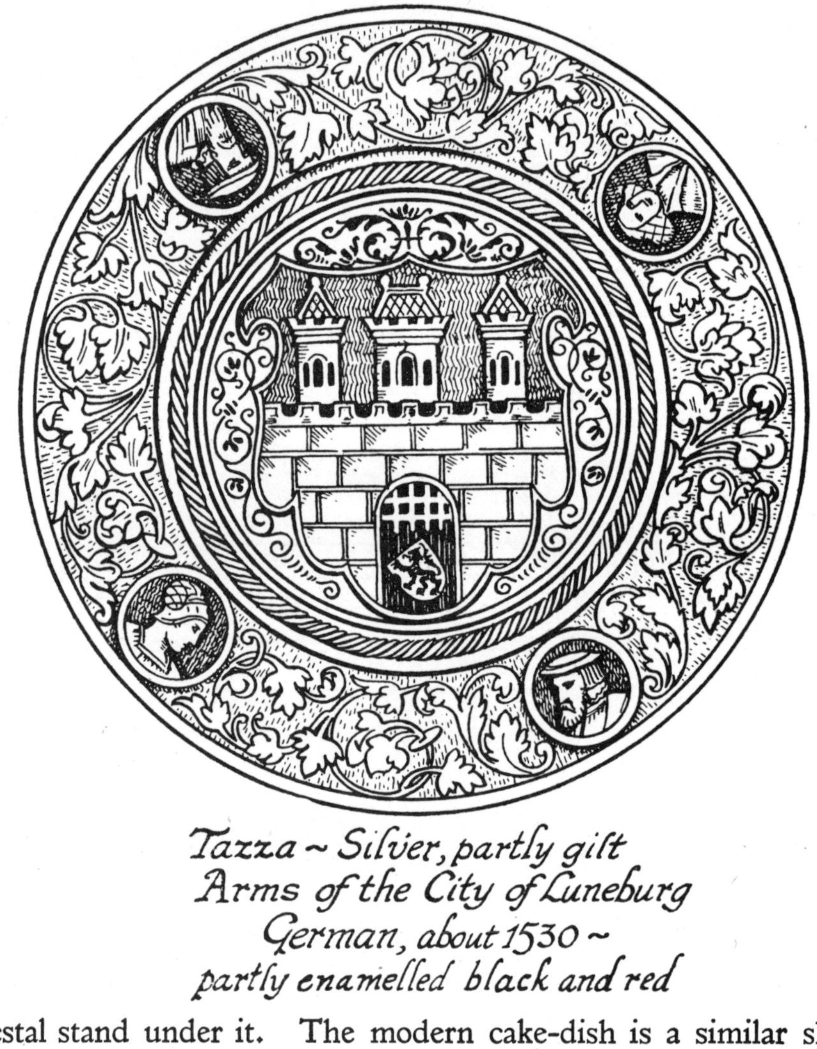

Tazza ~ Silver, partly gilt
Arms of the City of Luneburg
German, about 1530 ~
partly enamelled black and red

pedestal stand under it. The modern cake-dish is a similar shape, which would not lose in beauty if it took a few lessons in design from these fine examples of mediæval and Renaissance craftsmanship.

As a supplement to this chapter a few diagrams of some peculiar heraldic charges are given. Though they refer to some obsolete things these symbols are still in use on coats of arms. *Water-bougets* were mediæval vessels for carrying water and were formed of two leather bags appended to a yoke or cross bar. *Caltraps*—sharp iron instruments strewn on the ground to wound horses' feet or impede their advance, called also caltrops, galtraps and cheval-traps. *Clarion or rest,* an ancient musical instrument. *Chess-rook,* a conventional rendering of the chess-piece sometimes called a castle. *Pheon,* the barbed head of a spear or arrow engrailed on the inner side and pointing to the base of the shield, used in government stores and prisons and generally known as the unenviable "broad-arrow" mark of the convict.

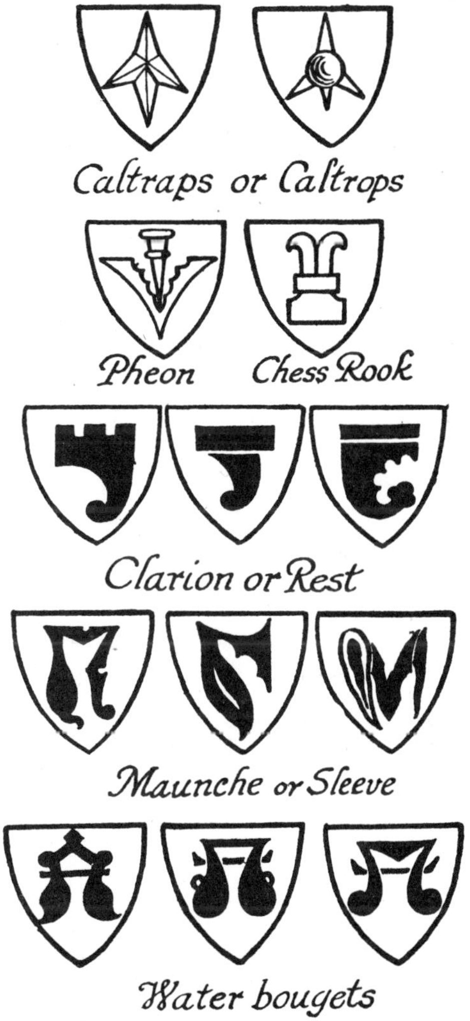

The *maunche* is frequently found in heraldry, being derived from the custom of the knights wearing a lady's sleeve as a favour when jousting at a tournament. The shape may strike a modern observer as peculiar, but on reference to ancient costume the conventional forms here depicted will be found to represent those large bell-mouthed sleeves with pendent drapery attached to the elbow, which form a well-known feature of costume on fair and fragile dames we have seen taking the air in the formal rose garden of many a mediæval illuminated manuscript. Truly the sidelights of heraldry are numerous, as well as instructive and interesting.

CHAPTER VII

IN searching for examples of heraldry in decoration it is astonishing how widely it has been used and how great the range of material in which it has been employed. Carving in wood and stone, weaving and embroidery, enamelling on metal, painting on glass, ironwork, cast and wrought, printed and painted book decoration are only some of the various ways designers and decorators have used in its expression.

In this chapter we have an example of heraldry in decoration in the form of a cast-iron fire-back, a favourite field in olden times for armorial display. There are many fine examples extant of this ancient industry both in public and private collections. The huge fireplaces in old palaces and mansions called forth the skill of the architect, the herald and the craftsman, sometimes singly, often in combination, and the results of their art are seen to-day in those splendidly decorated chimney-pieces in which carved, inlaid or painted heraldry is completed and supplemented by the metal fire-dog and fire-back of heraldic design.

This particular example is of the time of Charles II., whose monogram it contains. All readers of history remember how he escaped from the parliamentary forces by hiding in an oak tree. This story, true or untrue, has evidently inspired this design, and the royal badge of the crown, repeated three times in combination with this most beautiful decorative oak tree, makes a bold and striking piece of ornament. Decorative tree forms are to be found in many periods and many kinds of art work, but it would be difficult to come across one more beautiful than this, either in design and character, or boldness and richness of modelling. There was an ancient industry in Sussex about the seventeenth and eighteenth centuries, which concerned itself with ironwork of this character, but which is now extinct. "Sussex fire-backs" are now eagerly sought by enthusiasts in these days of collecting everything, and the pursuit of collecting, though it may engender in some minds a gentle species of monomania,

Cast iron fire-back with monogram of Charles II

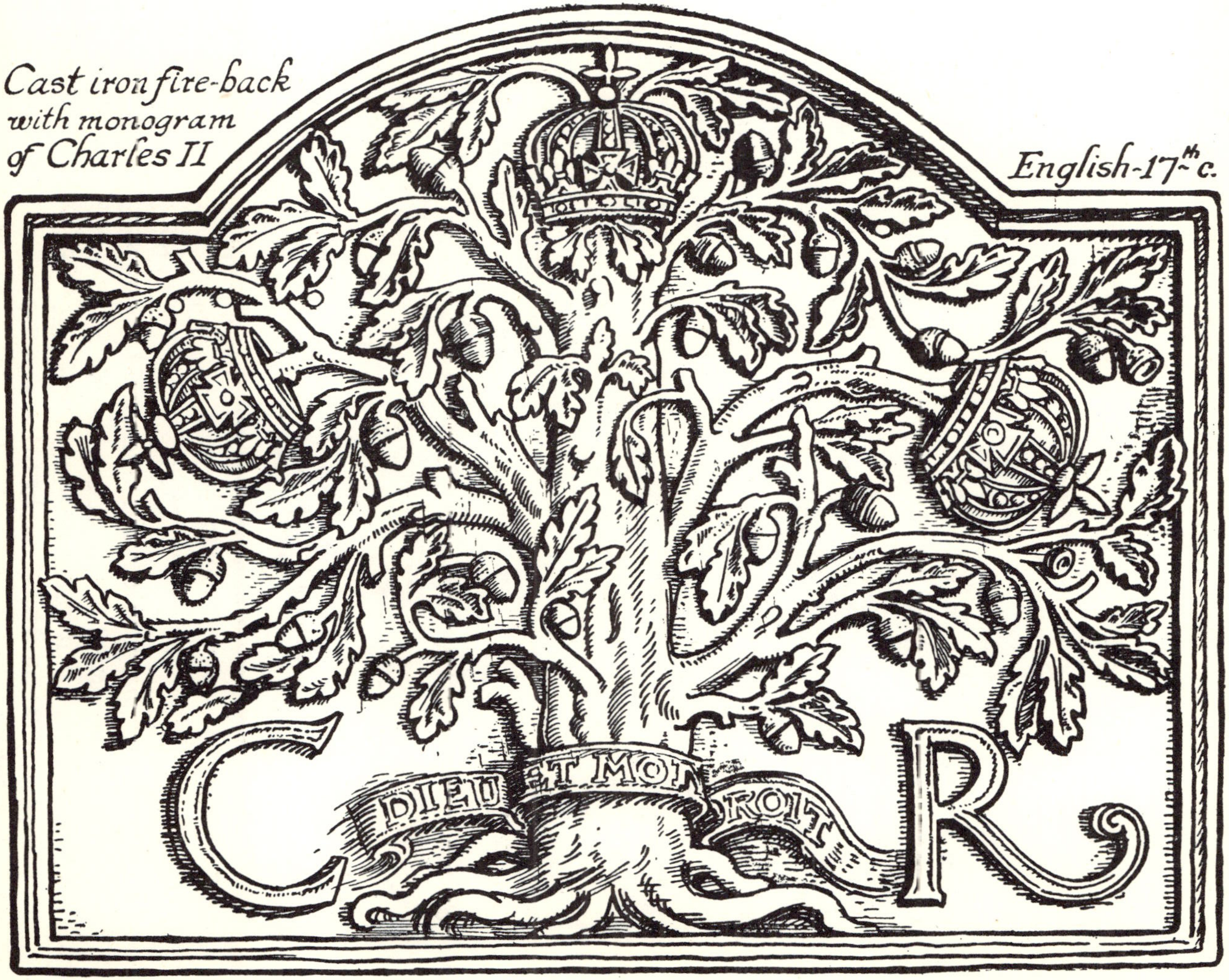

English–17th c.

is a good thing in the main. It all tends to the gathering of information, to the treasuring and appreciation of the work of other days, and it is a welcome and practical protest against the cold and callous vandalism which until quite recent times had been allowed a free hand in the destruction of many fine old monuments of the past. But there is also a danger that it may set up an exclusive worship of the old to the detriment of the appreciation which new work deserves, and we ought to endeavour to avoid a narrow conservatism with regard to the past while keeping alive an impartial expectancy for the merits of work done in the present. A certain amount of traditional conservatism in art is a safeguard against the loss or destruction of the knowledge our forerunners bequeathed to us. We have to-day new schools of Futurists and other violent enthusiasts urging us to break and burn all the doings of the past and to become entirely "new," but evolution, *not* revolution, seems to be the natural law upon which Art progresses. No one could claim, for instance, that heraldry is as important a part of life to-day as it was in the Middle Ages, but a study of it preserves many qualities of drawing, design and colour decoration which might otherwise be lost to our own time and to the future.

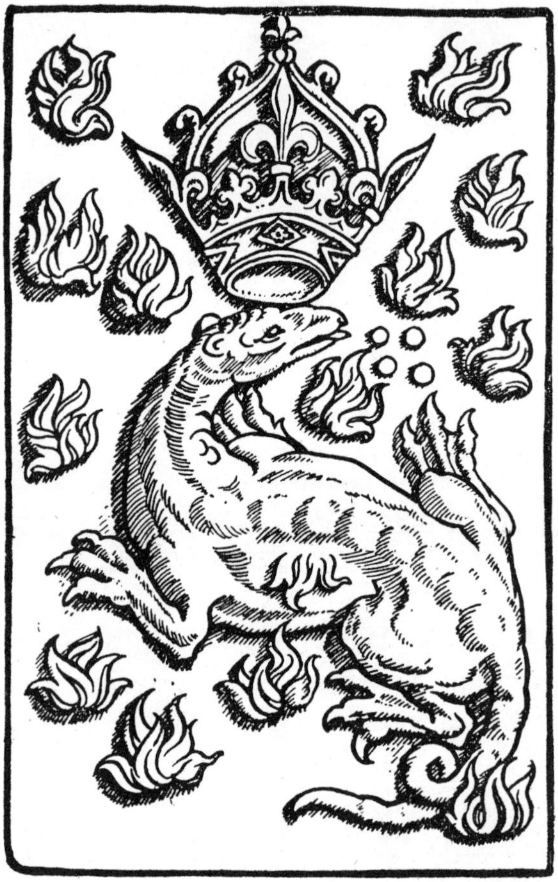

Oak panel carved with salamander badge of Francis I.—French, first half 16th century

Another beautiful heraldic design in the form of a badge is the

Salamander Panel of Francis I. of France. The Salamander was a mythical creature which lived in fire, according to the accepted belief in those ages of credulous wonder and superstition. Benvenuto Cellini, in his autobiography, solemnly records the "fact" that one day in his boyhood, he was called by his father to the fireside to see a real live salamander disporting itself in the flames. Creatures of this kind appealed to the mediæval imagination and their occasional use in heraldry need not surprise us. The Salamander is represented under two different forms, as a lizard like the one in the illustration, or as a kind of fire-breathing dog or dragon with flames issuing from the mouth. Probably the symbolical meaning was endurance and indestructibility, or ardour and fiery zeal. The panel in question whether symbolical or not is a very beautiful design. The animal is exquisitely drawn and modelled, the crown a lovely and effective secondary element, and the quaint little groups of flame form a most decorative background to the principal motive. The surface of the wood is highly polished and of a beautiful golden tint and the little panel is full of that subtle charm called "quality."

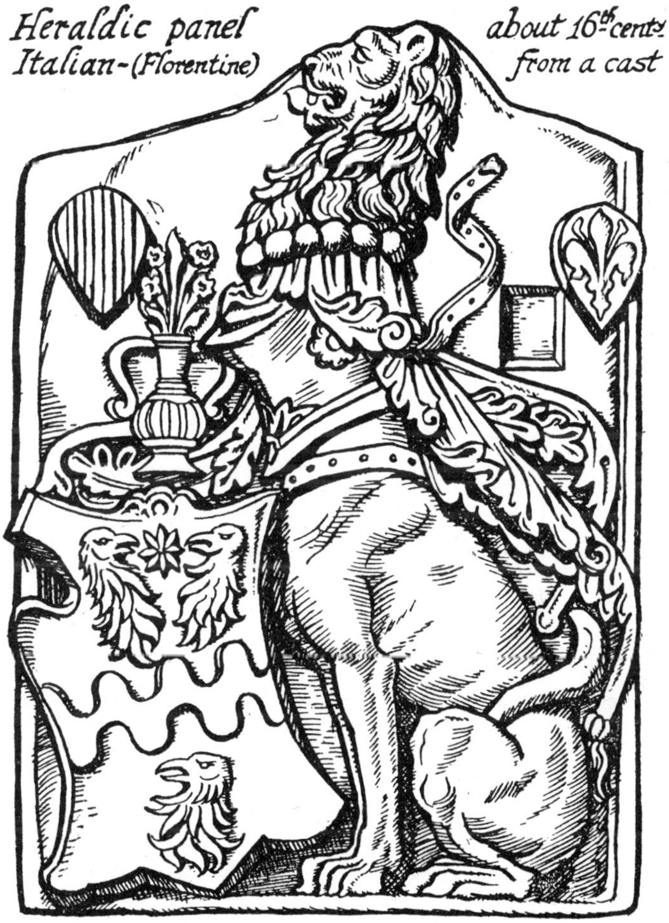

Another very fascinating piece of heraldic decoration is the Italian (Florentine) panel on p. 67. The drawing has been made from a plaster cast, but the original is most probably a piece of stone carving, marble perhaps being the material used. As a composition it possesses many beauties and much ingenuity of design. The shape of the shield, the unusual character of the mantling, the strong modelling of the animal forms, all commend themselves to the lover of heraldic ornament, and the two smaller shields with the decorative vase of flowers are very happy accessories to a charming armorial grouping. Consciously or unconsciously there is a sense of humour displayed by the manner in which the dog supporter is made to do double duty, holding the helm and crest as well as carrying out his ordinary function of supporting the shield.

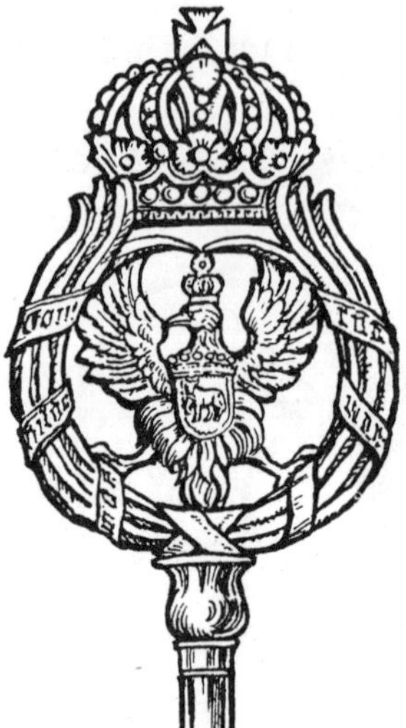

Chamberlain's Key
Silver, parcel-gilt,
Polish-2nd half 18th cent.

A fine example of heraldry in printed book decoration is shown in the frontispiece to *England and Wales Parliament,* a volume of statutes made and established from the reign of Henry III. to that of Henry VIII. It is a beautiful composition in line, mass and decorative effect. The arms are France modern and England quarterly, borne by the English kings from Henry IV. till the union of England and Scotland was consummated by the accession of James I. See Frontispiece.

It was not till the latter reign that the supporters of the Royal Shield took the permanent form of the Lion and Unicorn. Before that time the kings used a variety of supporters. The Tudors, for instance, favoured the Red Dragon of Wales, they themselves being of Welsh descent, and another supporter commonly used by Henry VII., Henry VIII., Mary and Elizabeth, was the greyhound *argent.* Both occur in the design under our notice,

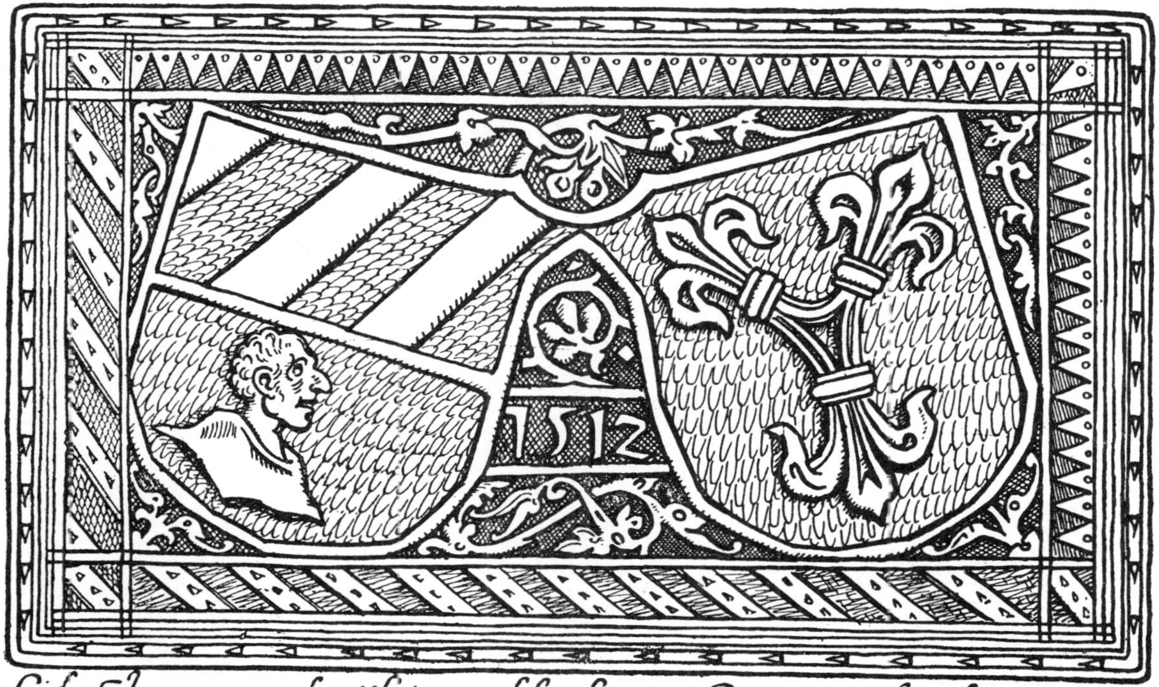

Lid of box covered with incised leather ~ German ~ dated 1512

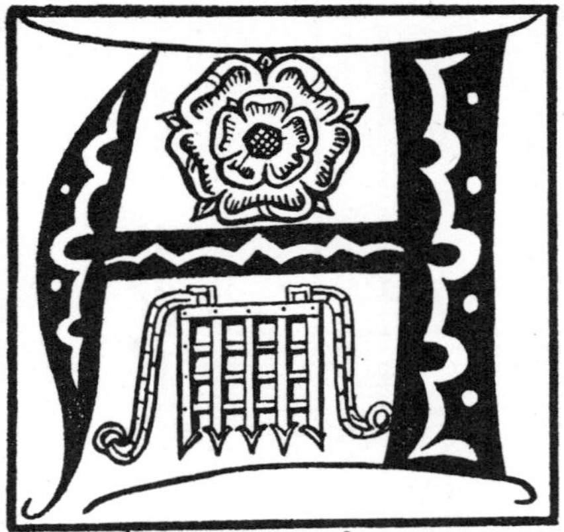

Woodcut initial from "England and Wales Parliament" Statutes made and established from Henry III to Henry VIII printed in 1543~

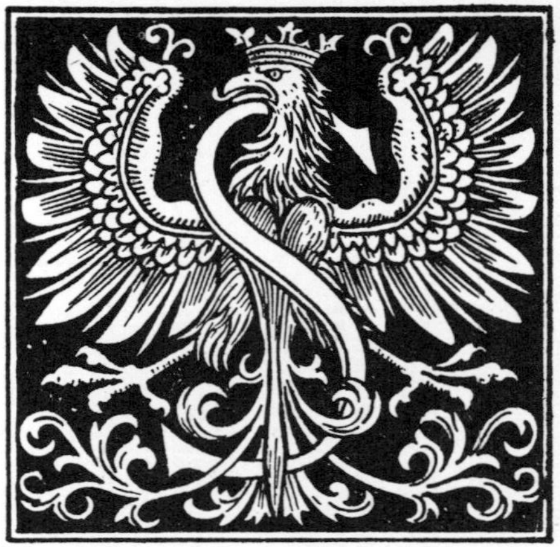

Woodcut initial letter German School~printed at Cracow-1521

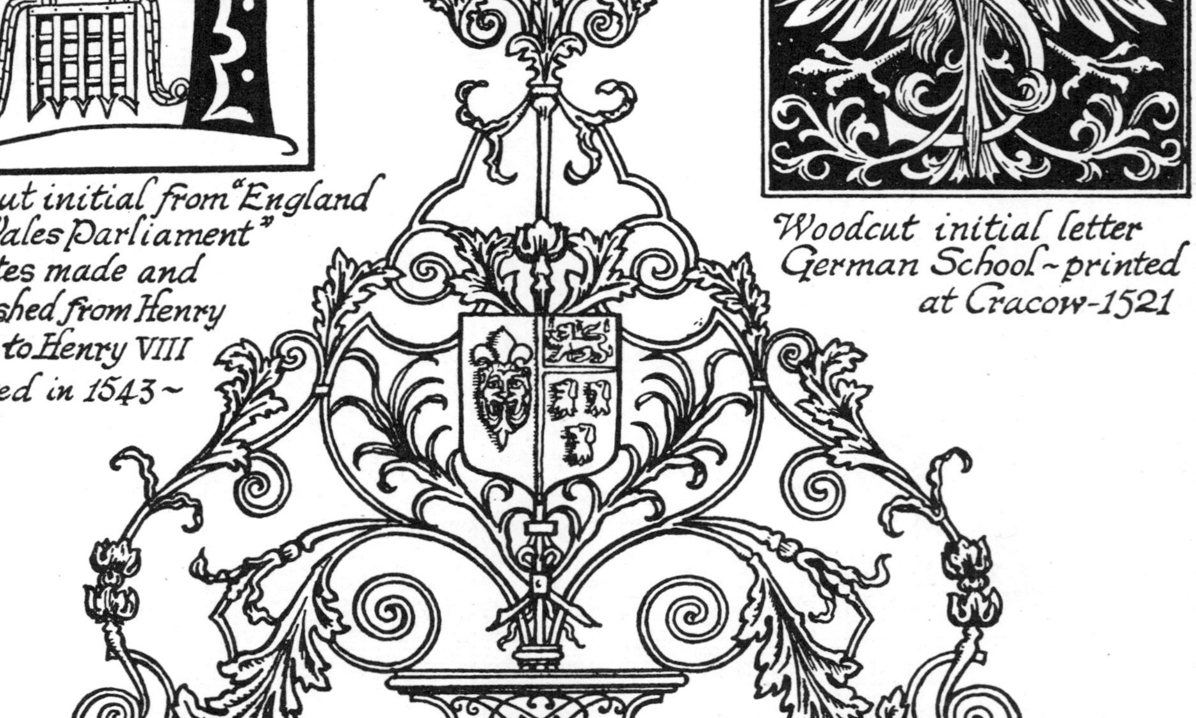

Iron screen from St. John's Church; Frome, Somerset. Arms of Leversedge-English-late 17th century (portion only)

with the Tudor badges of rose and portcullis. These two symbols were much employed as decorations in the buildings of that period—Henry the Seventh's Chapel in Westminster Abbey, and King's College, Cambridge, both contain them many times repeated. The designer of the frontispiece possessed a very refined and subtle sense of line and beauty of proportion in spacing. In proof of this the varied sizes and shapes of crown, rose, portcullis, and shield should be carefully noticed. Again, the relative proportion of the angels to the heraldic animals below, and the shape formed by the label which harmonises so beautifully with the curves of the base of the shield and the lines of the supporters, are all qualities belonging to a skilled composer.

The contrast of straight and curved line throughout the design is also cunningly played upon, while the lettering and the careful drawing of the sweet little plant forms help to complete a very noble composition. It would serve as a suggestion for a fine mural painting or composition in heraldic glass.

The initial A is from the opposite page of the same book and repeats the two Tudor symbols as ornaments.

The gilt key is another example of heraldic art. Here again all the masses and forms with their intervening spaces are interesting in shape and design. The straight lines of the shaft and wards enhance by contrast the richness and ornate design of the handle. The crown, wreath and eagle are all of somewhat unusual character, and the small rounded knobs in the shaft help to distribute the sense of curvature throughout the composition by acting as faint echoes of the main theme, which, of course, resides in the handle.

The incised leather box of German handiwork is richly Gothic in character. The fusing together of the two shields is original and ingenious and the curious charge of the man's head on the one, and the three *fleurs-de-lis* on the other, combined with the erratic foliage and the oddities of the border produce an amusing and unexpected charm. The scaly diaper pattern is probably not intentional, but due to the cracking of the leather through age. It makes, however, such a pleasant patterning of surface that I have drawn it as it stands. The initial letter S, with the eagle, is a rich bit of wood engraving as well as a fine piece of heraldic bird form.

In the screen from St. John's Church, Frome, which, by the way,

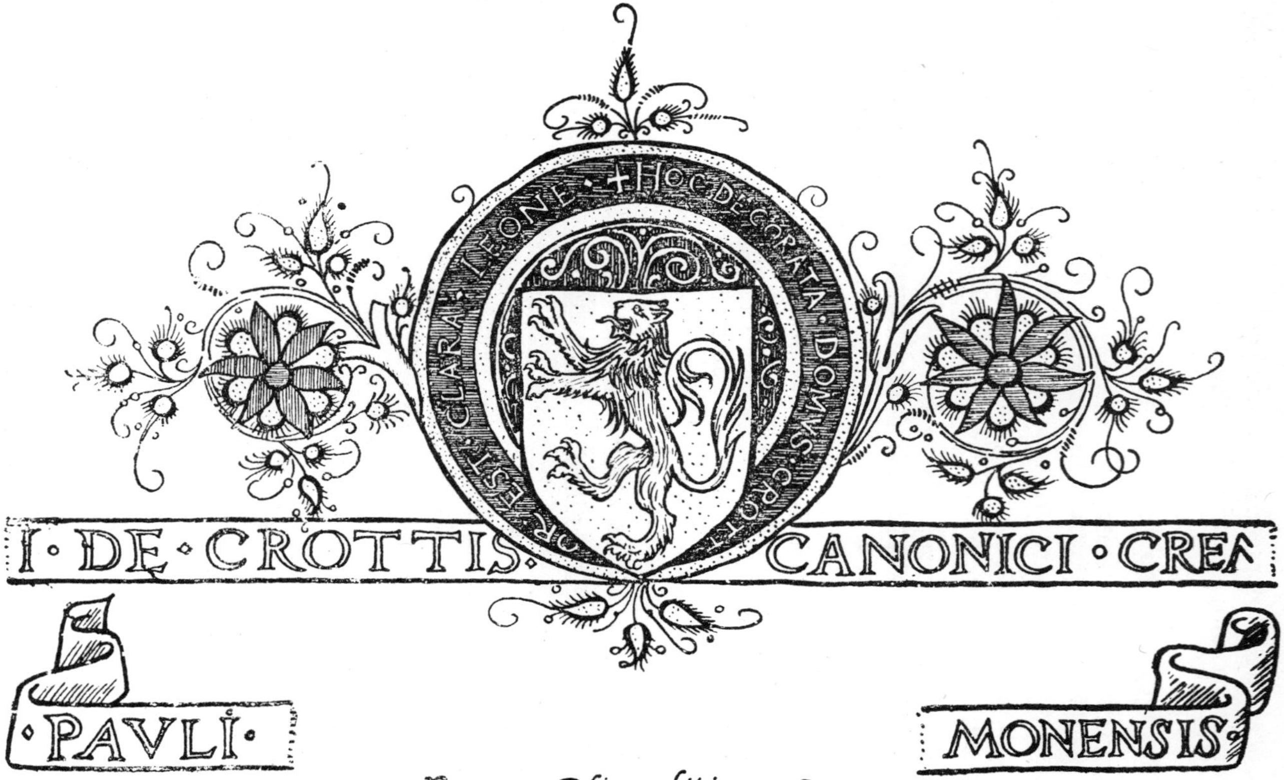

From a folio edition of
"TRACTATUS VISITATIONUM"
by J. F. de Pavinis - printed at Rome
in 1475 with decorations illuminated by hand -
Arms of Paulo Crotti ~ Canon of Cremona -

is a good piece of wrought-iron work, we have a curious charge on the dexter side of the shield which is divided pale wise or *per pale*. It represents a leopard's head, *jessant-de-lys*, that is a *fleur-de-lis* shooting forth or issuing from the head, the tail of the flower coming through the mouth. The sinister half of the shield contains three talbot's heads *erased* and on a chief ermine a lion *passant*. The shield serves a useful "centralising" purpose, and the graceful monogram below supplements the heraldic interest of the composition. The piece of Italian illuminating executed for Paulo Crotti, Canon of Cremona, is totally different from all the foregoing examples. The calligraphic ornament is the result of the craftsman's delight in the use of his instrument and bears a character all its own. It is a curiosity also in that it represents a partial survival of a dying art, for the book in which it appears is a product of the printing press. The scribes and missal-painters naturally would not all at once give up their craft upon the introduction of printing and thus for some time the printed book continued to receive decoration from the hand of the illuminator. In some books spaces were left open in order that painted initial letters might be added. No doubt books of this kind would be treasured by their possessors and the worthy canon tells us in the inscription that decorated thus the House of Crotti is made evident by the Lion. The device forms a tailpiece in the lower margin of the page and is in fact a species of heraldic book-plate.

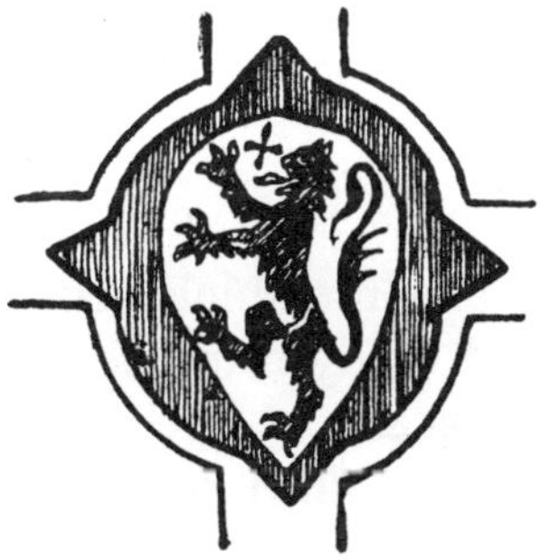

Small pendant cross with enamelled shield
Italian, 14th century

CHAPTER VIII

IN order to continue our notes on the principal elements of the Science of Heraldry, a few examples are given in this chapter of an important branch called "Marshalling." This consists in grouping or bringing together two or more coats of arms either into one shield or one connected heraldic composition.

As a simple instance a man might place his own arms and those of his wife side by side in one shield. The quartering of the Arms of

EXAMPLES of MARSHALLING

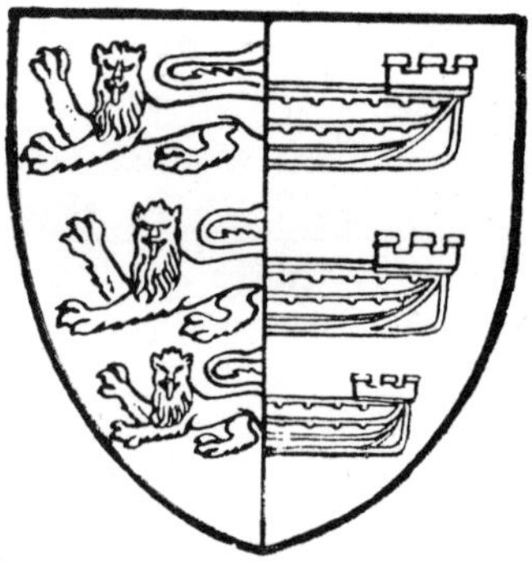

Cinque Ports.

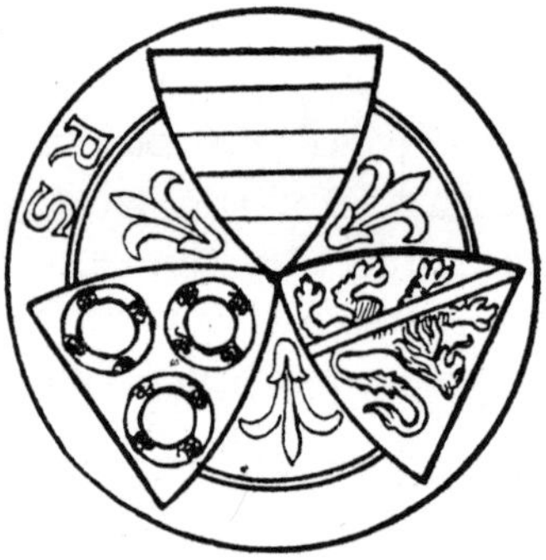

Seal of Matilda de Filliol.

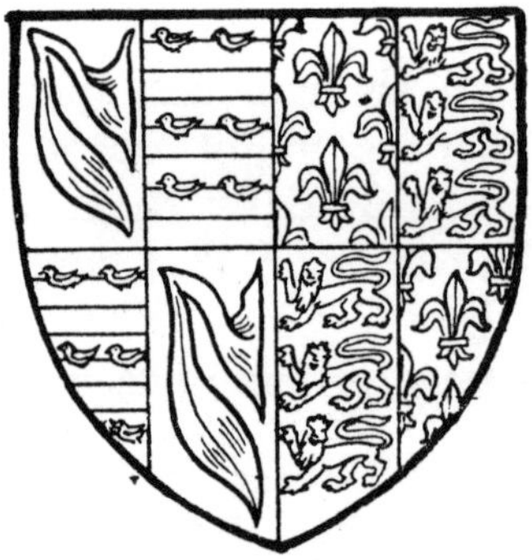

Quartering De Hasting and De Valence and impaling France ancient and England quarterly.

France and England in the same shield, commenced by Edward III., is another well-known and easily remembered example.

Marshalling also embraces the grouping of arms and appanages of various dignities, crests, supporters and other insignia into a complete heraldic achievement.

Until the reign of Richard II. the custom had been merely to use the single hereditary bearings on the one shield of the head of the family, but after that period the fashion of combining more than one set of bearings in the same shield became general.

FRENCH DOOR-PLATES of heraldic design

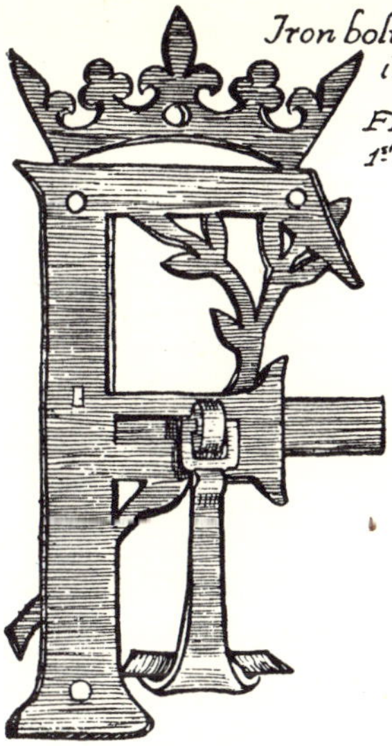

Iron bolt with crowned initial of Francis I
FRENCH
1st half 16th centy.

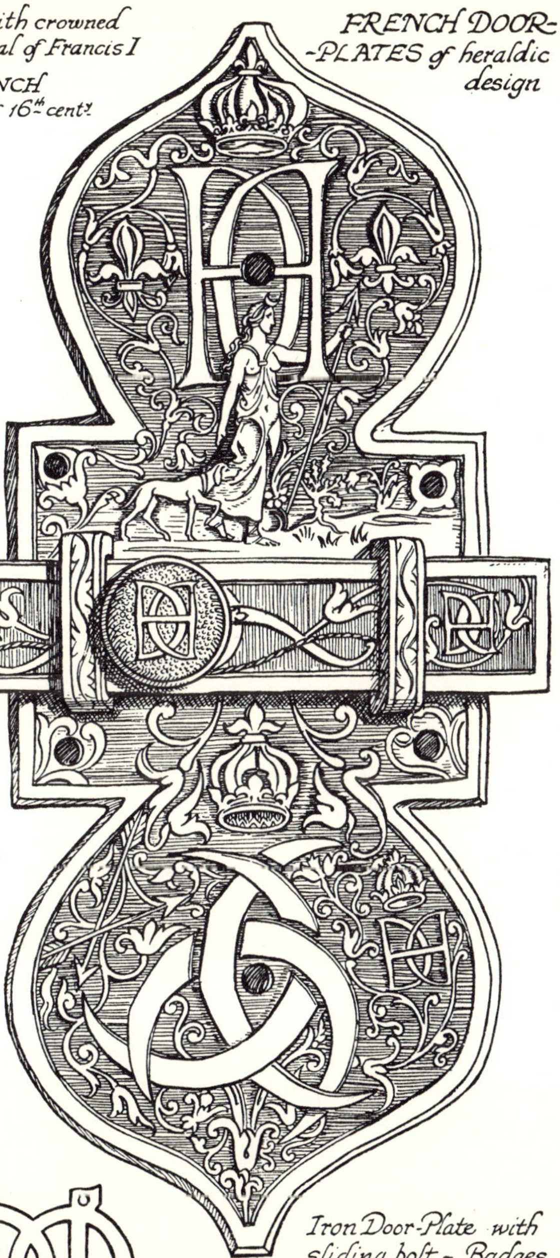

Iron Door-Plate with sliding bolt - Badges and monograms of Henri II & Diane de Poitiers ~ French - 16th c.

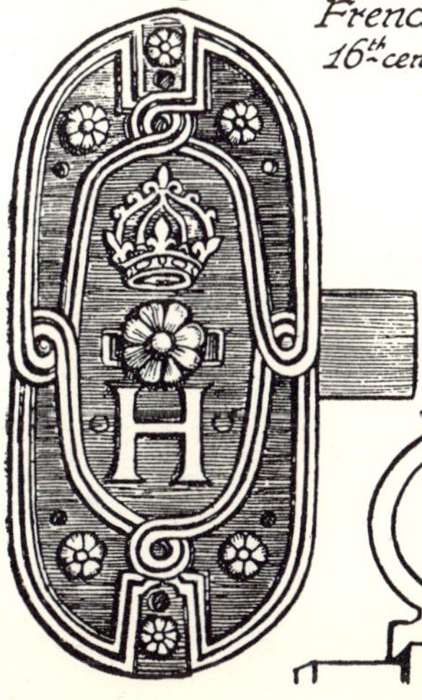

Bolt, iron with escutcheon plate containing crown and monogram
French
16th centy.

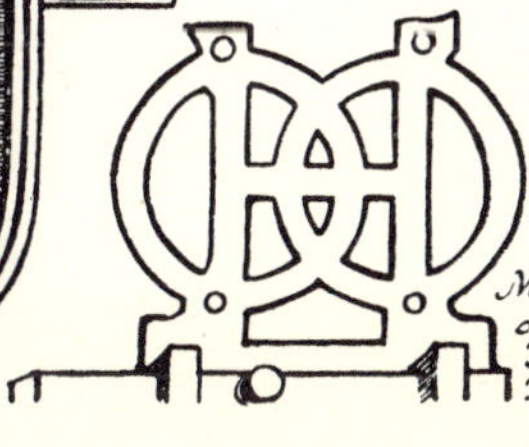

BOLT
Monogram of Henri II & Diane de Poitiers -

"Impalement," that is, placing two coats of arms side by side divided by a vertical line down the centre of the one shield, would naturally be the first method to be employed, and the earliest system was by *dimidiation,* which meant cutting each shield in half and joining the resulting halves together. An example of this is shown in the arms of the Cinque ports. Such combinations would result in rather awkward and unsightly forms, and would be abandoned for the better method of preserving the forms intact and adapting them to the change of space, and this is what actually happened. An examination of the other diagram, shield of John de Hastings, K.G., Earl of Pembroke, where the quartered arms of De Hastings and De Valence impale France ancient and England quarterly will show how the forms are fitted to their new spaces. The old heralds showed great ingenuity and skill in the way they designed their animal and other forms for these difficult positions. A well-known example is the third lion in the lower quarter of the Royal shield, where the curve of the base necessitates a different treatment from that of his companions shown on p. 26.

The maunche or sleeve in the De Hastings quarters it will be noticed is elongated in one instance to accord with the different proportion of space, and on the dexter side of the shield one of the De Valence martlets is sacrificed altogether. As the arms are stated fully in the upper quarter it is left to be understood in the lower one.

The marshalling of arms on seals is very common and sometimes very complicated. An extremely beautiful and simple arrangement is the seal of Matilda de Filliol here shown. She was the daughter of Roger de Lascelles, and was twice married; to Sir W. de Hilton, in 1288, and, secondly, to Sir R. de Filliol, in 1293. Her seal, therefore, contains the arms of LASCELLES—*argent, three chaplets gules;* HILTON—*argent, two bars azure;* and FILLIOL—*gules, a lion rampant argent, over all a bendlet azure.*

Sometimes six, seven or eight shields are grouped round a central one in a seal, the one in the middle representing the principal title and the others the different dignities and estates to which the owner has succeeded. Lack of space forbids the addition of other examples but the reader's attention will be drawn to notice this very interesting and fascinating part of heraldry.

More than one chapter could be written upon, and more than one

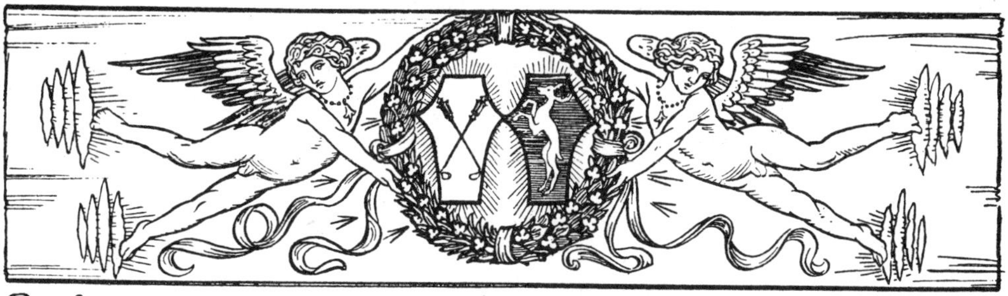

Panel from marriage coffer ~ painted with arms of Condi & Corbinelli ~ Italian, late 15th cent.y

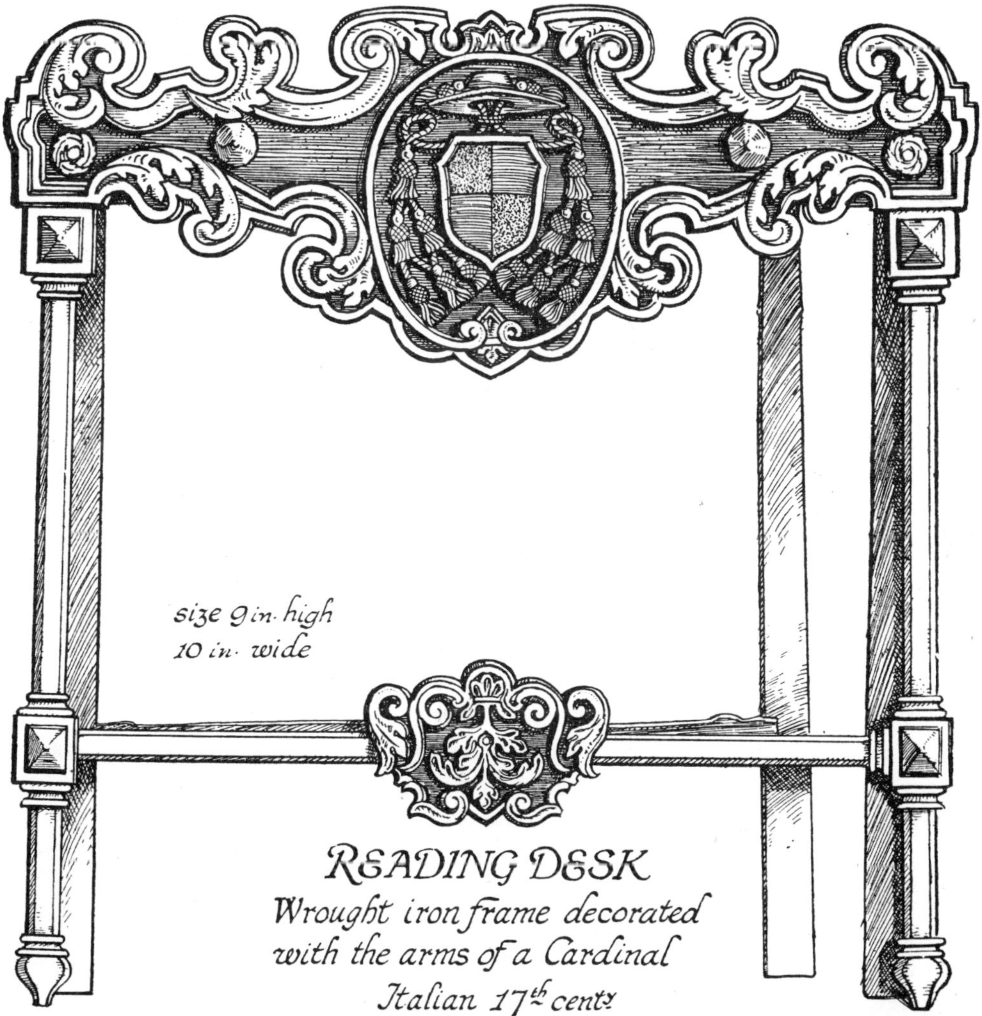

READING DESK

Wrought iron frame decorated with the arms of a Cardinal

Italian 17th cent.y

page filled with illustrations of monograms as badges or heraldic accessories. Some of them are most graceful and ingenious in design, and they often form a valuable decorative note in a composition.

In the bolts and door-plates of French design they are much in evidence, in fact, they are most important elements of the compositions in which they occur. The large one of somewhat eccentric but beautiful shape contains the initials conjoined of Henry II. of France and his mistress Diane de Poitiers. This lady, twenty years older than the king, for when they first met she was thirty-six, while he was but sixteen or seventeen, exercised a remarkable influence, not only on her royal lover, but on the architecture and other arts of her time. Thus we constantly find her badges and monogram in connection with those of the king and also frequent references to her great namesake, the Goddess Diana, pale huntress of the starry heavens, for under this guise the ancients symbolised the silvery moon shooting out her beams of light like arrows across the dark blue sky.

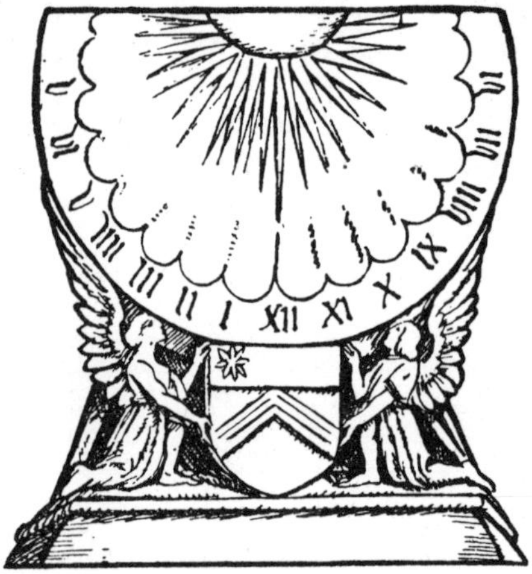

Stone sundial—Northern French, 15th century

So we find in this chiselled iron door-plate besides the crown and *fleur-de-lis* of Henri II. the bow, arrows and intertwined crescent moons of this great court lady, Diane de Poitiers. The little figure of the huntress with the hound is very charming, but it is somewhat dwarfed by the immense monogram above. To have reversed the proportions, making the figure larger and the initials smaller, would have greatly improved the composition. The interwoven initials formed merely by straight lines and circles in the smaller bolt are also a cunning arrangement simple though it seems.

Marshalling again occurs in the panel from the front of an Italian marriage coffer, where the arms of two families are grouped together in a very sweet little wreath of flowers. The amorini, who act as decorative supporters, have all the grace of design and drawing we expect from the period to which they belong.

The Italian marriage coffer or "*cassone*" was a recognised institution in those days as a wedding gift. Gorgeously gilded and often decorated with figure paintings by the prominent painters of the time, it was filled with wearing apparel, household linen and other domestic treasures useful and ornamental. What more natural than that the arms of the great families to which the loving couple belonged should appear as part of the exterior decoration? In this example the arms appear on the front panel, in others a Triumph of Love or Chastity, a scriptural or mythological subject resplendent with colour and gold, takes its place, while the family arms adorn the ends of the chest.

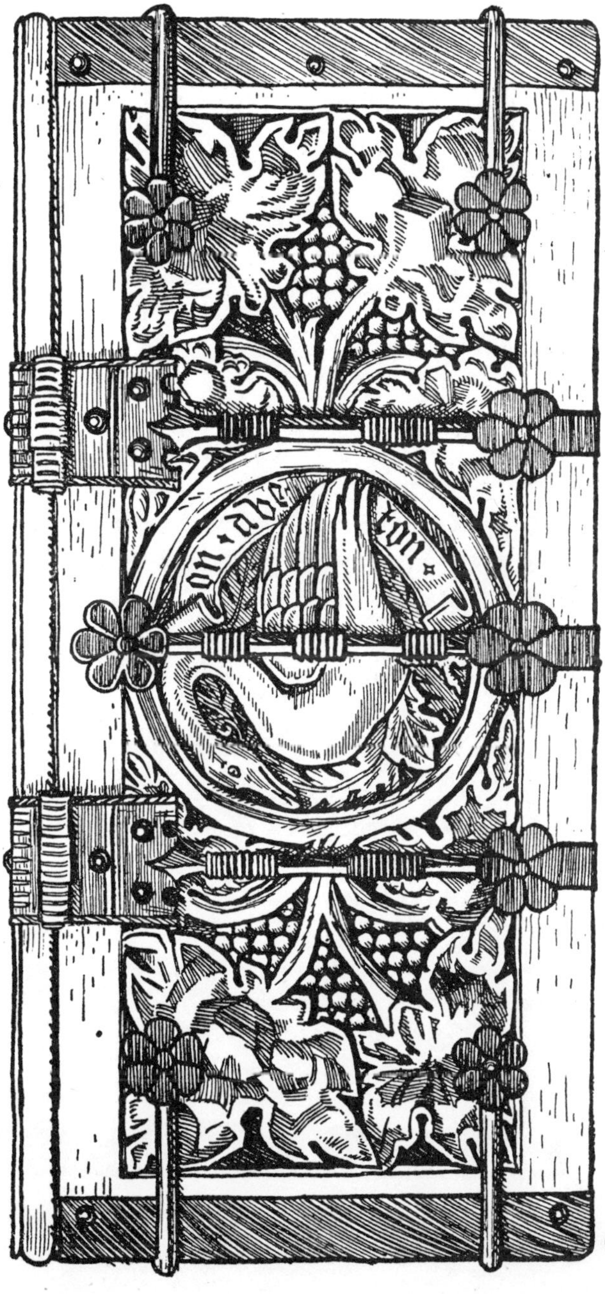

Box in carved beechwood German-15th centy.

The reading desk, decorated with the arms of a Cardinal, is also of Italian workmanship. How decorative the Cardinal's hat and tassels can be made when displayed round a shield this example will show. The ornamental framework is of somewhat

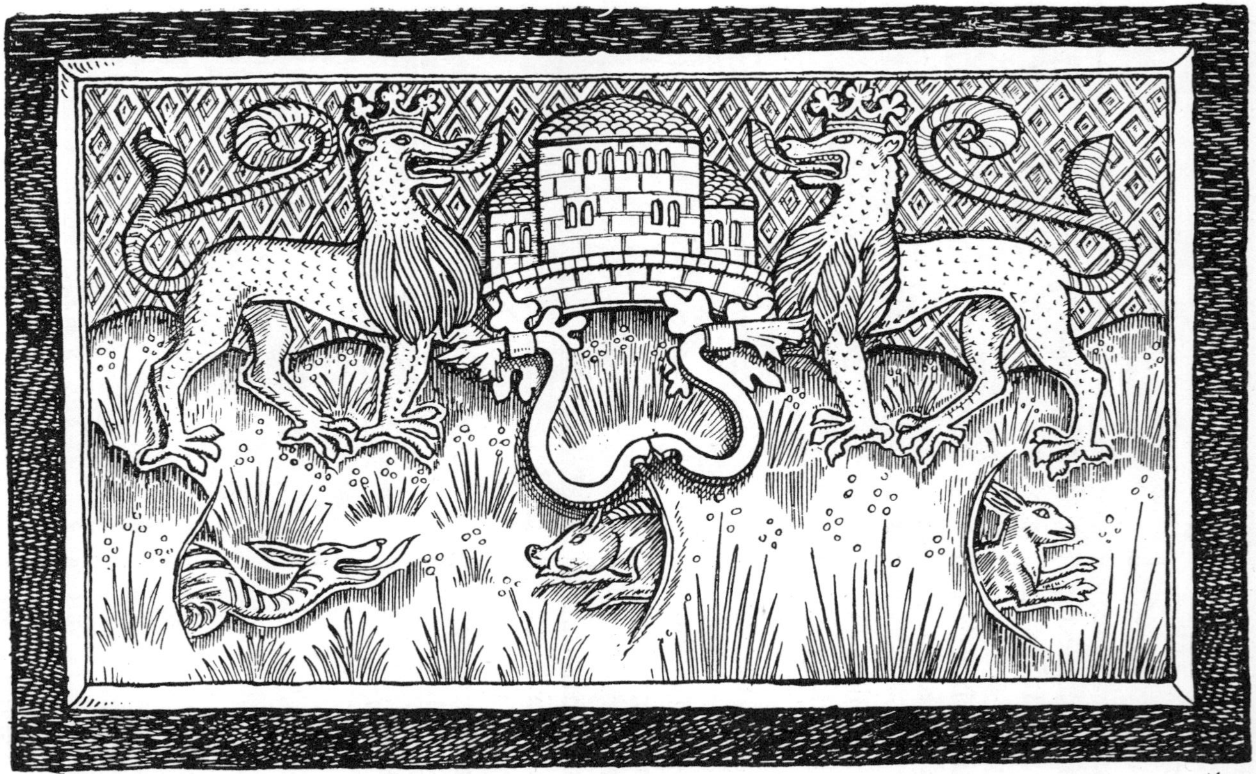

Lid of box in carved beechwood — *German or Swiss 16th cent.?*

meretricious Rococo character, but the whole object is well-proportioned and elegant in general appearance.

How different in style and spirit are the two carved boxes of German and Swiss design. The one containing the "Swan" crest may be called a harmony in black and gold for the beechwood is a rich yellow tone and the metal bands, clasps and hinges are of wrought iron. How strong and vigorous is the carving! The vine foliage is of bold design, deeply cut—a "strong-box" in more senses than one—and such is the impression it leaves on the mind.

The second box, with the crowned lions guarding the decorative city, may or may not possess any heraldic significance, but it is admirably heraldic in character, and a production of unsophisticated genius, just the sort of thing a gifted peasant-craftsman would do if left to himself. The boar, the rabbit and the third mysterious creature all emerging from their respective burrows make an interesting incident of decoration wherewith to support the main theme above, while the "lozengy" background and the tufts of grass and flower add a pleasant variety of surface to the design. It has been painted in black and pale grey green, with red spots in the flowers and animals' tongues. It possesses a simple old-world charm, which is very pleasing besides its merits as a piece of effective decoration.

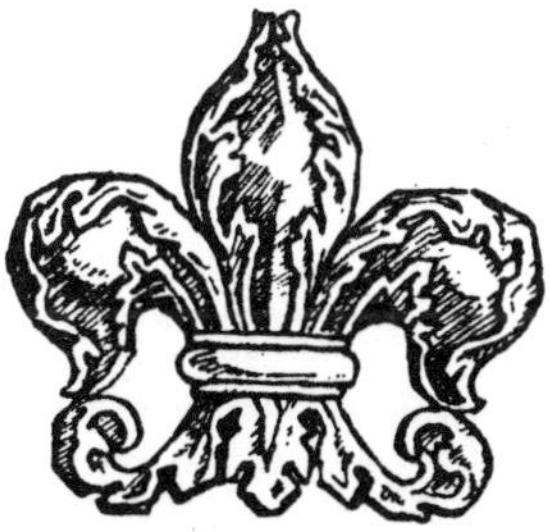

Fleur-de-lis from a mace
English, 17th century

CHAPTER IX

ANOTHER important branch of the technical side of heraldry may be briefly noticed by way of general information. This is Cadency, and with it may be taken its allied subject, Differencing.

Heraldry, like most other things, arose from simple beginnings, but as it progressed difficulties arose, needs had to be satisfied and problems solved, and the invention and resource of the herald had to be exercised accordingly. Marks of Cadency were therefore distinguishing signs or additions made to a shield of arms, in order that the different branches and members of a family should be known from one another, while still retaining the original devices common to all.

Seeing that the function of heraldry was primarily to mark off each individual by an obvious sign or device on shield or helm, two men bearing the same arms would inevitably produce confusion.

Therefore the sons of a family had to resort to some plan by which they could be distinguished from each other, while still bearing the arms of the father or elder brother who succeeded to the title or estates. Something had therefore to be added to the shield, while keeping it still recognisable as the mark of the particular family.

This was at first done in various ways, and not till about the sixteenth century was a definite rule and sequence of signs adopted. Modern cadency now adheres to the rules which had then become general, and a list of nine diagrams is given on the page opposite for information and reference.

Boutell's *Heraldry* gives the following definitions of these two branches of the science:

Cadency.—"That heraldic distinction of the several members of the same family, or of the collateral branches of the same house, which is indicated by some special device."

Differencing or *Brisures.*—"Distinguishing marks introduced into

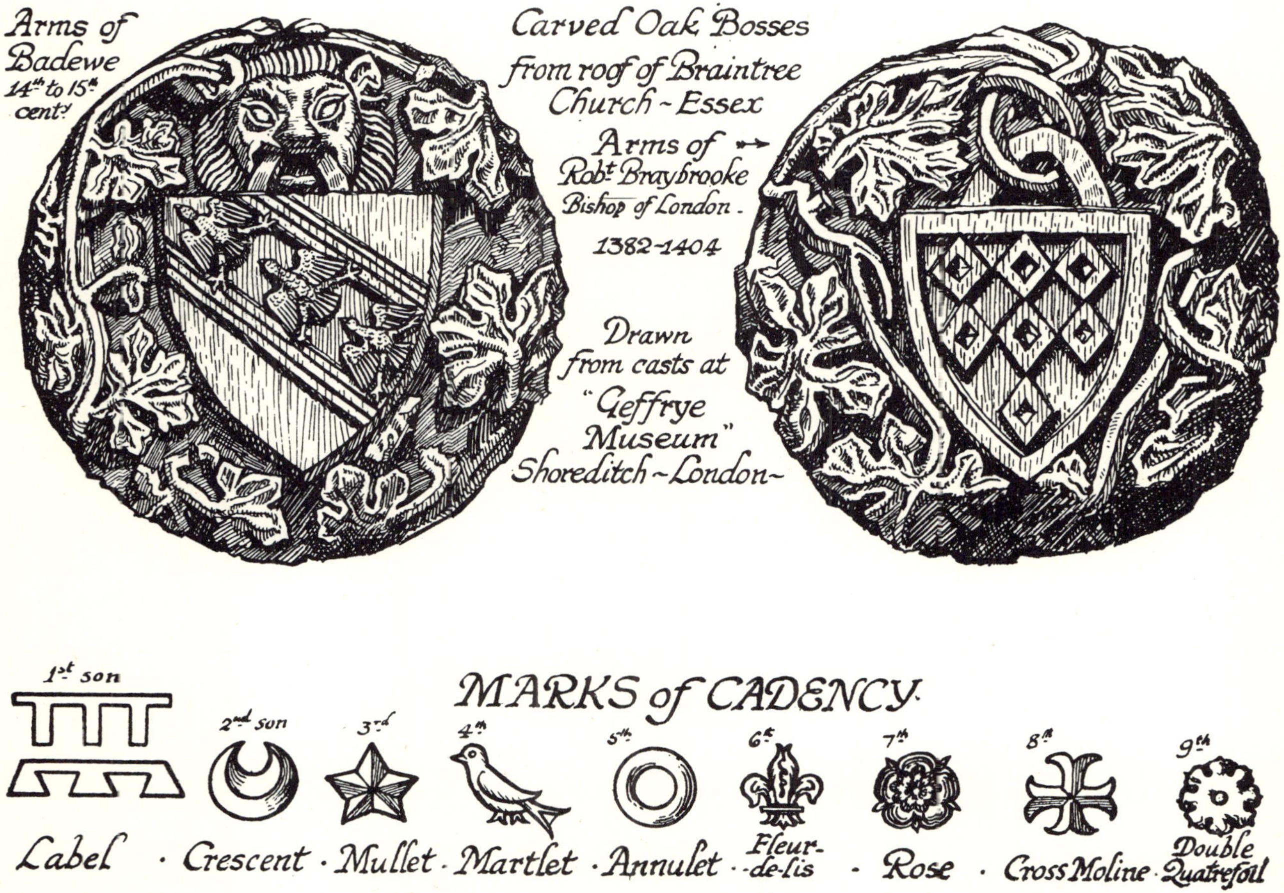
Arms of Badewe 14th to 15th centy.
Carved Oak Bosses
from roof of Braintree Church - Essex
Arms of Robt. Braybrooke Bishop of London.
1382-1404
Drawn from casts at "Geffrye Museum" Shoreditch - London -
MARKS of CADENCY.
1st son
2nd son
3rd
4th
5th
6th
7th
8th
9th
Label · Crescent · Mullet · Martlet · Annulet · Fleur-de-lis · Rose · Cross Moline · Double Quatrefoil

heraldic compositions, for the purpose of identifying different persons who bear the same arms."

It must be borne in mind that the list of diagrams given in this chapter does not apply strictly to the earlier heraldry, and as an instance we may refer to the shield of Edmund, Earl of Lancaster, second son of Henry III., given in Chapter I. He bears the Royal Arms, differenced with a label of five points, each charged with three *fleurs-de-lis*. Prince John of Eltham, son of Edward II., employed the Royal Arms, but added a *bordure* of France, thus compounding the arms of his father and mother (Isabella of France). This is, therefore, an example of both Cadency and Marshalling.

The *bend, chevron, canton,* and other forms, have been used as well as the *bordure* and *label,* as marks of cadency and differencing. The *baton sinister* is the best known mark of illegitimacy, but in earlier times other methods were used for this purpose. Sir Roger de Clarendon, son of the Black Prince, bore—*or, on a bend sa., three ostrich feathers, labelled, arg.*—a sort of parody of his father's badge, the Prince of Wales's Feathers.

Altering the colours either of the field or charges was another method of differencing, in the case of alliances and other similar connections. The subject has many ramifications, but this brief summary will enable the reader to understand the foundations upon which it has been built up.

With regard to the illustrations which accompany this chapter we have in the Collar of Office, made for a Dutch Archery Company, a very beautiful and striking example of the use of heraldry in decoration. On a chain of elegantly designed plates and cartouches the arms of presidents or prize-winners are enamelled in colour, or alternately varied with relief designs of the badges of the craft.

The two principal cartouches are very beautifully designed to compliment each other, and the little coats of arms are most lovingly treated and carefully drawn. At the top of the larger cartouche a figure of Saint Sebastian, the martyr, pierced by arrows, stands tied to a tree trunk. Supporters, represented by a "savage" man and woman, refer no doubt to sylvan sports, while the pendant of the whole chain is the "Popinjay"—the archer's mark, to which his aim and skill were directed.

Shooting at the Popinjay was an ancient sport, which out-lived

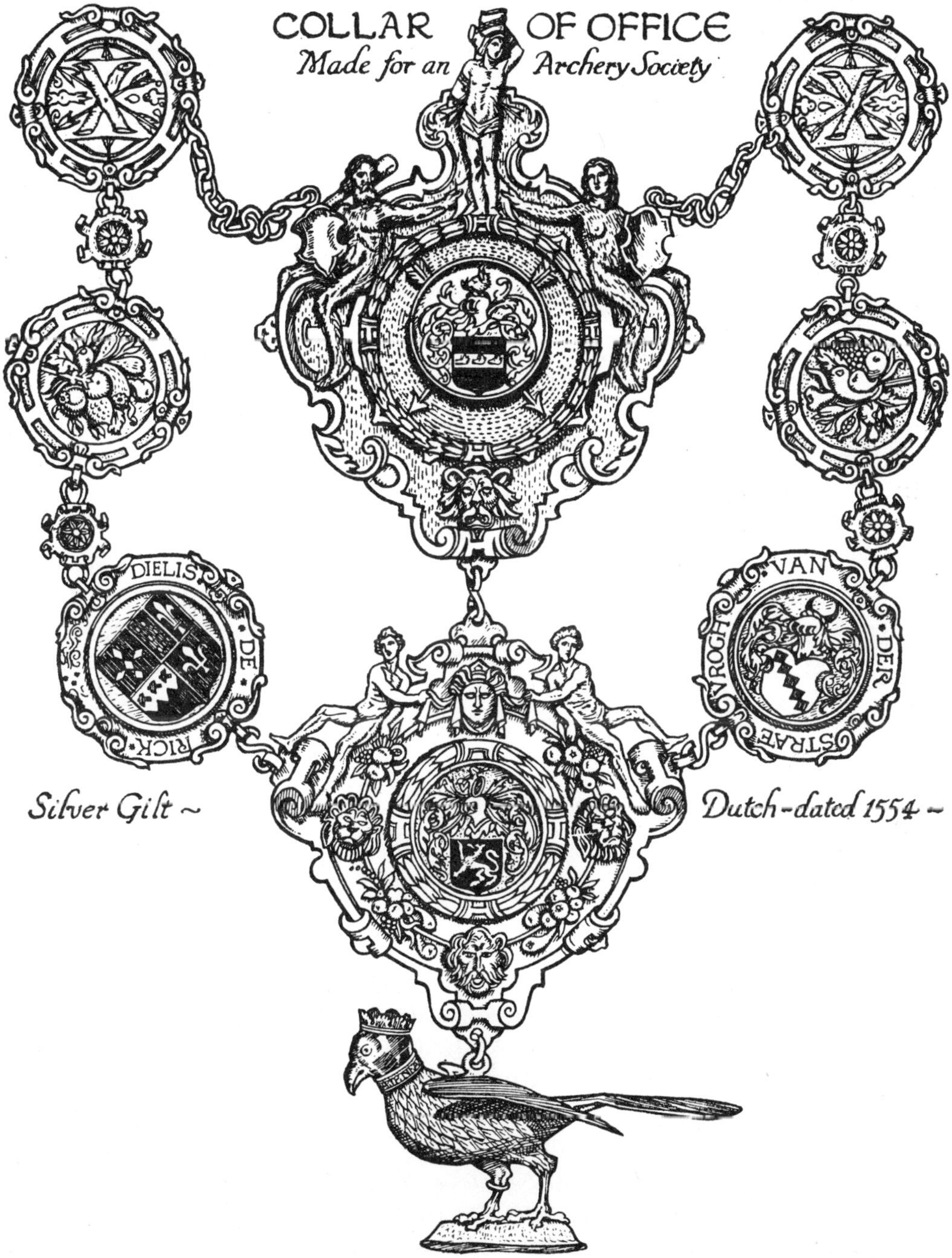

COLLAR OF OFFICE
Made for an Archery Society

Silver Gilt ~ Dutch-dated 1554 ~

the days of archery, and was practised long after the introduction of firearms. Sir Walter Scott mentions its survival in Scotland in his own time, and he gives a short description of the game in his novel *Old Mortality*. The passage quoted below is from the second chapter of that splendid tale. The date given is 1679, more than a century later than that of our Dutch chain of office.

"When the musters had been made, and duly reported, the young

Mount of a Sword sheath
hammered & chiselled iron

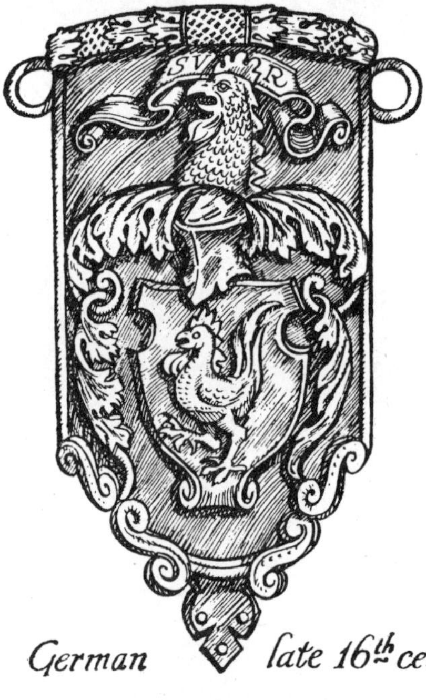

German late 16th cent.

Pair of Scissors

Steel
pierced & engraved
with the arms of
Cavendish
English (Sheffield)
about 1840

men, as was usual, were to mix in various sports, of which the chief was to shoot at the popinjay, an ancient game formerly practised with archery, but at this period with firearms. This was the figure of a bird, decked with party-coloured feathers, so as to resemble a popinjay or parrot. It was suspended to a pole, and served for a mark, at which the competitors discharged their fuses and carabines in rotation, at the distance of sixty or seventy paces. He whose ball brought down the mark, held the proud title of Captain of the Popinjay for the remainder of the day, and was usually escorted in triumph to the most reputable change-house in the neighbourhood, where the evening was closed with conviviality, conducted under his auspices, and, if he was able to sustain it, at his expense."

These shooting guilds were a public institution in Holland, nor

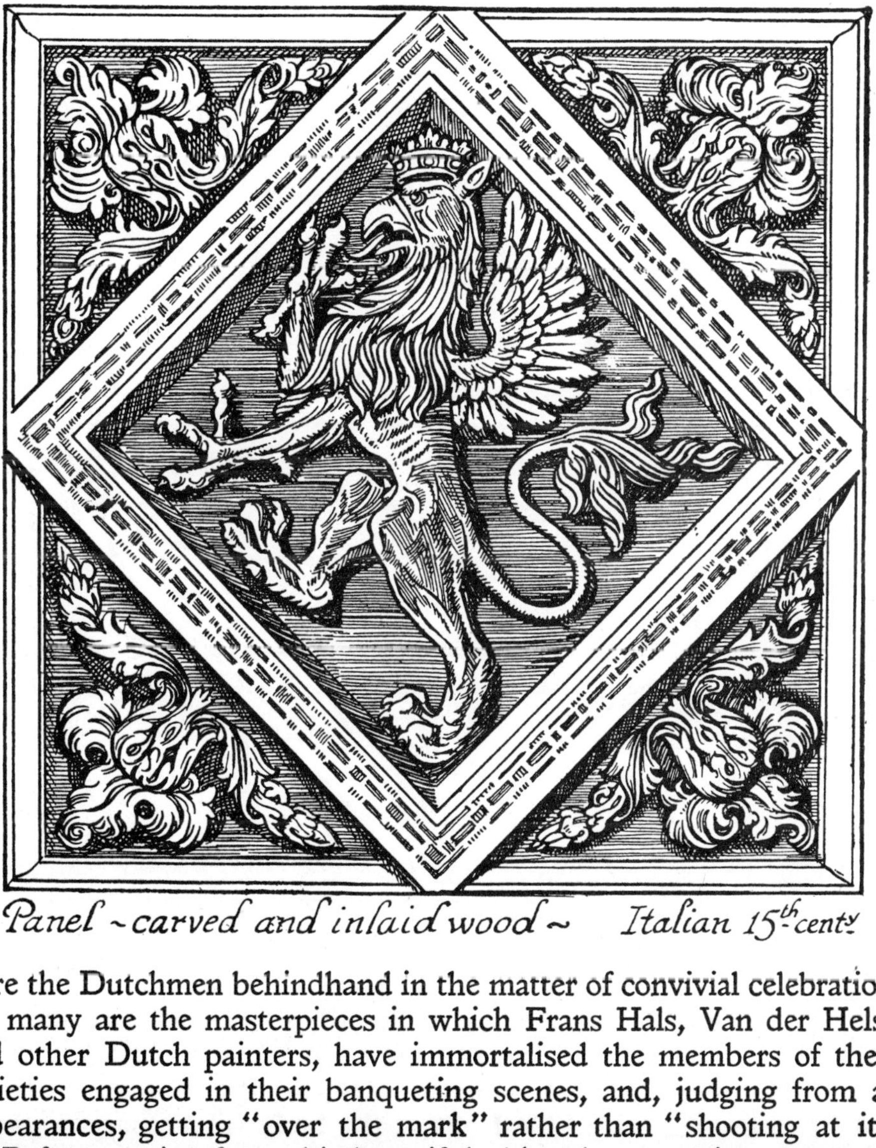

Panel ~ carved and inlaid wood ~ Italian 15th cent.

were the Dutchmen behindhand in the matter of convivial celebration, for many are the masterpieces in which Frans Hals, Van der Helst, and other Dutch painters, have immortalised the members of these societies engaged in their banqueting scenes, and, judging from all appearances, getting "over the mark" rather than "shooting at it."

Before parting from this beautiful object let us notice once more the decorative value of the fine lettering on two of the small plates. The whole composition is greatly enhanced by these inscriptions.

The mount for a sword sheath of German workmanship is a

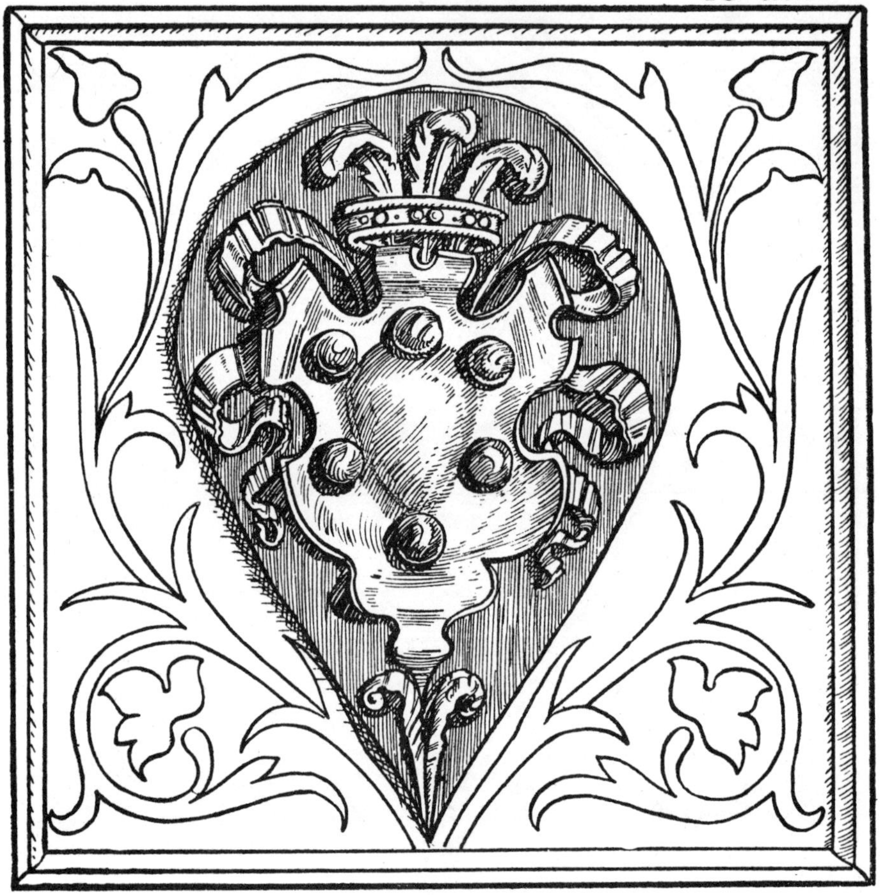

Panel from a walnut coffer. Medici arms ~ Italian 16th cent.

pleasing little composition, rich and compact in design. The cantle or piece cut out of the shield at each side may be noticed here with advantage. This shape originated with a notch cut out of the dexter side of the shield for the lance to pass through, thus enabling the knight to protect the whole front of the body while charging, and a shield of this form was said to be *à bouche*, i.e., having a mouth. When two shields were grouped together in a composition, it sometimes pleased the herald's fancy and sense of symmetry to give one of them the dexter notch, and the other the sinister. Afterwards a notch on both sides was considered an ornamental addition, but where a shield is represented alone it is always safer to place the notch on the dexter side, in accordance with the regular use for which it was designed.

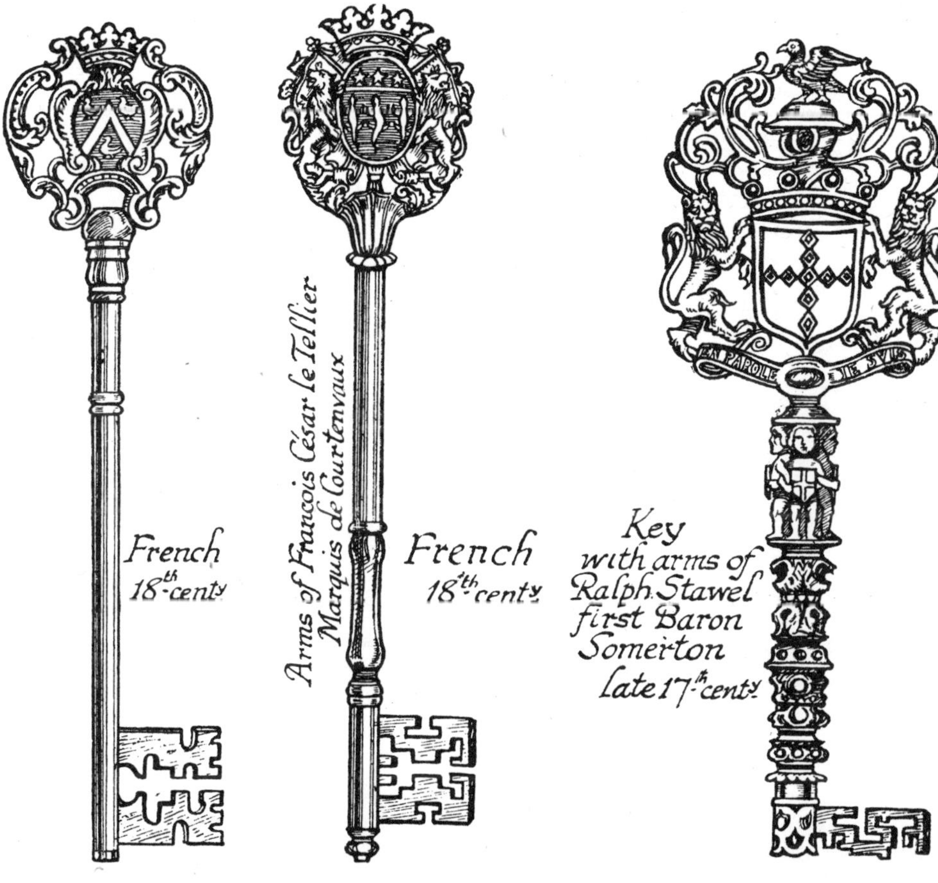

A very pretty result is obtained by the use of heraldry in the pair of scissors, containing the arms of Cavendish, and moreover, the late period, 1840, is not one from which we might hope to see so excellent a bit of decorative design.

The carved and inlaid panel of fifteenth-century Italian design is a fine specimen of heraldic animal drawing. Though it belongs to the period of the Renaissance it is a powerful rival ot the true Gothic griffins in the matter of sinewy strength and rampant ferocity, while the technical qualities of the carving are excellent in finish and completeness.

The panel containing the Medici arms is also a very pleasing and elegant composition. Part of its charm lies in the colour harmony produced by the gilding and yellow inlay on the rich walnut brown background. The gilded pills are punning references on the family

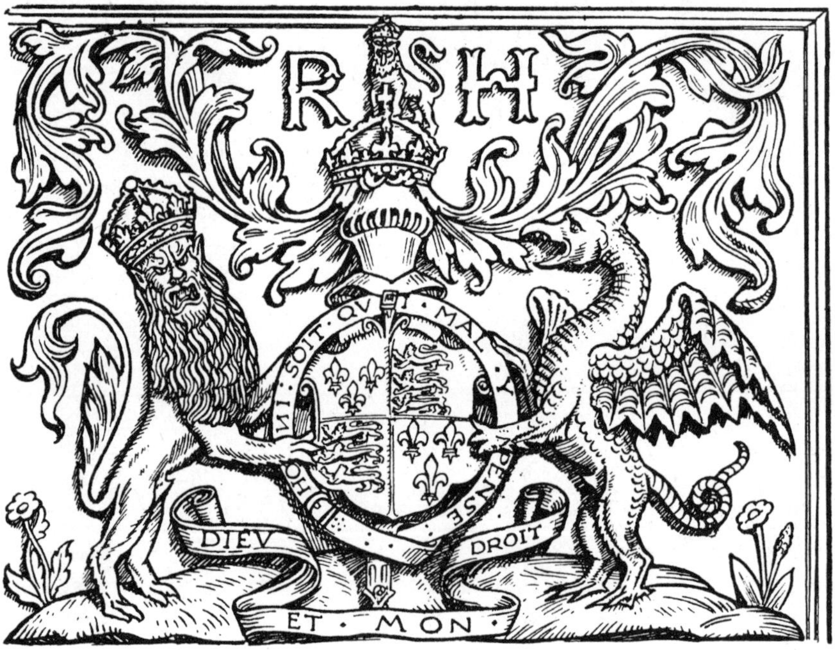

Carved oak panel from Beckingham Hall, Tolleshunt Major, Essex English, dated 1546

name, which is the plural of *medico* or doctor. This illustrious Florentine family contained members who by their great wealth as merchants, became bankers and money-lenders, and it is said that the three golden balls of the pawnbroker's sign are derived from this source.

Three keys with heraldic decoration are added in this chapter in order to do justice, if possible, to the beauty of design which was expended on such objects in those days. The earlier one, of English make, is the best, and will bear a close scrutiny in detail, with every satisfaction to the eye. The other two belong to the Rococo period, but are pleasant in shape and sufficiently simple in mass, therefore they do not offend by over-elaboration. Debased as the Rococo style no doubt is, there is a quality about it which suits the glitter and reflections of gilded or polished metals, and which has a charm of its own.

A fine specimen of Tudor heraldry is the panel of the Royal Arms of Henry VIII. The dragon again occurs here as one of the supporters. Tudor heraldry may be called the second best period of the art before the decay set in, and this panel contains many fine qualities. The mound which serves as a base for the composition, and the decorative plant forms at each side, are all very happily thought out.

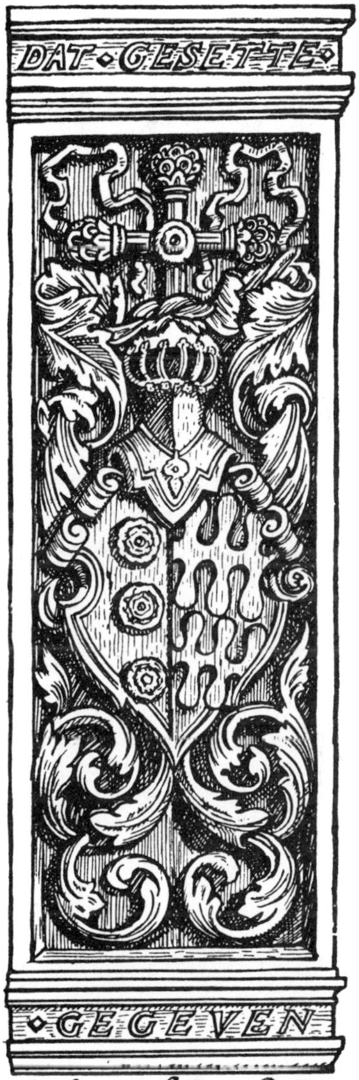

Oak panel from Coffer-front-North German-1584

The oak panel from a German coffer front is a bold and manly piece of wood-carving. The shield is beautiful in shape, and the mantling, crest and charges are all carried out with strength and thoroughness of workmanship. With its companion at the other side, it flanks an elaborate figure panel, giving an effective completion to the design without competing in interest with the central composition.

The two ceiling bosses of carved oak from Braintree Church, Essex, are excellent examples of Gothic work, though we possess them in a somewhat damaged condition. The spontaneity of design and rich decorative effect compel our admiration, and again we are forced to say what fine effects are produced by the combination of heraldic devices and decorative plant forms. They were drawn from casts at the Geffrye Museum, Shoreditch, London, a most interesting but not very well-known collection, devoted to furniture and woodwork. The objects are lodged in a picturesque group of old almshouses of the "Wren" style of domestic architecture, founded by one of the city fathers, Sir Robert Geffrye, early in the eighteenth century. It is well worth a visit, and permission to sketch can be obtained from the curator, who is always most willing to assist those interested in his special subject.

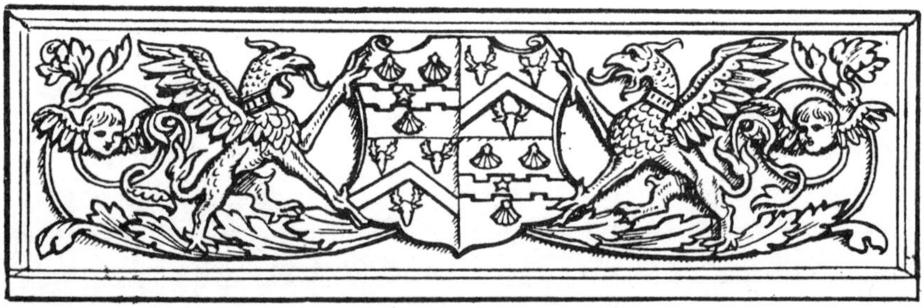

Carved oak panel from Beckingham Hall, Tolleshunt Major, Essex
English, dated 1546

CHAPTER X

IN the last chapter mention was made of the "cantle" or piece cut out of the dexter side of the shield for the lance to pass through. We saw from examples how the heralds began to cut notches on both sides of the shield, prompted, no doubt, by a desire to obtain symmetry in ornamental effect when grouping two shields together in one heraldic composition. From these ornamental scoopings of the edge of the shield the cartouche was no doubt developed.

As most decorators are aware, any ornamental shield shape or similar form capable of containing a coat of arms or heraldic device, is now called a cartouche, whether it contains armorial designs or not.

The cartouche being a form frequently employed in decoration, particularly in relation to heraldry, the examples given in this chapter will doubtless be found welcome and useful.

The German specimen at the base of p. 94 shows, perhaps, the first stage of development from the shield, with the ornamental scoop on right and left side, towards greater elaboration. It will be noticed that the two notches have grown into large and subtly-designed concavities, while the top and base of the shield have likewise been treated with ornamental curvature.

As the eye travels from this example to the other forms on the same page, we can readily imagine the processes of elaboration which finally resulted in the scrolls, strap-work and foliated edges, curls and volutes, which distinguish the endless varieties from one or the other.

The word is derived from *Carta*, the Italian for paper, and the words *card* and *cartridge*, and the French *cartouche*, come from the same root. Cartridges were so called because they contained powder and ball wrapped up in card or paper.

Very useful suggestions for the drawing of cartouches can be obtained by cutting ornamental shapes out of thick paper, and then curling and twisting the ends into volute forms.

SOME EXAMPLES of the CARTOUCHE

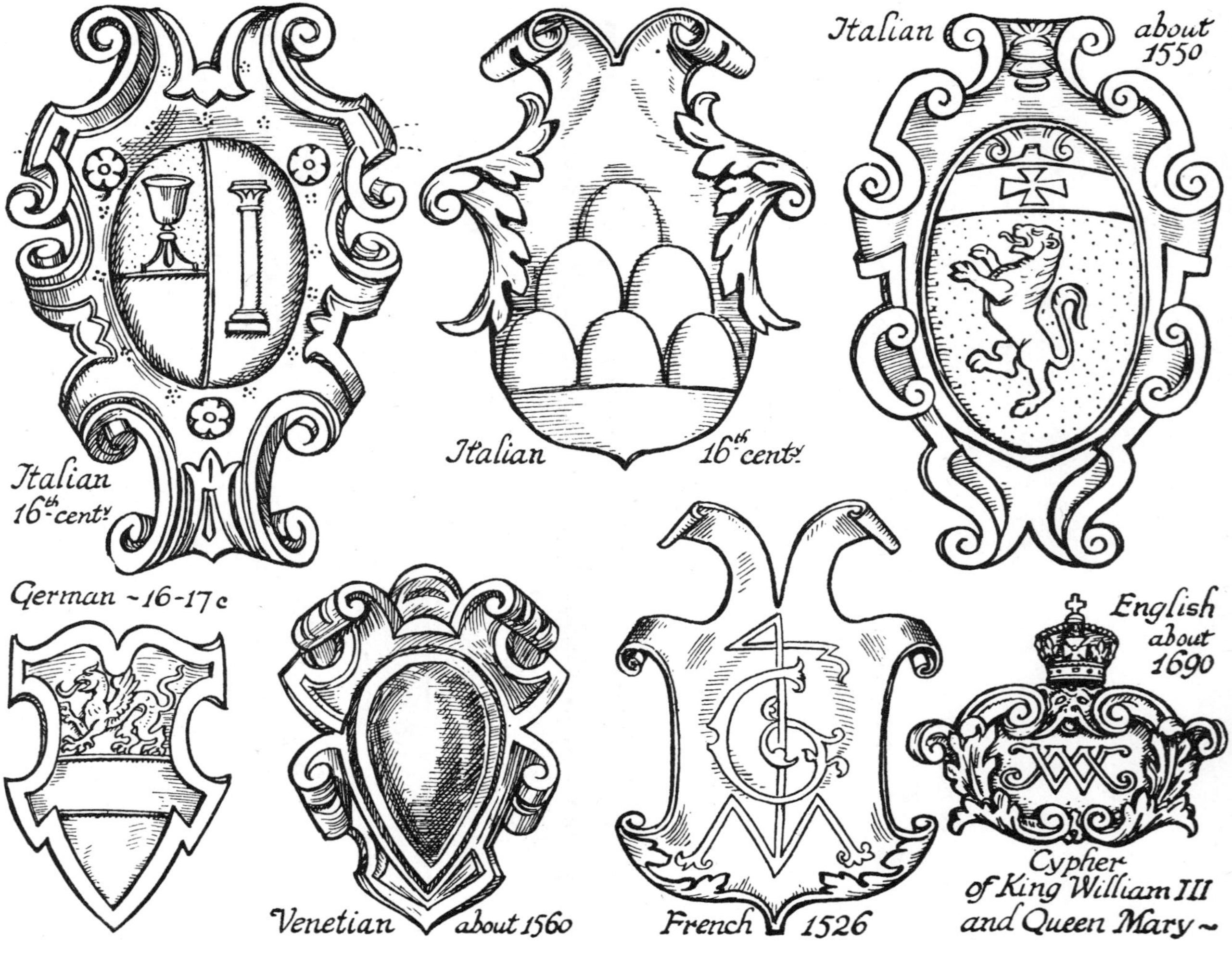

Carved decoration on back of folding Arm Chair of walnut wood
Italian ~ 16th cent^y

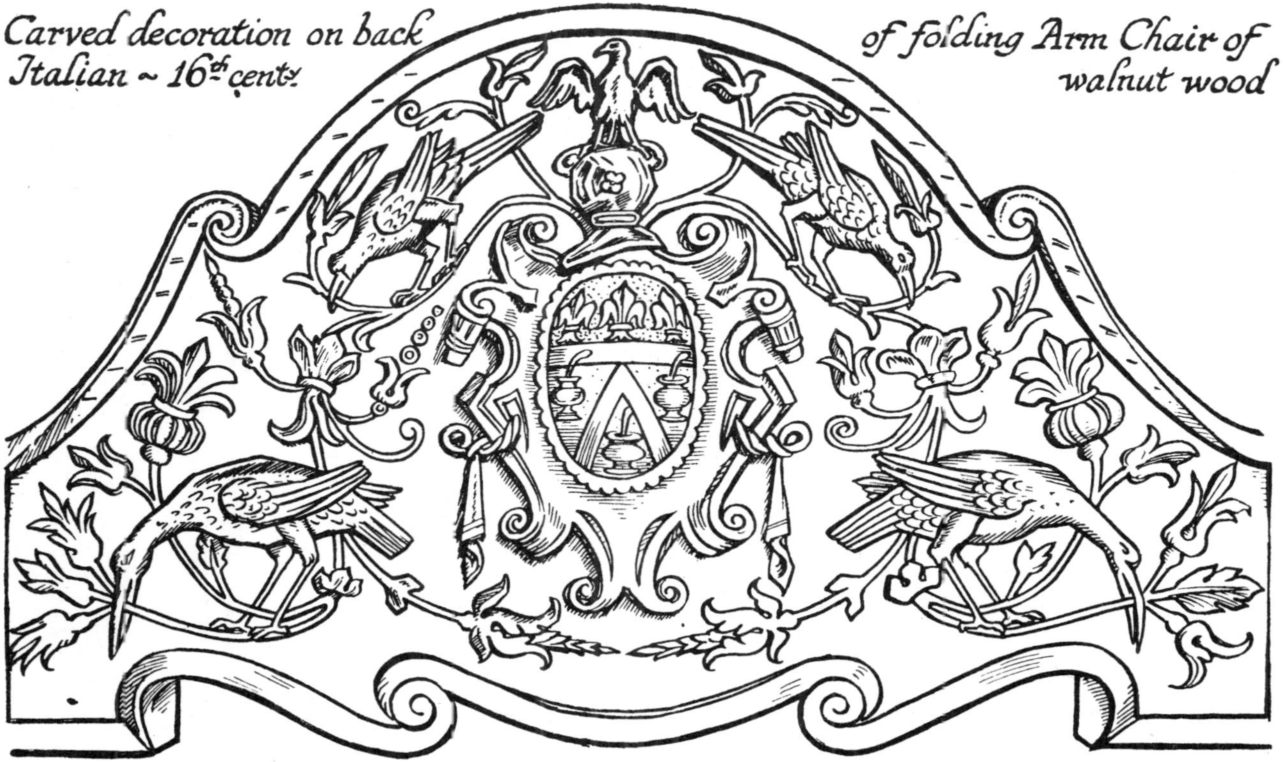

Probably this was done in practice by some of the old designers; it can, at any rate, be seen frequently in thin metal, both in old and modern work, where ornamental shields and cartouches have been used.

The French and Italian craftsmen designed and drew these forms very beautifully, as our illustrations will show, though the heraldic work belongs to a poor period. The podgy and pusillanimous rampant lion on one of these examples has sadly degenerated when we compare him heraldically with his fiery and ferocious ancestors.

The ingeniously designed monogram of King William III., and his consort, Queen Mary, may be noticed in passing. In combination it represents both their initials: taken apart, neither.

The Italian carved chair-back contains a cartouche charged with a coat of arms as the central feature of the decoration, and shows how the shield may be framed off by this means from the surrounding ornament. Much beautiful work will be found in this panel; the birds have life and action combined with firm drawing, the ornament is graceful in line and contains pleasant suggestions of rose-bud forms, which redeem it from any dull conventionality.

The panel, in carved oak, from a French chimney-piece of the sixteenth century, is a design full of freshness and charm. A pleasing variety of treatment will be observed throughout the different elements of which it is composed.

The Spanish panel, containing the arms of a prelate, is another rich piece of heraldic decoration, in which all the various forms and details combine to produce a very happy result. The bold and rounded forms in high relief catch the light on their well-modelled surfaces, the colour of the rich brown wood adding to the effect.

The other walnut panel, of Spanish workmanship, contains the arms of the ancient kingdoms of Castile and Leon, play upon words again being used here heraldically by the devices of "castle" and "lion." The crown above the shield is interesting and uncommon, and draws attention perforce to the wonderful variety of form in the matter of crown designs to be found in heraldic work of different periods. The two strange birds pluming themselves present an unexpected element, which adds a somewhat peculiar beauty and charm to the composition.

The French carved wood panel opposite containing the degenerate,

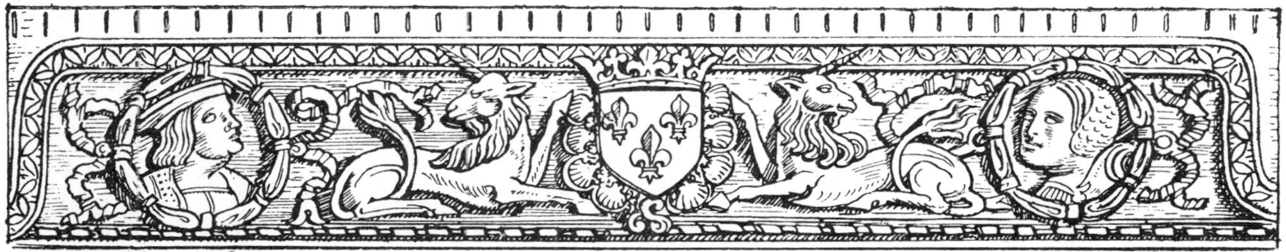

Portion of Chimney-piece ~ carved oak French ~ 1st half 16th century ~

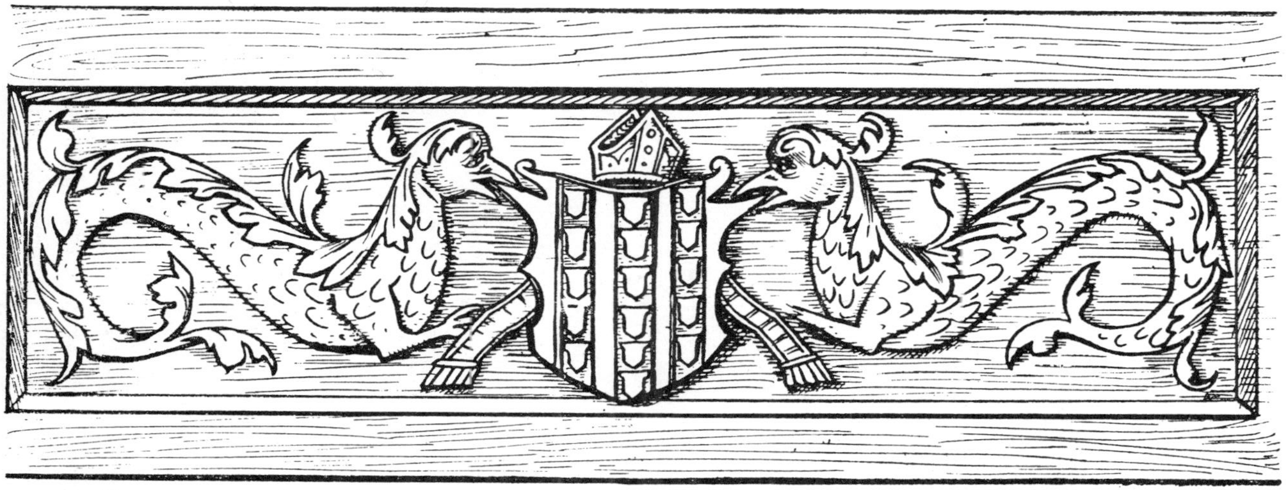

Panel ~ carved walnut ~ French 1st half 16th cent.

but ornamental creatures, holding a bishop's mitre and shield is more curious than beautiful, but as a piece of decoration it is typical of the period.

The remaining illustrations are all taken from objects of still later date than the preceding, but they are good examples of heraldic decoration. The quaint spoon, with the owner's name and coat of arms on the handle, is a good specimen of German goldsmith's work of the seventeenth century.

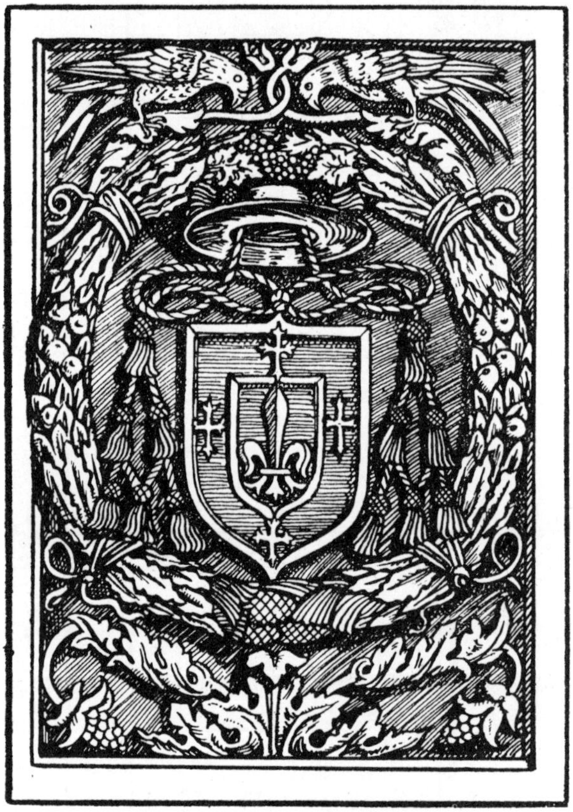

Walnut panel with the arms of a Prelate ~ Spanish ~ 16th cent.

In mass, outline and proportion, it shows fitness and beauty, plain and decorated surfaces are well contrasted and relieved against each other. The well drawn, elegant lettering on the handle, has a great decorative value in the scheme of the whole, while the shield, helm and mantling are adroitly grouped together to form a pleasing juncture, ornamental as well as structural, between the bowl and the handle. The displayed wings at each side of the helm are a common feature of German heraldry, but whether the three feathers at the top of the handle have any armorial significance it is impossible to say.

Two very stately objects of English design and craftsmanship are to be seen in the silver staff-head of the Clothworkers' Company and the gilded mace of the town of Retford.

The former is one of many of the same kind possessed by the

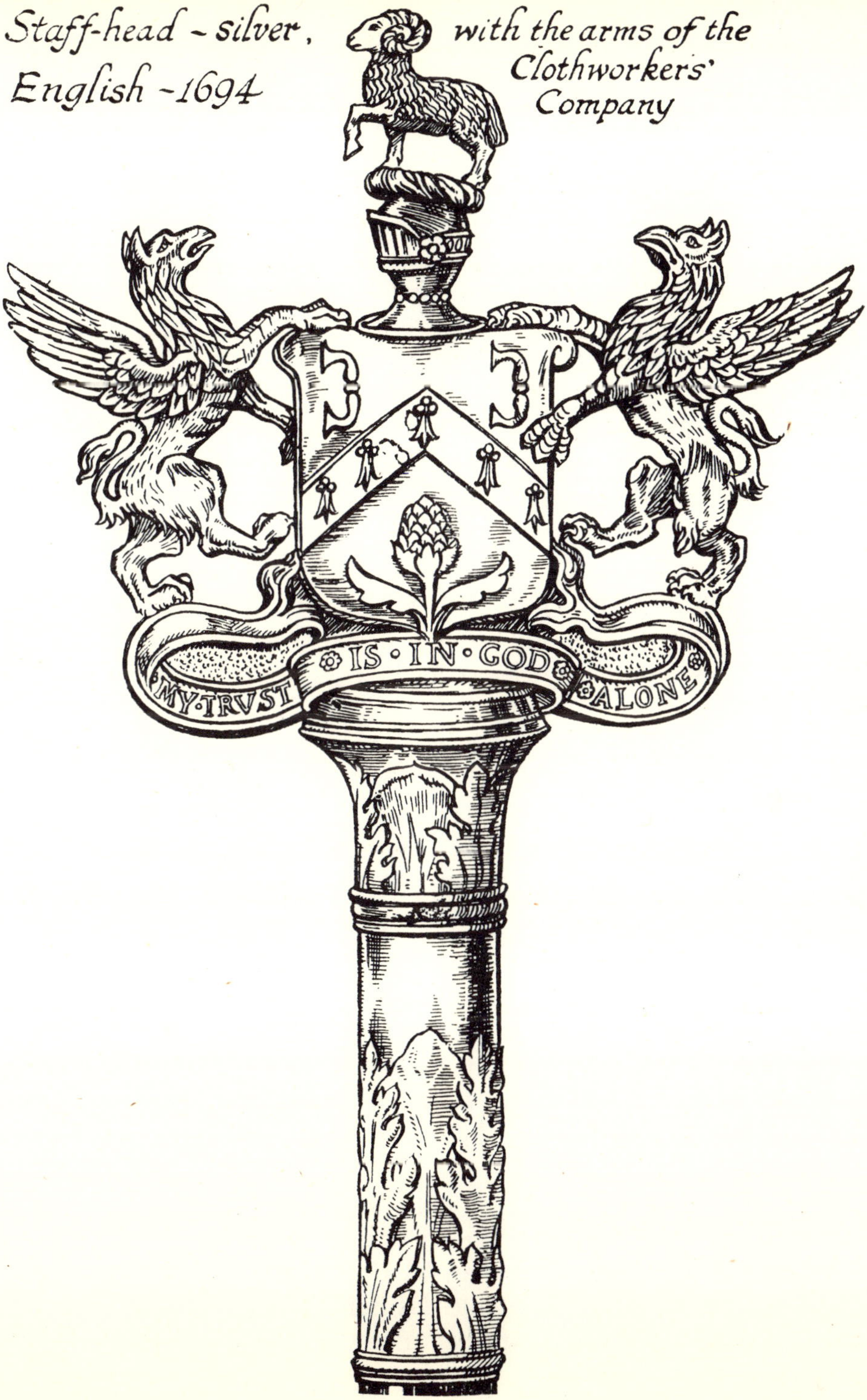

Staff-head - silver, with the arms of the Clothworkers' Company
English - 1694

great city companies of London. The drawing is from an electrotype copy in South Kensington Museum, and the original object will, no doubt, have many times played its part in the stately ceremonies of the ancient guild it represents.

The arms of the Clothworkers' were granted in 1530, during the reign of Henry VIII., and the crest and supporters in 1587, by Queen Elizabeth. In the old blazonry of the time they are thus described:

"Sables a Cheueron ermynee between two hauettes i' the fece siluer and a tasell cob in the poynt golde Vpon the healme on a wreathe Siluer and Sables on a mounte vert a Rame gold the Supporters two Griffens (gold pelle) tye mantled Sables doubled Siluer."

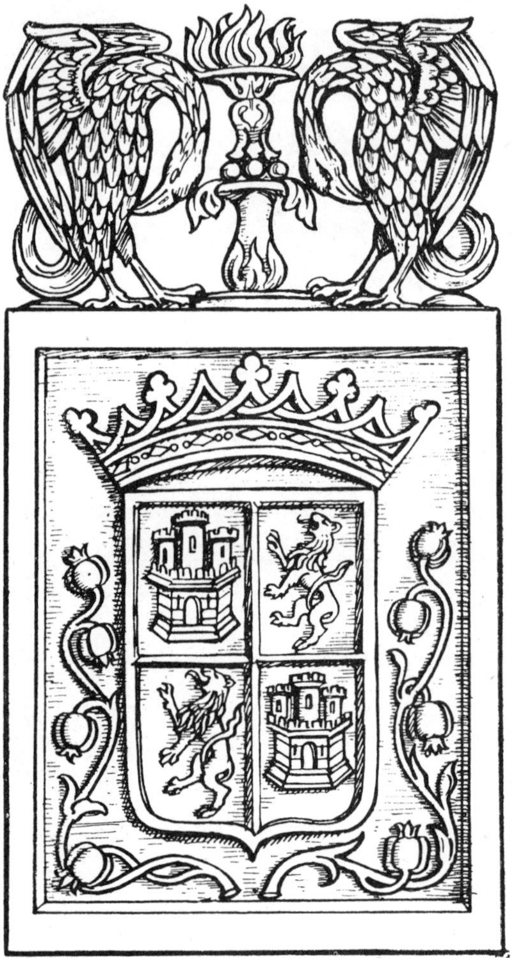

Walnut panel ~ Spanish 16th cent.

The two curious hooks or handle-shapes in the upper half of the shield are called "habicks" or "havetts," tools used in the trade. The "tasell cob" mentioned in the description above is the head of the "teasel" or "teazel," and the form on the shield is a very conventional rendering of that noble plant.

In ancient days it was always cultivated near to cloth and fustian mills, as its prickly, hooked spines were used for raising the nap on the surface of the material, a method now performed by machinery. It may even now be used in old-fashioned places where primitive crafts still survive, and I remember many years ago an old cloth mill

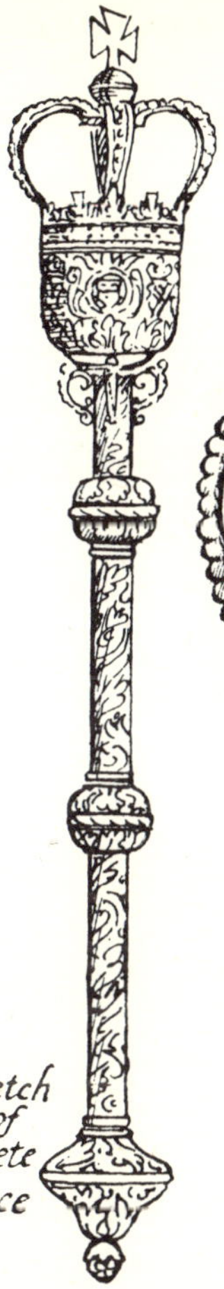

Sketch of complete piece

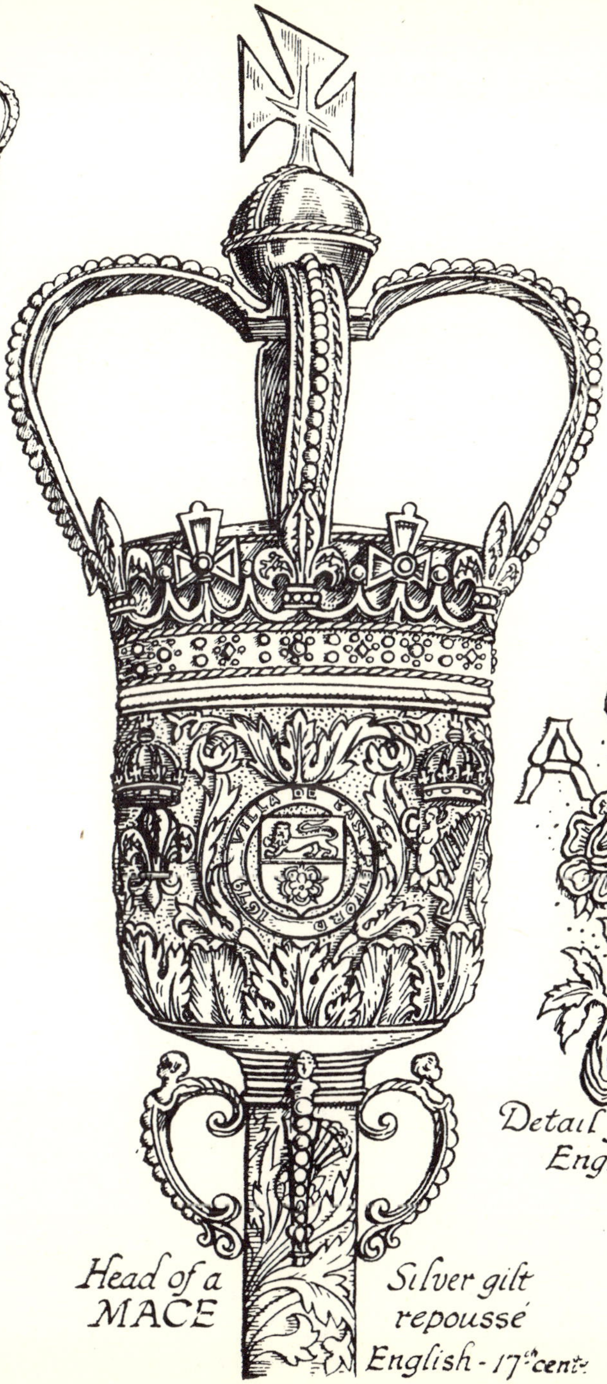

Head of a MACE

Silver gilt repoussé English - 17th cent.

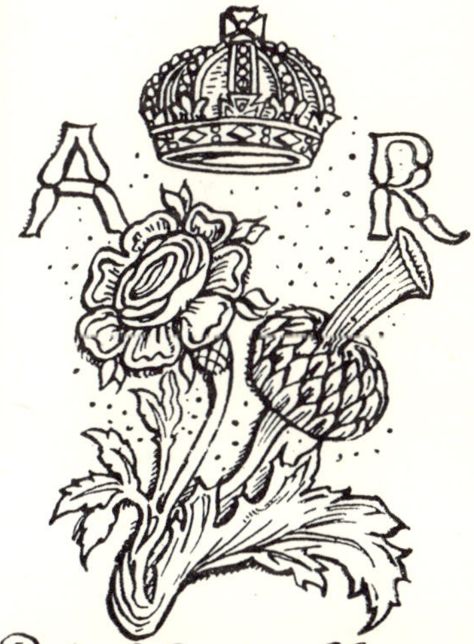

Detail from a Mace English ~ 1710 ~ Initials of Queen Anne

in the north part of the Isle of Man, near to which the plants were growing profusely. They may then have been still in use, or perhaps were merely the descendants of their ancient and local ancestors.

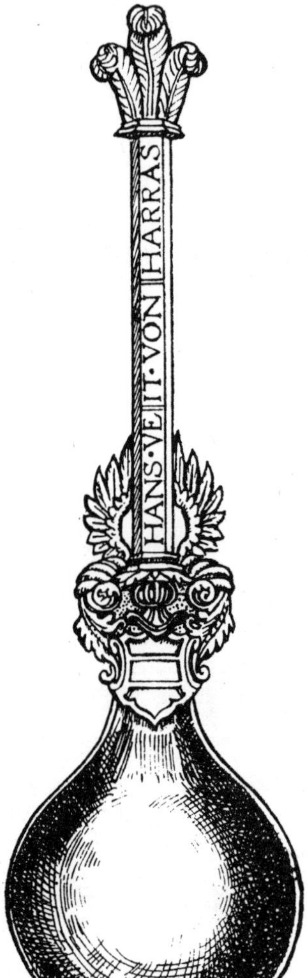

Spoon - silver. parcel gilt German 17th cent

The Griffins which support the shield and the ram crest are boldly and decoratively treated, but the helm is somewhat poor in design. We miss the mantling, but perhaps it was sacrificed in this instance to secure clearness and intelligibility in design. Nevertheless, the whole object is fine in modelling and silhouette, and the ebony staff is an effective contrast to the silver-work.

The Mace, as a symbol of mayoral or magisterial authority, would naturally be an object upon which the decorators and heraldic designers would lavish their skill in those days of pageant and ceremony.

The results of their art and craftsmanship are still to be seen and admired in these beautiful survivals of the past, and the drawing in this chapter from the Mace of Retford shows a good average specimen of its kind. Although it is lavishly decorated, the various degrees of relief, and massing of the different ornaments, are so nicely managed that there is no sense of unrest or irritation, each part is interesting in itself, but the massive crowned headpiece dominates the whole. The openings of the crown act as plain spaces, which give value to the rich ornaments. The remaining detail, with the initials of "Good Queen Anne," is a pleasing and original combination of Rose and Thistle, badges of the two countries, and a symbol of the union of England and Scotland poetically and heraldically expressed.

CHAPTER XI

ALTHOUGH we are more concerned in these chapters with the artistic and decorative side of heraldry, a reference may be made in passing to another interesting part of blazonry called Augmentation. A couple of examples illustrating the principle are given on this page. These two specimens will show the reasons why and how certain changes have been made to already existing shields by some additional device.

Augmentation, therefore, means in heraldry some honourable

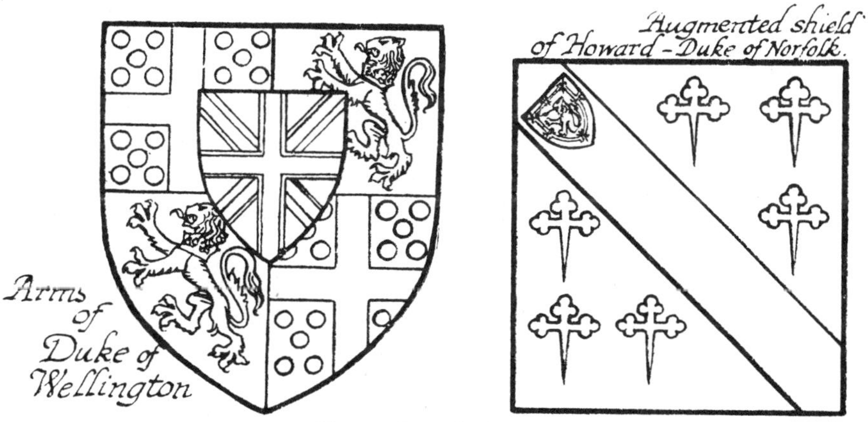

Examples of Augmentation

addition to a coat of arms granted by the sovereign to a subject for some heroic deed or distinguished service. A method frequently adopted is to emblazon this special device on a shield of pretence over the original arms as a commemorative distinction. As before explained, the word "pretence" is here used with its original meaning of something "held forward," not with the somewhat sinister use we now make of it by meaning a mask behind which we conceal some deception.

The arms of the Duke of Wellington are a striking and appropriate use of the principle of augmentation. To distinguish and commemorate his notable services to his country a shield of pretence, or inescutcheon, charged with the Union device of Great Britain and Ireland, was added to the arms of his family. Our second example is still borne by the Duke of Norfolk in the first quarter of his shield. Henry VIII. granted to Thomas Howard, Duke of

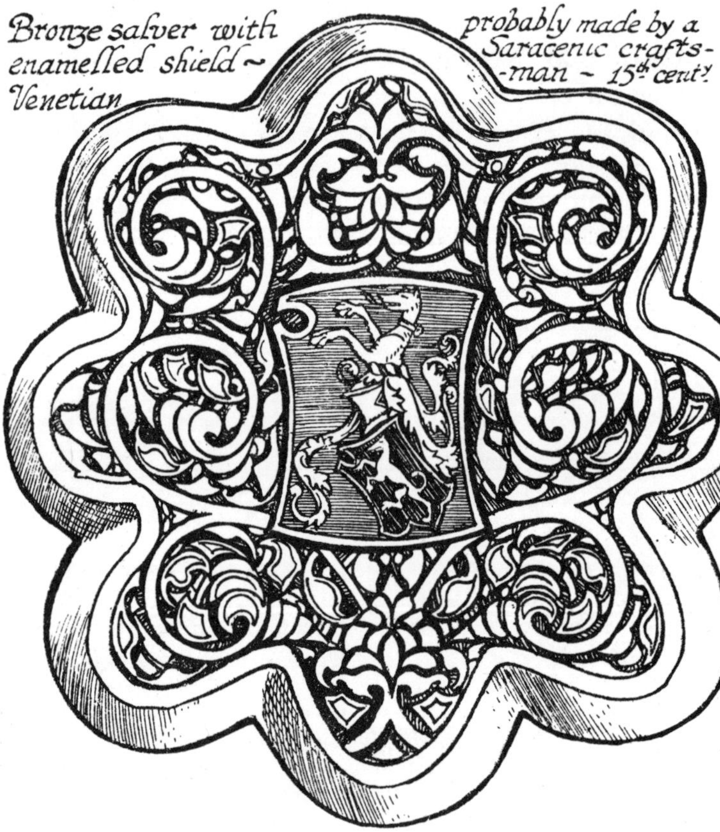

Norfolk, and his posterity, for the victory at Flodden Field on 9th September, 1513, in which battle James IV. of Scotland was slain, a commemorative augmentation to his shield. The Howard arms, as they then stood, consisted of a bend between six cross-crosslets fitchée.

To this a small shield containing an adaptation of the Royal Arms of Scotland was placed upon the bend as shown in the illustration. It differs, however, from the Scottish arms by having in place of the rampant lion, a demi-lion only, which is pierced through the mouth with an arrow.

Let none of our Scottish friends take offence at these historical

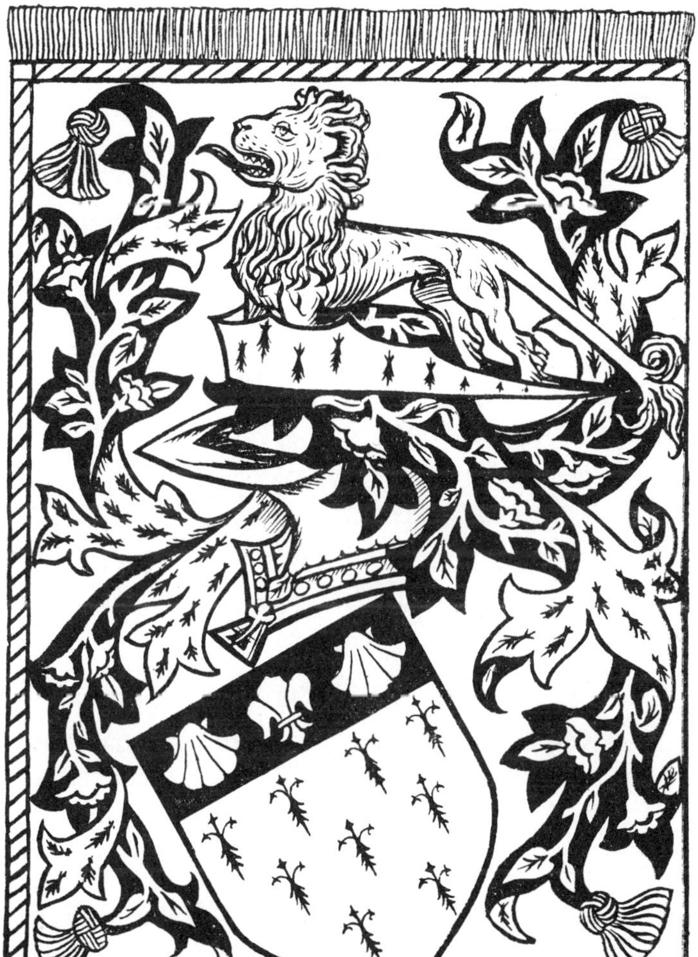

Example of "flowered" mantling

allusions, for no doubt among the nobility of their own land more than one commemorative augmentation granted for heroism displayed on the field of Bannockburn will be found. An interesting augmentation in Scottish heraldry, by the way, may be instanced in the crowned heart on the shield of Douglas, granted about 1330 to Sir James Douglas, who conveyed the heart of King Robert Bruce to the Holy Land. The story requires modification, however, as Froissart of the *Chronicles* records that Douglas journeyed *via* Spain, and hearing that fighting was there proceeding against the Saracens joined in the fray, and he and his companions were all killed. Some say that as he perished he threw the heart forwards that it might at any rate rest as near the Holy Sepulchre as it remained in his power to perform. Augmentations were sometimes granted in the form of crests or alterations and additions to crests. Many more examples could, of course, be given, but enough has been said to enable the reader to understand how these interesting changes and additions have come about.

Panel - Iron Gates of Bridewell Hospital - early 18th centy

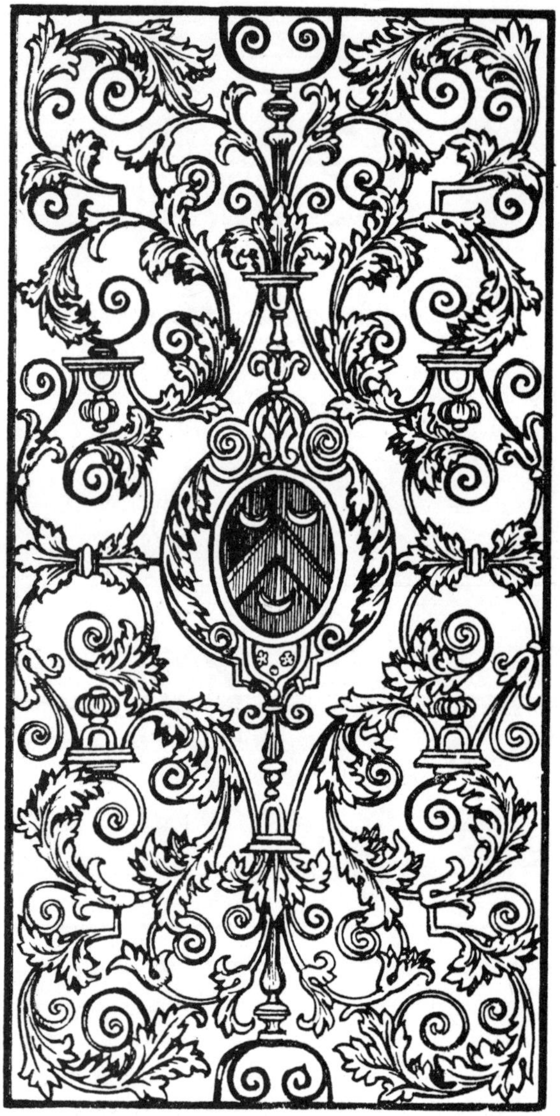

Talking of the Saracens, we have on page 104 an illustration, of a portion only, of a very beautiful piece of Saracenic craftsmanship, containing an heraldic device. Not that there is anything extraordinary in such a combination, for as Washington Irving tells us in his most fascinating story of the Conquest of Granada, the

Moors in Spain imitated their Christian opponents in everything concerned with the pomp and circumstance of war, its mimic form—the tournament, and even the system of heraldry, with its rules and cere-

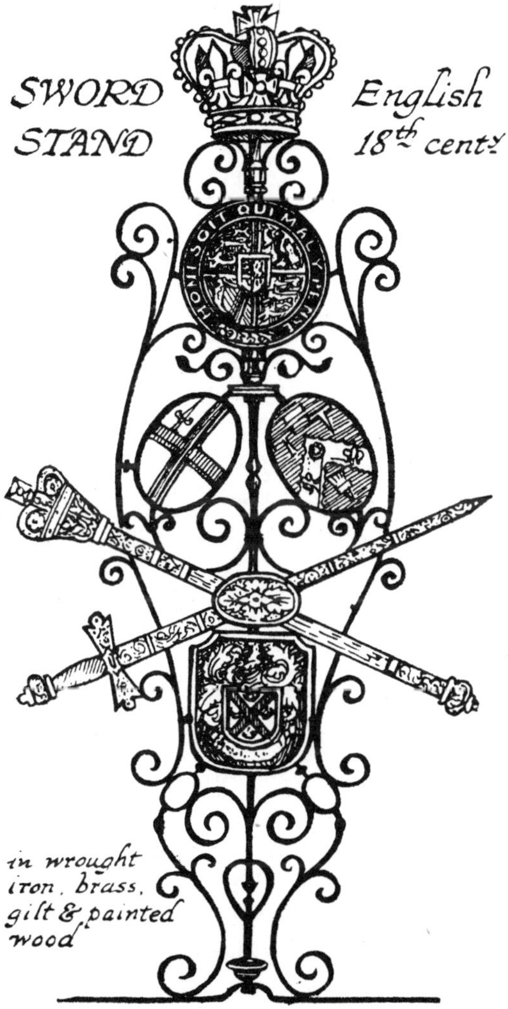

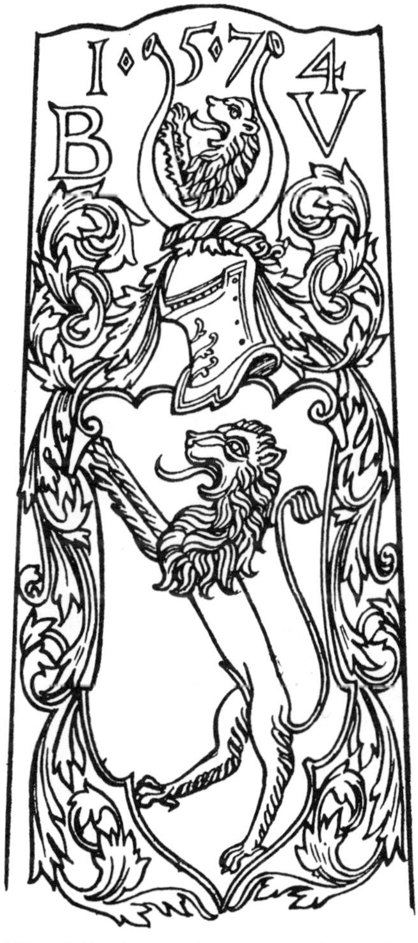

Heraldic decoration on earthenware beer-jug—German, 16th century

monies consequent thereon. We need not, therefore, be surprised that our Saracenic craftsman knew how to engrave or enamel a coat of arms on a salver amidst the more purely Eastern type of ornamentation with which he decorated its surface. The piece shown in the illustration is only the centre portion of the salver and the effect of the red coppery

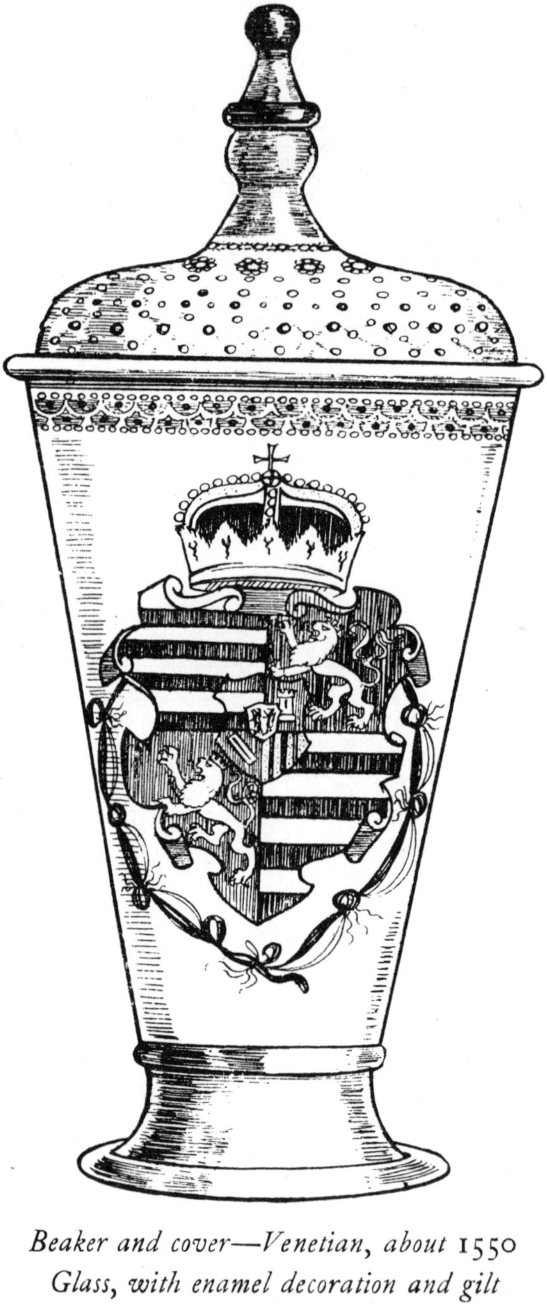

Beaker and cover—Venetian, about 1550
Glass, with enamel decoration and gilt

bronze with silver and gold ornament damascened in intricate arabesques is splendid in itself, but the small shield enamelled and engraved in cerulean blue, red, white and black, shines like a lovely jewel in a sumptuous setting. Taking it on the merits of our title, "Heraldry as used in Decoration," nothing could be more effective. On the other hand, decoration as used in heraldry is strikingly exemplified in the drawing of "flowered" mantling on page 105. It is taken from some of the early Gothic sources and shows what splendid decorators the old heralds were. What a quantity of later ornament has been inspired by that trailing flower pattern superimposed on the bold leaf forms of the mantling! The "cap of maintenance" or "estate" is seen to advantage in this specimen, and the care with which the old craftsmen designed the ermine spots, tassels, helm and other details will be noticed also.

The iron-work panel from the gates of Bridewell Hospital is a fine example

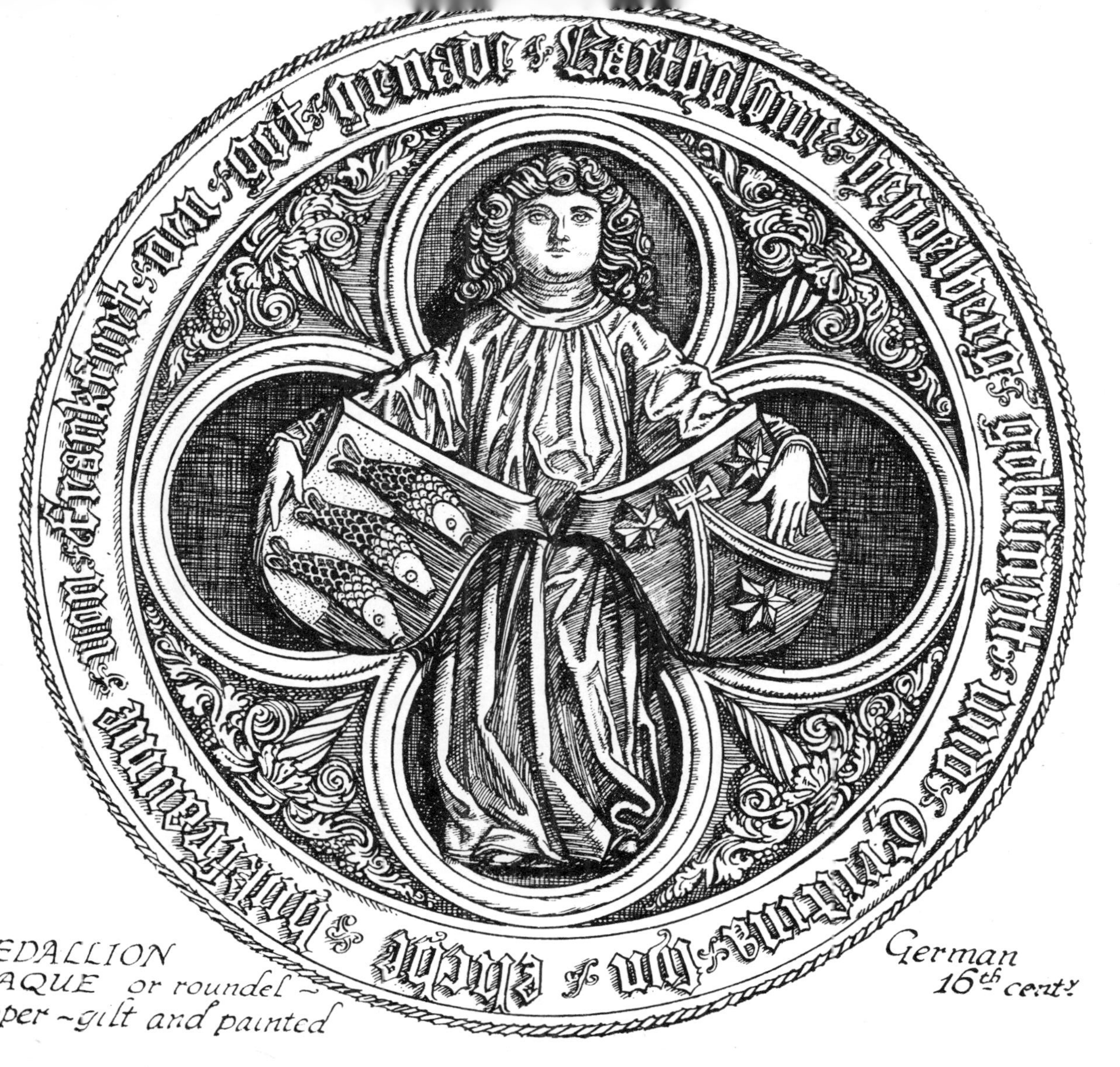

MEDALLION
PLAQUE or roundel ~
Copper ~ gilt and painted

German
16th cent.y

of the crafts of the period, early eighteenth century. It has a rich and elaborate effect though inclining to the Rococo style, but the central panel being filled with an heraldic device, entitles it to our consideration.

The sword stand, also of English workmanship, is of the same period, but is more effective as a piece of heraldic decoration.

The combination of materials, iron, brass and wood, gilt and

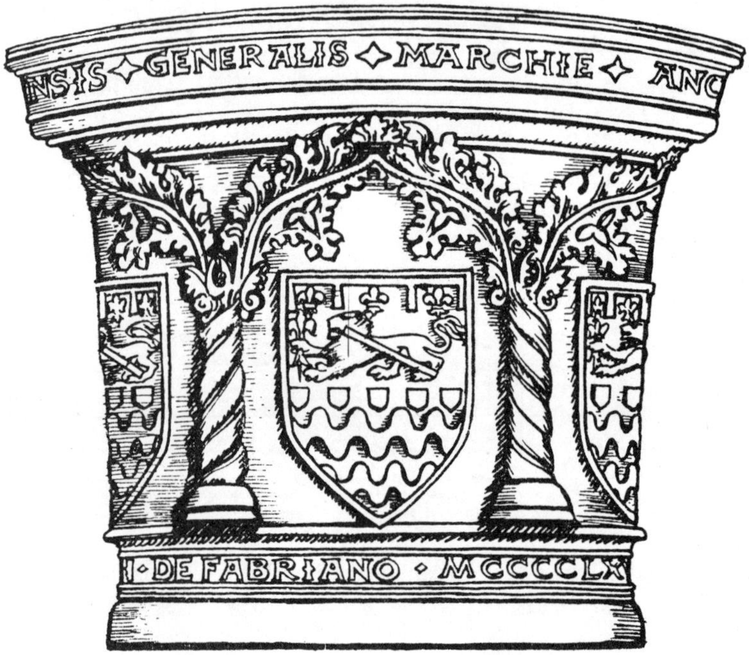

MORTAR ~ cast bronze - Italian-1468-

painted, is very interesting and might be used with advantage to-day. The crown is of brass, the shields, sword and mace of wood, painted and embellished with gold. It probably stood in some city church and was most likely used in civic functions and ceremonies combined with church service.

The beaker-shaped ornament of Venetian glass gives us a widely different material and effect. It possesses a happy combination of transparent delicacy with rich colouring and gold. The glass is a very pale golden green, the coat of arms is enamelled in strong orange

Leather covered Despatch-Box tooled in the style of book-binding ~ English 18th c.

and brown reds, while the handle of the cover is a deep ultramarine blue, the transition from one to the other being pleasantly assisted by the little beads and rosettes in colour and gold which run as borders between the two principal items.

The heraldic decoration on the German beer-jug is a distinguished bit of ornament with a character all its own and the German roundel or plaque is another fine piece of heraldic work. It is of copper, gilt, and painted, the angel—or is it a chorister?—who holds the shields is but a decorative accessory without heraldic meaning, but his robe of full red is the chief piece of colour in the composition, the scrolls in the spandrils are in dark cool green, black and gold come in the charges in the shields and also in the beautiful Gothic letters of the inscription which plays a not unimportant part as a border to the whole.

The leather despatch box with crown and monogram of King George III. shows how a very rich and elaborate effect of decoration can be obtained by combining and repeating a few simple elements either heraldic or otherwise.

The Italian mortar on p. 110 shows that even a simple household utensil can be made beautiful and interesting by thoughtful design. The principal item of the ornament is a family coat of arms. The character of cast metal is admirably kept throughout, even to the details of the bands of lettering which help to enhance the decoration. Good lettering is decoration in itself.

Badge Monogram James II.

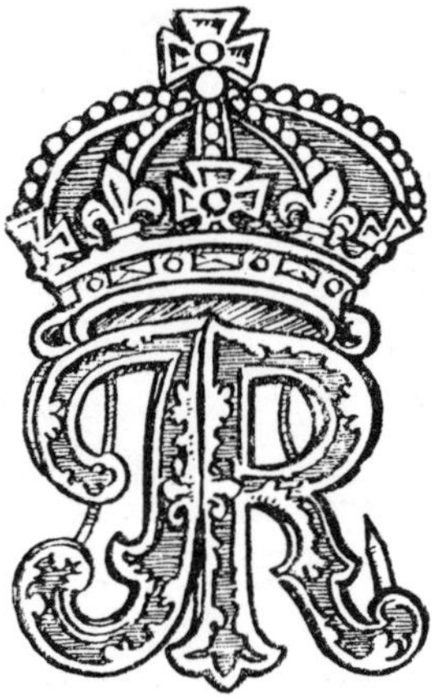

Latter half of 17th century

CHAPTER XII

IN days gone by heraldry came more into the domain of the craftsman and the decorator than into that of the pictorial artist, but much could be brought forward in the way of evidence to show that it was well understood by all workers in the arts. Experts have shown that in modern times many easily avoidable mistakes have been made through lack of a little knowledge of the subject. On sculptures, monumental tablets, in windows, seals and other decorative works heraldic knowledge is still required, and in these short chapters we have seen how varied and common its application has been in the past. Lack of space, difficulties of access, questions of copyright have prevented the inclusion of modern heraldic work much to my regret, as of late years a great improvement has taken place. As far back as the designing of the present Houses of Parliament good heraldic work can be pointed out as "modern." The windows in that building contain some excellent heraldic drawing and design, but no great effort was made after that time, with the exception of isolated examples, till the modern Arts and Crafts movement called forth workers of intelligence, skill and taste in all the arts and crafts relating to decoration. Since then much excellent work has been done—one has only to look over the shop-fronts of London and other large cities to find the arms of royal or distinguished patrons displayed in beaten metal or coloured enamel, or carved in stone or wood embellished with gold and colour over the portals of our later public buildings, all treated with excellent heraldic knowledge and individuality of feeling and design. Does not this show that heraldry, instead of being a dead art, has entered on a new phase of life and vigour, and that it behoves the modern decorator or craftsman to acquire a general knowledge of the subject as part of his business equipment?

This, in the main, has been the object of these twelve short chapters, and it is to be hoped they will lead many readers towards an interesting and delightful as well as a useful study. No treatise on heraldry would be complete without a reference to the masterly and beautiful renderings of heraldic design which came from the hand of

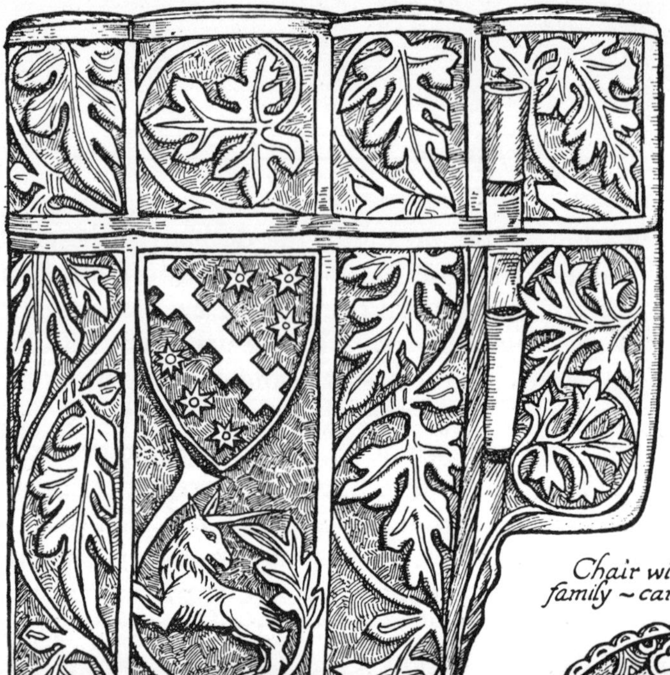

Case for a crozier with the arms of a bishop of the Aldobrandini family ~
Cut and embossed leather (cuir bouilli)
Italian-14th cent.

Helms from engraved heraldic plates by Albert Dürer d. 1528

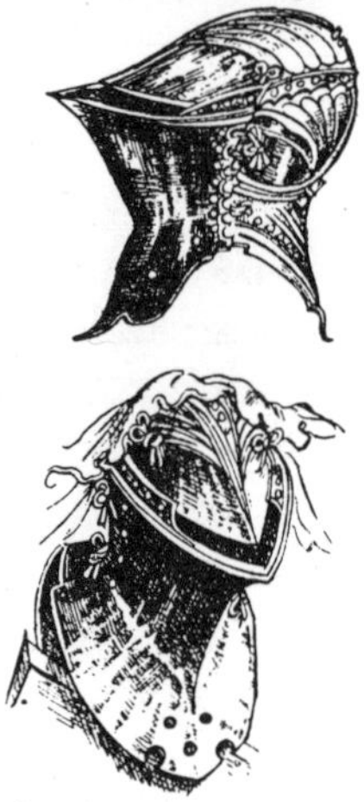

Chair with arms of Cavendish family ~ carved & inlaid oak ~ English about 1660

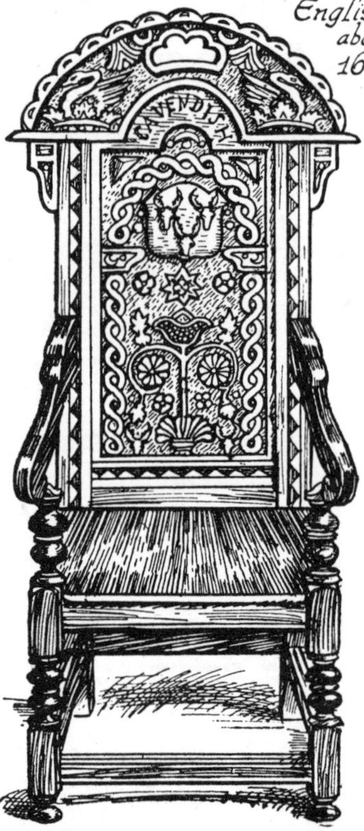

Albert Dürer. That great line draughtsman put the same amount of pains and love of good workmanship into a coat of arms as he did into an altar-piece or one of his more serious copper-plate engravings.

This, however, is by no means a complete treatise on heraldry, but I have copied two helmets from Dürer's handiwork in order to show not only something of his excellent workmanship, but also their own beautiful forms which may still be used.

It must be remembered that they are from highly-finished engravings, for more ordinary purposes a bolder and simpler method would be advisable if not imperative—but there they are, as most beautiful models of drawing, a guide for all time.

The specimens of Della Robbia ware on p. 116 are again instances of the use of heraldic design in the hands of great artists. Luca della Robbia, a great Italian sculptor, born in 1400, commenced life as a goldsmith's apprentice, but soon became a worker in marble and bronze. Towards middle age, however, he invented a process of enamelling and glazing his clay models in colours, which rendered them impervious to atmospheric conditions, thus giving them a durability greater than that of marble or bronze. The fact that they could be so effectively used for open air decoration soon brought him in huge quantities of orders, and after a time, his nephew Andrea joined in the work, which was again continued by the sons of the latter. Consequently it is difficult to distinguish the work of all these artists and the generic term, "Della Robbia" ware, is applied to all the productions which continued to emanate from their workshops for about 150 years. The process was a secret one, carefully guarded by the craftsmen, and though attempts have been made to re-discover it, none of them have been quite successful. Beautiful white tints, which sometimes approach cream colour and sometimes a milky grey, give key and basis for the other colours employed, the chief of which are grey blues, greens and yellow tones.

The large roundel, about three feet six inches in diameter, has a border of this kind, the shield is white on a dark purple brown slab and the ribbons are golden yellow.

The other illustration on p. 116 forms the base of a large scriptural figure subject. With two armorial shields, one at each end in strong colour, it adds a rich embellishment to the central panel under which it stands.

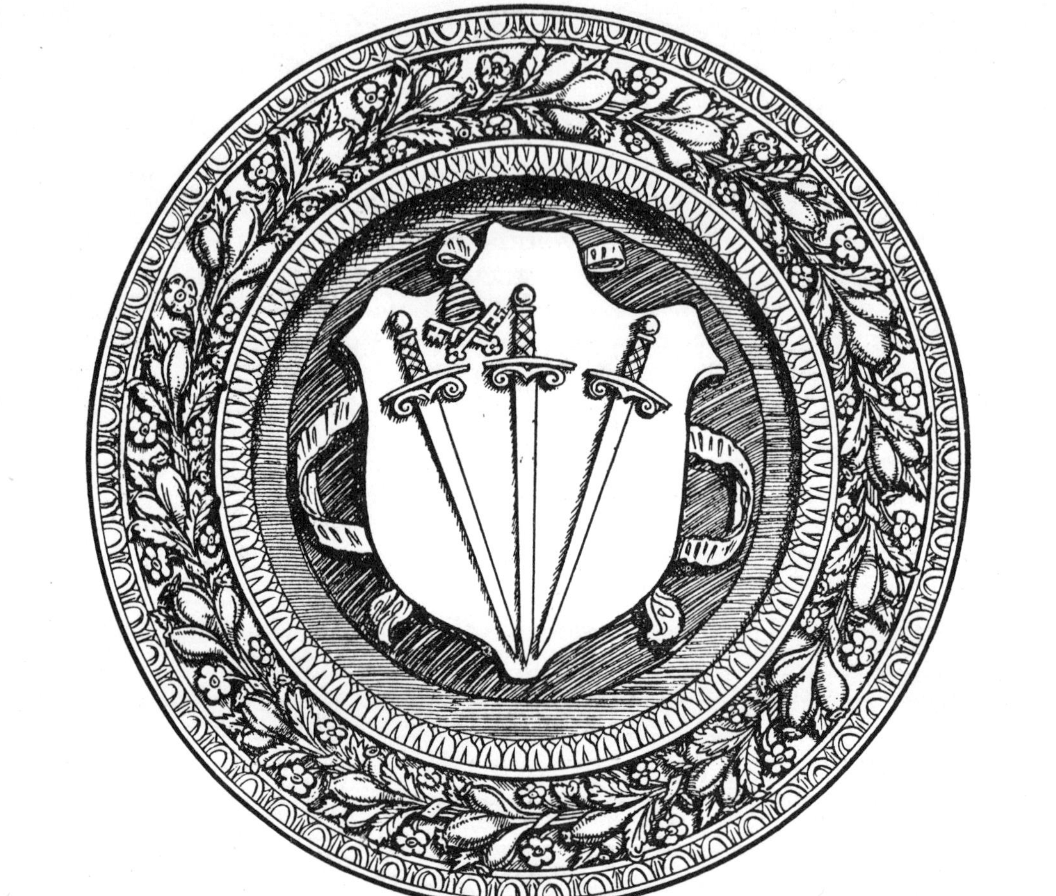

Two examples of heraldic decoration on Della Robbia ware
Italian ~ 15th cent.

The panel from a French sideboard in carved oak is a typical example of the style of the time. Plant form has been abandoned for an ingenious arrangement of strap-work interlacings, flanked by meaningless and ugly grotesques, but the little shield employed as the central figure is beautiful in contour and design.

A much more beautiful panel is the front of an Italian cassone on p. 118. In a similar manner the shield, charged with three dolphins, possesses a centralising effect, it "plays first fiddle," so to speak, and the beautiful vine scroll is a running accompaniment to it. Unlike much Italian wood-carving of the Renaissance this piece has a direct and obvious touch of the gouge and chisel which redeems its graceful lines from any charge of over-polished smoothness. The grapes are

Carved panel – Oak sideboard – French – second half 16th cent.

conventional, but there is merit in their conventionality. Rounded forms like grapes are laborious to complete in wood; the carver, therefore, patterned them in faceted surfaces and allowed his chisel marks to decide the shapes of the fruits and their groupings. The small borders quietly echo the motive of the central panel.

The crozier case in tooled leather with the arms of an Italian bishop is a rich piece of Gothic work. The heraldic unicorn and dragons are grotesques of the kind so much relished by the old Gothic carvers and craftsmen. A sense of humour pervades the evident enjoyment in the workmanship. The leather was wetted and then pressed into shape with various tools, the main forms were incised before being modelled and the tooling of the background has a pleasant "crackle" appearance which contrasts effectively with the ornament.

The old English chair with the arms of the Cavendish family, Dukes of Devonshire, belongs to a style of which we ought to be proud. It was a development native to these islands and no decoration exactly like it is to be found elsewhere. It might with advantage be more studied to-day than it is.

The casket with knights tilting makes a fitting close to our series. How evident is the enjoyment in design and workmanship. How clever the space-filling and decorative effect! In spite of the quaintness there is great beauty of drawing and modelling, and the surfaces of bone, leather and brass are a delight to behold.

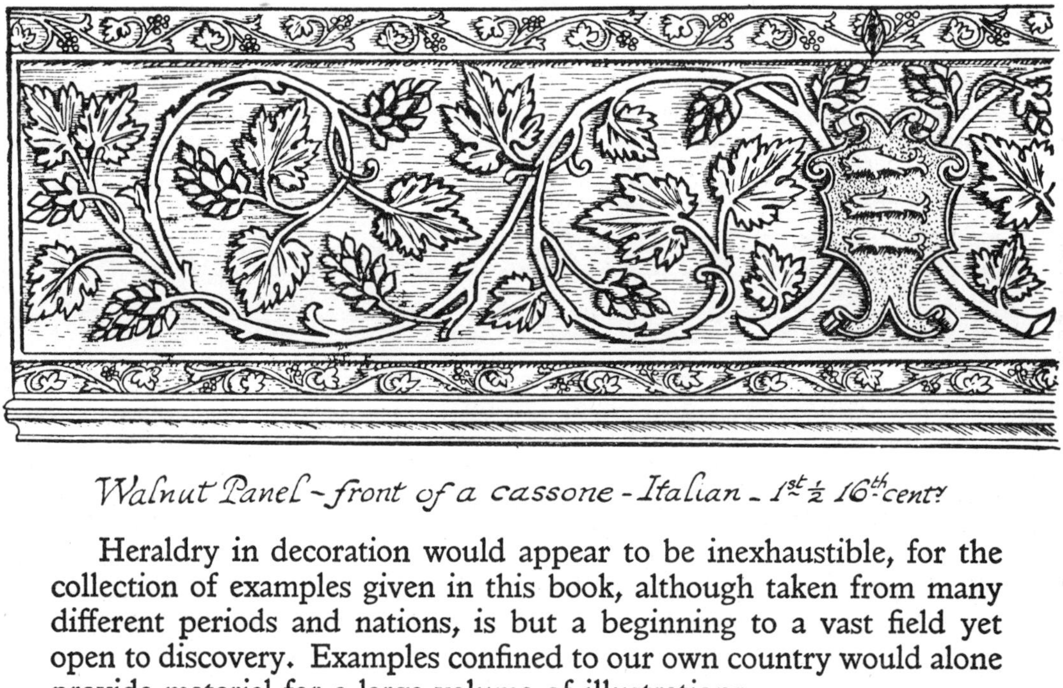

Walnut Panel - front of a cassone - Italian - 1st ½ 16th cent.

Heraldry in decoration would appear to be inexhaustible, for the collection of examples given in this book, although taken from many different periods and nations, is but a beginning to a vast field yet open to discovery. Examples confined to our own country would alone provide material for a large volume of illustrations.

The student of ornament, whether painter, carver, metal worker or textile designer, will find that in the practice of his craft heraldry will somehow creep in. To realise this we have only to recall the frequency with which the craftsman encounters coats of arms and heraldic detail in nearly all kinds of decoration. Public halls, courts and municipal buildings all require royal or civic arms to be painted on their walls or in their stained windows, or carved in wood or stone, or perhaps beaten or cast in metal as decoration either interior or exterior.

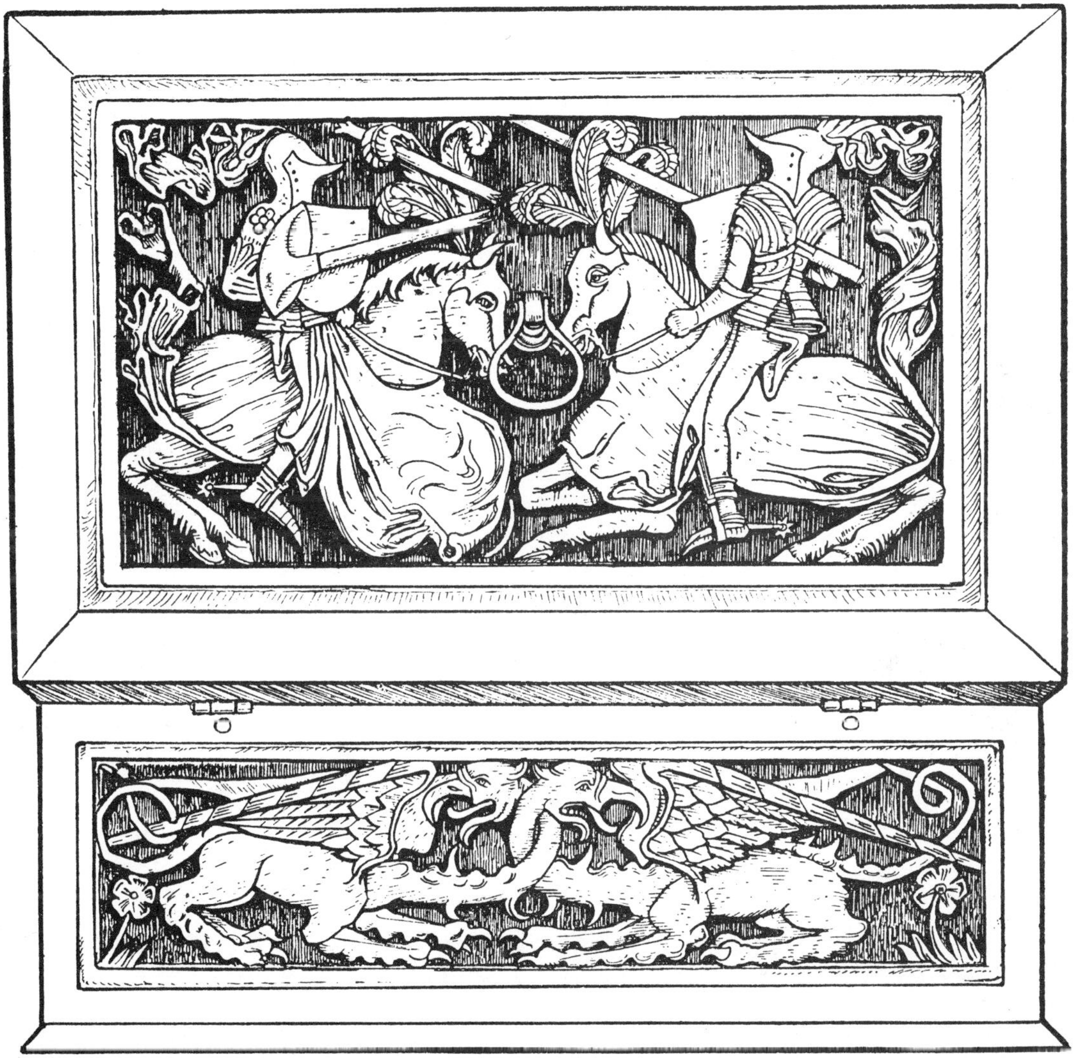

Casket - knights and heraldic monsters - carved bone on red leather, - brass frame - German - 15c

Guilds and city companies still use armorial insignia and in special cases their arms or badges are engraved on plate, painted on pottery, or woven or embroidered on curtains and other textile fabrics.

The bookplate designer, the craftsman in metal or the illuminator have often to embody heraldic detail in their work when commissioned by private individuals, and they will find help and suggestion in the drawings here given, but the reader is reminded that our subject has been "Heraldry as used in Decoration," and no attempt has been made to write a complete text book or technical treatise. The artistic aspect of heraldry in conjunction with other ornamental design has been the main consideration.

FLORAL FORMS

AS USED IN DECORATION

FLORAL FORMS AS USED IN DECORATION

CHAPTER I

FLORAL pattern is one of the commonest and yet one of the highest kinds of decoration. No one will deny that the forms of flowers and plants rank high among the loveliest of nature's phenomena.

It is small wonder then that they have been used as material for ornamental design from time immemorial, and an immense amount of research and illustration would be required to make anything like a complete survey of the history of ornament in which they occur. The use of floral forms is spread over many periods and is found in almost every national style.

Now, as the subject is so large, I cannot attempt to treat it in full—the most ambitious of text-book writers on ornament would shy at it; but if you will accompany me on the Magic Carpet of the old fairy tale (which could travel wherever one desired to go) we will take certain flower forms with us and observe and compare their treatment in decoration by designers and craftsmen in many parts of the world. You will, therefore, not think me irrational if we glide from Gothic England, Renaissance Italy or Germany, and, regardless of century or space, arrive in the peach-blossom gardens of China or Far Japan. We should have to go back a long way if we tried to trace the evolution of floral form in ornamental art, for it may be easily guessed that when the savage began to amuse himself by carving on his weapons and primitive utensils he would soon progress from straight lines to easily cut curves, and rough attempts at floral form would not be long in developing. It is not, however, till a more civilised state is attained that we see floral decoration in full beauty, in fact, a high state of culture and refinement seems a necessary condition for its growth and well-being.

It required a cessation from war and strife; learning, leisure and happiness being necessary to produce such marvels as a Persian carpet or the lovely green, blue and purple tiles against which bloom the rose, the peony and the carnation in the "Gorgeous East." The craftsman has then time to look around, and the beauty of his cultivated garden becomes a living poem to him, from which he quotes his floral stanzas and inserts them in his weaving, his carving, or his lovingly illumined manuscript.

We Westerns are too often apt to think of our civilisation as the only one, and forget that the nations who have produced a large share of the world's finest ornamental art represent the results of culture and civilisation in many ways as fine as, sometimes finer than, our own, though different in their nature.

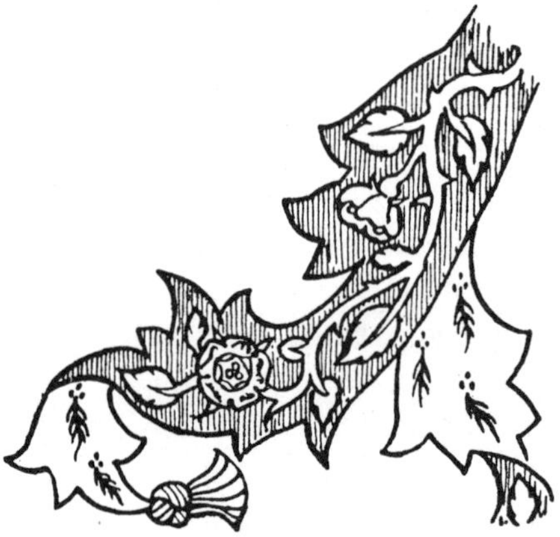

Floral patterning on heraldic mantling

Every designer becomes tempted sooner or later to weave into his imagined patternings these beautiful flower forms. In fact, it is highly interesting to see how they creep in as soon as decoration begins. The mediæval herald first jagged, then scalloped the edge of the mantling, which fell as a veil over the knight's helmet to protect him from the heat of the sun. From this it was a short step to foliating the edges, and finally, he yielded to the fascination of floral form, and when he had the opportunity, covered the cloth with a trailing flower or a diaper of flower and leaf as a variation from the ermine spots or other heraldic symbols on the reverse side.

Certain forms of flowers have always been favourites with designers, and the reason of this is obvious and familiar to the practical decorator. The primary object of decoration being not imitation but ornament, it becomes clear that those flowers or plants which can be bent and twisted to the requirements of geometrical pattern would be used in preference to others of a more intractable nature. If imitation alone were desired this aspect of our subject need never have been considered, but it has been felt by the good craftsmen and decorators of all periods that strictly imitative renderings of natural

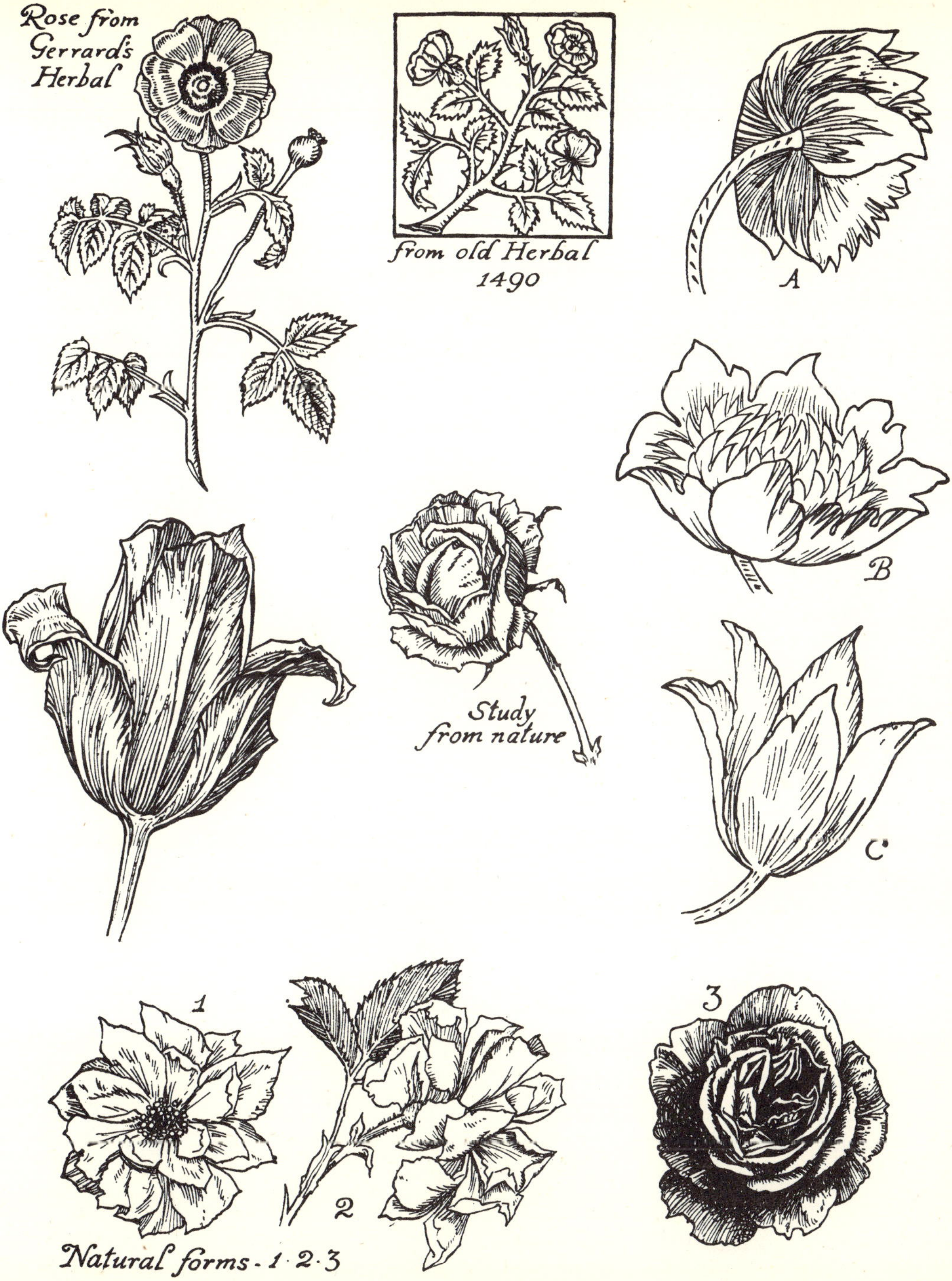

Rose, peony and tulip forms

forms are neither fitting nor desirable in ornamental art. Therefore, we find some floral forms common to the decorative arts of nearly every country and period, and it is mainly of these I propose to speak and illustrate.

There are several reasons why ornament and not imitation should be the first consideration of the decorator. In the first place we may say most ornament has a connection in some way with an architectural

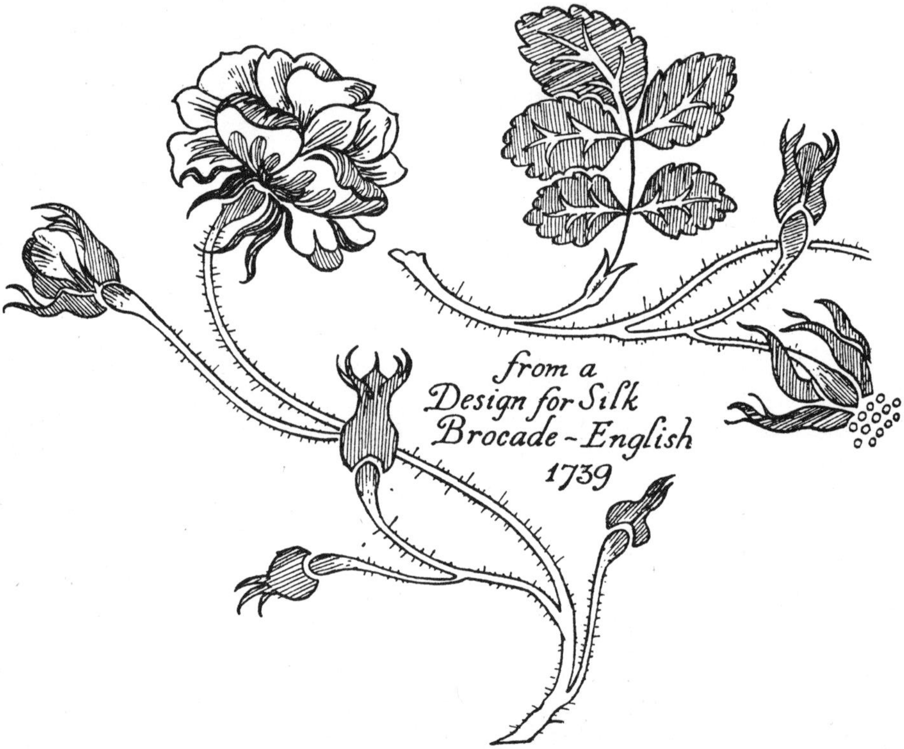

scheme. This involves limitations; repetitions have to be made in order to bring about unity of motive and harmony with the building conceived as a whole. This precludes an absolutely separate treatment for each individual item of decoration. Thus close imitation is ruled out, and a pattern or symbol of the form chosen takes the place of pictorial representation. All this is supposing that the form could be rendered imitatively, but now we come to the question of material, and it is easy to see that what could be painted on a wall would present an impossible problem for the designer to solve if it had to be carved in stone or wood, or woven into a tapestry or a carpet. Floral forms are, therefore, modified in their treatment to fit in with the conditions under which the decorator is working, and it is a subject of great interest to note how this has been carried out in various times and places. Again, in our carpets, wall-papers and utensils of daily life we do not wish to have close imitations of the flowers of the field; they are essentially out-of-door things, but pleasing reminders of them which do not enter into competition with them in degree of interest are tolerable and satisfying. We do not like allegories of grief and death talking to us from our clock cases and furniture, and a landscape picture repeated as a wall-paper pattern, with the same trees and the same windmill constantly recurring to our eyes would be insufferable. Ornament is aggressive if it becomes too insistent or too serious, but forms which decorate without intruding on other spheres of interest are restful to live with.

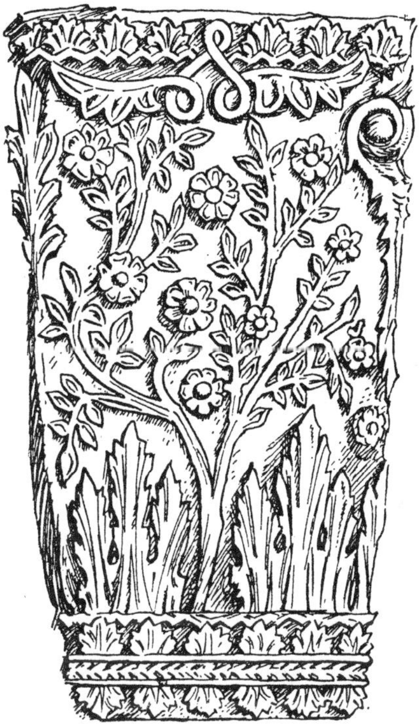

Byzantine capital, carved wooa

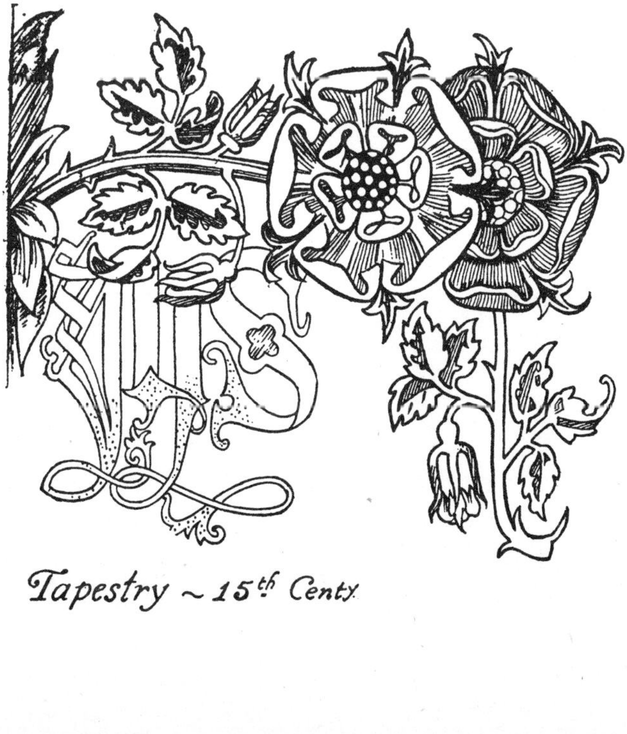

Tapestry ~ 15th Centy

We have now some ground to work upon, and for the convenience of generalisation (not being a botanist) I will group the floral forms under a few charac-

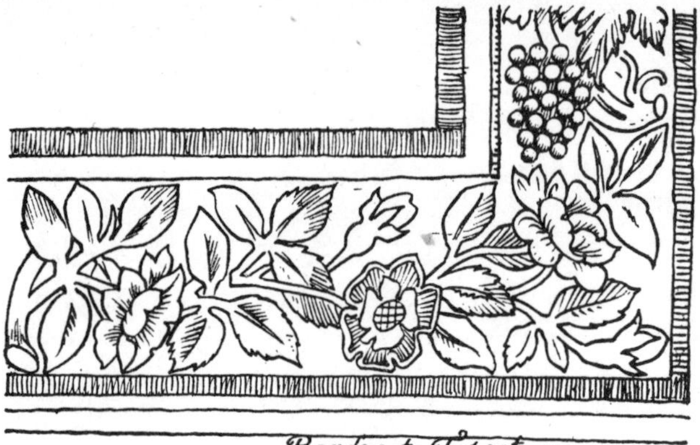

Border to Tapestry.

teristic types, which we shall find have been employed in some of the most splendid works of art accomplished by the human hand.

By general consent the rose has ever had first place as the most beautiful of flowers, and under this heading we must include the rose-shaped blossoms of all kinds. The wild rose, dog rose, briar, the full blown red rose of a Gothic illuminated initial letter, the delicate little tea roses of a Chinese vase, or the ivory petals of one on a Japanese lacquered screen.

Yes, whether you look abroad or at home, you will see how and why the rose has been so great a favourite—it bends and turns at the will of the designer, its parts and stages of development are ready for use at almost any time—it can be placed on scroll lines, or it looks equally stately when carved stiffly in a stone border—leaves, blooms, buds too, can all be so conveniently massed and grouped; there is such an endless variety of size and shape that the designer's resources are practically unlimited—he can do as he likes with it.

The tulip, the peony, and the pink and carnation family have

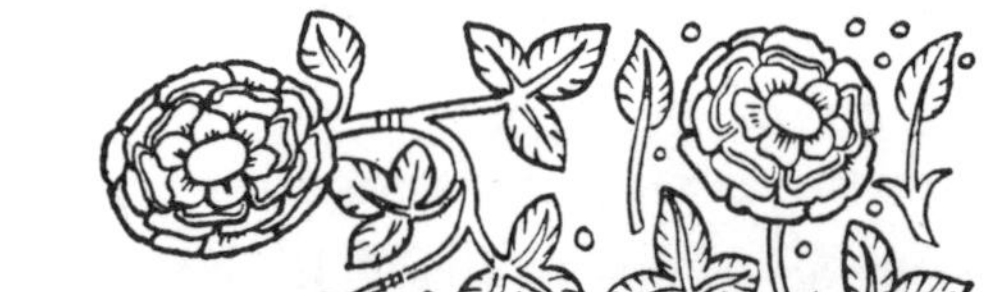

Border, illuminated law writing.
Temp. Henry VIII.

also been great favourites with designers and craftsmen, both Eastern and Western. The pink and carnation forms are absent from the sketches to this first chapter. As they give a character of their own to so much Eastern decoration they will require a chapter to themselves. The tulip, however, can accompany the rose—we find it a very frequent companion of the latter in both European and Asiatic designs. Like the rose, it is tractable in line and lends itself to many schemes and materials.

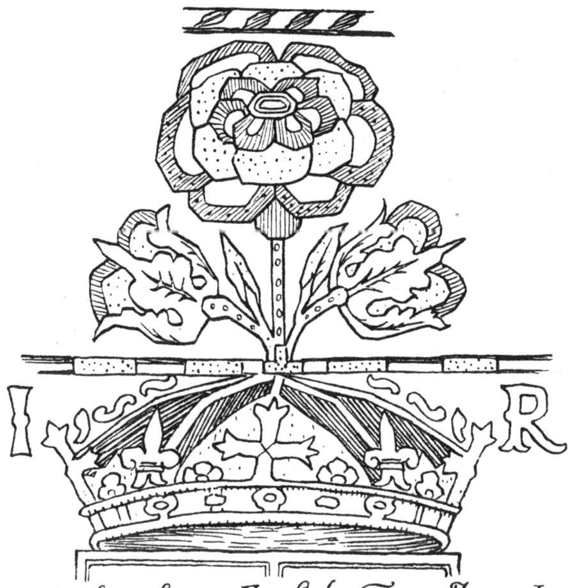

Embroidery – English – Temp James I

In my illustrations I have endeavoured to give as varied an assortment as possible, particularly in the matter of treatment or the manner of presenting the forms chosen for different pieces of decoration. Also, I have sought rather the byways than the highways in looking for specimens to illustrate these short chapters. Instead of giving a drawing of a whole piece or entire scheme I have chosen what I think are interesting bits from the designer's point of view. Two small examples are given from *Old Herbals*. No designer should fail to look at these books from time to time. The flowers and plants in *Gerard's Herbal*, a seventeenth century book, are most beautifully drawn and engraved, and what is more to us, they are arranged decoratively on the page in a cunningly skilful manner—in fact, they are for many purposes already designed. The eighteenth century designers of the "sprig" patterns for silks and cottons evidently knew them well.

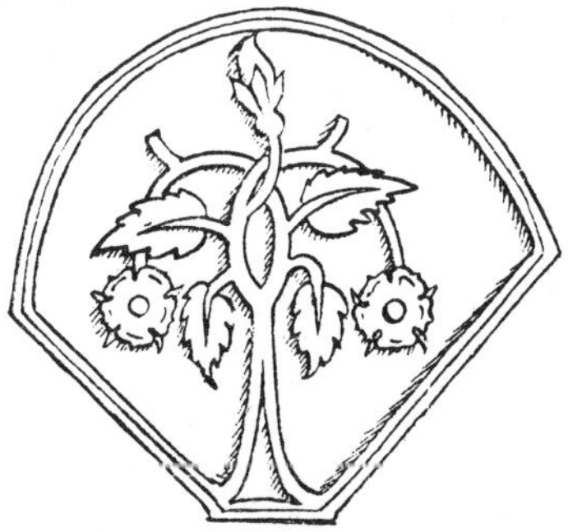

Detail from old plaster ceiling

The Byzantine Capital, given on page 127, is a delightful example of the treatment of the rose. What beautiful balance and spacing is combined with childlike waywardness and hint of symmetry! How true these old craftsmen are to nature's principles. While there is no attempt at direct imitation, how like a casual bit of natural plant and flower life! We look into a wayside hedge and find a trailing briar against some dock leaves, beneath, among the grass and spike-formed growths a series of small and serrated leaves attracts our attention, the criss-cross play of light and shadow amongst them all gives one just the impression the old Byzantine carver has obtained.

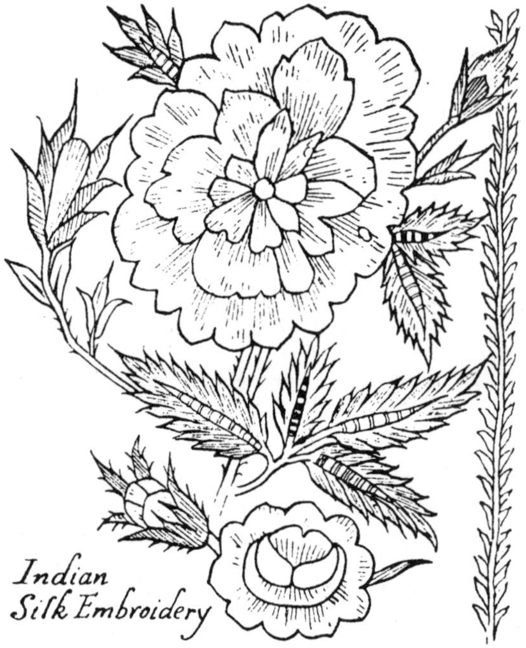

Indian Silk Embroidery

The large roses in the tapestry with I.H.S. monogram show, on the leaves particularly, a very interesting treatment; light and shade on the respective halves of the leaf seems to have suggested a decorative effect—but there is no shading in the pictorial sense. The overlapping of one form on the other, as seen in the two roses, is a risky thing in design, but this is on a very large scale, the flowers being ten inches or more in diameter, and one is white against the other's red; consequently, confusion of form is avoided. The border design to a piece of tapestry and an illuminated deed, on page 128, are good examples of the initiative and fearlessness of attack possessed by the old designers. How many "moderns" fed on rules would have dared the solution of "corner-turning" difficulties shown on the one by boldly carrying the terminal leaf of the rose into the domain of the vine, or by the frank little device of the single leaves to fill the blank spaces on the other? Fancy an illuminated border to a "deed of conveyance" at the present day! There would not be time, but for such a charming piece of ornament one could forgive the "law's delay," lamented by Hamlet in his famous soliloquy.

In this example, and also in the crown and rose embroidery of James I. time, the very beautiful forms of buds and half-opened flower should be noticed. The bit from an old plaster ceiling again

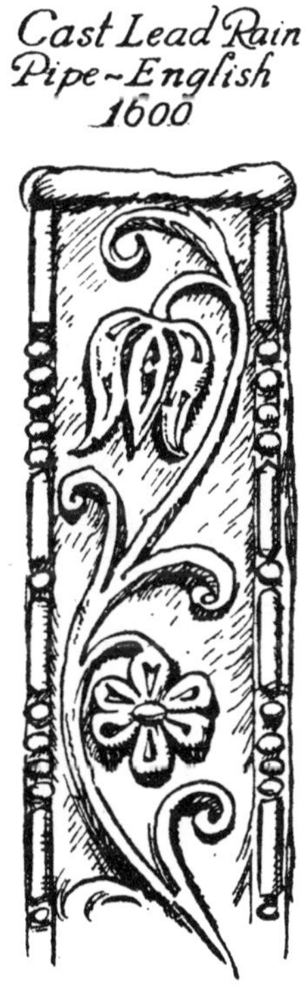

exemplifies the freedom enjoyed in design by the old men. Geometric arrangement, symmetry and space filling are present in the craftsman's mind, but they are at the back of his brain, while his fancy plays with the forms of his decoration—perfectly decorative in result, but miles removed from cast-iron rules or mechanicism. In the fragment of Indian silk embroidery the serrations of the leaves are seized upon by the designer as a means of contrast to the smoothness of the flower petals.

There is an inexhaustible mine of interest in floral decoration—each piece we look at represents thought and feeling, shows us the preferences and personality of its originator. We follow his ingenious mind as he puzzles out his problems in the adaptation of his forms to his material. In the suspension rod for a chandelier, page 131, we get a fresh element in the combination of rose and tulip forms—the nature study with the curling petals given on p. 125 shows how readily the iron-worker has availed himself of this feature, and the way he has backed up his twisted rods with a large smooth tulip leaf gives a sense of body and solidity to the central part of his group. The tulip and rose combination in the lead rain pipe gives a very pleasant effect suitable to the simple blunt character of the material. The way colour is obtained by perforating the petals of the flowers is both ingenious and beautiful. The flower in the old French brocade, here shown, is a "parrot tulip," one of the frilled-edge kind, with streaks of brilliant colour. To realise how well the markings give lustre and play of surface the original must be seen, in shades of old rose on a rich green ground. The Louis XIV. designer could not resist the temptation to serrate his tulip leaves or to add the gay flourishes of a florid age, but 'tis a dazzling and sumptuous bit of work in silken bravery.

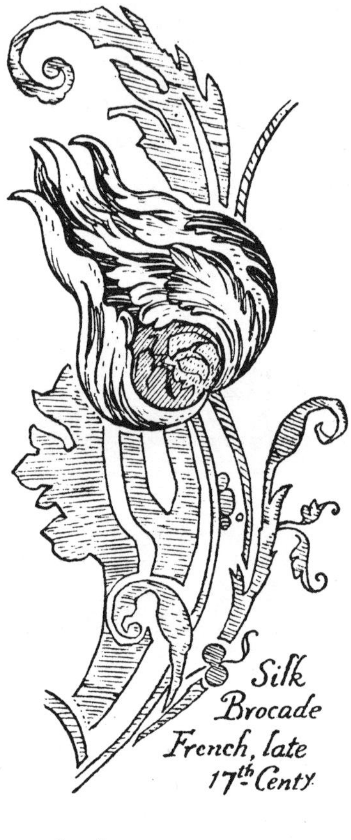

Silk Brocade French, late 17th Centy

And now to speak of the Italian embroidered altar frontal—a line drawing of it conveys but a skeleton idea of its glories, and if I used every colour in the rainbow to describe it the words would but remain what they are—the poor symbols only of the real thing. Still, the mind's eye can picture the crimson tulips and roses streaked and veined with silver white or palest gold—copper-coloured peonies and crocus and snowdrop in grey white and dusky blue. These are grafted on to scrolls of generous form, whose greens range from dark peacock to the fresh pale yellow-green of an April bud. The field or ground is a quiet grey, low toned, and as a contrast to the work upon it a foil of consummate taste.

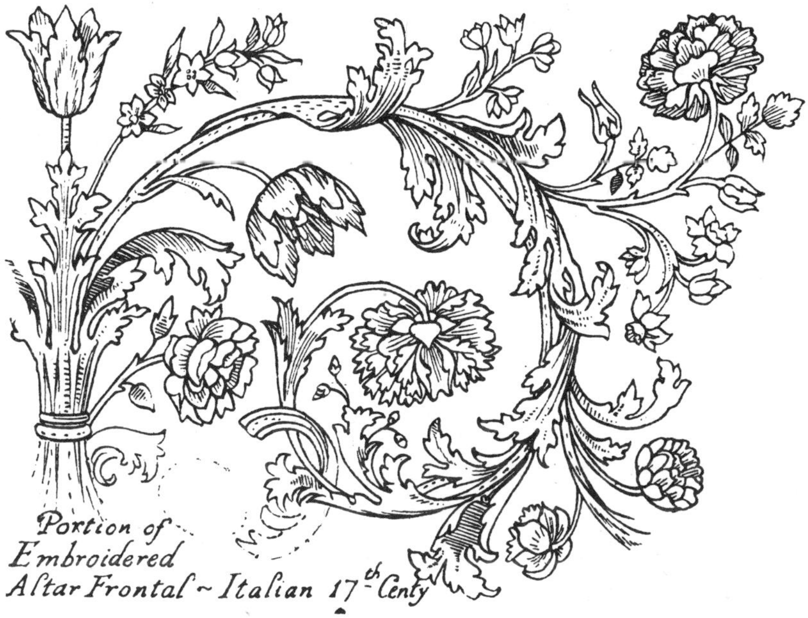

But I have strayed from my province and wandered from floral form into colour; nevertheless these word paintings of the various tints may prove useful suggestions.

CHAPTER II

IN the first chapter I spoke of the intention I had in mind of classifying the various groups of floral forms used in decoration, not in a botanical manner, but under a few broad general types. The rose, the tulip, and the peony claimed most of our attention, and they will no doubt appear again as we journey on once more upon our imaginary travels. Owing to the evolution of floral decoration from primitive to complex forms it will be impossible to classify all of them in any strict sense of the word, either botanically or ornamentally. Still, it is interesting to track the course of some of these flower forms as they evolve under the hands of the decorators of old, and notice how, their object being ornamental, not botanical, mixtures and overlappings occur. Sometimes we are perplexed to name the exact flower used on a tile or a carpet, and even unable to name them in any way. Seemingly, they have become purely ornamental forms, and nothing more. This is the opposite extreme from imitation, and I cannot help feeling that when the designer has strayed so far from Nature he has to some extent lost his grip on us, and we are not so intensely fascinated by his work as in those examples where we find both ornamental beauty and the more intimate love of, and close interest in, natural form.

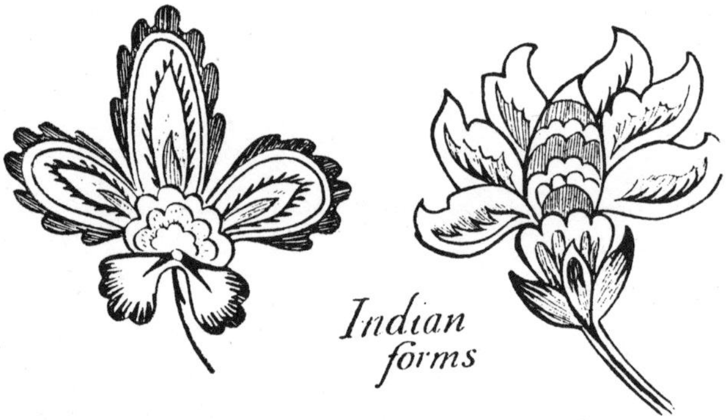

Indian forms

Some of the forms which evade our nomenclature, on Indian or Persian fabrics, for instance, are extremely beautiful in shape; but here I am on uncertain ground, and fear a lack of botanical knowledge may prevent me recognising flowers common enough in the East and familiar to the learned eye.

Be that as it may, I have given some drawings of these forms, and if they are deviations from nature, the manner of their development may be easily accounted for. The Eastern craftsman was (and is, we hope) trained on traditional methods, a father taught his carpet-weaving or tile-painting to his son or pupil, thus handing his art down from generation to generation. This conservatism, taken all round, is a fine thing in the arts; it inculcates a feeling of reverence for that which has been learned from the past and preserves the beauties discovered by previous thought and skill. Still, by mere repetition, it generates a too easy formula, carelessness creeps in by the hand of some inferior craftsman, and the shapes gradually assume less and less likeness to the source of all artistic inspiration—natural form. Many of these Eastern forms were brought by the traders of the sixteenth, seventeenth and eighteenth centuries to Europe, and were so closely imitated in the products of England and Holland that often it is difficult to say whether they are pieces of true Oriental art or not.

Border—Turkish Embroidery 17th Centy

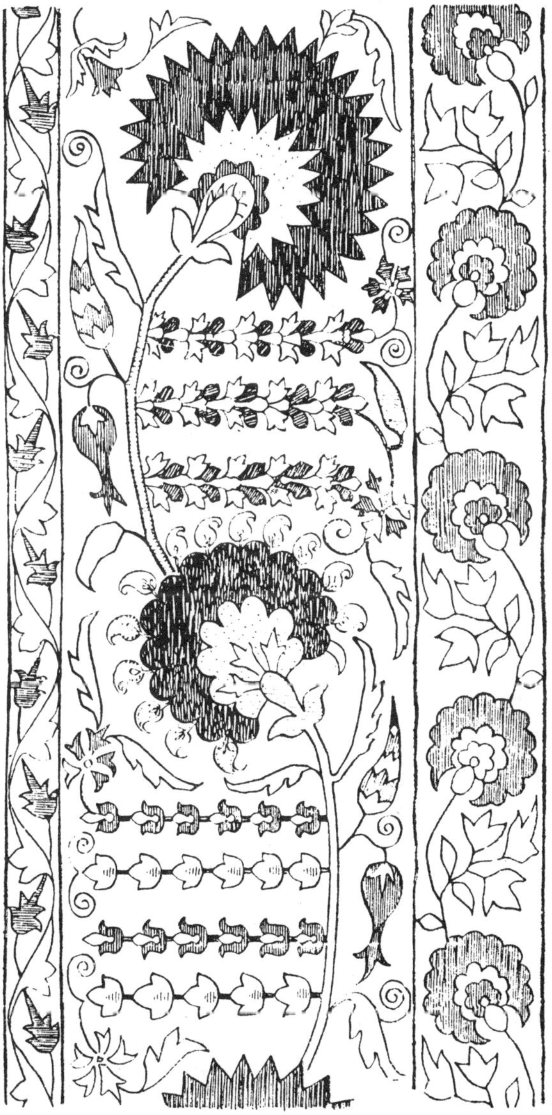

They influenced the marquetry and the hangings of silk and

cotton embroidered or block printed by ourselves, and the Dutch, to such a degree, that they are classed as Dutch-Oriental or

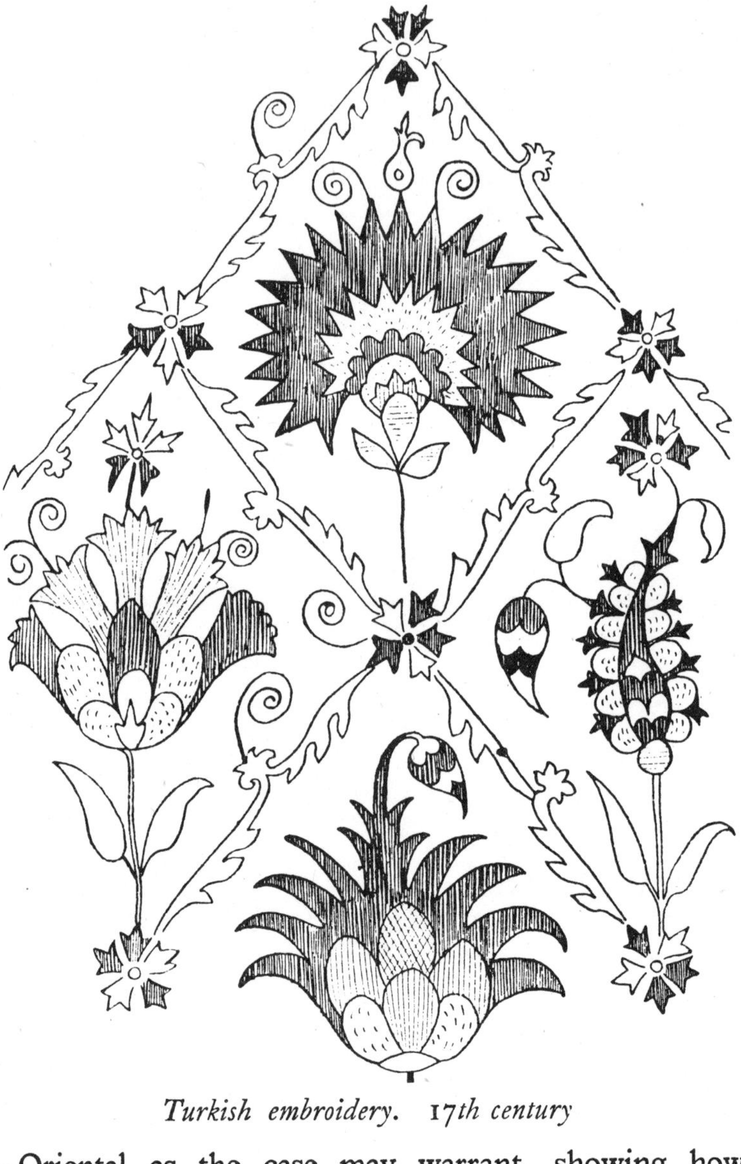

Turkish embroidery. 17th century

English-Oriental as the case may warrant, showing how far a floral form may be carried on its travels and become acclimatised in different parts of the world.

The two examples marked "Indian forms" in this chapter are specimens of ornamental flower form of the kind under discussion. They are taken from a piece of block-printed cotton hanging in my possession, which is either English or Dutch, of the seventeenth or eighteenth century. The seventeenth century carved wood chair back is another example of this Oriental influence on the crafts of the West—there is a distinct family likeness in the carving on chests and chairs of the Jacobean times to the forms brought by traders from the East. I hope to give more illustration of this style both in carving and embroideries later on.

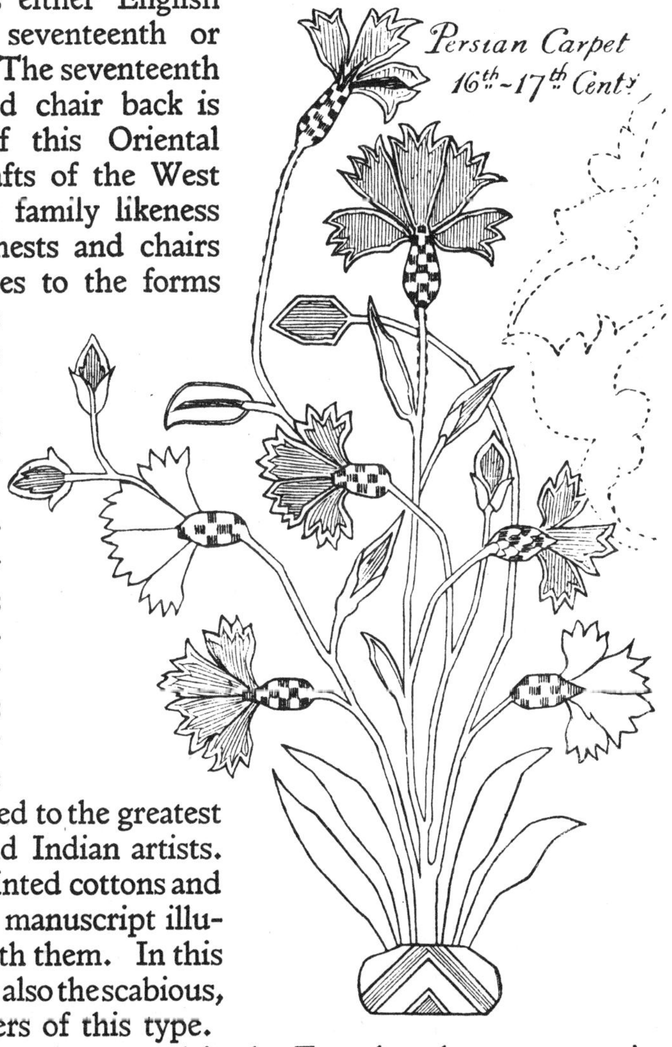

A group of flower forms largely used by designers is the class into which pinks, carnations, cornflower and similar shapes may be conveniently placed. They have perhaps been employed to the greatest extent by Persian and Indian artists. Their carpets and printed cottons and linens, and also their manuscript illuminations abound with them. In this group we may include also the scabious, knapweeds, and others of this type.

So much have these been used in the East that they seem to give the character we know as "Oriental" to a large part of the surface decoration executed in Persia, Turkey, India, Egypt (modern), and Asia Minor.

In the examples I have given of Turkish embroideries it is

interesting to notice the rendering of stamens and other small details, and the scale forms on the calyx of the cornflower in the Persian carpet examples give some very interesting conventionalisation. In the

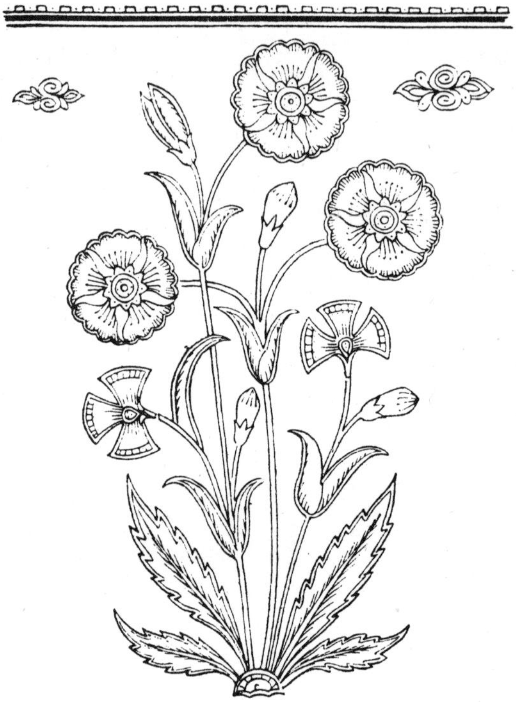

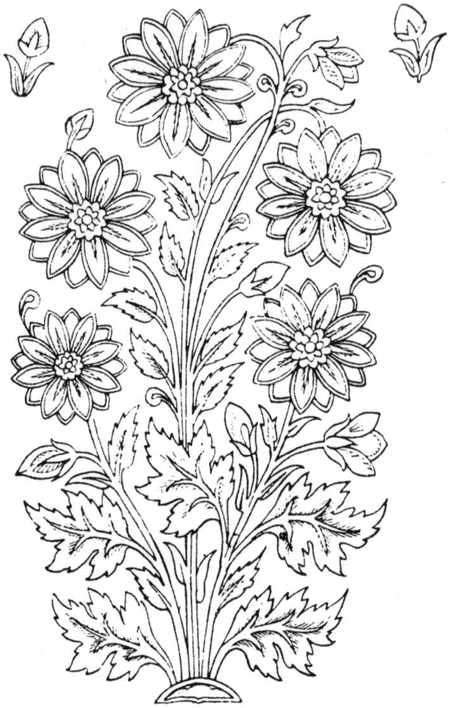

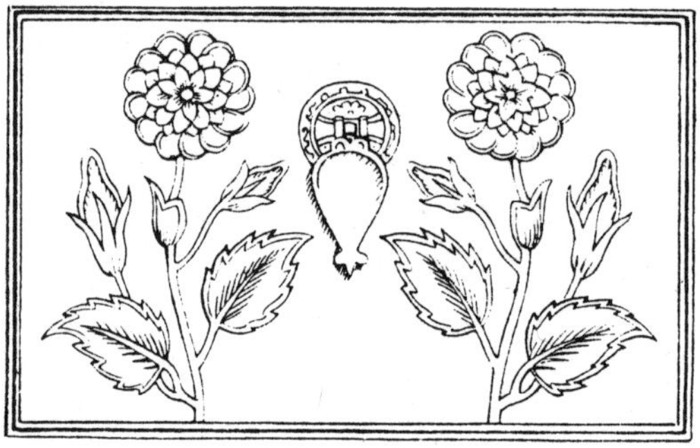

Details from a Persian cabinet

Inlaid ivory on rosewood

three portions of an inlaid ivory cabinet I have included our old acquaintance the rose, but as it completes the scheme of decoration in this exquisite piece of Persian craftsmanship I felt it would be a pity to lose its value as a contrast to the other two larger forms. These latter are placed in alternating succession with each other on the front, back and sides of the cabinet, and the small drawers of the interior are decorated with the rose. The fine lines on the flowers and leaves are engraved and blacked in.

As a piece of fine finish in workmanship it may with advantage

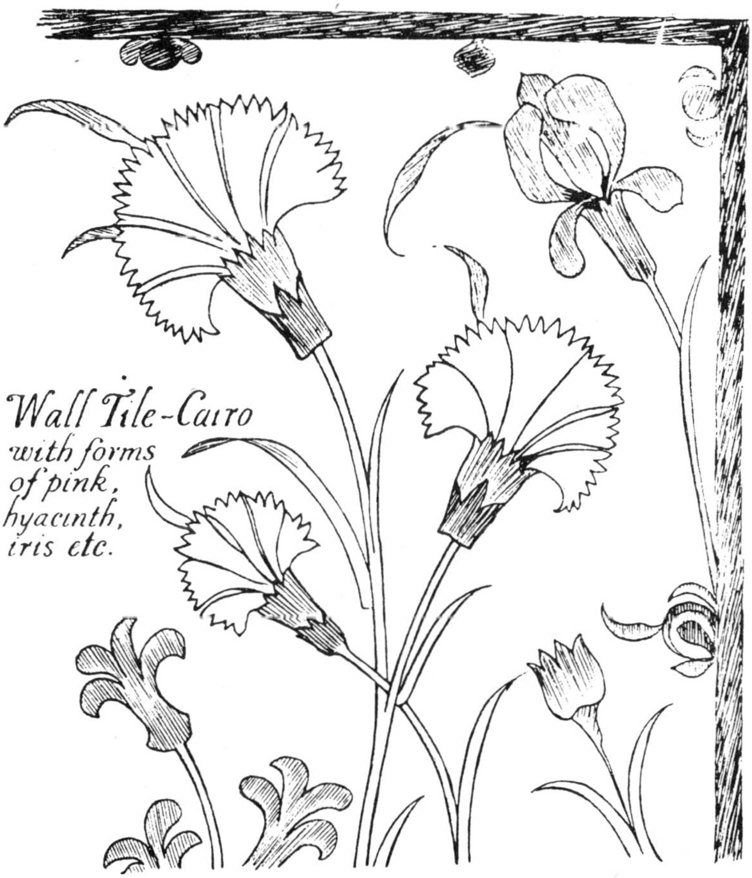

Wall Tile-Cairo with forms of pink, hyacinth, iris etc.

be compared with the free, rapid and spontaneous brush work of the Cairo wall tile, which is none the less interesting in other ways.

The hyacinth seems to be a favourite form with the Persian and Turkish tile painters and decorators of pottery, and it, or some kind of rendering of it, is found again in the horizontal bars in the border of the Turkish embroidery given here. The fritillary or snake's head flower, a kind of spotted tulip shape, is also largely used by the

Eastern designers, particularly on pottery. The spotting gives them the opportunity of displaying one colour on another, and such inventive artists as they are would not be long in discovering the beauty of dappled surfaces. I have often wondered whether the "inhabited leaf," as Morris called it, was invented in this way—that is, a large

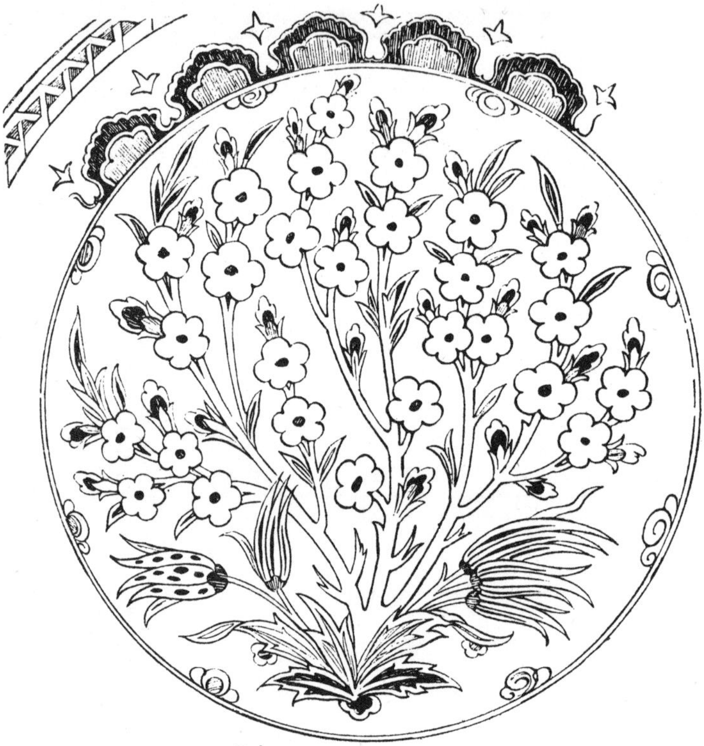

Turkish plate with blossom forms and fritillary

leaf upon which the designer places a group of flowers as a space-filling—or as a reminiscence of a spotted flower he had just used, or perhaps he may have been imitating an effect we often see out of doors when a large leaf serves as a background to a group of flowers of a smaller scale. It is one of those interesting little problems with which a study of floral form abounds when we come to investigate it. To revert again to the question of the evolution of floral forms, it is obvious how easy it would be for designers to modify or generalise

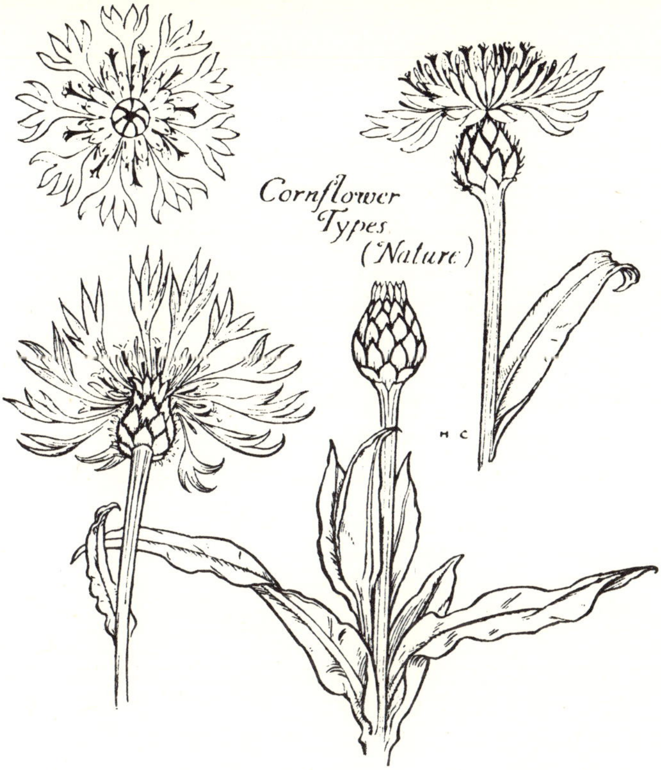

Cornflower Types (Nature)

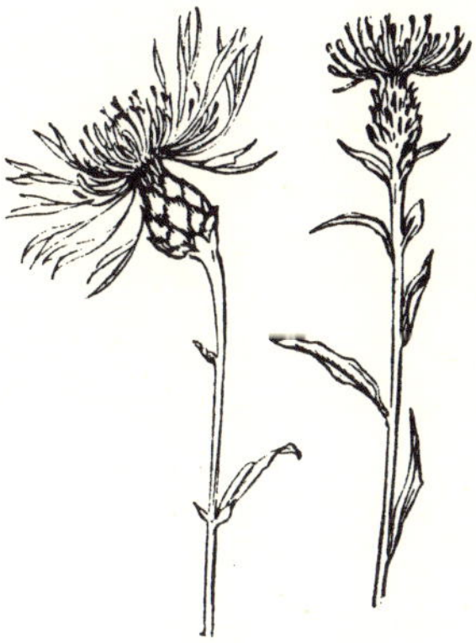

Knapweed (from Nature)

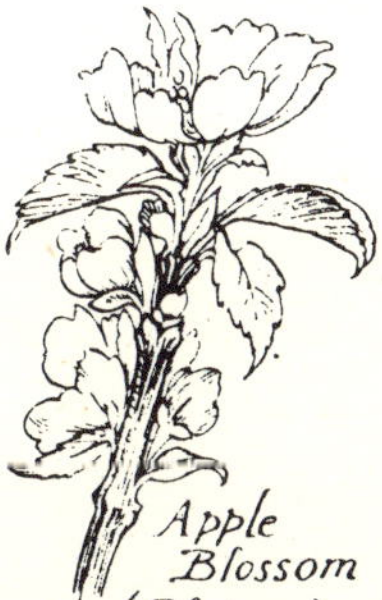

Apple Blossom (Nature)

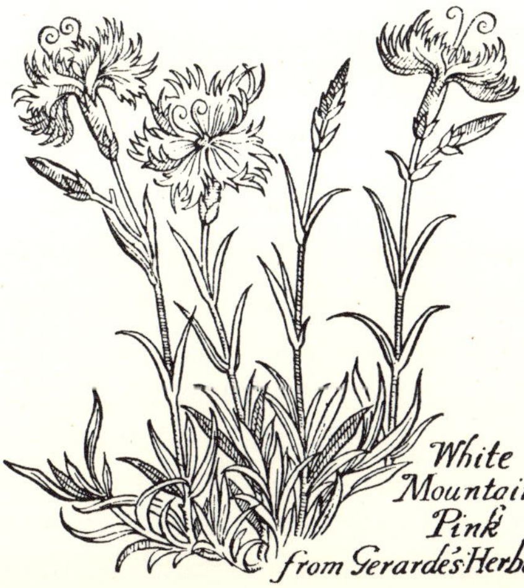

White Mountain Pink from Gerarde's Herbal

the shapes they were using when we consider the similarity of structure in flowers. A glance at the top view of the cornflower shape here given will at once suggest a whole series of rosette or star-shaped floral forms—in fact, this view would be the one most likely to form the answer to the question—what is the commonest shape of a flower? Most people would reply, if they could put down their ideas in form,

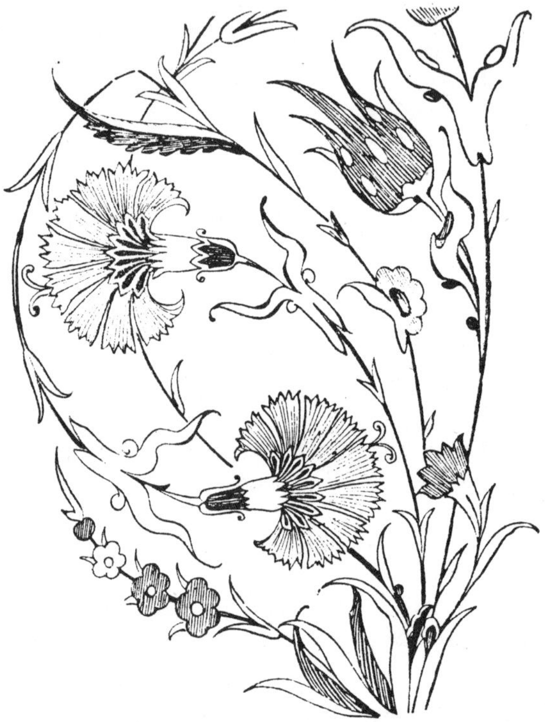

Rhodian Dish with carnations &c

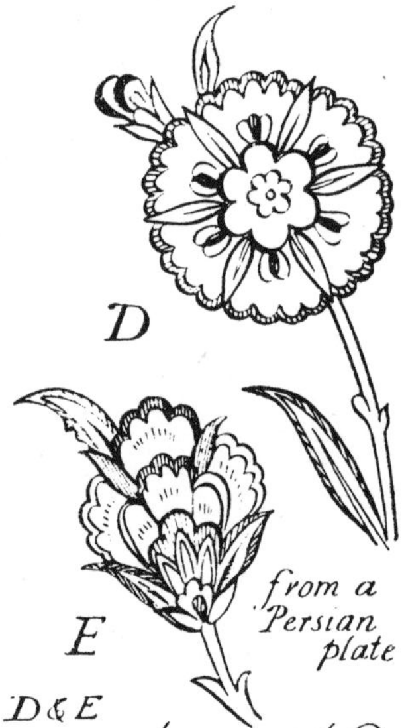

D & E Persian renderings of the Pink

with a central mass from which came radiating petals. Thus we can easily understand how the infinitely varied shapes of flowers in top view or rosette arrangement evolved, and, by the way, it may enable the reader to excuse my very loose methods of classification in floral form by exhibiting the difficulties of the subject to him.

The pink and carnation forms on the Eastern fabrics and pottery given in this chapter should be compared with the example from *Gerard's Herbal.* Every part of the flower has been brought into the service of decoration by these wonderful designers. The Persian carpet, from which the cornflower shape and the smaller primrose type have been taken, abounds with interest when considered under the heading of our subject. It is impossible to give even a sketch of the whole in the space I am entitled to, but to give a general idea of its plan I may mention that the carpet is centralised and sub-divided by those large forms we know as characteristic of Persian art, and the remaining spaces are filled by these wonderfully beautiful natural

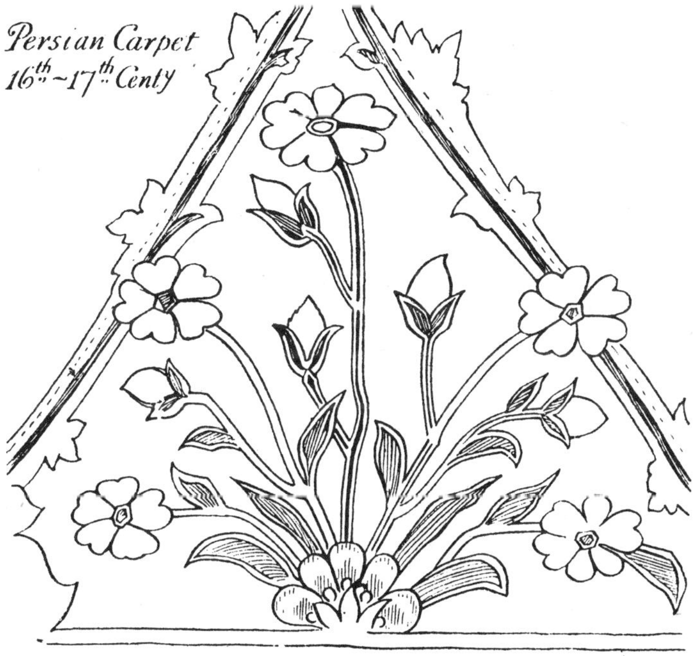

forms, of which a few examples are given here. Even though they are withdrawn from their surroundings they give a good idea of the skill of space-filling, power and beauty of drawing, and knowledge of nature possessed by the old Eastern craftsmen.

In translating these examples of decoration into black and white from their native hues of azure and vermilion, emerald and purple, I have felt like those wicked fairy godmothers in the old stories who turned charming and lovely princesses into maids-of-all-work, only with a soreness of conscience and pity for my victims, which those malevolent viragoes were not supposed to feel.

Before closing this chapter I would like to draw attention to the interesting device employed by the designer of the Rhodian dish in breaking the stem of the carnation to compel it to fill the circular space. This is just one of those resourceful touches I wish to emphasise—it gives us a glimpse of his personality, an insight into the conditions of the period, and a sense of the rightful liberty enjoyed in the making of a work of art by these designers of a decoratively delightful age.

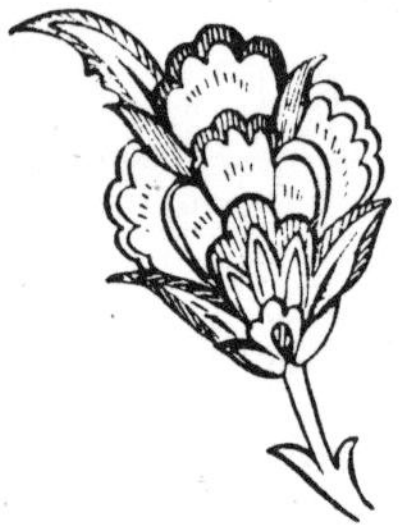

CHAPTER III

WE may now return to some of the favourite forms used in floral decoration and make a still more intimate acquaintance with them to our mutual benefit.

In this chapter I have added some more forms from the piece of block-printed calico spoken of in our last. It is of either Dutch or English design and workmanship of the seventeenth or eighteenth century, and made under the direct and exclusive influence of Eastern pattern.

At the risk of repetition I will remind you that at this time the traders from the East had found a lucrative market in Europe for all the precious products of the Orient—pottery, lacquer work, carpets, silks, cottons, textile fabrics of all kinds, carved ivories, weapons, metal work—all these things had a vogue in the wealthy fashionable world and influenced our arts and crafts in a characteristic and distinctive manner.

On many an old-fashioned sideboard may still be seen the ginger-jar or "China" bowl handed down to its present owner from the time we are considering, and at Ightham Mote, Kent, one of those historic houses which visitors are allowed to view, the drawing-room walls are covered with a genuine Chinese paper of splendid design, one of the first ever brought to this country. Specimens of Chinese wall-papers may also now be seen in the London Museum and the Geffrye Museum, Shoreditch.

Those interested in furniture will remember that Chippendale had a period when he designed some of his pieces "in the Chinese taste," introducing fretwork and other devices taken from this source. The splendid lacquered cabinets of the eighteenth century, made principally in France, Holland and England, are decorated with floral ornament copied from Eastern specimens.

The Persian carpets and other Oriental objects at South Kensington Museum, from which my illustrations are mostly taken, no doubt made their first appearance in England through the hands of

ORIENTAL FORMS

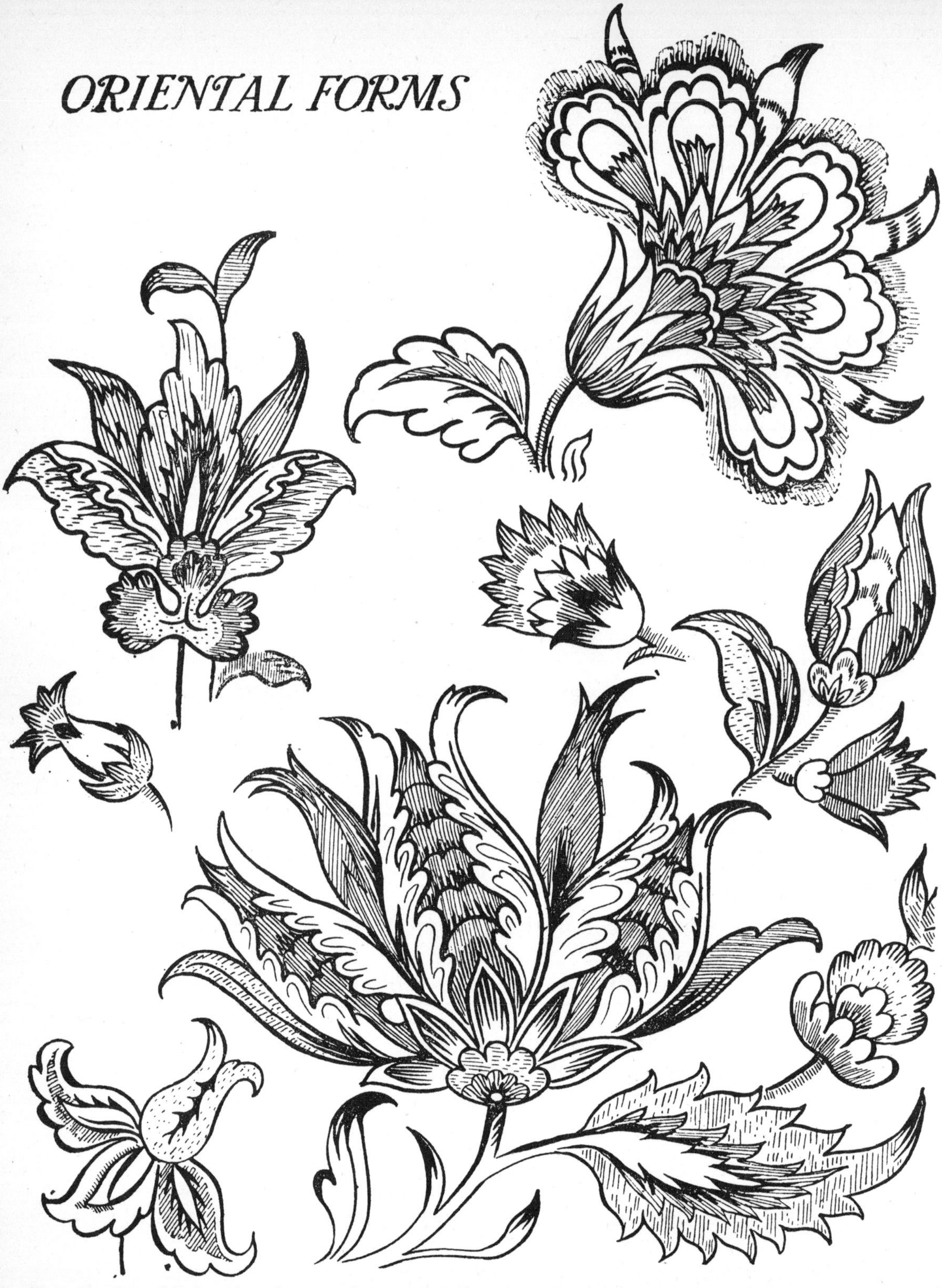

Details from block-printed cotton hanging. Dutch or English of about 17th or 18th century, showing strong influence of Eastern design

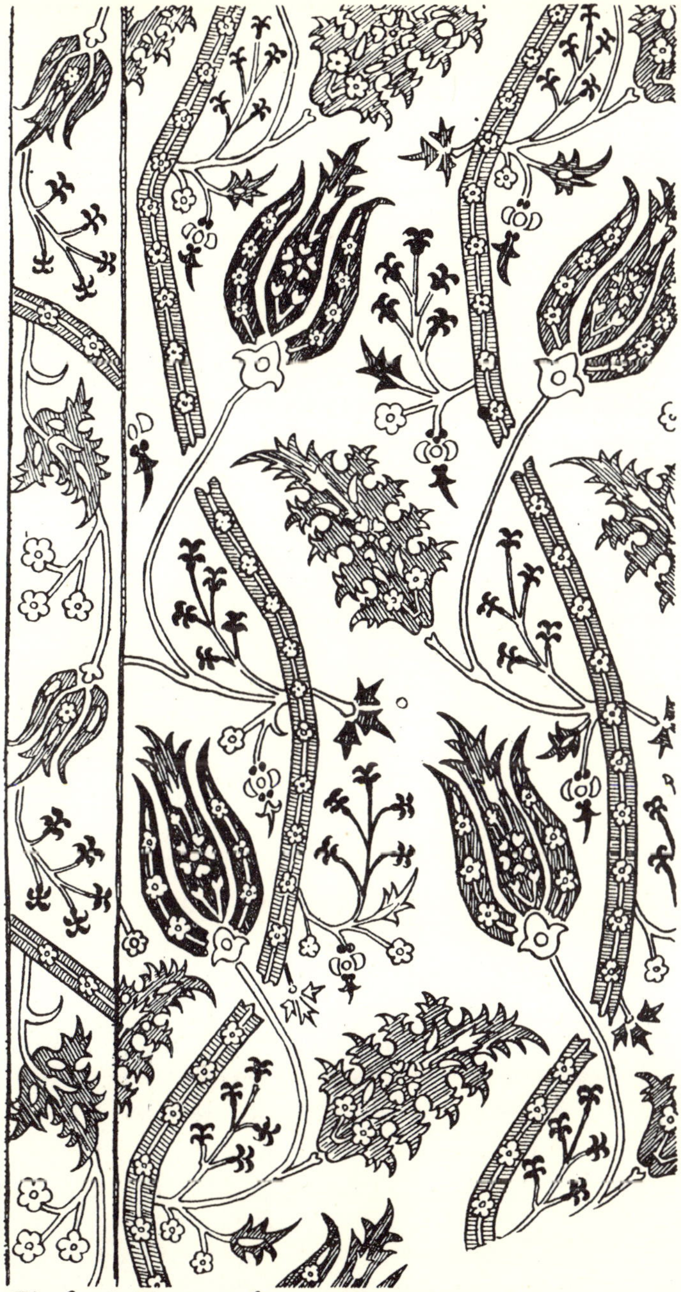

Turkish Embroidery 16-17 Centy.

Eastern traders, and if these short chapters induce readers who live in and near London, or those who make an occasional pilgrimage thereto from the provinces, to visit the Museum and examine afresh these beautiful works of art, a gratifying result will have been obtained.

The pattern mentioned above is full of interest for us. The designer has not only devoured, with a voracious appetite, all the Eastern floral forms he could find, but, more wonderful still, he has managed to assimilate them. His inventive powers have thriven on the nutritious material, for look you how he wields his brush-line! how joyously he revels, even to the point of exuberance, in the quantity and variety of the shapes he has found. Yet he has added a spirit of his own to the treasure-trove which the merchant navies of old time brought, under their swelling white sails, across the rolling blue seas from India and quaint Cathay—countries which had not then lost the charm of remoteness in arts and customs.

In looking at works of this kind, and especially at the marvellous facility of invention displayed in the Persian carpets, there is to be found that sense of "enjoyment in the doing" which is characteristic of most great art—there is no sign of fatigue or labour in them, and they give in return to the intent observer the same pleasure their makers experienced in working them out. There will not be wanting those who would reply that it was work done for a living, but there is a vast difference between the old conditions and those of modern times. Machinery, well enough if kept under control, has taken much of the variety and incidental invention away from the craftsman, allowing him less individuality of expression and destroying to a large extent the artistic interest the old designers were able to enjoy in their work.

In Chapter II. I quoted Morris's phrase, "the inhabited leaf," and we have now before us some additional examples of it in the Turkish embroidery of fritillary and hyacinth—a favourite combination of that style and period—and the Persian carpet of sixteenth and seventeenth century design (see pp. 149 and 152). To such an extent was this ornamental motive carried by the Persian designers that it developed under their hands into an elaborate and systematic principle. Notice how form is superimposed upon form, colour of course being used to differentiate each mass. The shape of every form is intelligently considered, with the result that wherever the eye wanders

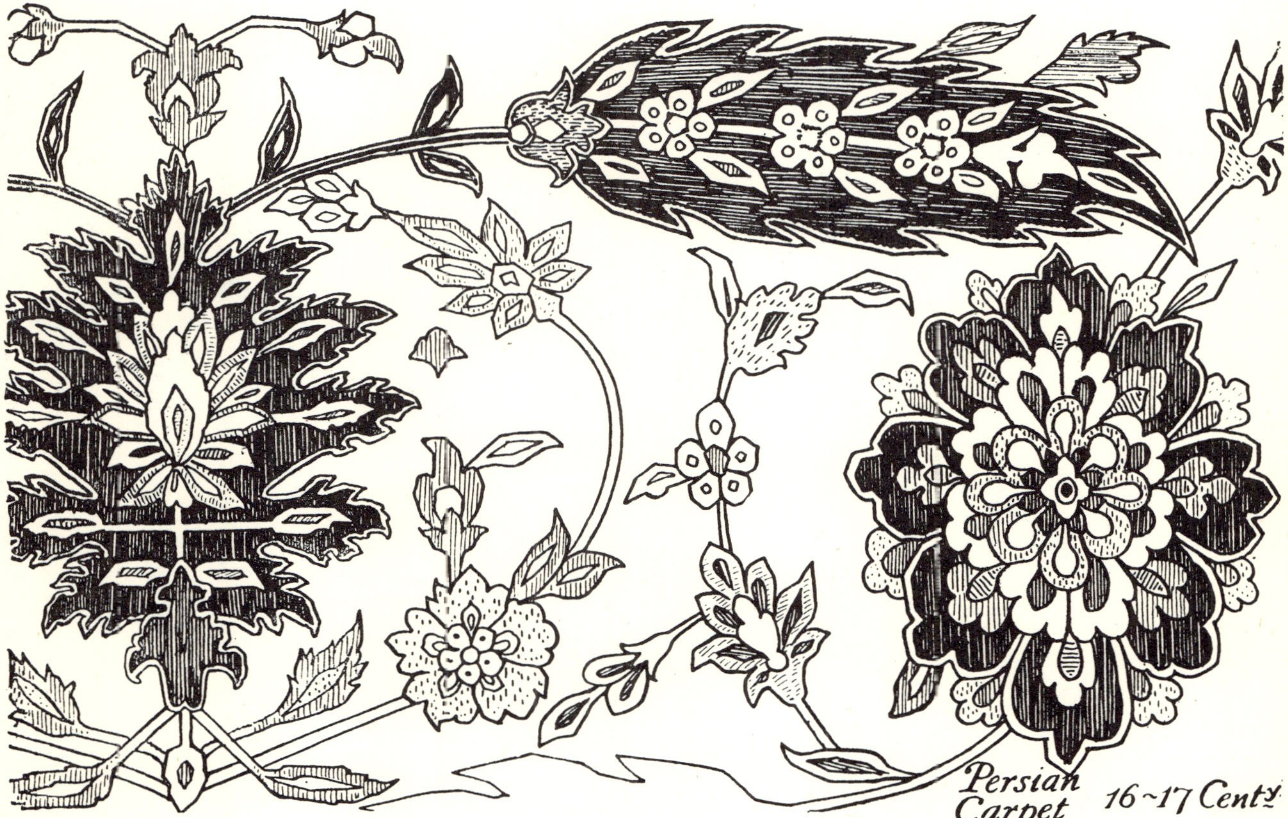

Persian Carpet 16~17 Cent.y

beauty of patterning is the result—from the outside edges of the largest mass as it tells against the groundwork to the smallest detail spotted over any part of the interior.

This is a triumphant issue from the severest test in pattern design—and to my mind the Persian scores heavily in this branch of art over the Japanese and Chinese, who are too fond of massing their forms in an accidental silhouette, a treatment suited to the landscape painter rather than the surface decorator.

It will be noticed how intense is the love of floral form in the Persian designer, when the whole carpet is analysed—he has even foliated the edges of the geometrical centre piece and then placed upon the dark forms a trailing flower pattern.

In fact this carpet is an astounding piece of decorative invention, for not only does it abound with an infinite variety of floral forms, but it also contains animal and bird forms, full of life in drawing and skilfully designed to accord with them—there are lions, tigers and leopards devouring deer and gazelles upon which the dappled markings are shaped into rosettes, giving us this time not an "inhabited" leaf, but an animal "inhabited" with floral forms—to such a degree did the old designer carry his love of floral ornament.

I only show these incidentally, and do not mean to trespass on the domain of animal form in decoration. That is another affair. The debased form of the peacock I have given as an illustration of the long life which traditional forms enjoy in the hands of the Eastern craftsman. It has degenerated into a sorry caricature of its gorgeous predecessors by means of vain repetition. But there are other factors to blame. The Western merchant has introduced the Eastern craftsman to the benefits of the factory system, and the peacock's tail becomes a rude semblance of a leaf terminating in a still rougher rosette. It is taken from a cheap modern rug made in the East, but which still contains enough remnants of fine Oriental pattern to make it preferable to the mechanical designs mostly turned out of our carpet factories.

It is generally supposed that the forms on Persian carpets are geometrical and conventional shapes, but an examination of the sketches here given will show how their evolution has probably occurred, and that when all is said they are not so far from nature. A full-blown tulip, a peony or poppy seen from above, will exhibit

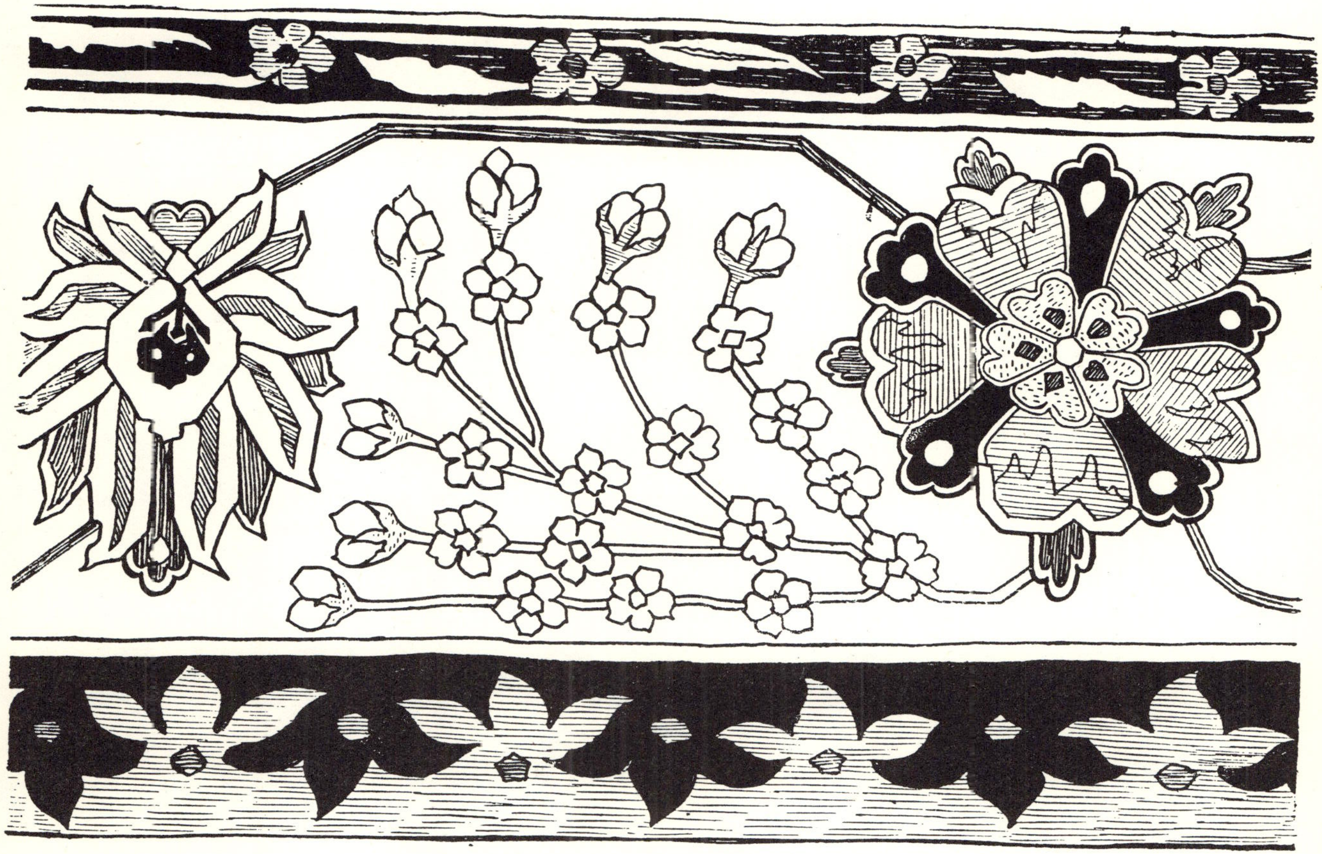

Border, Persian carpet, 16th–17th century

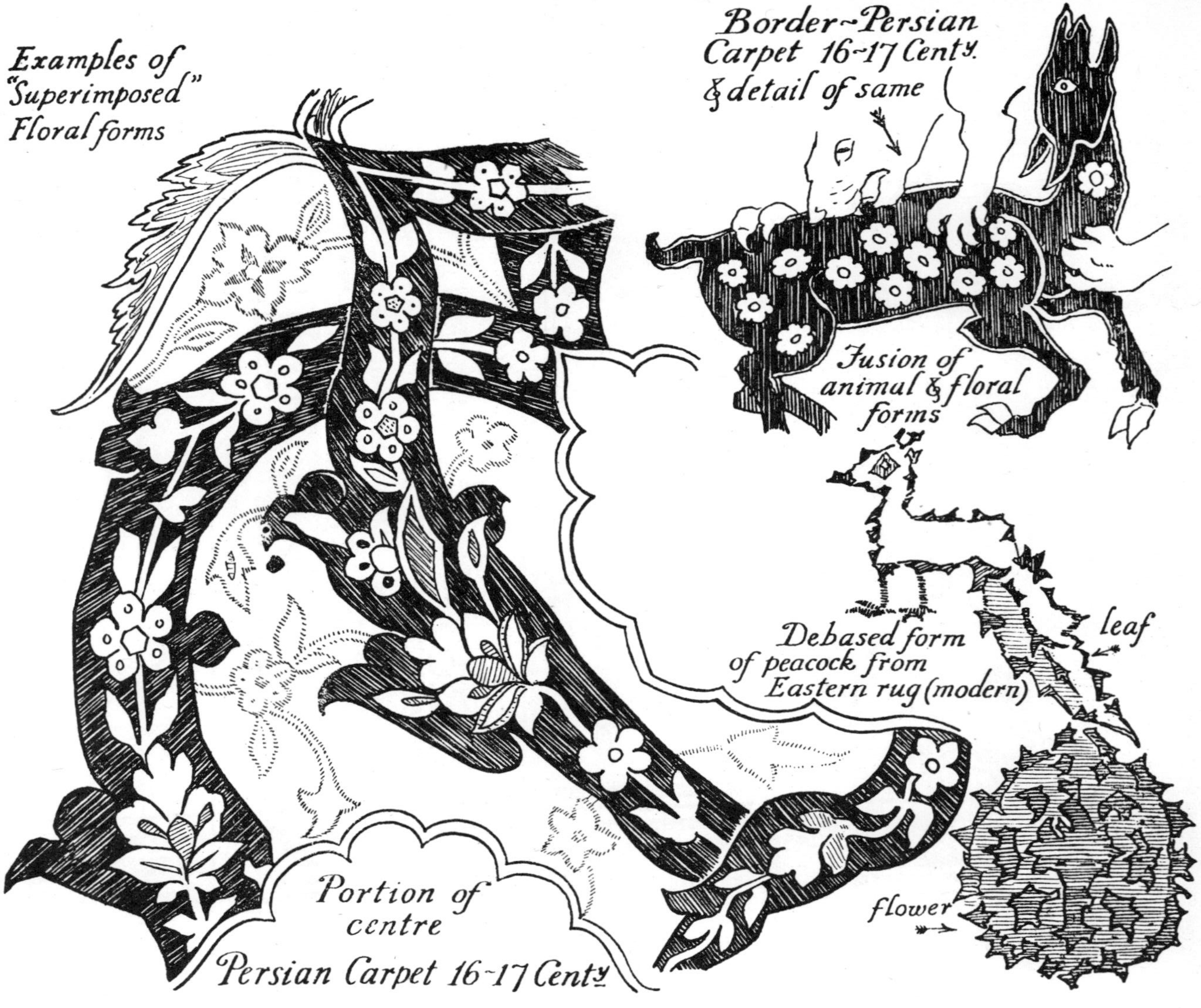
Examples of "Superimposed" Floral forms
Border~Persian Carpet 16~17 Centy. & detail of same
Fusion of animal & floral forms
Debased form of peacock from Eastern rug (modern)
leaf
flower
Portion of centre
Persian Carpet 16~17 Centy.

detail of seeds, stamens, stripes and markings relieved against curling petals very much like the top-view forms used by the Persian designer.

The diagrams in the lower part of page 154 should be compared with the forms in the examples selected for our main illustrations.

Although colour is not my present concern, it will perhaps be helpful to readers if the general scheme of the large carpet which contains the forms here illustrated is roughly sketched by a word-picture. The ground is of a maize-coloured yellow—the lions tawny orange, the deer a dark blue with lighter blue for the rosettes. The large leaves are of a dark plum blue, "inhabited" with leaves and flowers in greens, yellows, white, crimson or brown reds. But the most curious part of the whole design is the outer border, which I have reserved to the last. It contains a succession of shapes which at first sight look like floral forms joined by running stems. On further investigation they prove to be grotesque animal heads artfully designed to imitate the former and echoing the animal forms of the interior portion.

It strikes me "that devil of an apprentice" had a hand in this—we know him, he has survived many a period of decay and renaissance in decorative art, and he still abideth with us. It was his prototype, no doubt, who designed the border we

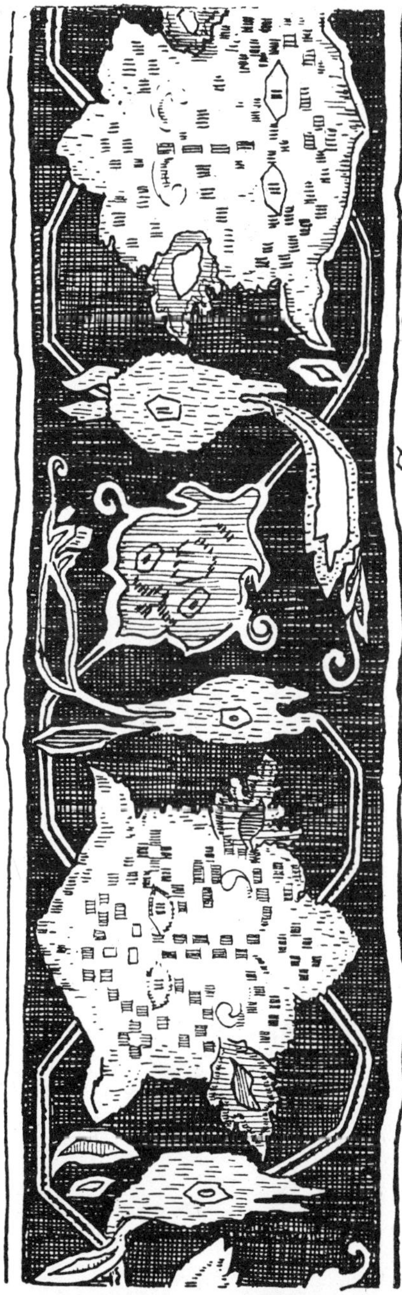

Fusion of animal & floral forms

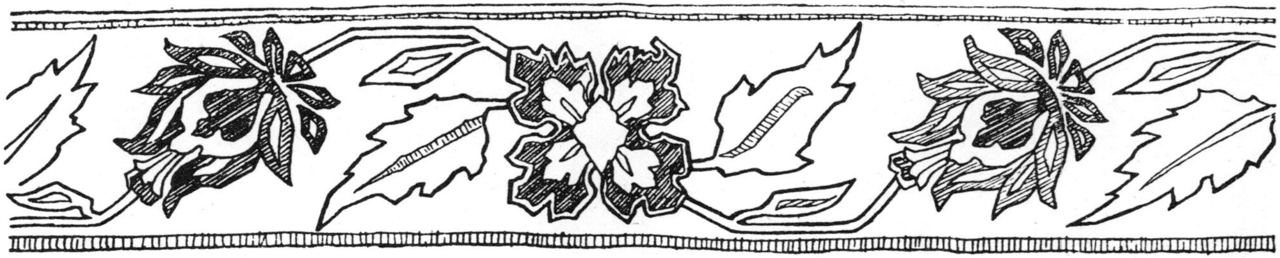

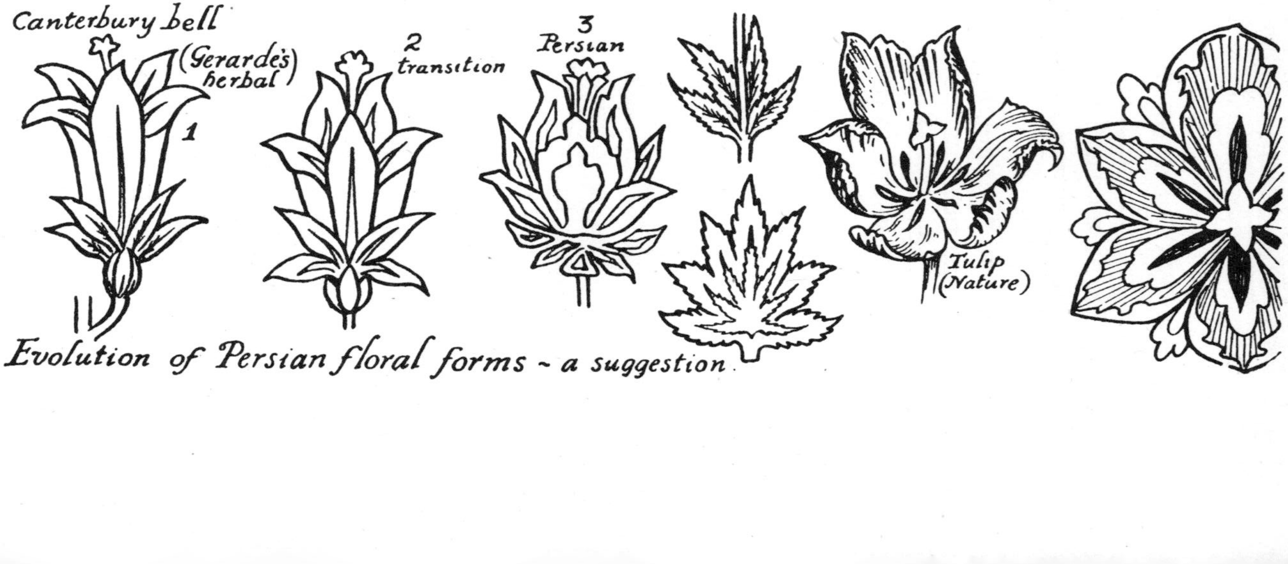

Evolution of Persian floral forms ~ a suggestion.

are looking at. Evidently he determined to work this touch of humour in while the master craftsman went to inquire what time it was at the caravansary round the corner. But, since writing this, I have again examined the carpet minutely, and find the grotesque heads are scattered over its surface, partially concealed in the flower forms, so I did him an injustice, or perhaps flattered him too highly.

We, in our part of the world, do not associate humour with the dignity derived from the tall turban and long beard of the grave Oriental, yet there are droll stories in the *Arabian Nights*, and here in this carpet is a reflection of the same comic spirit. To throw out a thought at a venture, did the craftsman of "old Iran" ever dream that we of the twentieth century would smile at his decorative jest—we, who are made companions of his thought by the freemasonry of art? 'Tis as hard a question to answer as many another in this field—for who *were* these wonderful designers, where are their drawings, how did they learn to render nature's forms so exquisitely in such varied materials? However, after this, who will deny that floral decoration has its human side?

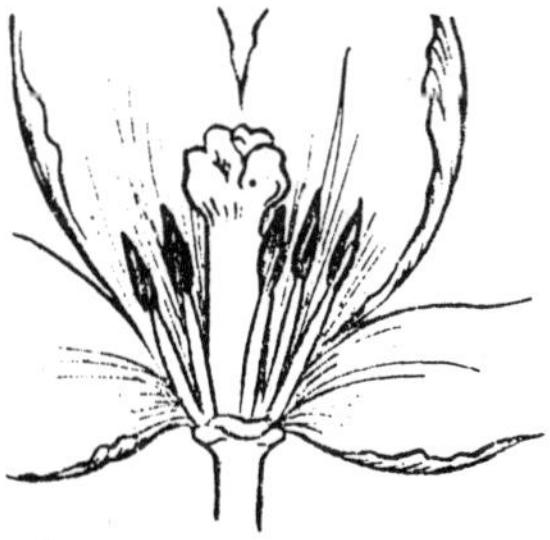

Interior forms of Tulip

CHAPTER IV

READERS of these short chapters on floral form have no room to complain of me in one respect at least. I have used the magic carpet as much as I promised, and they have flown from one side of the world, or from one century, to another, without the slightest delay or inconvenience.

There are good reasons for this method. Comparisons can be made readily, variety of interest is stimulated and monotony of style and treatment avoided. And I hope it will widen the field of enquiry and excite the curiosity and interest of the general reader, student or prentice hand in this very ancient but still fascinating subject.

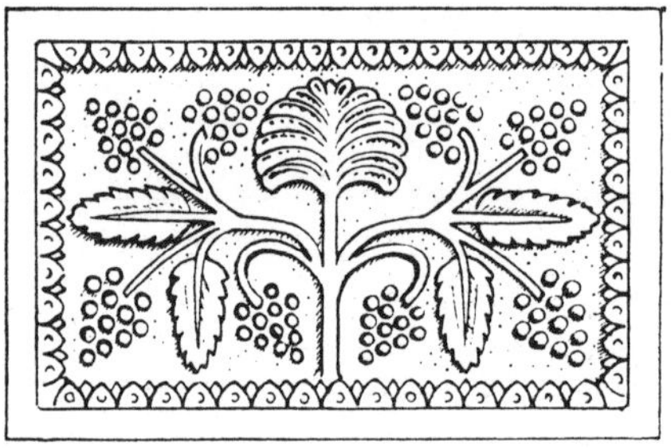

Chair-back panel, carved wood, showing Oriental influence—English, 17th century

It is strange to note the attitude of the average person walking through the museums where our national treasures are on view. To him a Persian carpet is just a carpet made in Persia—that is all. He reads the label, and wanders on to the Flemish tapestry or Jacobean embroidery with the same lack of interest. There are movements now of guides and lectures on such things, it is true, but what interesting chapters on these matters could be written for school readers! By this means general culture would be greatly helped, an appreciation of beautiful objects aroused, and an understanding of good workmanship acquired.

Now, with apologies for sermonising, let us look at the examples which illustrate our present chapter.

The piece of floral decoration from the Rhodian vase gives us still another example of the treatment of the rose, something quite different, in fact, from foregoing examples. The stage of the flower chosen is beyond the full-blown; the petals seem about to drop. The peculiar form in the centre of the design is a conventional cypress tree, and a very beautiful and uncommon form it makes. Neither in this nor in the two large leaves on the outside of the group has the old

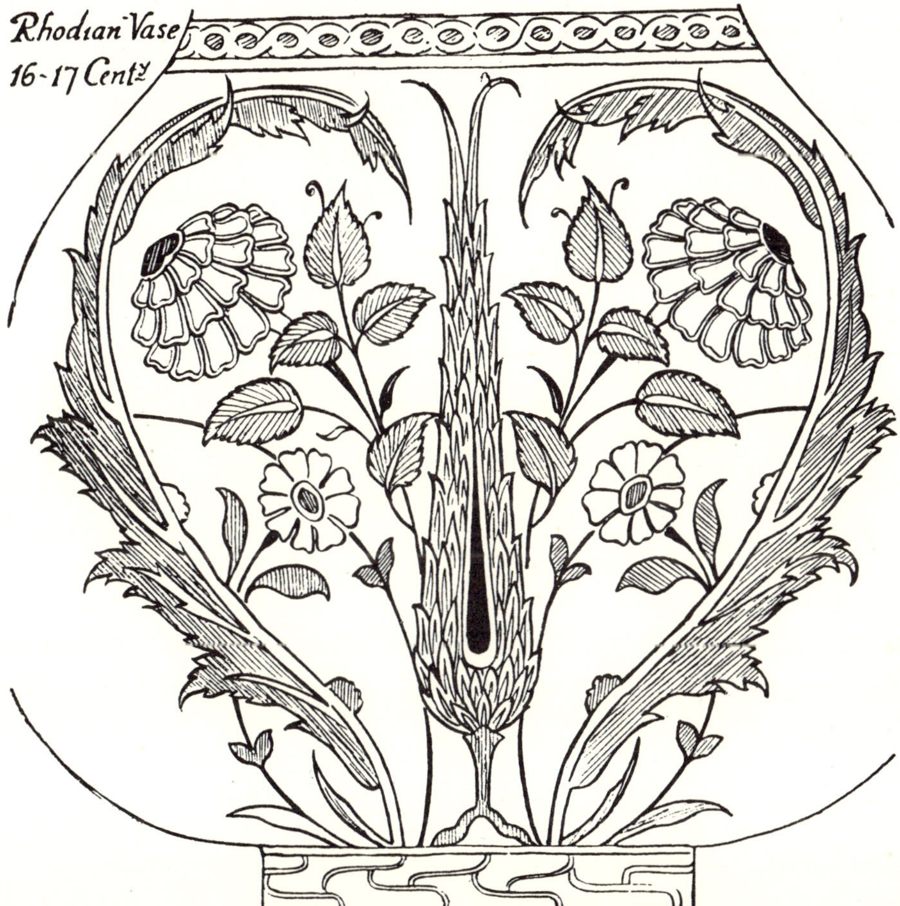

Rhodian, who painted this vase, worried about the differences of size and scale. We need not do so either, for the shapes are all so far removed from imitation that they do not challenge comparison in this respect, and so satisfying is the pattern and arrangement of line, form and colour, that we would not have it otherwise. Strong reds and greens on a white ground make the colour scheme. A love of frank, bright colour is a characteristic of this fine Rhodian pottery, and what skill and accomplishment, what grace of line and drawing, contrast of rounded and sharply serrated forms are placed on it!

The sure hand and flowing brush are more in evidence on the

Carved wood panel - Jacobean - early 17th cent.

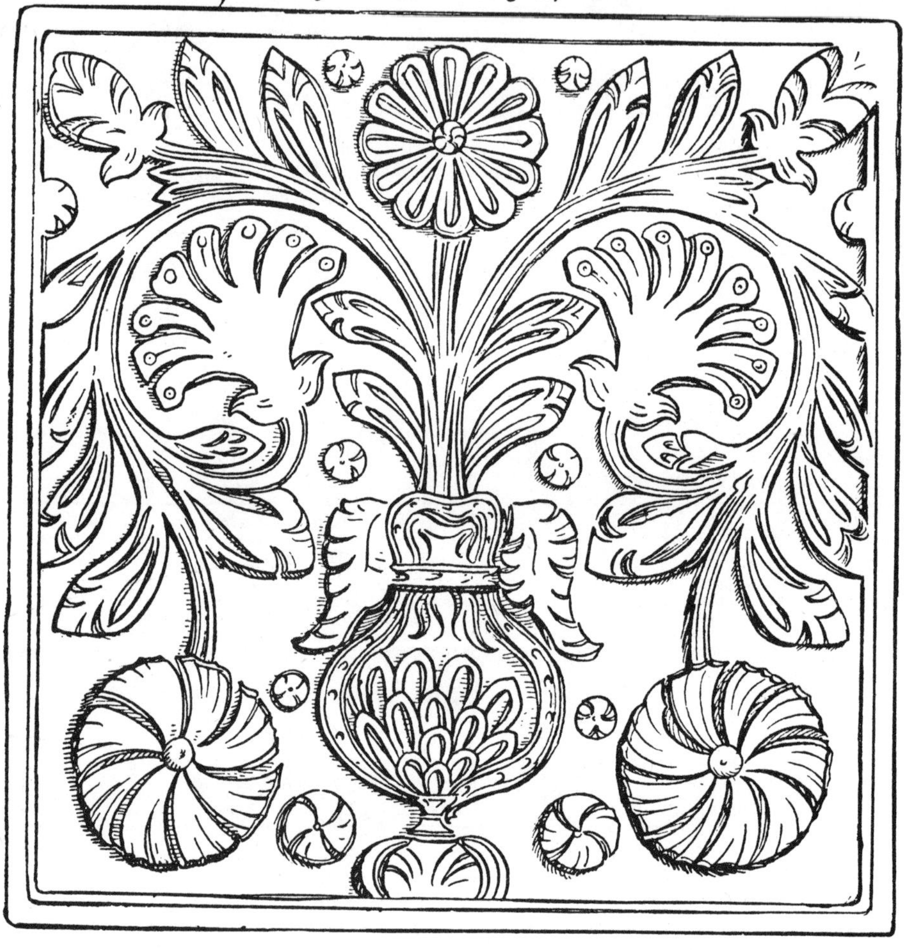

thing itself, of course, than in my drawing; with a pen it is scarcely possible to give the liquid appearance or gradation and variety of surface which endows it with so much charm.

The Jacobean panel, in carved oak, is from a court cupboard, a piece of furniture somewhat after the fashion of a sideboard.

It is interesting to compare it and the border and panel of the oak chest with the Rhodian vase, if only for the sake of contrast in temperament. In the pottery there is more skill of hand, but the carved

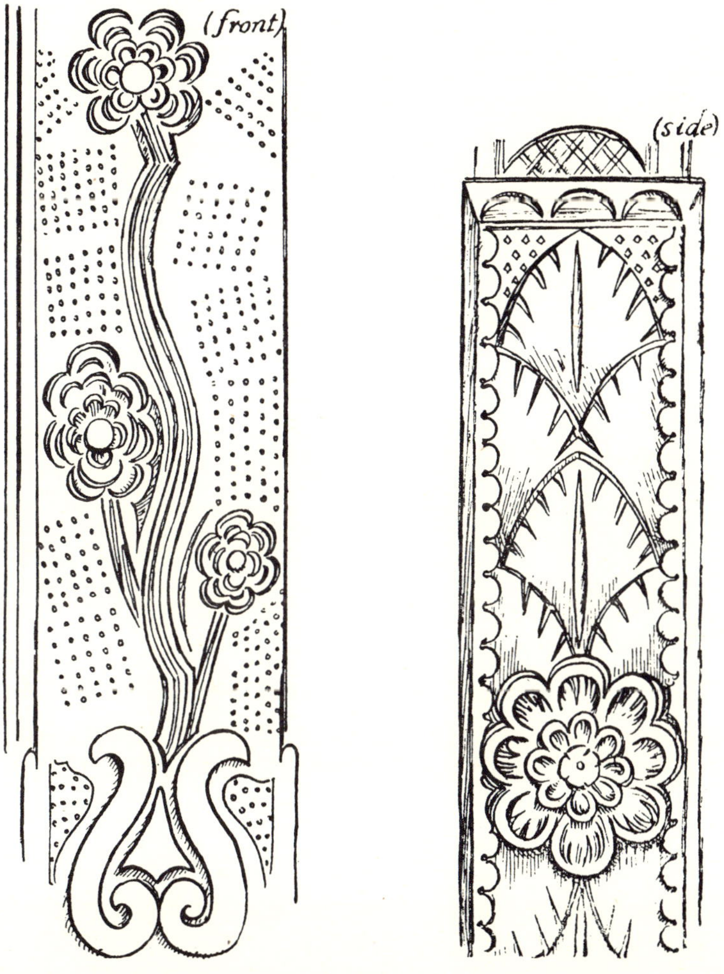

Carved decoration on joiner's plane—German, 18*th century*

panels are very lovable in their homely and childlike simplicity and frankness. Allowing for the difference of material and what can be accomplished in each, there is a certain similarity to be found in them.

These old English examples of woodwork seem to me to be executed in the true spirit of wood-carving; the gouge and chisel marks

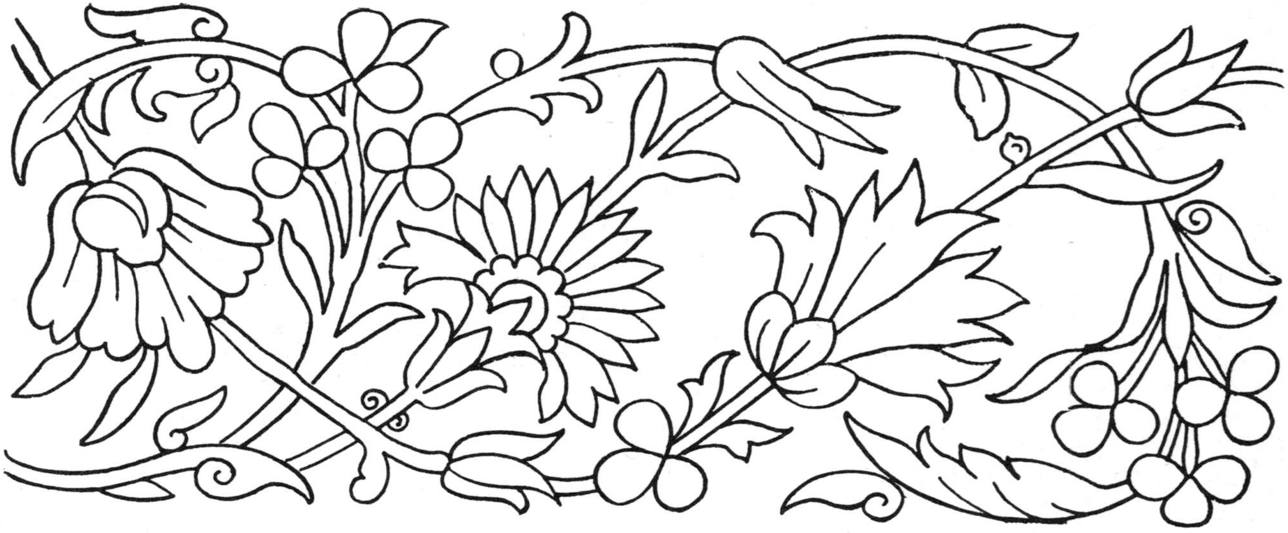

Carnation forms. Wood block for printing on calico—Turkish, 18th–19th century

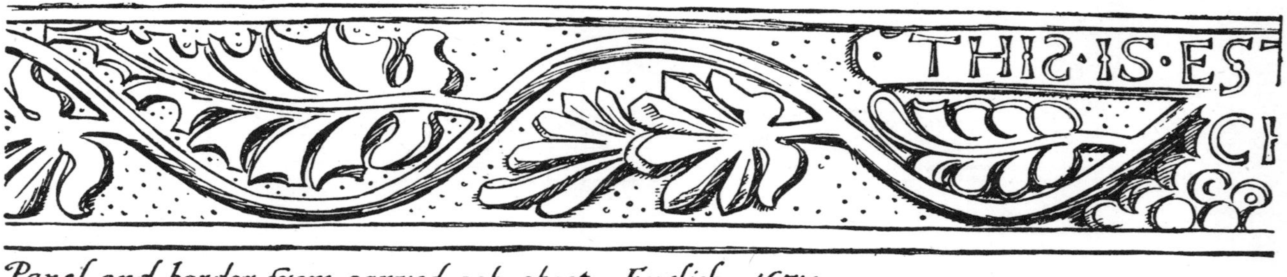

Panel and border from carved oak chest ~ English ~ 1637 ~

are quite candidly shown, the forms and their details are just such shapes as can be easily cut out with these tools. In so much of the

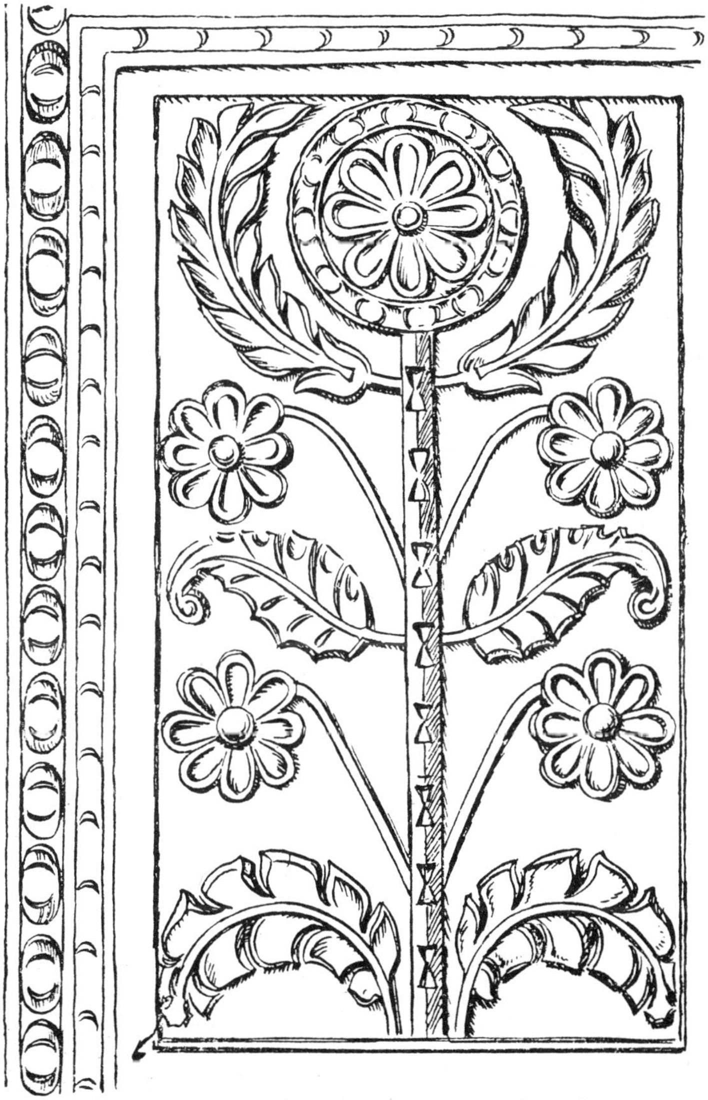

Panel from carved oak chest—English, 1637

Italian wood-carving of the Renaissance period the effect obtained is either like marble or metal, or it suggests modelling in a plastic material, and though it is hard to draw a definite line of restriction as to how far delicacy of modelling should go, there is no doubt that these old English panels give the right effect when the material and its treatment are considered. Stepping aside from our subject for a moment, the forms of the letters carved on the chest are well worth attention. They are very beautiful in shape, and as the drawing shows, carved "intaglio." So again the chisel and the gouge have decided the forms and the treatment. No doubt the purist will object to the letter S turned back to front, but I have an idea that the good old craftsman felt there was a balance and symmetry of design in placing it thus, as it is followed closely by another S. Also it must be remembered that this was carved in the golden age of spelling, a century or more before Dr. Johnson compiled his famous dictionary. In those days, as regards orthography and similar problems, the Englishman was truly a freeborn Briton, and did that which was right in his own eyes, however wrong it may seem in the opinion of later days.

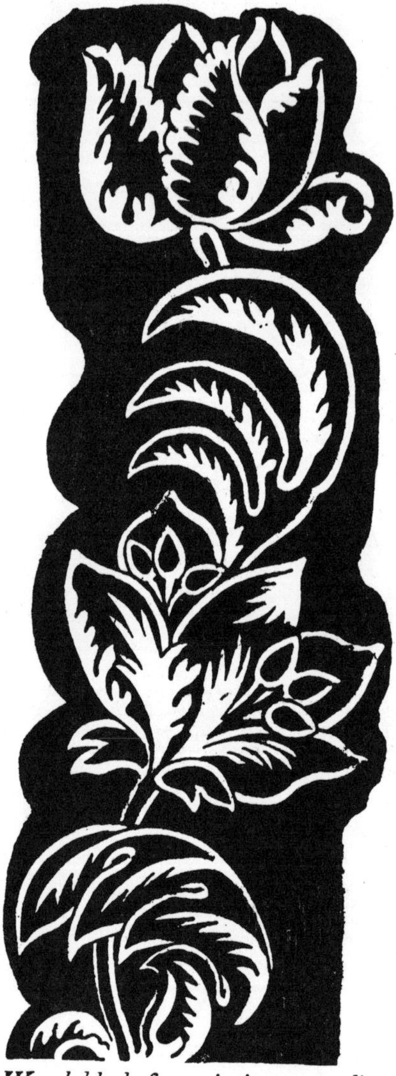

Wood block for printing on calico. Turkish, 18th–19th century

The complete inscription reads: ESTHER HOBSONNE CHEST, 1637, which is as downright in statement as the gouge and chisel method of the carving.

The "pot of flowers" motive seen in the panel from the court cupboard is a favourite one in both Eastern and Western decoration. It is found on Chinese and Japanese plates, Persian and Indian tiles, or carved in their wood and stonework. Embroiderers and textile printers and weavers have used it, too; showing again how one touch of decoration makes the whole world kin and how ideas travel from one country to another.

I remember a very beautiful design of Morris's for embroidery with the same motive, but then no man knew the world's art better than he, and this was what made him such an original designer.

There is a delightful air of inconsequence in this panel in the parts where the carver has run his leaves into the corner or the side just as it pleased his momentary fancy or convenience. It is a bit of self-expression which forestalls criticism in a manner similar to that of the encounter between the navvy and the pugilist. The navvy, it will be remembered, scored the first hit, and there was no more to be said.

The carving on the joiner's plane shows how artistic common things *used* to be "made in Germany," and also what beautiful decoration can be obtained by very simple means. The method is the same as that of the English oak chest and panels. How these craftsmen must have loved their work, when we see the very tools they worked with decorated so charmingly. People are worked too hard nowadays and have too little leisure to express their feelings in this way. Under modern pressure and "speeding-up" this kind of democratic art has disappeared. Art in the broad sense is the outcome of "work-pleasure" and should not be a luxurious or aristocratic thing, but a people's possession, and shorter hours of labour would restore national art, for human beings do not really like idleness, and, given the chance, self-expression will assert itself.

The tulip forms taken from nature studies are used here to supplement the Turkish wood block for textile printing. By comparing them it will be seen how the block designer has

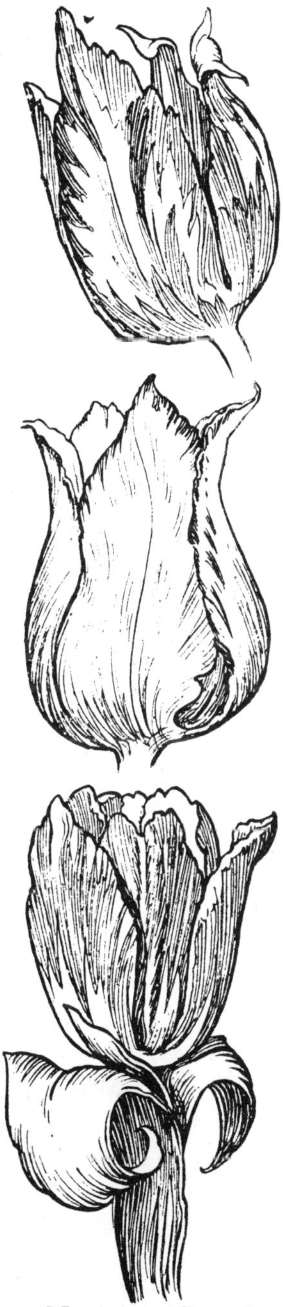

Nature studies of tulip forms

Silk Embroidered hanging ~
Japanese ~

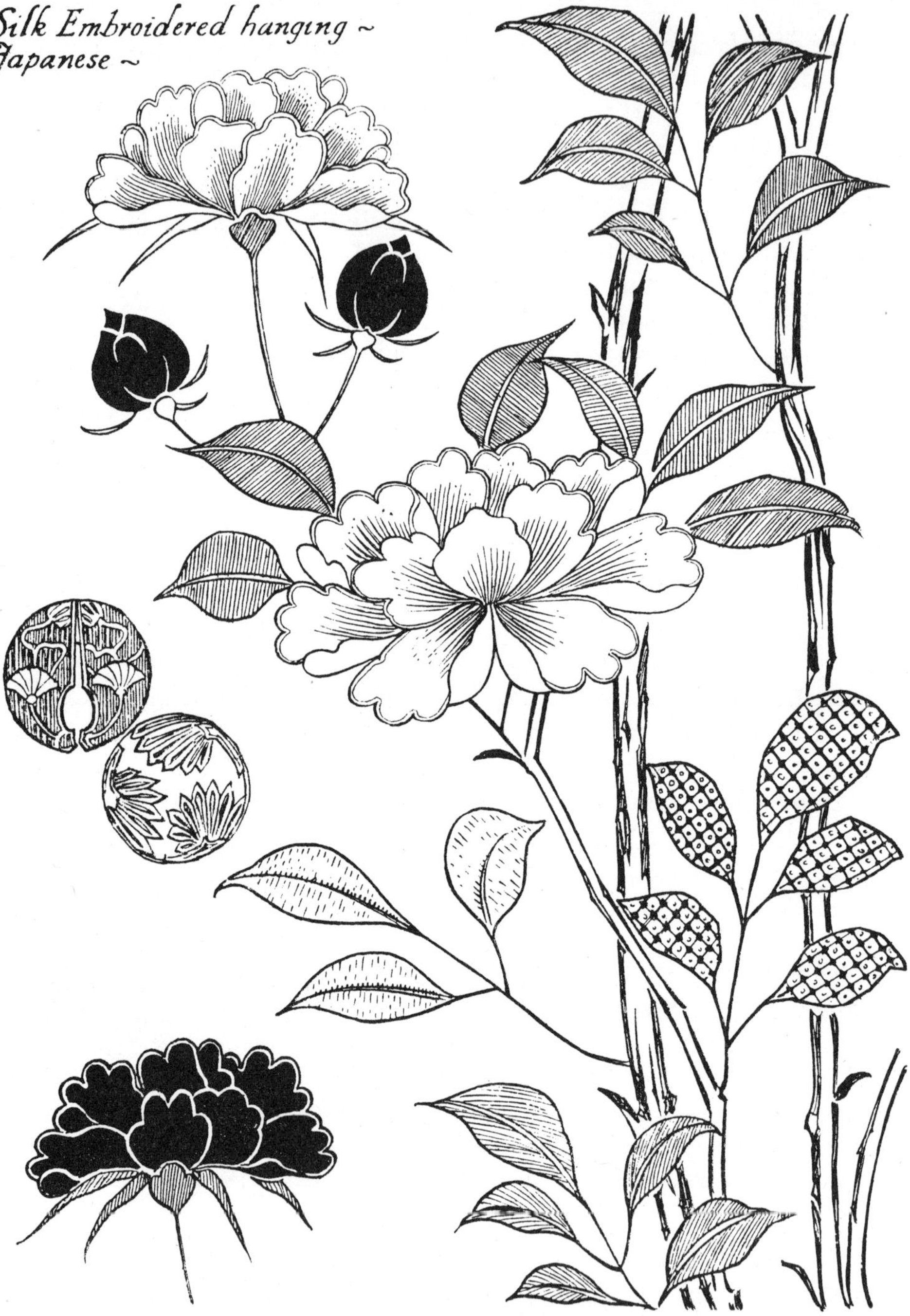

"patternised" his material. He has very evidently succeeded in getting the decoration he required from it.

The Japanese silk embroidery is a specimen of that wonderful people's skill which can only be spoken of in the superlative. Ordinary praise cannot do justice to the subtlety of the drawing and delicacy of finish lavished on these exquisite forms.

The flowers are a dainty shell pink, except those blacked in which are a dark blue, the leaves generally considered are a pale apple green,

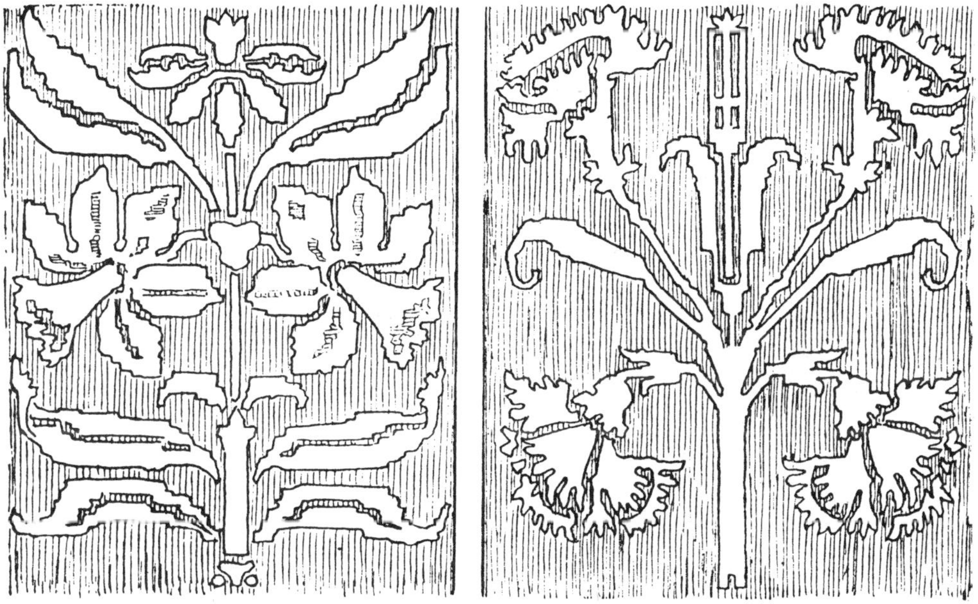

Daffodil and pink from linen damask—Flemish, 17th century

but the three in light tone just over the dark flower are a wonderful apricot-orange tint—a touch of genius. The leaves with the chequered pattern on their surface are in brown-gold and so are the large stems. The former are an instance of that curious mixture of the almost natural with the ultra-conventional so often found in Japanese work. The whole design savours far more of plant drawing than of pattern, yet these leaves and the little roundels are severely conventional. In closing I may mention that the ground is a delicate watered silk of silvery grey-white, and we come to the end of this chapter with the two quaint little sprig patterns of daffodil and pink taken from an upright running border of Flemish damask.

CHAPTER V

IN the last chapter attention was drawn to the "pot of flowers" motive so often found in ornamental decoration all over the world. In looking over the various periods it is astonishing how often it occurs, so I have given a few more examples of it for the sake of comparison.

A very primitive instance of it is seen in one of the two examples

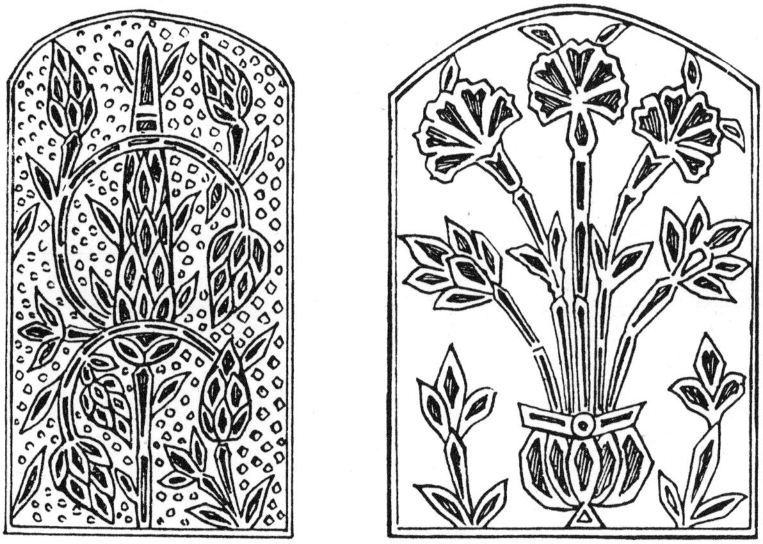

Arab lattice windows, coloured glass in plaster, Cairo

taken from fragments of Egyptian grave clothes. No historical plan has been followed in these very discursive notes on floral decoration, that has not been their object, and we have strayed from periods to countries the most remote from one another without any logical sequence. But in order to understand the examples under discussion, let us cast back our minds for a moment in order to take a slight historical survey in reference to our subject.

The Greeks, although conquered by the Romans, impregnated them with their art, and Roman art is therefore an evolution or development of Greek art. When the Roman Empire decayed it is generally thought that art decayed with it. This is only partially true, for artistic activity was still in progress though not so evident

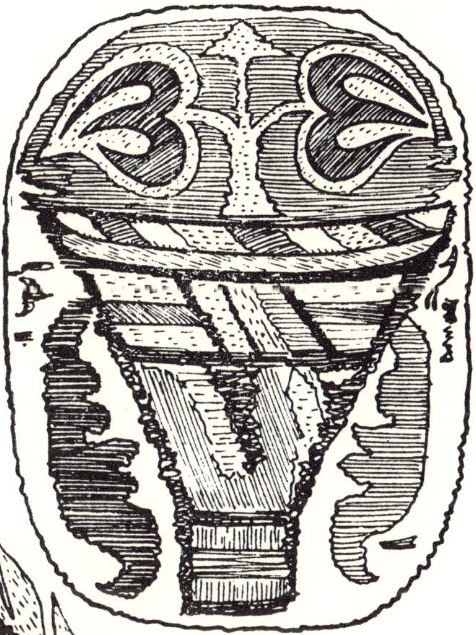

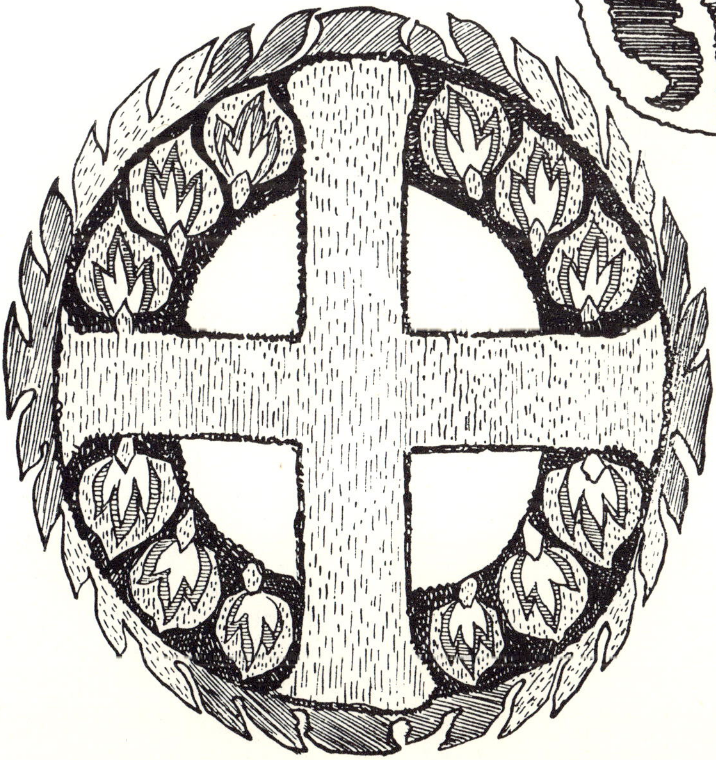

Details on grave clothes

Egyptian, Coptic and Arab period

A.D. 300 *to* 900

as when the great Empire demanded palaces and temples to be reared and decorated in accordance with its pride, wealth and luxury. Greek workmen, sculptors, painters and craftsmen of all kinds were largely employed by the Romans, and Greek artists and craftsmen again were they who travelled northward and eastward as well as Romewards and carried their fine design and excellent craftsmanship to Byzantium, the ancient Constantinople, to Asia Minor, Syria and northern Egypt, nay more, for the stream of their influence flowed onwards to Persia and India as well.

When Christianity became established at Byzantium, and the

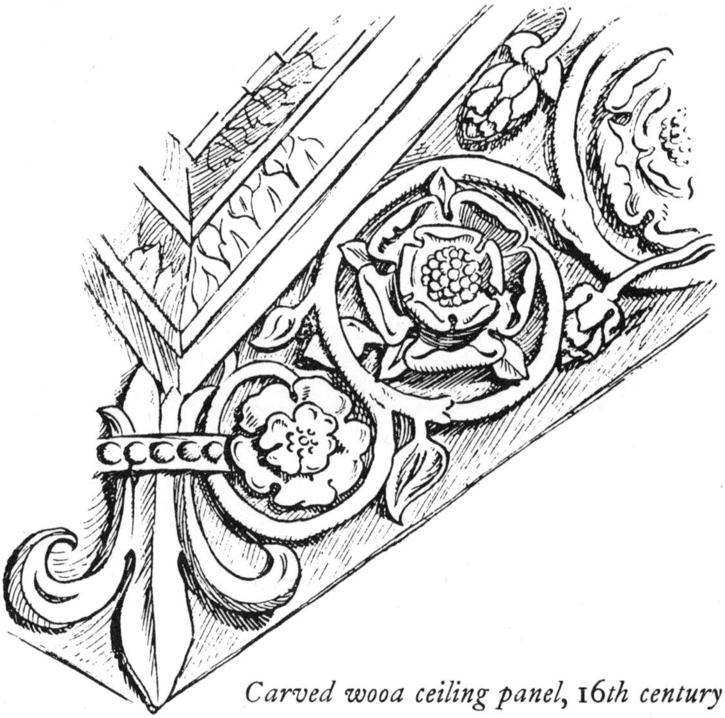

Carved wooa ceiling panel, 16*th century*

Church grew in power and magnificence, these artists and craftsmen supplied its demands. A new demand, too, it was that then arose—symbolism became one of the chief features of the new creed—the cross, the dove, the halo, the evangelical signs, the figures of the Zodiac and other details of sun worship which Christianity absorbed from its surroundings, and many of which it retains to this day, were all employed in the art and decoration of the time. So the two examples of embroidery on grave clothes on page 167 are specimens of the early Christian art of the Coptic peoples in Egypt, the head of the Church in that part of the world being at Alexandria. These two crude specimens are therefore about the earliest in date of any examples illustrative of our subject which I have so far given. They are extremely interesting if only for this reason, and it is also a coincidence that the pot or basket of flowers should form one of the

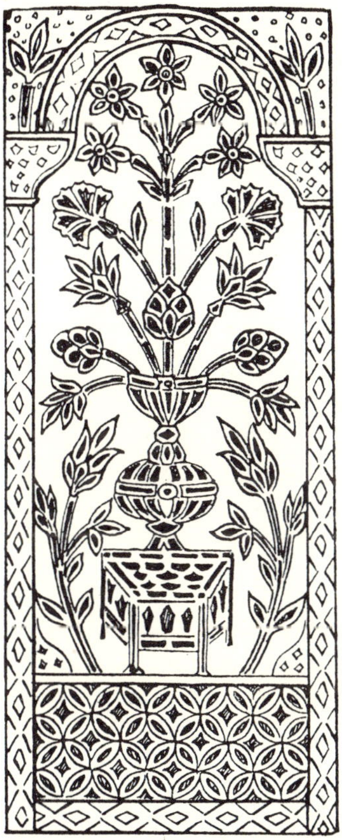

Arab lattice window, coloured glass in plaster, Cairo

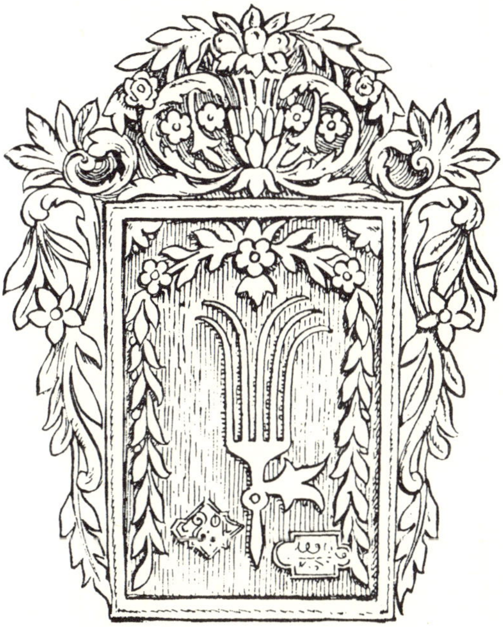

Tradesman's Signboard from Constantinople — Carved & painted wood.

schemes of decoration; whether it has any symbolical meaning I am unable to say, but the cross in the surrounding circle with the flaming flowers seems to speak a fiery zeal, crude though it may be reckoned in workmanship. Art here is down at zero, but symbolism glows fiercely above it. These two very simple attempts at floral decoration are both worked on linen in coloured threads of coarse quality, and they are singularly like the quaint old samplers executed by our grandmothers as exercises in needlework. History repeats itself, in floral decoration as in other things. The Arab lattice windows from Cairo again contain the same motive, though here the material is utterly different. These are the jewelled lights of dazzling colour we see in the pictures of Eastern interiors. Where the light glares so strongly outside, small openings are enough to illuminate the grateful and welcome shade indoors, we can therefore understand how admirably designed they are for their purpose and how rich the floral

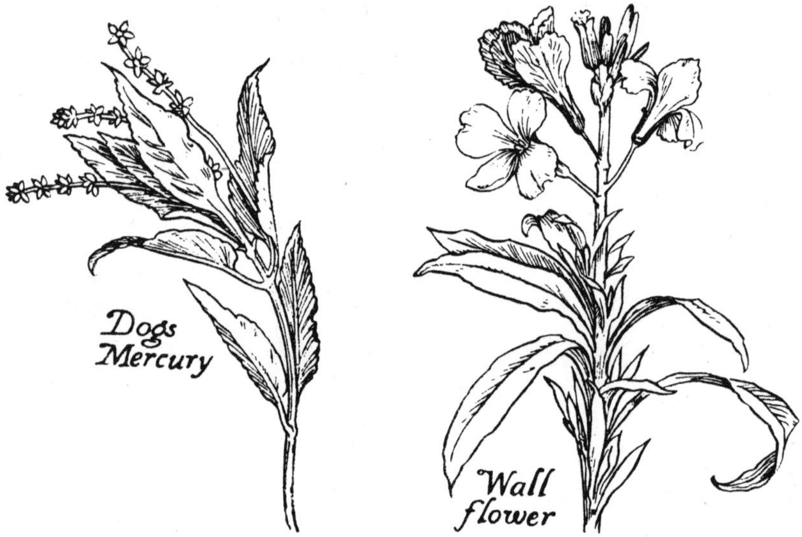

Nature studies

forms must look in this lovely material. The pieces of glass are embedded in the plaster while it is in a partially soft and wet condition. The exact process by which the work is done I have been unable to ascertain. The small holes between the flower forms of the design are perforations which not only admit additional light, but also the cool draughts of air so necessary in that sultry climate. They are not shown on the other two specimens as they obscure the clearness of the design in a pen-and-ink drawing.

In the tradesman's signboard from Constantinople the pot of flowers is a vase of fruit, though this is a very "Celtic" mode of describing a bit of Oriental decoration.

It is a rich and interesting piece of floral ornament for such a homely and businesslike purpose, but why not? Art and use should go hand-in-hand and here we so find them. Though the flower forms are conventional, I have supplemented this piece on another page by the two little nature studies of wallflower and dog's mercury, to show how many an ordinary flower and many a wayside weed suggests forms and groupings from which conventional ornament like this may have been derived. In the lower part of the panel there are two small cartouches containing Arabic or Turkish inscriptions, and much as I have longed to read them, I shall have to disappoint my readers of the hope of a translation. Had I possessed the power to give one, who knows but that I might have elucidated the meaning of the extremely ornamental gridiron in the centre of the panel? Was it designed to call the attention of the turbaned crowd to the craft or "mystery" of Oriental cooking, or what? Guesswork is dangerous, and we shall have to content ourselves with the beauty of its form and the part it plays with its accessories in the excellent space-filling of the panel. Speaking of the Turkish writing on the little cartouches, how decoratively beautiful the Eastern forms of lettering seem to us. Perhaps it is but that they are less familiar than our own, for strangeness has always a charm.

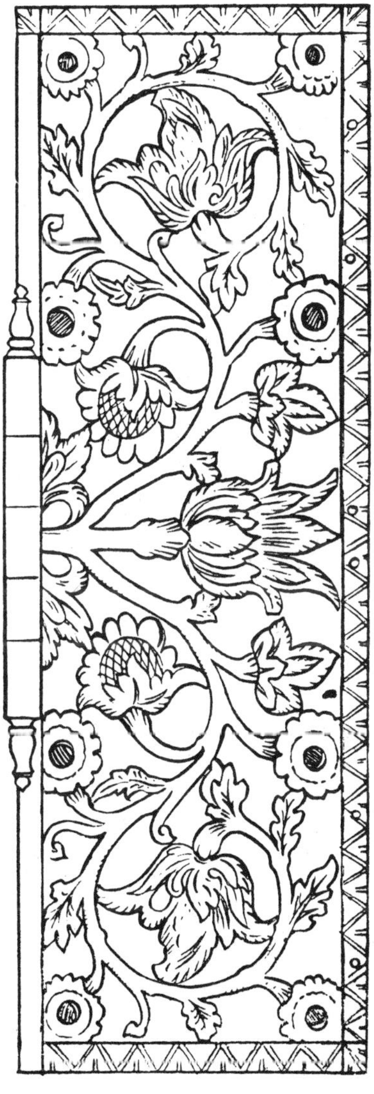

Engraved brass hinge—English, 17th century

There are those who assert that the "unspeakable Turk" has never enriched the earth with anything constructive or artistic, that he is but a barbaric conqueror who has subjected other more artistic peoples to minister to his demands. Whether this is so or not there is virtue in the decorative products which come from his quarter of the globe, so the foregoing indictment does not seem entirely true.

Panel, carved wood, on court cupboard—early 17*th century. Pink or carnation motive*

The engraved brass hinge of the second half of the seventeenth century shows the excellent conditions of the crafts in our own country at that date. The flower in the middle is of a tulip type, and the way the fastenings have been arranged in the centre of the smaller flowers is both ingenious and resourceful. The surface engraving exhibits the skill of a craftsman who knew what effect he required and the most expeditious and direct way of attaining it. The brass scrolls are placed over a steel plate, the dull grey of which is a very effective background to the golden pattern.

From this date onward to the beginning of the nineteenth century

Rainwater pipehead in cast lead ~ 1611

English craftsmanship reached its highest perfection. Think of the Chippendales, Sheratons, Hepplewhites, Adams and Wedgwoods, the goldsmiths, the silversmiths, and the potters who left us the chaste, the classic and the richly and elegantly designed objects these names recall. Alas, a little later came the débâcle of the lesser arts and crafts from which we have not yet entirely recovered, though sturdy and vital progress has been made.

A

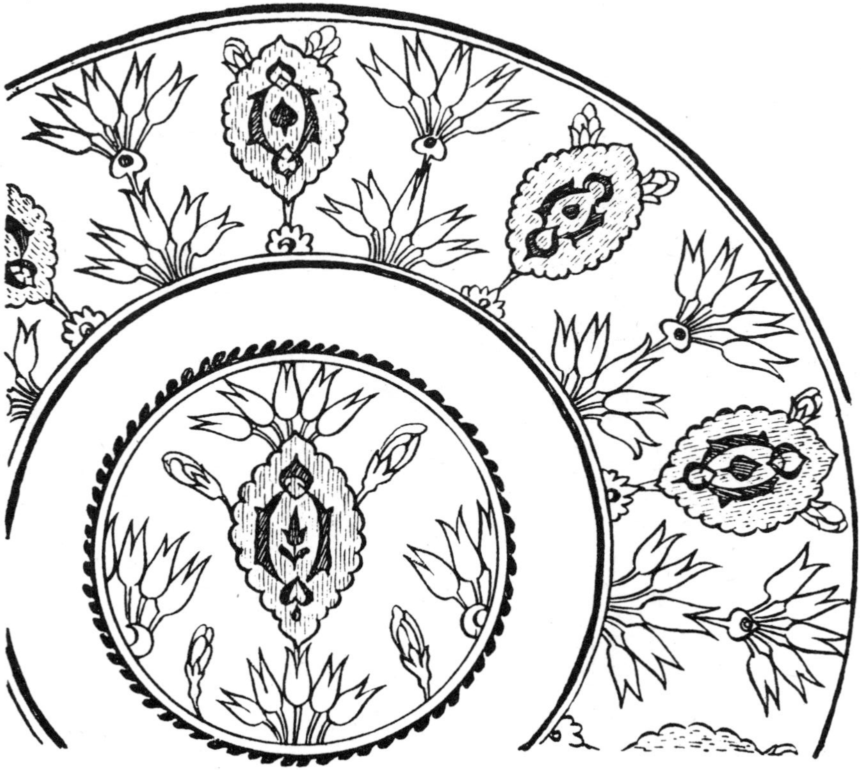

C

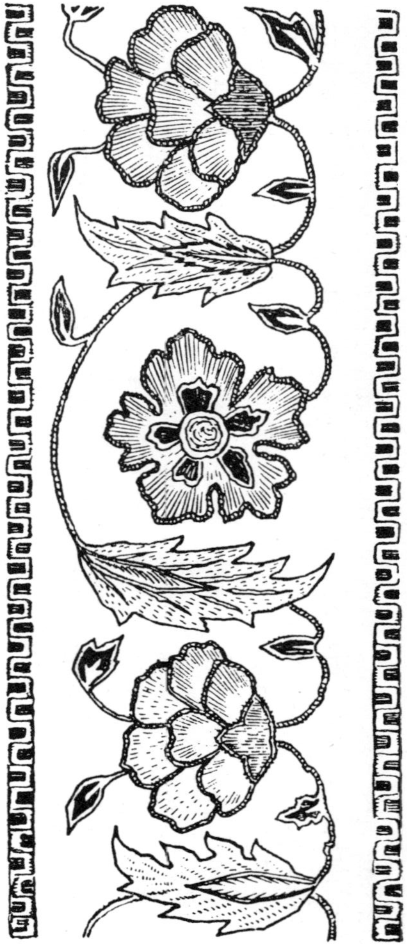

A & B – Two Damascus plates – 16th Century
C – Satin cover, silver & silver-gilt thread & silks – Persian 17th Century –
D – Padded linen coverlet – Sicilian, about 1400.

B

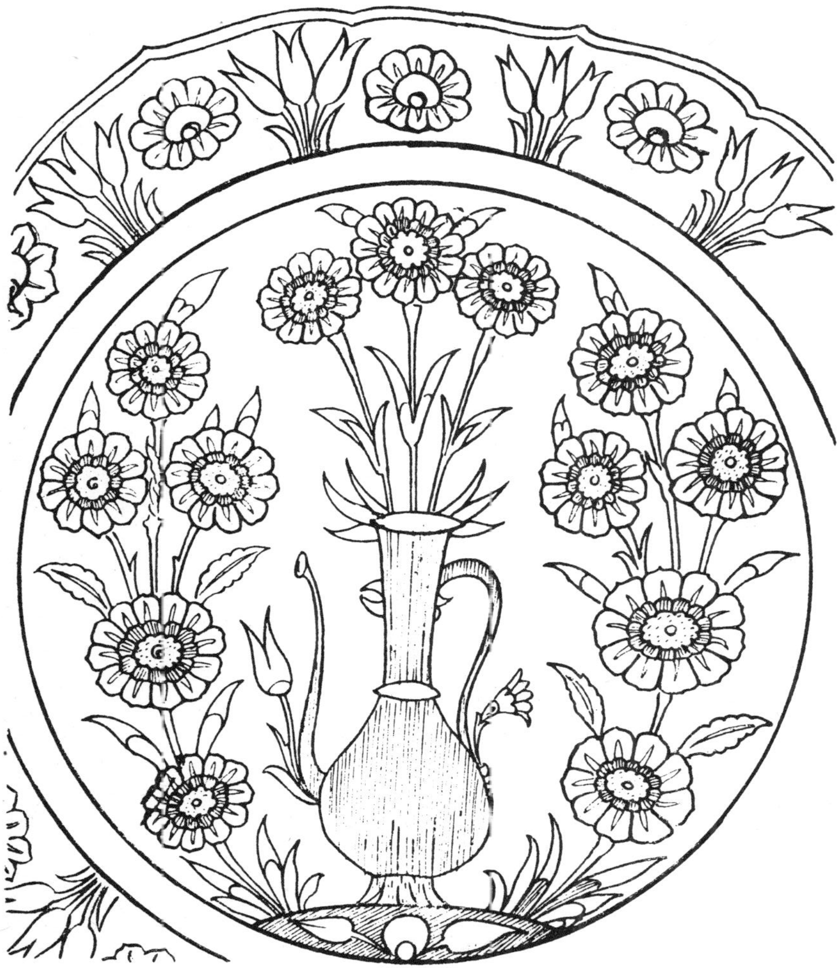

D

Another panel from the carved oak court cupboard is added here with a piece of lead work of about the same date, a very beautiful "Rose and Crown," a royal badge and a sidelight on heraldry, that realm of rich possibilities for the decorator and designer.

The Persian border charms by its waywardness, its liberty and apparent disregard of rule and law. But for all that it is very artful, and, in colour, daring and unusual. On a crimson satin ground the flowers and leaves are neutral umber grey, relieved by deep metallic blue in the touches of dark and by the metal threads.

The bit from the Sicilian coverlet tells by light and shade without colour, and is but a detail of a huge scheme in which are knights on horses, churches, forts and castles, separated here and there by a spray of rose, or oak, or quaint conventional tree.

The two Damascus plates again show us the abundant life of design and love of floral form under the hand of the Oriental decorator. The upper one is blue and white, the lower one with flower of marigold type contains dark and light blue varied with a sage-brown green. These and the Sicilian coverlet represent the two branches of the stream of Greek art mentioned above—eastward result, Byzantine and Oriental art; westward, Sicilian, Norman, Gothic and modern. So we owe all this to that wondrous land still inhabited in the imagination by gods, heroes and artists.

CHAPTER VI

BY way of variety, and also because they are closely allied to our subject, I have given in the present chapter some conventional tree forms. They represent a feature prevalent in decorative art of all periods, and they are designed in conjunction with floral forms so frequently that I feel they ought to form part of our illustrations in order to give completeness to this subject of ever-reviving interest to the decorative artist.

To go as far back as Assyrian sculpture may be considered a good beginning, and in these wonderful low relief stone-carvings, which date from nearly a thousand years before Christ, we get some interesting forms of tree, plant, and flower as settings and backgrounds to the scenes of war and the chase, which formed such a large portion of the lives of the Assyrian monarchs.

I must not stray far from our theme, but those who cannot easily visit the splendid collection of Assyrian sculptures in the British Museum will, perhaps, be glad to know the surroundings from which the fragments here shown are taken. (See page 178.)

These carved and graven wall-slabs formed portions then of the "picture palaces" of the mighty Assyrian kings of 3000 years ago. With more art, more decorative beauty, and certainly with more skill than the cinematograph of to-day can show, may still be seen life as it was lived in Babylonia under her despotic and luxurious rulers.

From these assertive and informing panels we may learn how their majesties went to war, besieged a city, hunted lions, or rode in pomp and circumstance to temple or banqueting hall. The horses and mules, hounds and lions are wonderful in the rendering of carved animal form. Horses prance, dogs strain at the leash, lions and lionesses crouch and spring, or, pierced with spear and arrow, drag themselves along in painful progress to the death-agony, clawing the air in powerless anger.

That the accessory detail is not less faithful to nature, or less

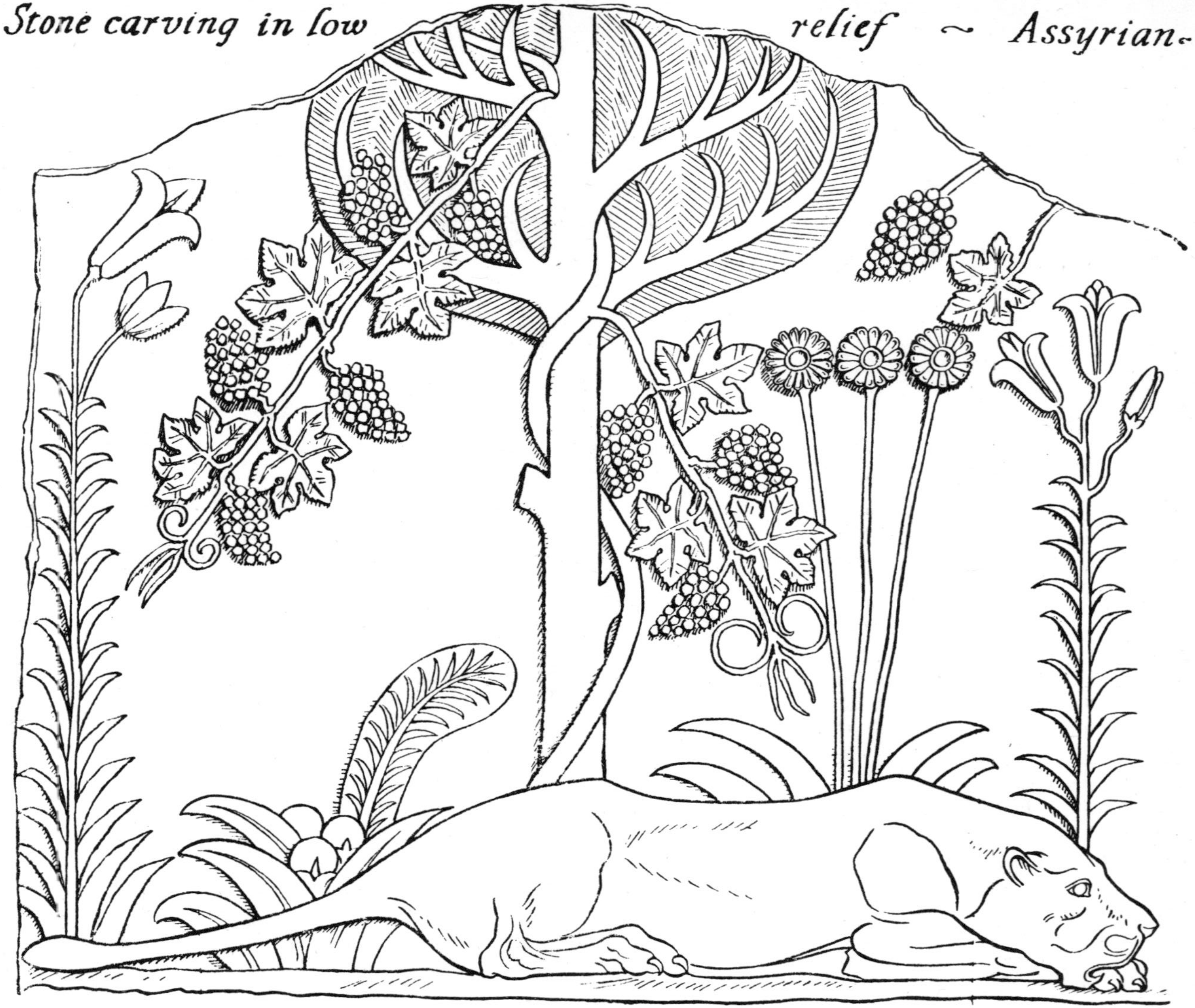

Stone carving in low relief ~ Assyrian.

interesting in design, the forms of the tree, vine, lily, or daisy given in the illustration will show, while the form of the crouching lioness confirms my praises of the animal drawing, though it is a comparatively unimportant specimen of the Assyrian sculptor's skill.

Have you ever thought how difficult a thing to render in sculpture a tree would be? Imagine yourself to be for a moment an Assyrian architect with a large number of carvers under your guidance. These men were most probably what we should call working-men stone carvers, not great and original sculptors. Tell them how, or give them a drawing or pattern showing how to carve a tree, and you will appreciate the methods by which the trees and plants are expressed in these carven stories. The branching of the pine trees is given by simple low relief, and the spaces between are filled by incised lines giving the effect of the needle-like

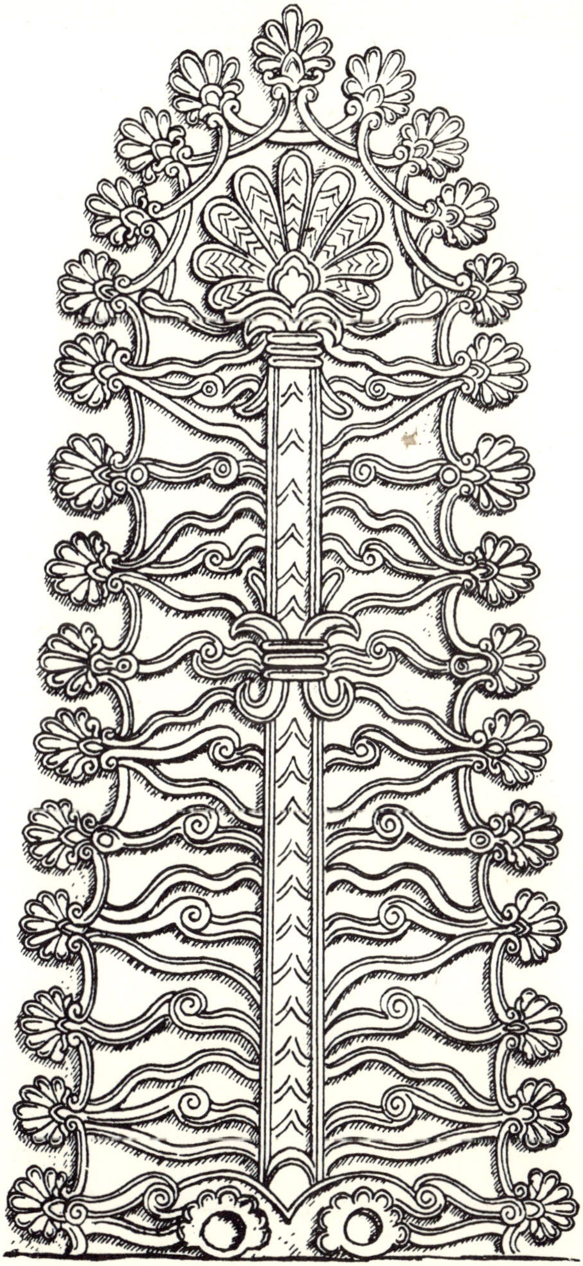

Symbolical Sacred Tree — Assyrian - 880 B.C.

spines. A more direct way of expressing a pine tree could scarcely have been devised.

Looking at these interesting decorative trees has made me wonder if they are the originals of the conventional shapes termed "pine forms" seen in Oriental decoration so frequently. It seems quite as

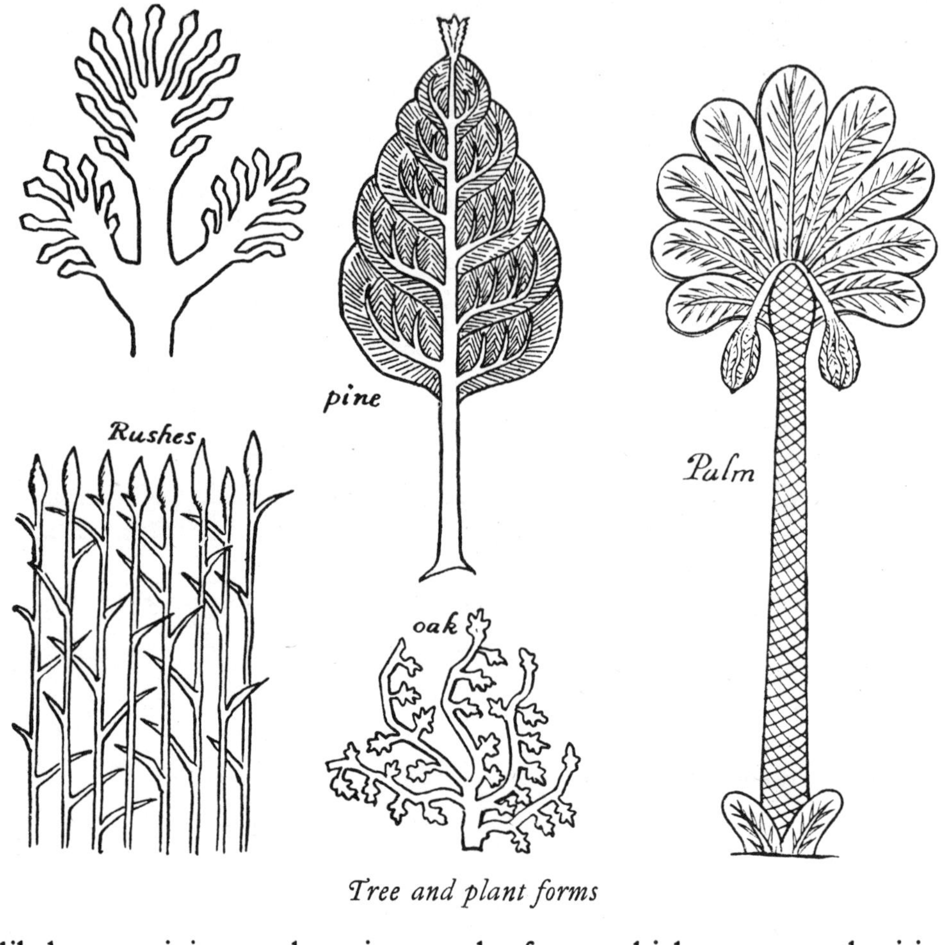

Tree and plant forms

likely an origin as the pine apple from which some authorities derive them.

Along with the great beauty of line and simple yet finished rendering of form in flower, tree and animal, there is in these bas-reliefs an incisive and direct way of stating the ideas or facts required which captures and convinces the mind at first sight. Everything in this "picture-writing on the wall" is presented in elevation—a group of rushes or row of trees stand in front of a river, the water being represented by wave-lines closely incised. Fishes are seen swimming in their natural element, while on the opposite bank, which is shown

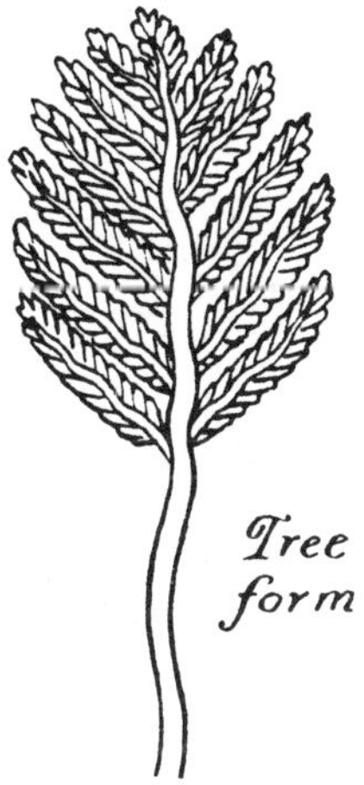

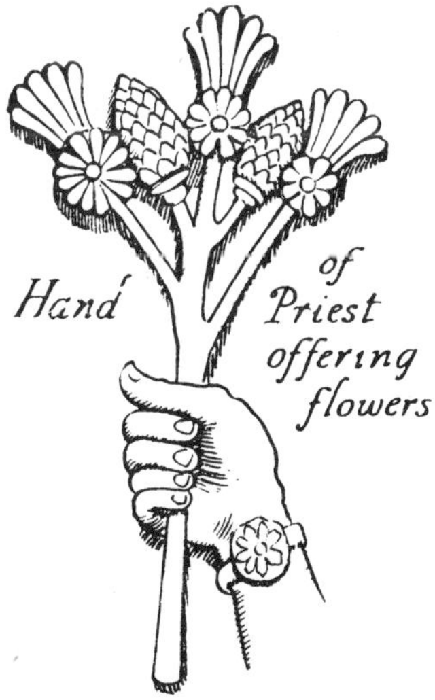

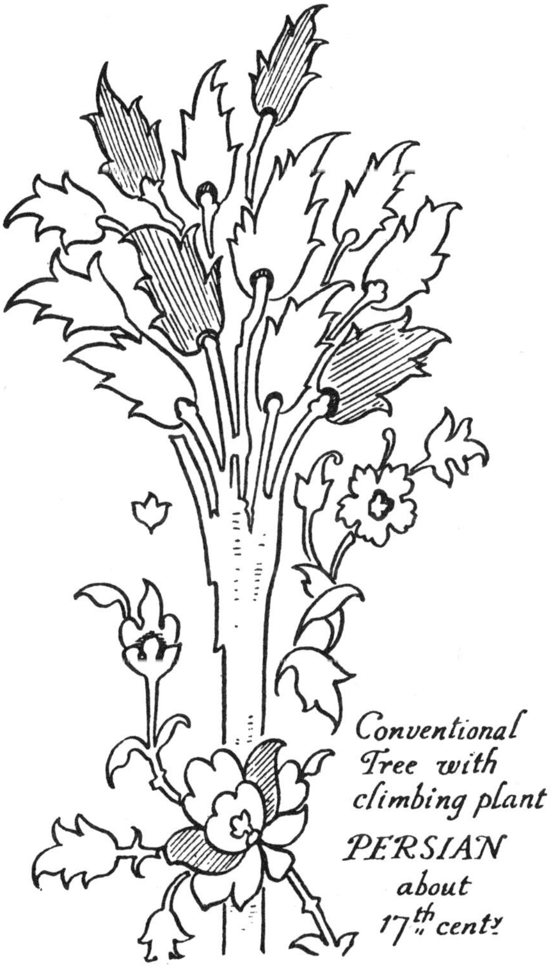

a couple of feet higher up the panel, a troop of hogs or a team of laden mules march along the river side; another row of pine trees above them forms a border to the towers of a palace or a city, and thus completes the picture. Then, if we allow our eyes to wander in a lateral direction, we shall see a lion hunt in progress or slaves lifting the gates of cages in order to allow a captive lion to escape, thereby giving the monarch in his chariot a chance to practise his royal sport. The Assyrian kings were not only supposed to lead their armies to battle, but to clear the land of lions as part of their obligations to their subjects.

Well, this is perhaps wandering from the point, but I have the excuse that floral forms play a part in all this decoratively sculptured drama.

The sacred tree (see page 179) is a splendid piece of decoration

Carved pavement in low relief—Assyrian

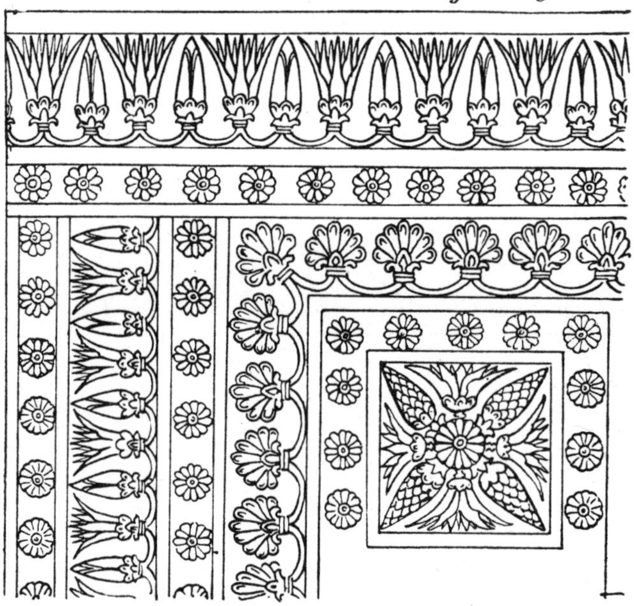

whatever its inner meaning may be. Most ancient religions originated in the worship of the sun or the reproductive powers in nature. A tree, through the wonder excited by its growth from a seed, would easily become a symbol of these forces, and an object of worship in consequence. The form in the centre is obviously a palm, the encircling leafage and stems probably a vine—both things therefore emblems of fruitfulness and sustenance.

Perhaps some of our ambitious young church decorators will see their way to adapt this piece of ancient sculpture to their requirements of to-day. It is almost ready to hand should a Tree of Life or cross with interlacing vine be wanted. The other examples of Assyrian tree forms are beautiful in shape and interesting in treatment. The palm in particular is lovely in design and instructive in its method of conventionalisation—a lesson to a beginner.

The other decorative tree is from a Persian textile, and may be compared with these Assyrian examples by way of contrast.

The pavement pattern of lotus flower, rosette, vine leaf (?) and pine cone is in very slight relief, not more than one-eighth of an inch above the surface. It has been said these patterned floor slabs were carved in imitation of carpets or rugs, but that is most likely merely conjectural.

I must ask pardon of my readers for so often bringing in the rose, the tulip, and the

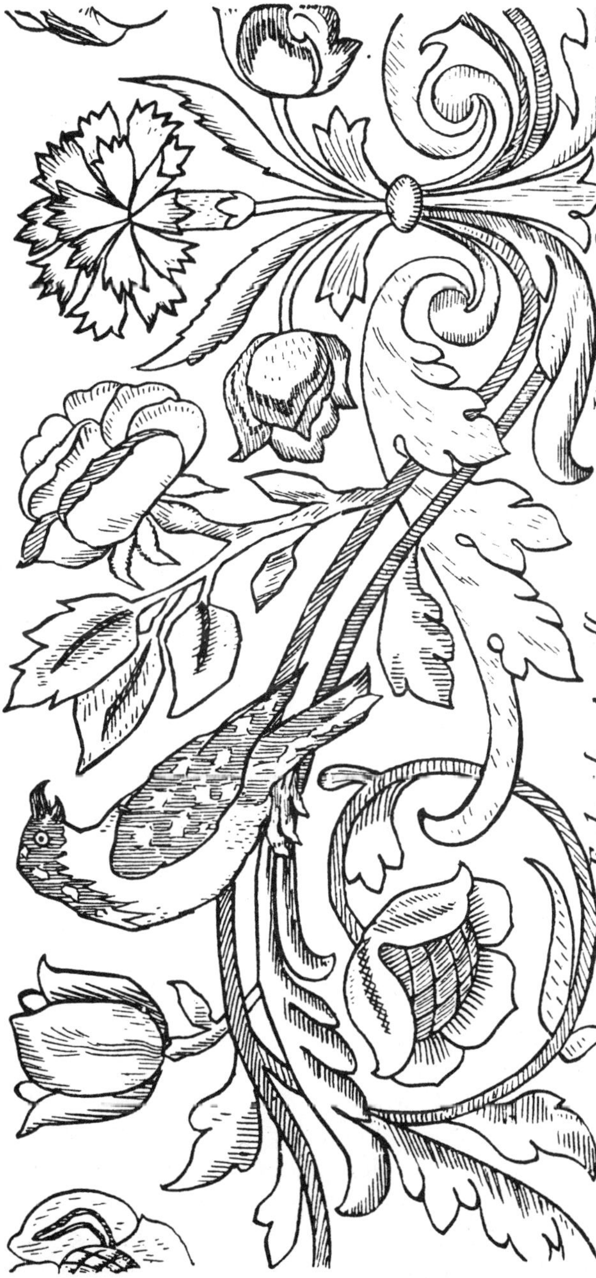

Embroidery in silks on canvas ~ Italian ~ 17 Centy.

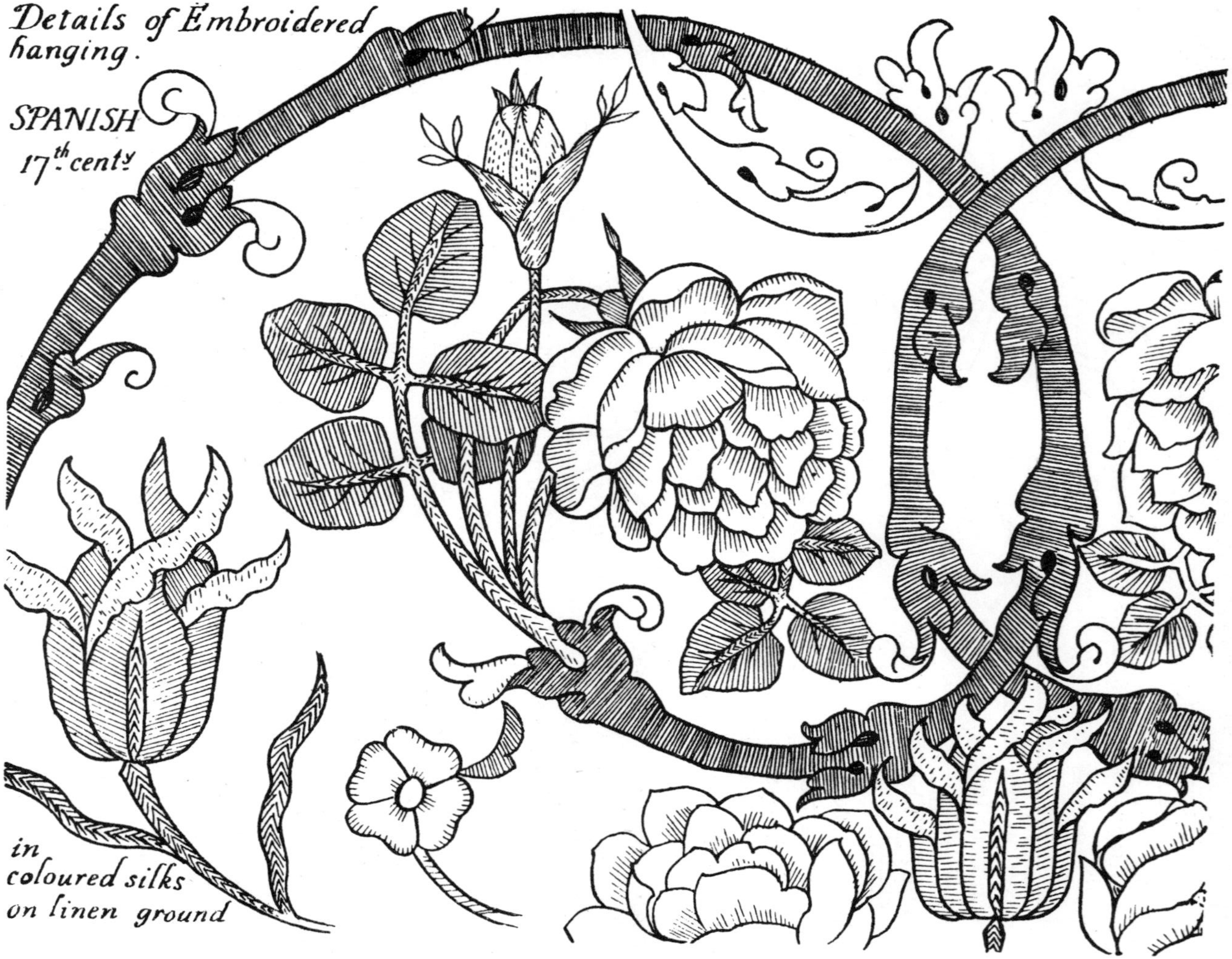
Details of Embroidered hanging.
SPANISH 17th cent.y
in coloured silks on linen ground

pink, but the fact is, these flowers are so frequently used in decoration that they are constantly to the front in fine designs, and after all their treatment is as various as their repetition is frequent.

In all my illustrations to these short notes on floral decoration, I have endeavoured to keep as close as possible to the feeling and spirit of the original. No attempt has been made to improve on the

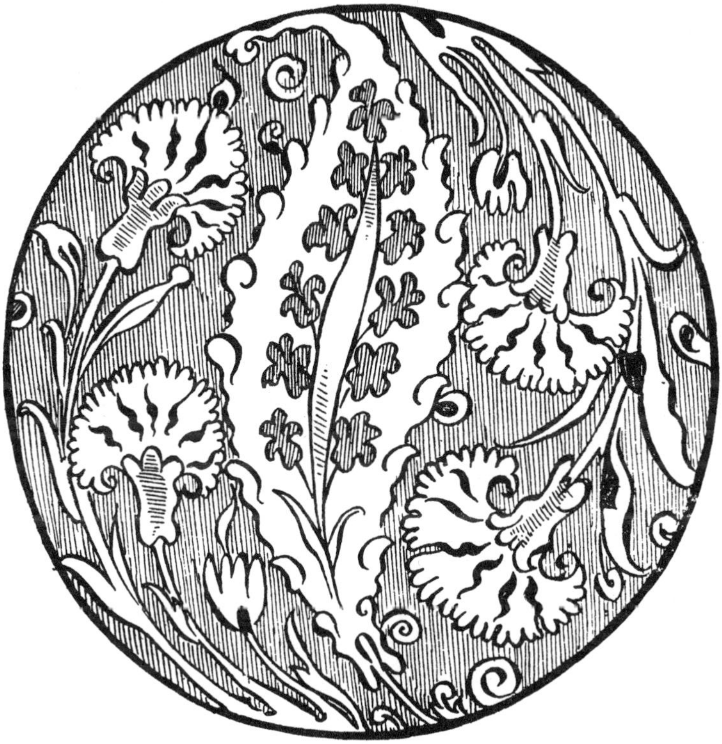

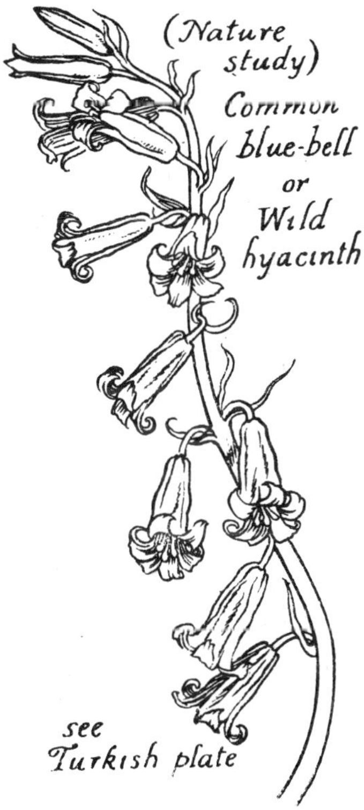

Centre of plate—Syrian or Turkish, about 17th century

imperfections or immaturity of the drawing. The border of Italian embroidery is a case in point. It is naïve, simple and childish in feeling, but that is what makes it so fresh and so human, so honest and delightful. (See page 183.)

Here again we have the rose, the pink and the tulip in a new presentment, and, out of proportion as he is, who would be without the jolly little dicky-bird? Something of the hawk he seems to be, and there is knowledge of nature in spotting of feather and drawing of claw and tail, wing and beak. The colouring of this piece is in soft suggestions of dull rose, pale golden green, bronze stem and yellow gold acanthus scroll. The Spanish embroidery is a grand and brilliant piece of colour in addition to its opulent splendour of design. The ground is linen, the scrolls are in parts blue, in parts gold; the roses terra-cotta pink of a coppery hue, as are also the tulips, though these latter are sometimes changed to a canary yellow: green leaves, and the blue of some remaining flowers, complete the impressive scheme. The centre from the Turkish plate gives us another pink, and a hyacinth on an "inhabited" leaf.

The colour scheme consists of a deep blue ground, and flowers in white touched with pale green; the hyacinth, and parts which appear black in the drawing, being of a dark purple brown. The whole design is bound together by the bold and daring, yet rich and beautiful line, and the inherited skill of the Eastern craftsman's brush.

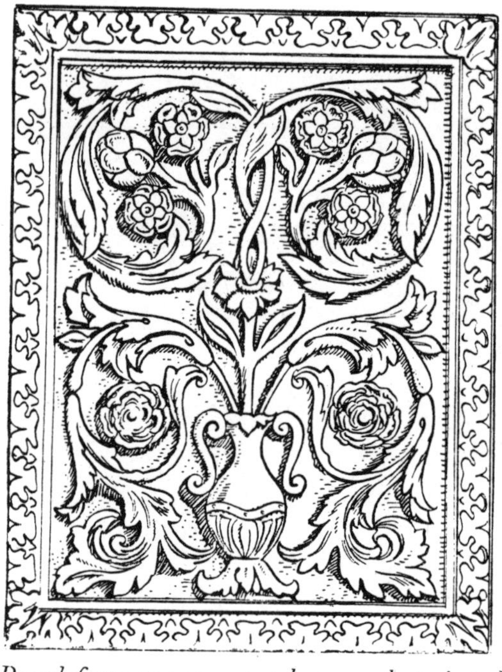

Panel from screen—wood, carved, painted and gilt—Greek, 1757 *to* 1762

CHAPTER VII

THE nature studies of roses in the bud and half-open stage are given in this chapter in order that they may be compared with the various examples of decoration we have had under our notice. By common consent the rose is considered the most beautiful of flowers, and as I have remarked before, it has always been a great favourite with designers and decorators. As the studies show, its details are also most interesting. There is such a variety in the shapes of bract, opening bud, calyx, leaf and petal—not only on the same plant, but in different kinds of roses—that the designer has a wide choice in the matter of forms to select from, and the accompanying sketches show the sources of many conventional forms, as well as characteristic details which have been seized upon and appropriated by craftsmen and decorators of all periods. The buds of the wild rose again exhibit different features from the cultivated varieties, and are smaller as a rule.

The drawing from Syrian wall tiles, page 190, is a fragment only, and it was selected mainly because of the iris forms it contained. A nature study of the flower will be found on page 189. Of course, the flower is "patternised" by the Oriental designer, it is rightly not a natural drawing of the plant, as he remembers his flat surface, and that it must tell by beauty of massing for its effect at a distance. This is one of the best tests of good pattern designing. A natural or imitative treatment includes all the little accidents of form, the crossing of one piece over another and confusion of lights and shadows. The result is a jumble of irregular shapes as soon as the spectator moves far enough back to lose the detail. Not so with a well-massed conventionalised form; it has to be cleared up and simplified in its manner of presentation to the eye, consequently it makes beautiful and intelligible shapes of decoration at whatever distance it is viewed.

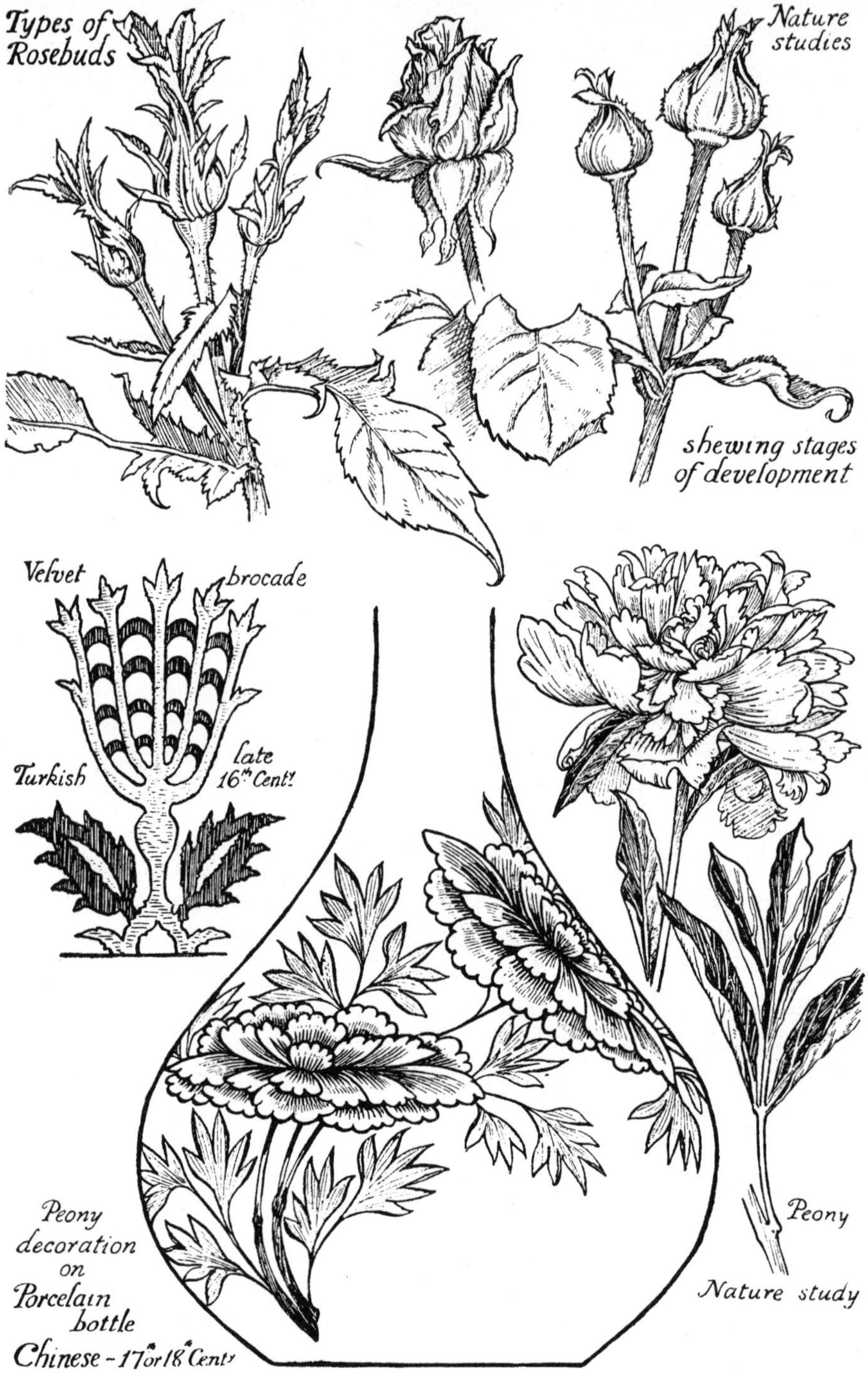

Types of Rosebuds
Nature studies
shewing stages of development
Velvet brocade
Turkish late 16th Cent.
Peony decoration on Porcelain bottle Chinese - 17th or 18th Cent.
Peony
Nature study

That the tile painter has secured this effect is quite evident in the example before us. It is highly interesting to see what he has made of the flower. The colouring of the piece consists of dark and light blue (ultramarine and turquoise) and emerald greens on a white ground. The little spots of decoration on the petals are a reminiscence of certain features of the flower, but they were evidently prompted by the desire to break up the big blots of dark blue and so prevent heaviness of effect. The rose will be found in the lower part of the panel, and a very interesting treatment it is too—the designer's fancy has played with the petals and the serrating of the leaves, and the little leaves and other details which he has distributed impartially over the stems of all the flowers help to bring the whole into harmony of design though not strictly true to natural drawing. The iris, however, does possess details of this kind in real life—the dried-up shields which protect the bud may be seen curling round or hanging from the stem in a similar manner. These old craftsmen probably worked from memory only when introducing a plant form into their decorations, but there are extant some Hindoo pattern designers' specimen books, of which I have seen reproductions, representing various plants in decorative arrangement ready for employment by the textile worker or potter.

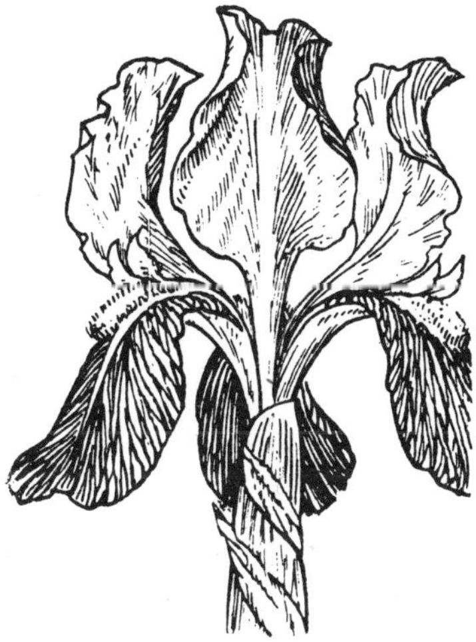

Iris (*Nature study*)

Iris - Nature study

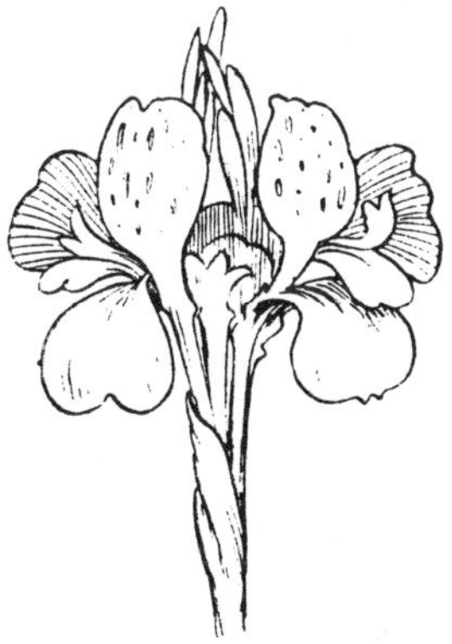

The conventional cypress tree appears also in the illustration as it did on a Rhodian vase given in a previous chapter. Imagine the wall spaces of a palace or mosque decorated with these wonderfully designed and coloured tiles. Think of the effect under Eastern sun-light of sapphire blue and emerald green, combined with amethyst and turquoise tints in a glazed surface, and

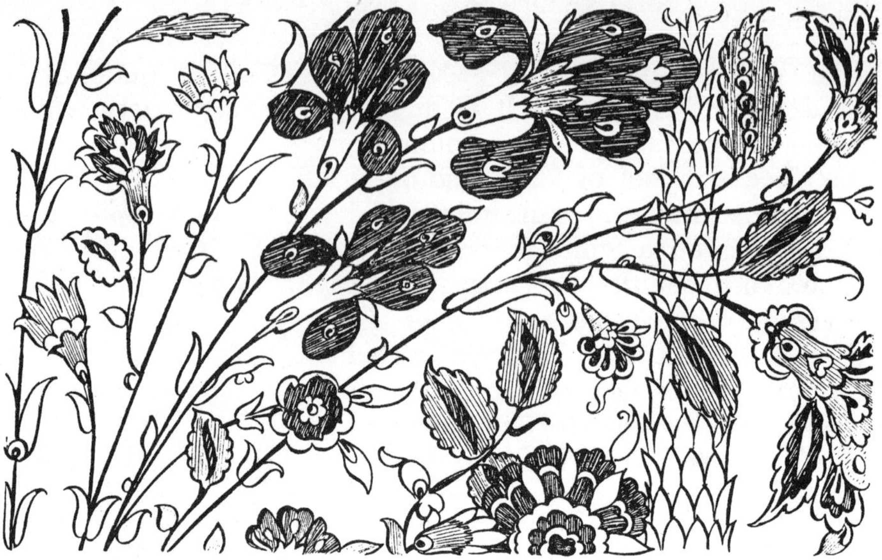

Syrian Wall Tiles 16th to 17th Centy

IRIS, ROSE & COLUMBINE FORMS

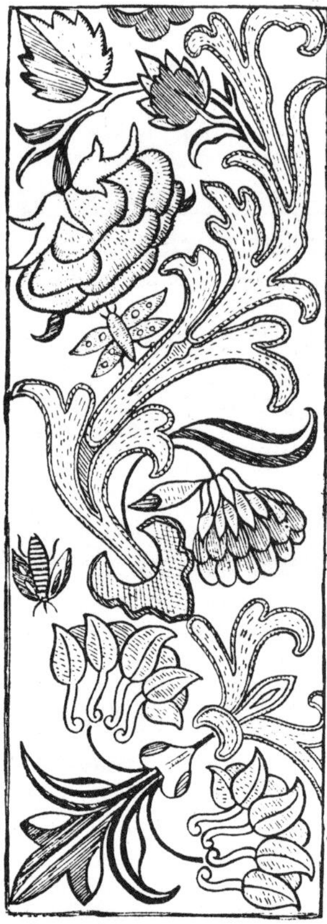

Border Italian Embroidery late 17th Centy

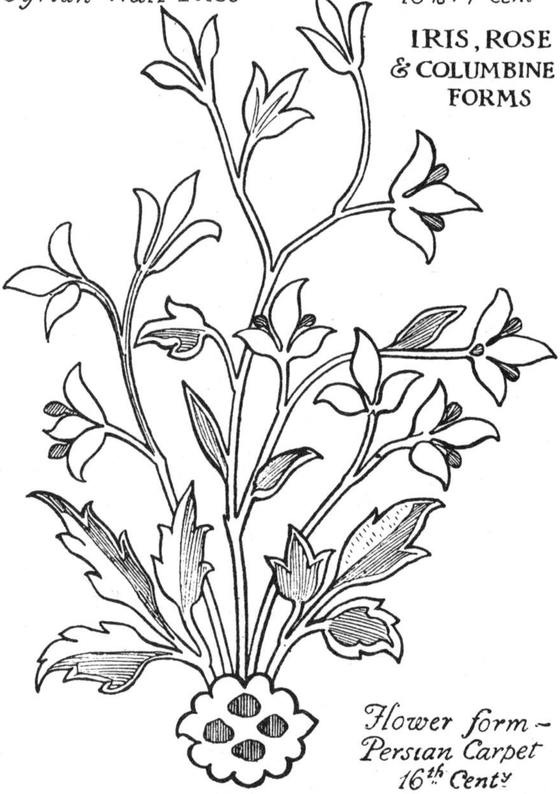

Flower form – Persian Carpet 16th Centy

it will not be difficult to account for the enchanted palaces covered with jewels which the romantic story-tellers of the *Arabian Nights* so eloquently describe.

The flowers taken from Persian sources in the ivory inlay on rosewood and the carpet I am unable to name, but everyone with an eye for graceful pattern will appreciate their beauty of line and the skill shown in their composition and arrangement. Let the beginner put a piece of tracing paper over them and follow with his pencil the boundary lines of the groupings, and the manner in which they connect with or flow into each other, and he will be surprised at the beautiful arrangements of line contained in them. The detail from the inlaid ivory cabinet shows with what excellent taste and feeling for effective contrast the Persian craftsman framed in his floral ornament with a simple geometrical border. Its severity is a most pleasing and useful foil to all the play and flow of natural line in his flowers and sprays—but they were artists indeed, these old Persian workmen.

The bowl of Damascus ware is another piece of beautiful Eastern handicraft. A simple form of rose, a crocus form and a sort of lily of the valley type of flower are the elements, simple, but sufficient, which go to make an arrangement full of charm. The sense of lifelike growth, of movement almost as of swaying in the wind, and adaptation of line and form to the curved surface is altogether admirable. The body of the bowl is a deep sky blue, the large flowers white, leaves green, and the crocus shapes and small flowers are a faint and faded tone of old rose. A wash of thin brown madder will, perhaps, explain the exact tint. The borders, top and bottom, are pale green and white.

Altogether these make a sparkling and vivacious harmony which accords well with its other decorative merits.

There is a curious and somewhat eccentric use of the budding or half-opened rose in the piece of Turkish velvet brocade, but its unusual qualities appeal strongly to me. It makes one wonder whether it is an experiment by a rebel against traditional forms or some freakish bit of nature coming by accident under the designer's notice. Anyhow, there it stands as it forms a repeat border, each item panelled off by a framed space from its companion. The colouring is dark crimson and bronze green.

Nature study

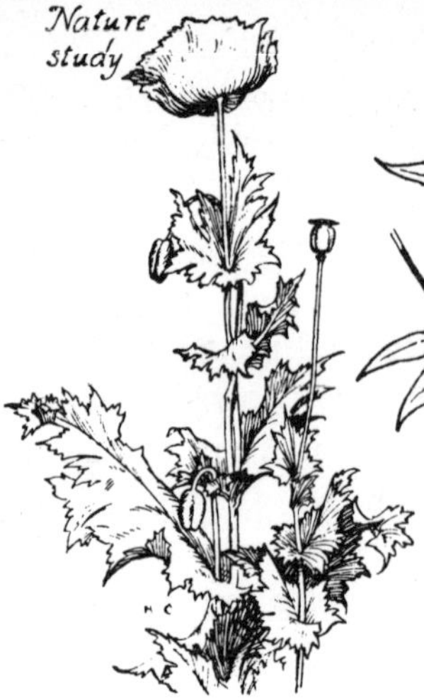

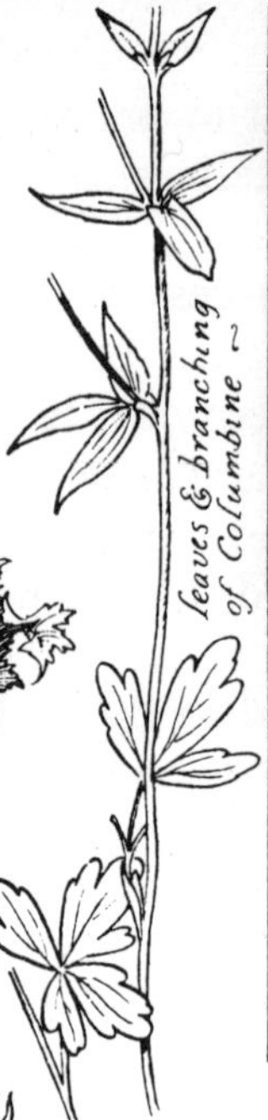

leaves & branching of Columbine ~

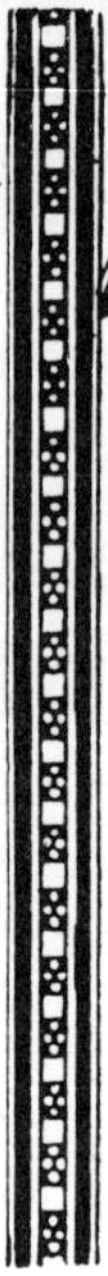

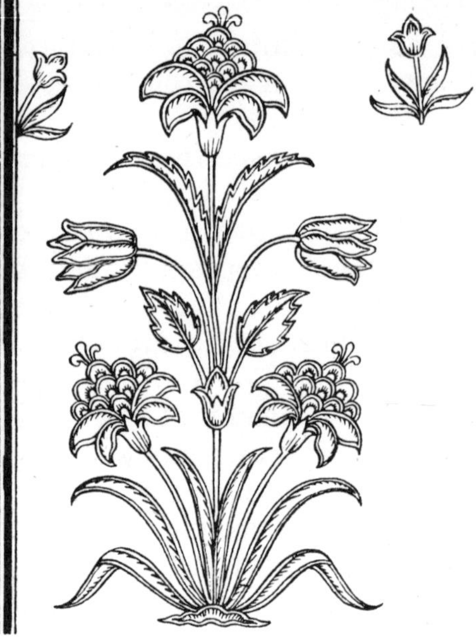

Flower forms inlaid;-ivory on rosewood-
17th centy-Persian ~

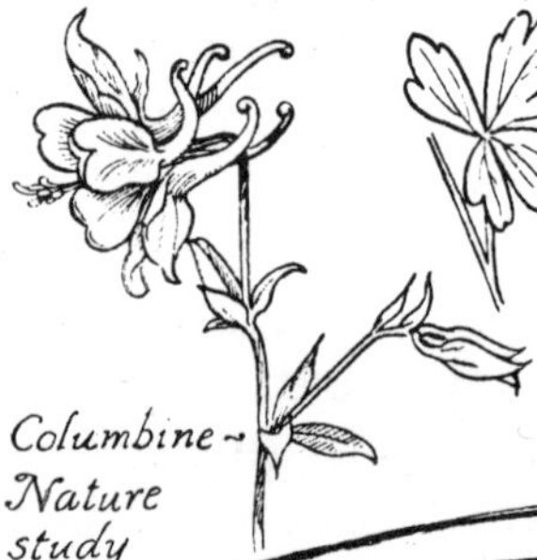

Columbine -
Nature study

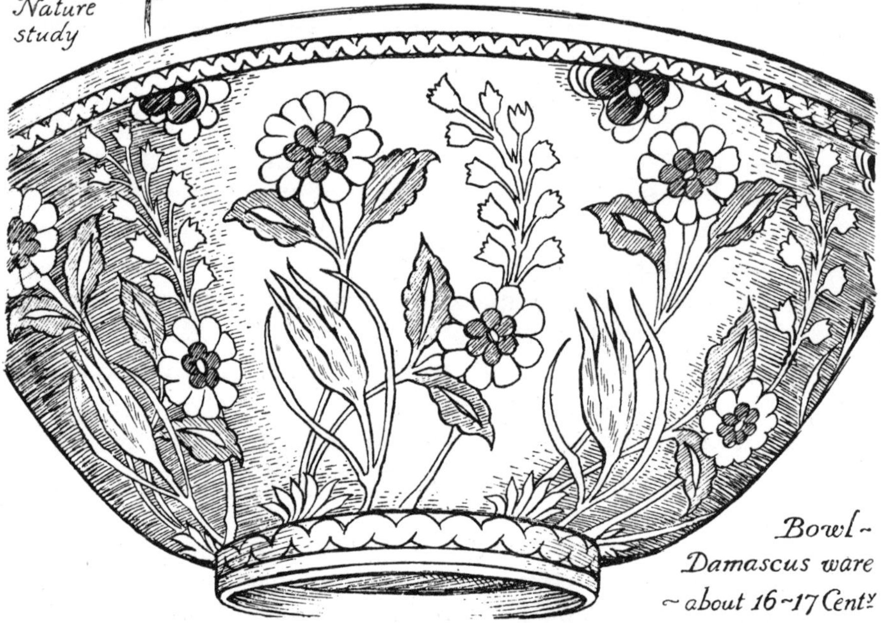

Bowl -
Damascus ware
~ about 16 ~ 17 Centy

The border of Italian embroidery work is interesting on account of the columbine placed in the corner. It is one of the few instances I know of the use of this flower in decoration, and it is only a fragmentary sort of treatment as we find it here. It is strange that so many beautiful flowers are and have been neglected in decorative design—and the columbine is surely one of them. The running pattern of conventional stems in this design is gold thread work. It forms a convenient basis for throwing out the various flowers as the pattern travels along—a need often felt by the designer who embodies more than one element in his scheme of floral decoration. The insects are a quaint touch and open up another field of suggestion (see page 190).

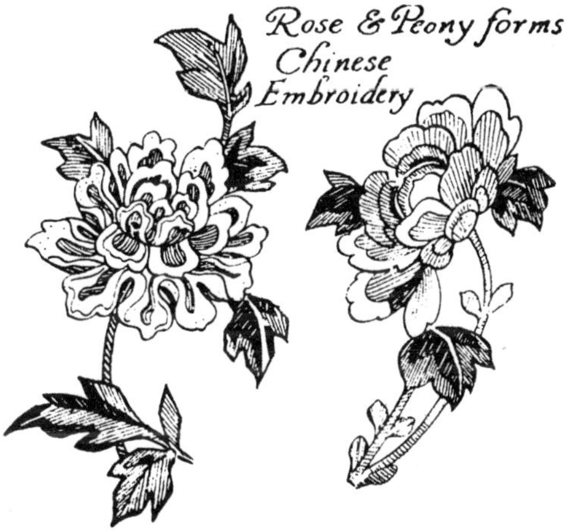

The peony study which accompanies the Chinese porcelain bottle is considerably reduced from its natural size, but it will serve for comparison with the conventional rendering on the object itself. How beautifully the Chinese artist has drawn the flower, stems and leaves, is surely obvious to an outsider. The designer or craftsman will see further and notice the art and inventiveness which renders not only the form, but the glow and inner richness of the colour of this most gorgeous flower, though the example before us is in blue and white only (see page 188).

The five-pointed leaf is kept subservient to the flower and gives us an instance of decorative judgment and selection of material. The deft-fingered Celestial wanted to emphasise the flower rather than the leaf and he dared to do so, obtaining by this means the preponderance of interest which colour gives in the natural flower over the leaf. This was legitimate in method as he had only one colour to work with.

The ground tint of the bottle is a bluish white, not a pure white, a feature which is characteristic of most of the old pottery, whether Chinese or European imitation of their products. Many of the Old English vases and bowls of the eighteenth century have a lovely greenish white ground like the shell of a pale green duck-egg.

All white pottery is now made "raw" white—are the delicately tinted whites of old China a lost art? I wonder. That they are *not* the result of age I am convinced. Must we attribute it to a lack of sensitiveness to delicacy of tint in these days?

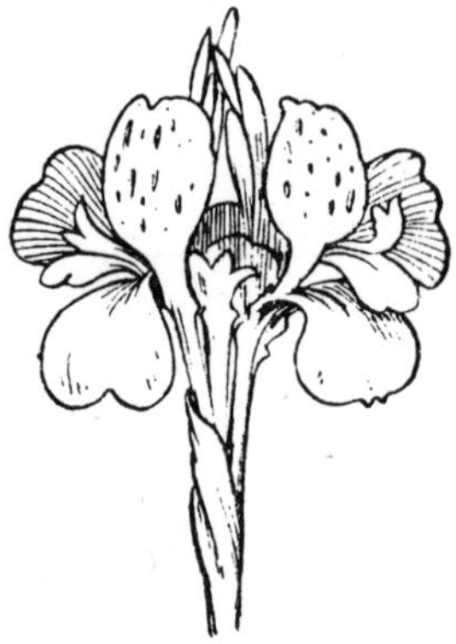

CHAPTER VIII

IT will be obvious upon looking at the illustrations to this chapter that there is no difficulty in finding plenty of examples of the treatment of the vine in all kinds of decoration and material. It has been a great favourite with designers from time immemorial, and on looking at it we cannot help being reminded that its waving lines, curling tendrils, serrated leaves and rounded fruits must have been a temptation not easily resisted to the stone or wood carver, while its opulent beauty of colour, added to the variety of fine forms it possesses, gives the tapestry weaver or embroiderer the opportunity for any degree of richness and splendid display.

The early examples of its use in carved decoration from the Romanesque doorway at Nivelles exhibit all the vigour, roughness of finish if you like, of a strong and vigorous period. It is the work of men who went straight to their task and did it. It is not "sicklied o'er with the pale cast of thought" in the sense of that feeling of hesitancy which stays the hand in work which is too fastidious or over-refined. Yet thought there is in it, and great skill of design, too, accompanies the conception. Take each bend of the scroll-line singly, and notice the ever-varying treatment of the detail; no two pieces are alike, every leaf is different in expression. The treatment of the tendrils is decidedly fresh and original, if one may speak thus of work so many centuries old. True it is that the sculptor has departed from nature, but his object was decoration, not imitation, and the result justifies the liberties he has taken. Nothing seemed to worry these old craftsmen. What splendid courage of attack they possessed! It would be difficult to follow in our time their disregard of proportion, but we might imitate their simple and commonsense methods of solving difficulties of design sometimes. They always seem to go direct to a problem, their work has the look of being done in the most natural way possible. Under the pressure of too much criticism the modern designer or craftsman polishes up, and worries over

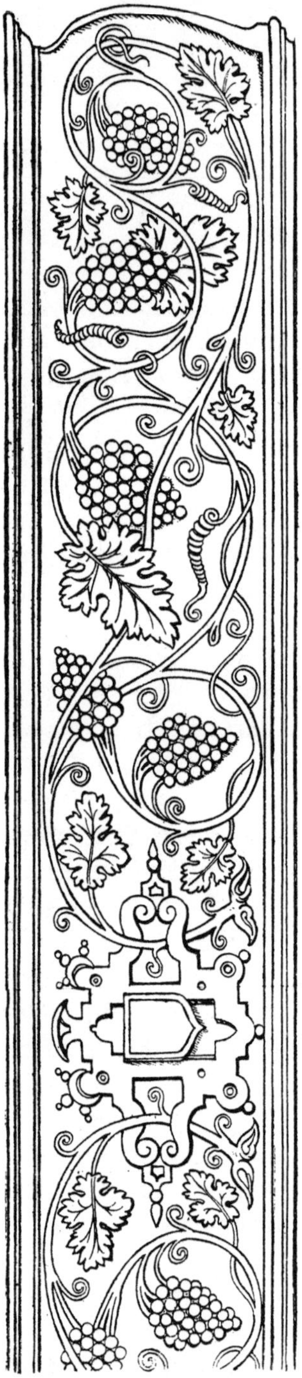

Frieze of chimney piece ~ carved stone ~ English, 17th century

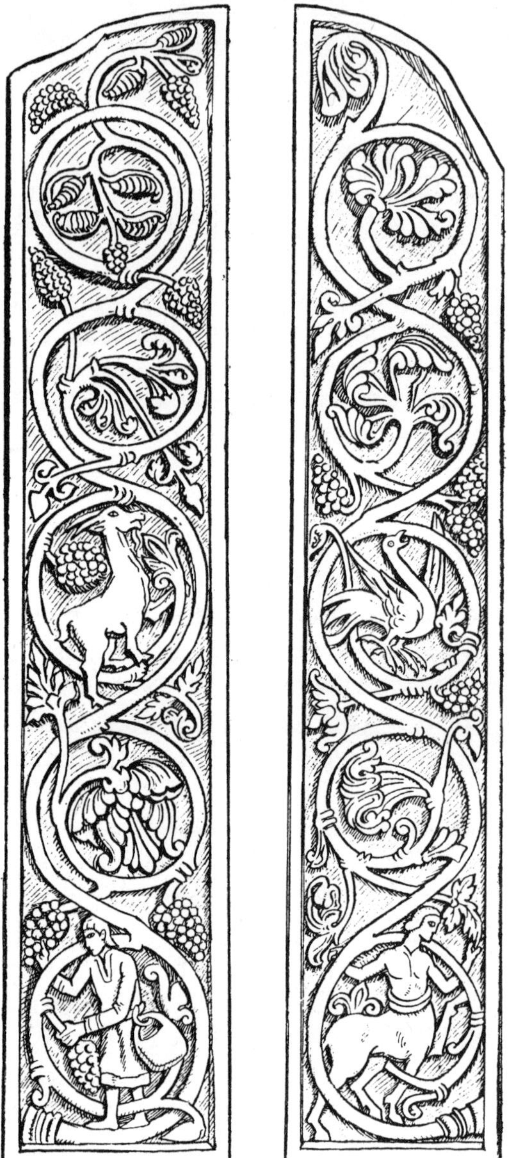

Two side panels Romanesque Doorway ~ from Nivelles ~ 11th cent^{y} ~ carved stone ~

THE VINE

its treatment in stone-carving ~

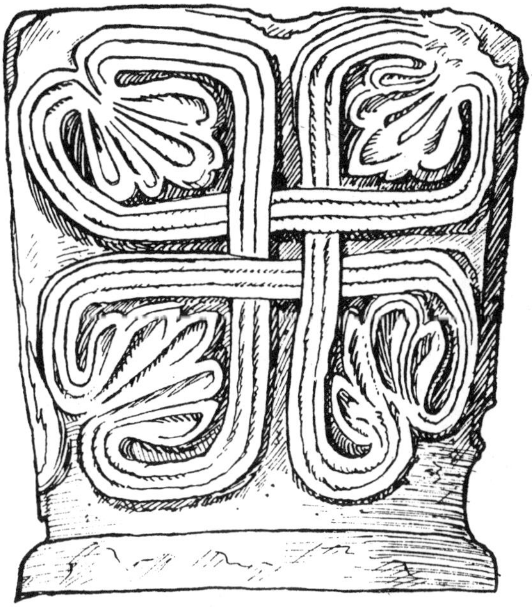

details and small perfections, while the old men let them slide a little in pursuit of a big effect. What would the designer, ancient or modern, do without his scroll-lines? How useful they are, and also how much easier to use are the flowers and plants which fit them!

The portion from the Old English chimney piece in carved stone is also a very beautiful rendering of the vine. Here we have a much greater amount of naturalism, but never once are the bounds of good decoration departed from; imitative skill in drawing and modelling is never allowed to take precedence of the decorative effect. It has more delicate grace, and more subtle play of line in stem and tendril, but it lacks the power and vigour of the earlier example. It would be unfair to both, however, to push this comparison too far, as they serve different purposes, and though they treat the same plant they are widely different in character and feeling. The cartouche in the centre

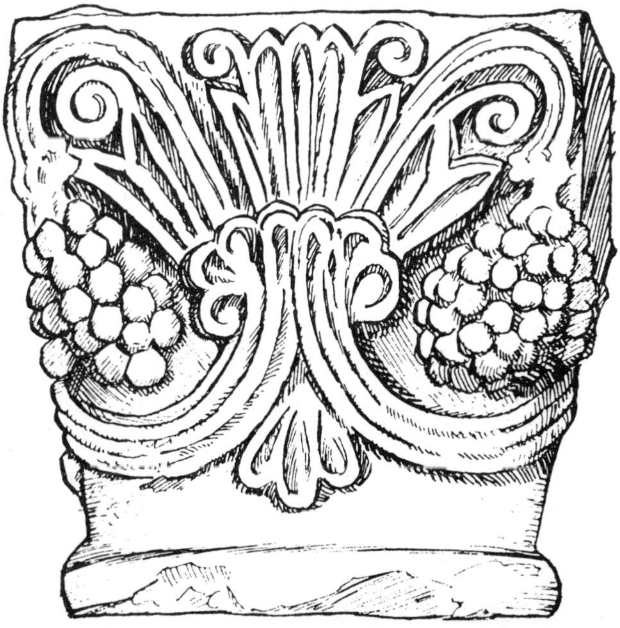

Stone capitals—French, 12th century

of the chimney-piece is not a particularly beautiful thing in itself, but it may be pointed out that it serves the useful purpose of a starting-point or basis from which to grow the ornament. This is a difficulty often felt by the designer, he is sometimes puzzled how to begin, and in the illustrations to this chapter it will be seen that the question has been answered in various ways.

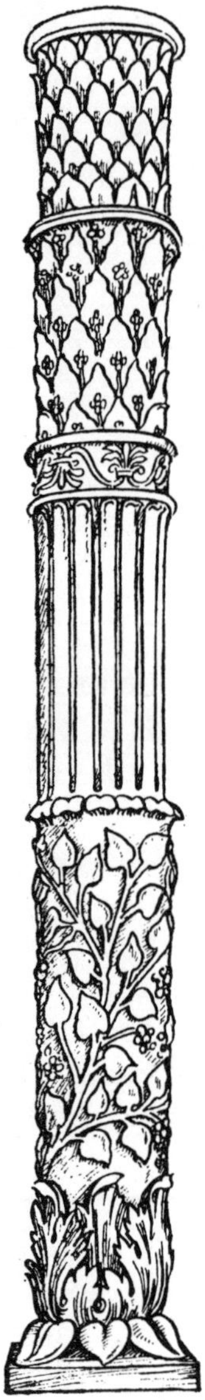

Carved marble column.
Ancient Roman

The two French capitals of the twelfth century, on page 197, may be considered in conjunction with the Roman column here. The old Roman sculptor (or Greek working under the Roman employer) was usually engaged in carving the severer forms of capital, cornice or frieze, with acanthus, volute, egg and dart, or conventional honeysuckle, as the case might warrant, and seldom felt his liberty outside those well-defined limits in the field of architectural decoration. Not often had he the chance to trail a piece of ivy or other wild plant round a column, but here we see how beautifully he could do it when it was required of him. Ivy leaves and berries have been used in the beautiful scale pattern in the upper part, forming a charming contrast to the free wandering of the whole plant in the lower portion, while the small honeysuckle band and the acanthus base seem to bring him back to his everyday duties. Altogether it is a very exquisite and out-of-the-way example of its period, and it contains the usual skill and refinement of design and execution, as well as great beauty in proportion of parts.

Now we come to the vine in the French Gothic capitals. Centuries have gone by since the Roman column was carved, art and skill have slept while wars have raged, but a rebirth has taken place, new ideals and new methods have arisen; fierce and rugged Northern liberty has supplanted Roman suavity and voluptuous grace. The Gothic carver is eager to express himself, roughness and unfinish trouble him not. Irregular, crude even, his work may be, but it is new and

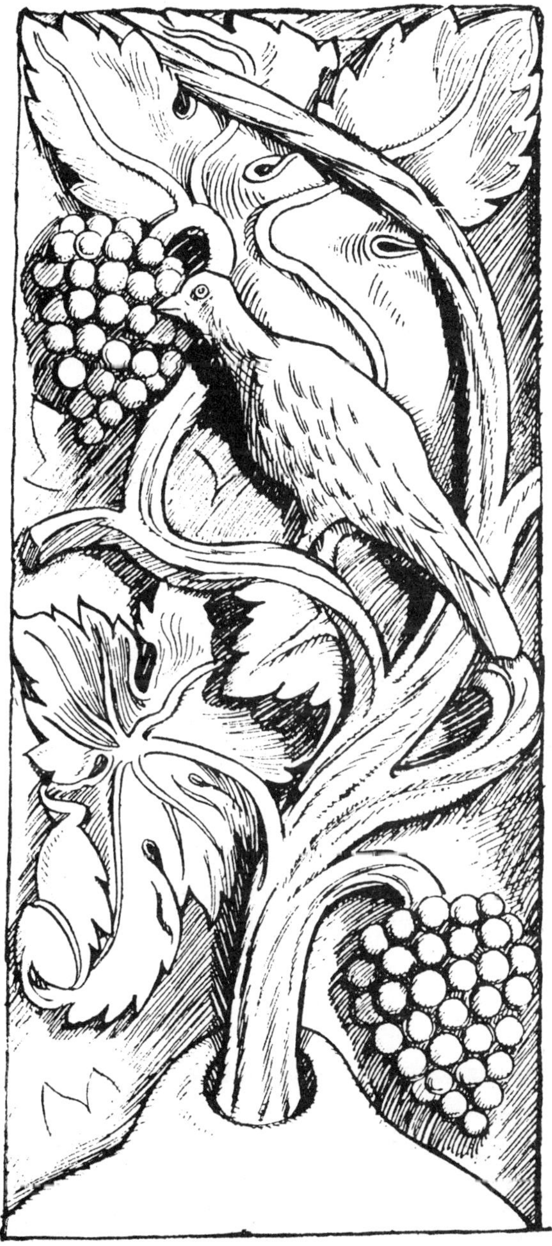

Panel of chimney-piece, carved walnut
French, early 16th century.

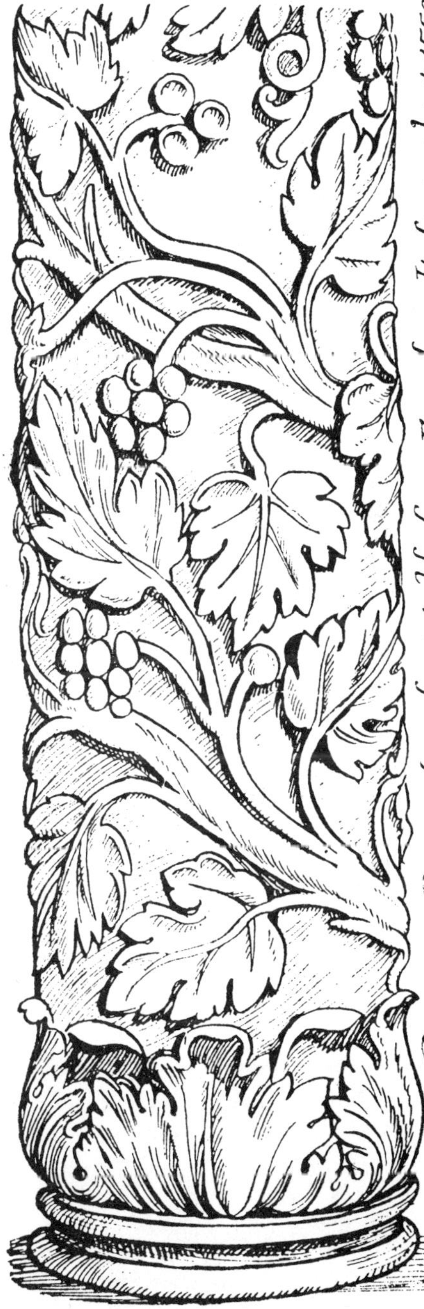

Portion of carved walnut table-leg ~ French or Italian - about 1550

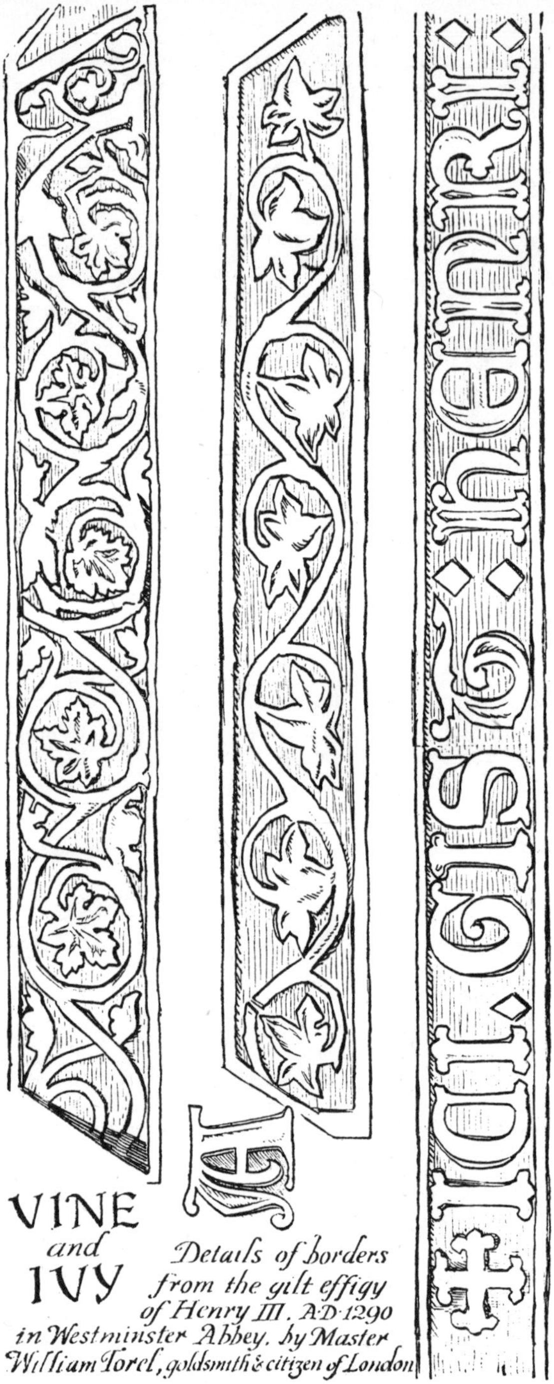

VINE
and
IVY

Details of borders from the gilt effigy of Henry III. A.D. 1290 in Westminster Abbey, by Master William Torel, goldsmith & citizen of London

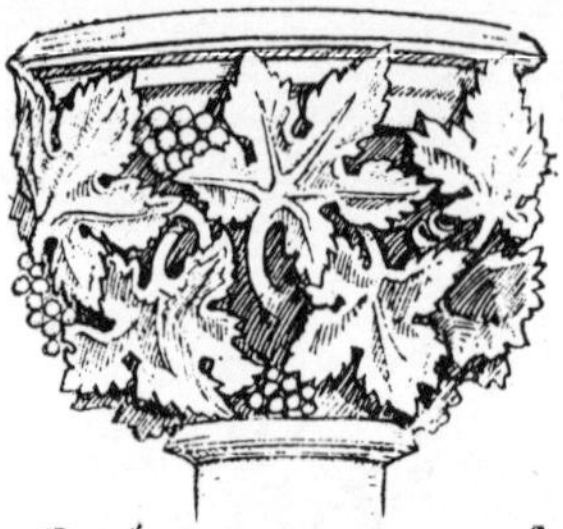

Gothic Vine Capital

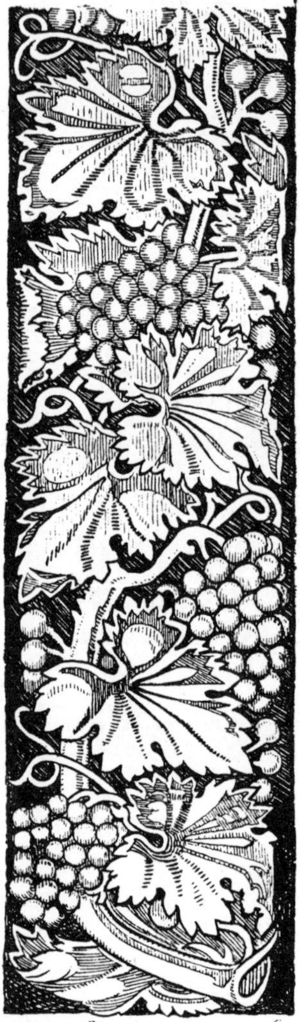

Brussels Tapestry - early 16th Cent.y

fresh, there are more decorative worlds to conquer, so with mallet and chisel he hews out the beginnings of other styles and leaves finish and smoothness to his successors. The later Gothic capital on page 200 represents the perfected state of the stonecarver's art before the decline set in. The forms are true, the design simple and clear, the execution eminently skilful as shown in the under-cutting and excellent modelling. Later on these qualities were abused by the Gothic sculptors, and leaves were bent and twisted into the semblance of wet rags, or some equally flaccid material.

The panel containing the bird is from a chimney-piece of carved wood, evidently a remnant of some old French country house or château—one of those huge hooded fireplaces forming a canopy which projected itself several feet into the room. Though centuries later than the two capitals, it retains the tradition of their vigour with an added grace of drawing and modelling not to be expected of the former. Probably it was executed by some good old country craftsman, far removed from decadent influences, who had his own way of doing things and his own ideas to express. Certainly it is unusual, and its peculiar merits are not to be met with at every turn.

The carved table leg is also a fine example of beautiful design and accomplished workmanship. It is from a Renaissance piece, and is, therefore, all the more refreshing as an elegant yet vigorous bit of natural form among the smooth and over-refined conventionalities of its period.

The vine and ivy forms on the gilt effigy of Henry III. from his tomb in Westminster Abbey appear somewhat simple and childlike in a detached drawing, but in the real thing, with their direct and spontaneous design and modelling, they form with the beautiful letters which accompany them a most effective finish to the figure of the recumbent king. The monument has all that simple and austere dignity in pose and expression, and in arrangement of rigid draperies, that belongs to Gothic sculpture at its best, and these little patterns of vine and ivy are almost all the decoration Master William, the goldsmith-sculptor, allowed himself. I have drawn some of the letters to show how the slight foliation of the serifs brings them into harmony with the floral ornament, and also because decorators are, or should be, interested in good lettering of all kinds.

The vine from the door of Notre Dame, Hal, is another specimen

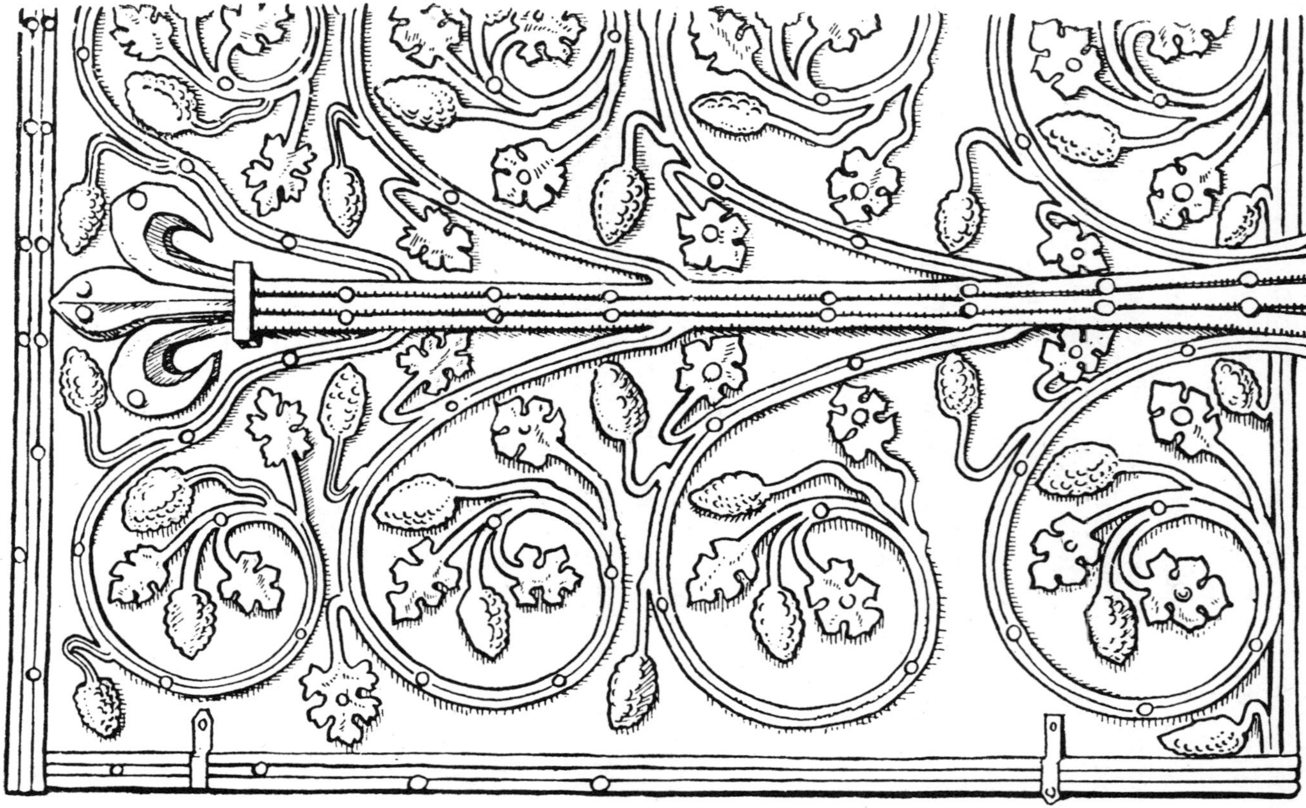

Ironwork from doors of Notre Dame & St. Martin-Hal, Belgium ~ early 15th cent.y

of my searchings for examples of the vine in ornamental art. It differs widely from those previously given and is a bold and massive piece of wrought-iron work from Belgium. The ornament is in high relief, the forms being about an inch in thickness and well rounded and modelled above the surface of the door which they strengthen and protect. The Flemings have always been famous for their work in this branch of art, and this is a fine specimen of their fertility of design and technical skill.

The vine in the Brussels tapestry is merely a small piece of the border, six inches wide, of one of those huge "triumphs" crowded with figures, animals, architecture and everything else which seemed to be so easy of accomplishment in those days. Kings, emperors, gods, saints and heroes march along or ride on gorgeously caparisoned horses or elephants, draperies are shot with colours innumerable, yet even the borders have a wealth of care and invention lavished upon them. The leaves are shaded in every tint of bluish and golden green. The grapes glow with purple, blue and gold, leading on to the next motive, a rose or some other contrasting form equally admirable in colour and design. What wonderful artists these tapestry designers were, yet their names are nearly all unknown.

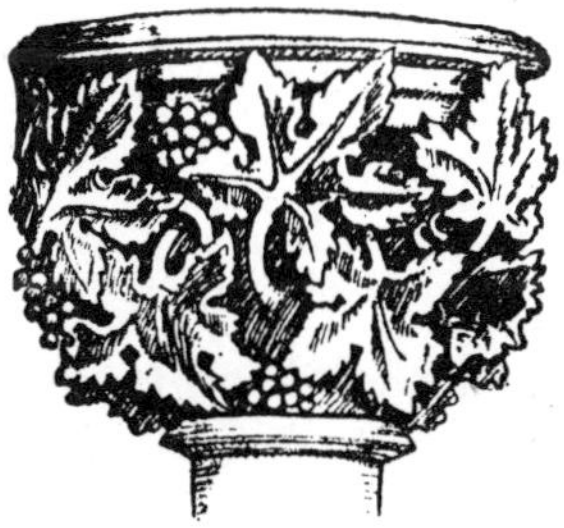

CHAPTER IX

IN our last chapter I gave some examples of the vine in different treatments, as used in various kinds of decoration. There is such a wealth of material, however, when one comes to look for specimens of this great favourite, that I have included some further drawings of it. On account of their beauty they cannot fail to be of interest to the decorator. Besides, the two given in this chapter are decidedly out of the common, both in character and design. The panel in carved walnut is from the chimney-piece mentioned on page 201—a huge wooden hood which projects over a fireplace into a room, and carved with quaint scenes of the chase by some local craftsmen—probably the joiner, carpenter and cabinet-maker of the district who had the ambition to be, and the pleasure of being, the woodcarver as well. One feels, on looking at the panel, that it is full of native talent, self-developed and self-expressive. The way the space is subdivided is unexpected, the little panel bearing thistle-like foliage at one end and the border of dot and dentil shapes at the other give an interesting note of contrast to the wandering lines of the large vine, and the decorative mound of earth from which the plant grows has that charm of directness which proceeds from a simple mind. And here let me say a word or two about the spirit of unrest and revolt of which we hear so much to-day. Do not expect me to explain "Futurism"—for how dare I step in where so great a philosopher as Mr. Dooley fears to tread. "Don't ask me what it manes, Hinnessey, for I cudn't tell it ye." But if the unrest and revolt in art means (among other things) that decoration should be simpler, less academic, less exacting in its demands on skill and finished perfection, there is reason in it. That nineteenth century ideal of machine-like perfection for a long time ruled over the designer and decorator with a rod of iron. No sign of human feeling or imperfection was allowed to show itself in its "rule and compass" domain. A mechanical exactness was preferred to spontaneity and artistic feeling.

Look now at the old work; its "freehand" quality is obvious at once, and in translating these examples into penline and black and white that is the aspect I have been most anxious to preserve.

We feel, on looking at the Persian or Jacobean embroideries, the painted tiles, the old chests or chair-back decorations in carved wood, the capital or panel cut by the Gothic stone carver, that they were not overburdened with rules and restrictions in those days. We are often asked why we admire the old work, the figures and animals are so funny, so out of proportion, the workmanship so rough, so crude, and many another fault is found. All these things may be true, but because the works in question were pieces of free self-expression, done to decorate or beautify some building or object of daily life, they are full of human

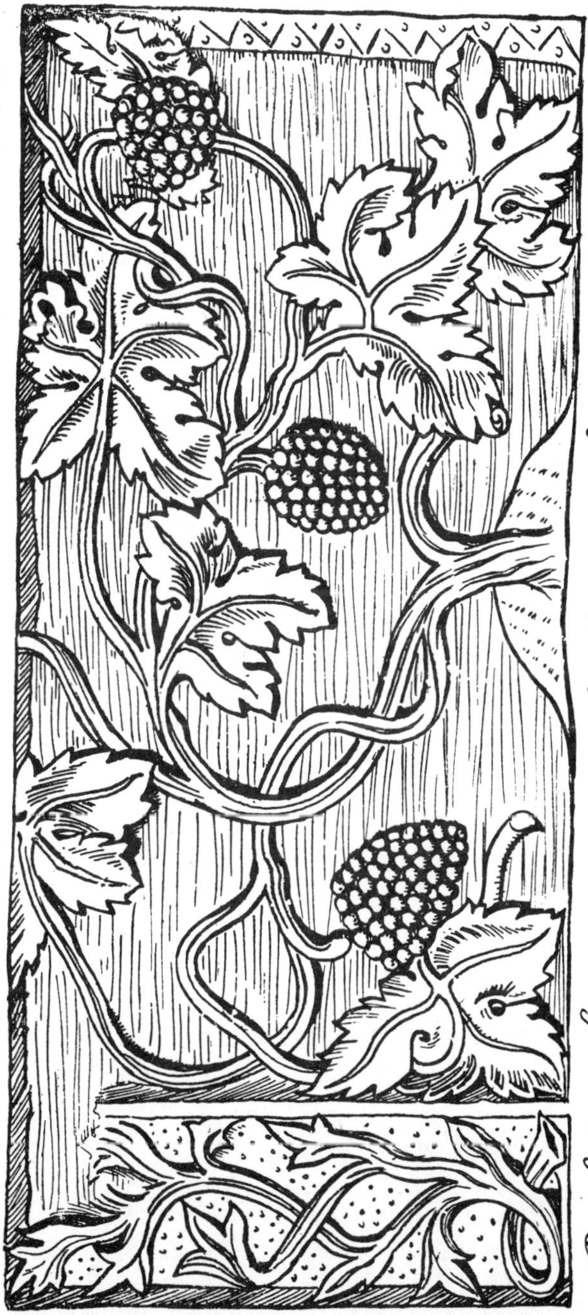

Panel from chimney-piece ~ carved walnut ~ French ~ (Brittany) · 1st ½ 16th cent.

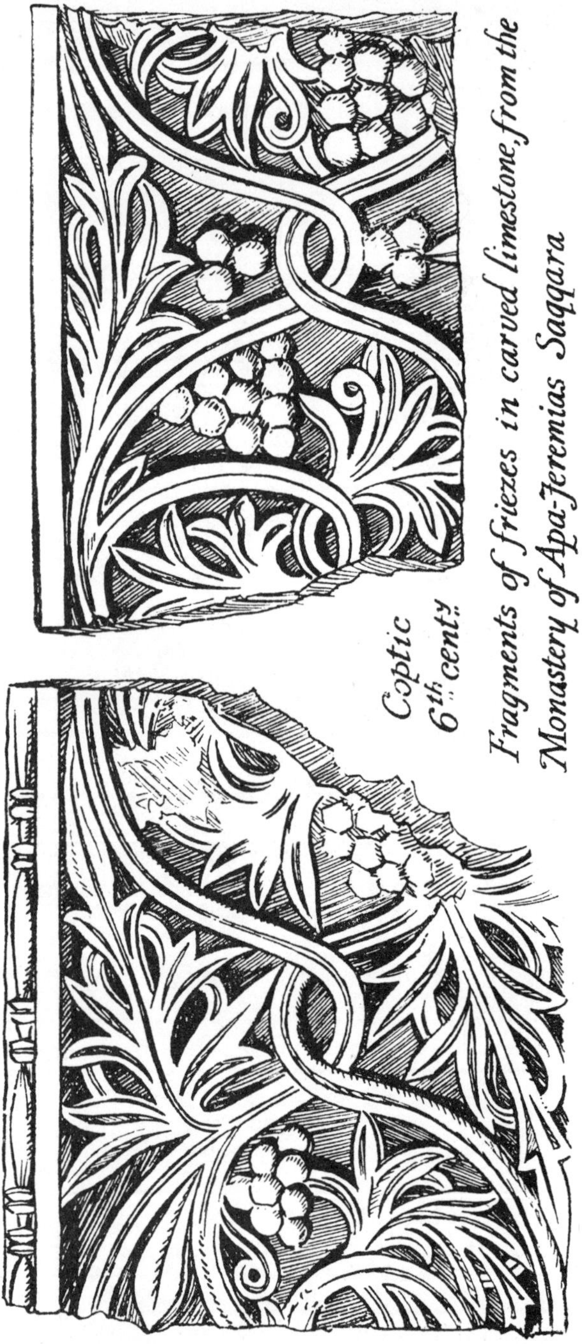

Fragments of friezes in carved limestone, from the Monastery of Apa-Jeremias Saqqara

Coptic 6th cent.

interest and have become works of art to us; and because, looking back over the centuries and eliminating present fashions from our view, we find in them nature seen through temperament. So we realise how the old French carver saw his vine, how he chalked it on his panel, what he thought a nice arrangement of lines in the stems, where he felt the bunches of grapes would come best, how he felt half a leaf would do where there was not room for a whole one. Now imagine the chimney-piece left plain, undecorated, then look again at the vine carved on the panel, with its wandering beauty of stem-line, its play of light and modelling on fruit and leaf, and the human interest expressed by the old carver's hand will set a sympathetic chord vibrating in the mind of the observer. It has been said that art is nature seen through a temperament, and we may add to this that a sympathetic mind is necessary in the receiver—the one who looks on the work of art when it is made.

The vine in the Coptic stone carving is a curious rendering of the

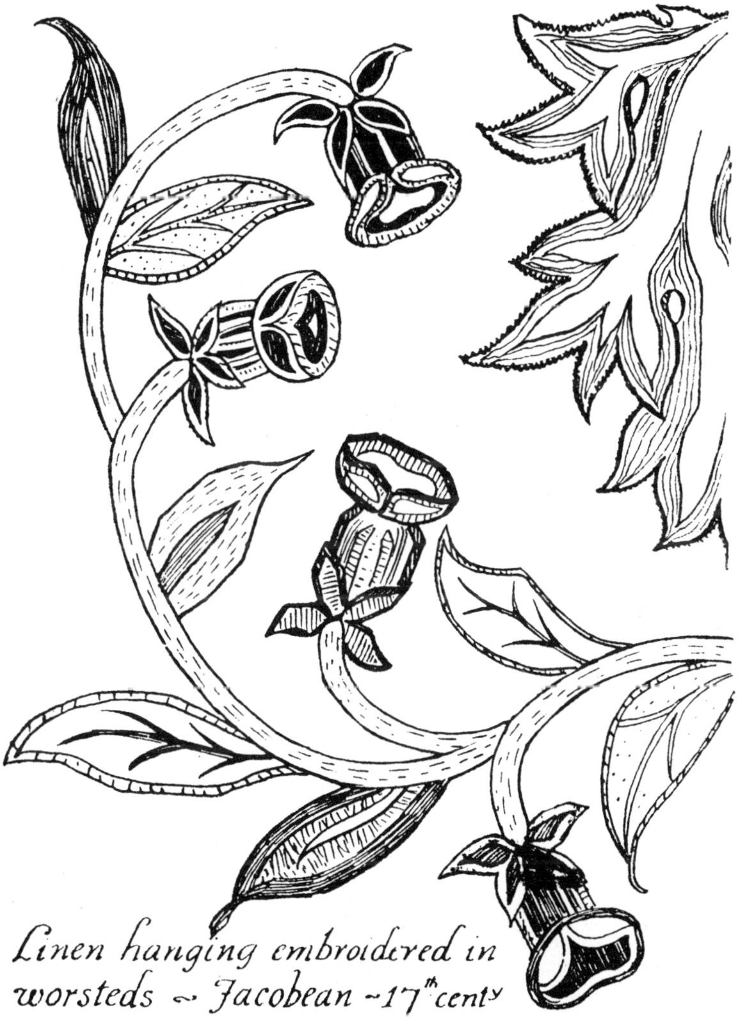

*Linen hanging embroidered in worsteds ~ Jacobean ~17th cent^y^*

plant, and it seems probable that, being very near in date to Roman and Greek art, the sculptor could not discard the traditional acanthus forms in the leaves when cutting it. It is nearer to Byzantine art than Roman, and in design and space-filling a fine piece of ornament; the sharp spikes of the thistle-like leaves, with

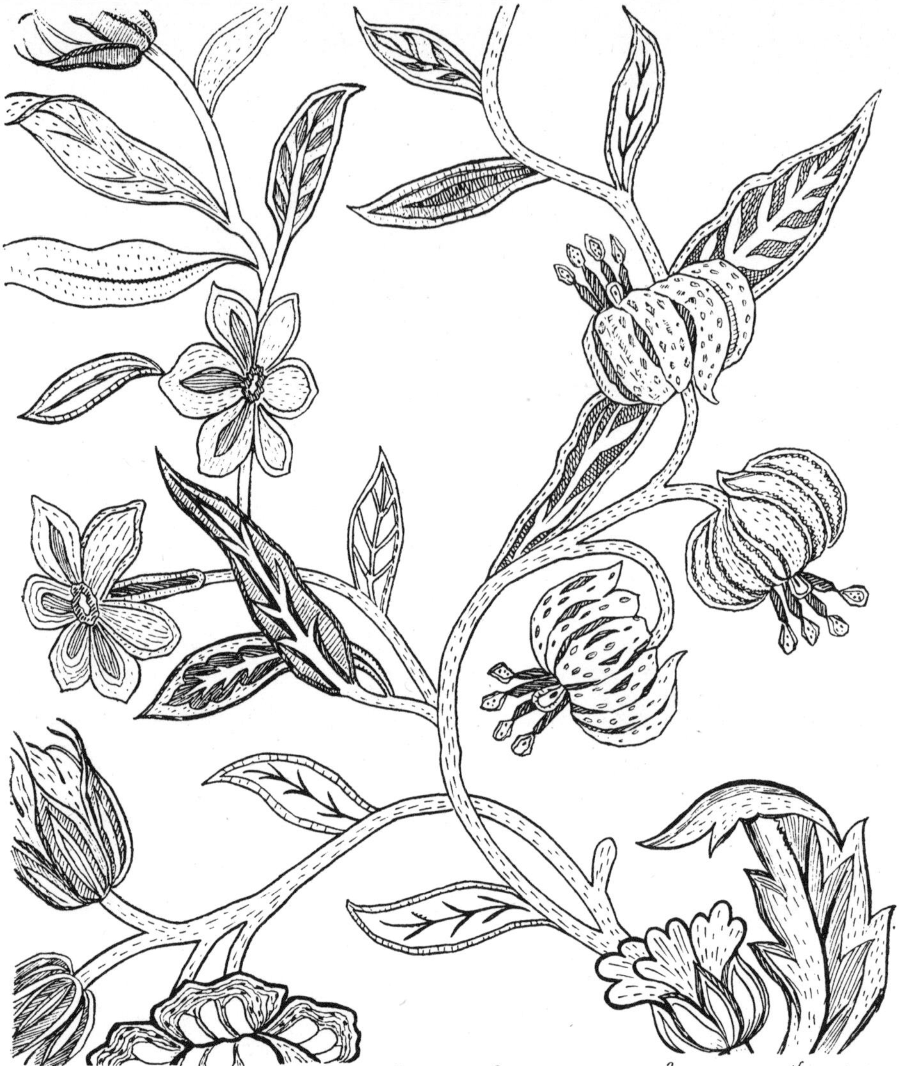

Linen hanging embroidered with worsteds — Jacobean - 17th century

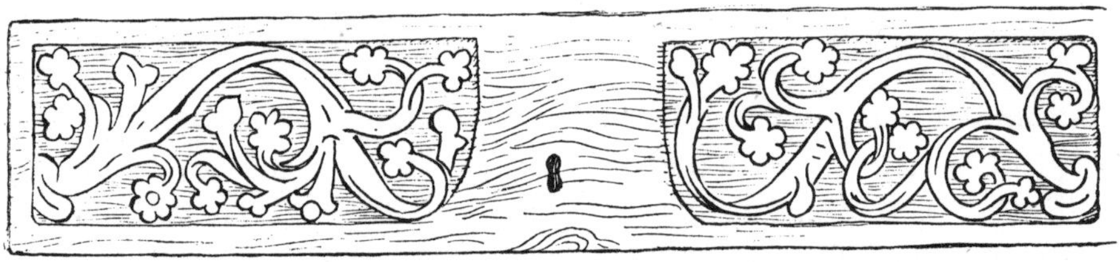

Carved panel - from pine-wood table ~ Swiss ~ 1532.

the rich darks deeply cut into the stone, giving a bold effect of light and shadow.

The two pieces of Jacobean embroidery given in this chapter are again typical of that frank, candid feeling for nature just referred to. A morning stroll through an old-fashioned garden would bring to notice a collection of floral forms like these—Turk's head lily, Canterbury bell, tulip, narcissus, and other blooms and buds. The captious critic will exclaim against such a variety being found together at one

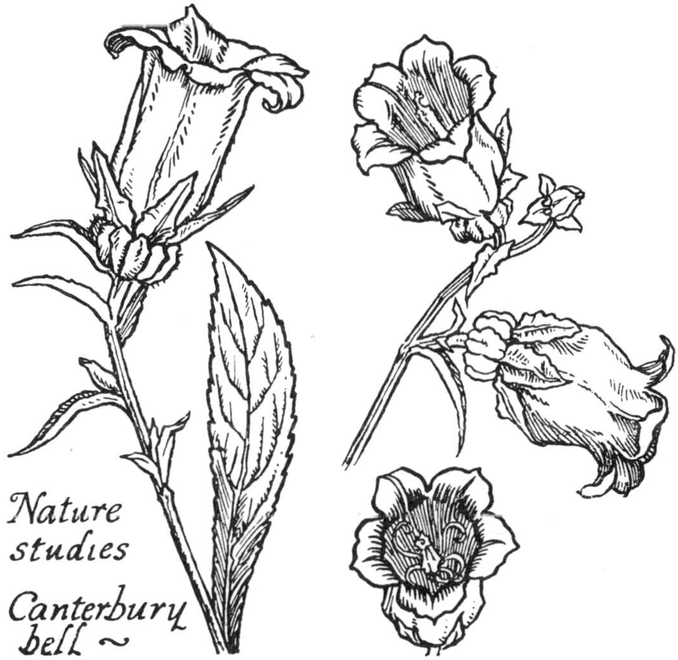

time—true, but little incongruities here and there did not trouble the old craftsmen and designers. Besides, the very character of the design is a wandering main line from which grow all kinds of flowers, and as the work progressed the forms were grafted on to it, each in his due season. And, as the design is made in several repeats, a narcissus might easily neighbour with a Canterbury bell or a Turk's head lily nod to a tulip across the way. The Jacobean embroideries are wonderfully interesting in treatment. Examine the leaves and flowers, and scarcely two will be found alike. They are also varied in colour—the Canterbury bells, for instance, are given as blue in one place and red in another. This does not offend one's logical sense, because decoration is the object of the design, and no attempt at real representation is made.

Wools and worsteds are largely used in the embroideries of this period, giving a sense of boldness and strength both in colour and design. If there is any fault to be found with them it is that the scheme is sometimes out of balance in the matter of tone values. A group of flowers and leaves of medium weight, as regards tone, will be crossed or broken by a heavy brown stem or other element

Border ~ stained glass ~ from Lincoln Cathedral ~ 12th to 13th centy

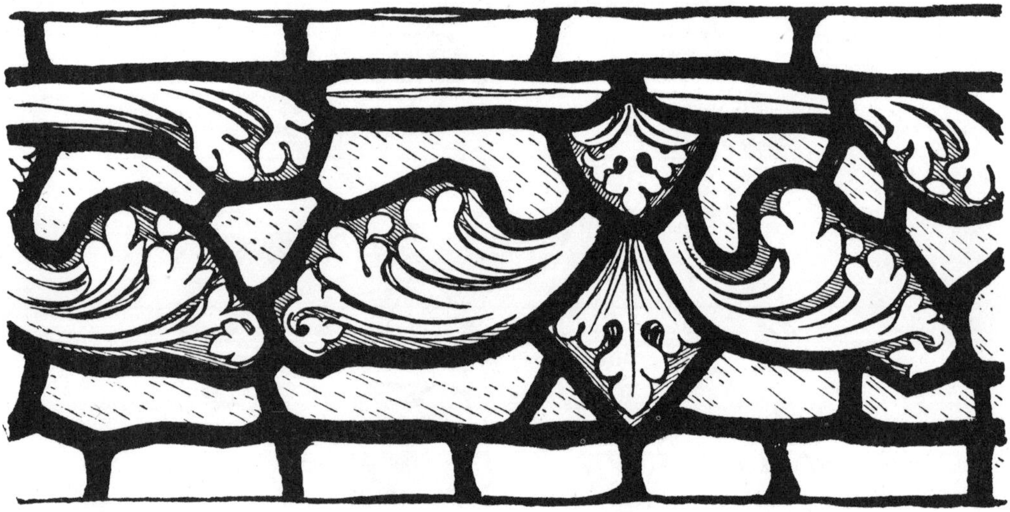

of the general motive, making too loud a note for the rest. This is a thing which requires watching by every designer. Not that a monotonous sameness of tone is necessary in the forms used in a piece of decoration, but a want of centralising or nice distribution of the strong spots of tone leads to a lack of balance and sense of weight evenly distributed.

The nature studies of Canterbury bells are given here that they may show what they look like when translated into the terms of Jacobean embroidery.

The border of stained glass from Lincoln Cathedral and the little panels on the Swiss table are given as examples of vine derivatives. A whole school or style of decorative foliage has come from the forms

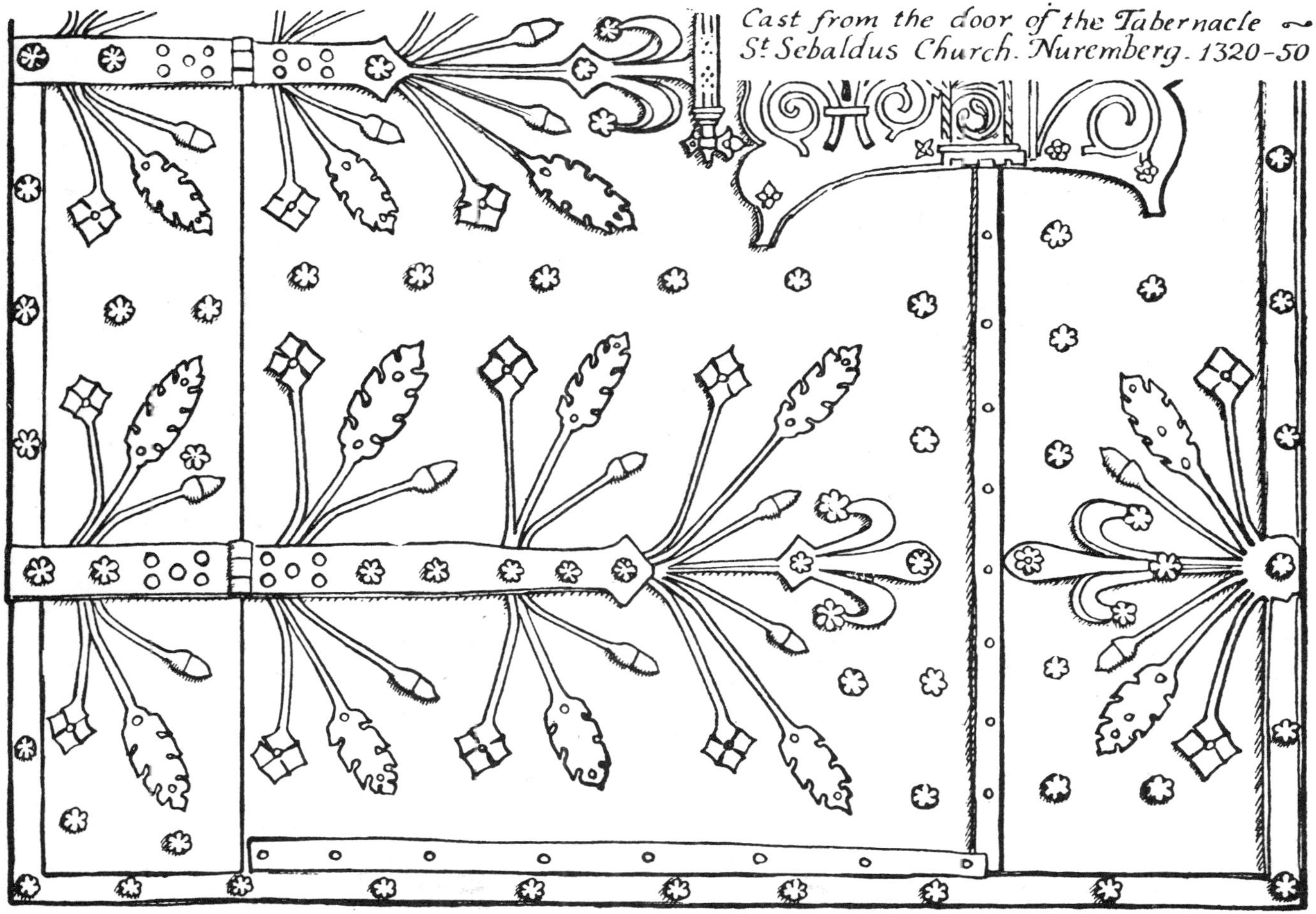

*Cast from the door of the Tabernacle ~
St. Sebaldus Church. Nuremberg. 1320–50*

of the vine leaf, gradually wandering from the original till it becomes quite a convention. Nevertheless they are beautiful pieces of decoration, and we can admire the way the glass craftsmen darkens his ground between the forms, and contrasts his coloured or decorated and plain spaces.

The carving of the Swiss table is a bit of peasant craft and is full of handwork charm. The table-top is a plain slab of pine placed over a square drawer or locker, the panels of this being carved on all the four faces. It is an excellent example of a beautiful thing made by simple means, the carving being merely incised outlines and the ground lowered a trifle. There are traces of colour, red and black, remaining on the ornament, and the uneven dividing of the panelled spaces with the keyhole not quite in the centre gives us a pleasurable insight into the conditions of the age. These are proofs that the old craftsmen were not so fearful of criticism on the one part, and that ideals of workmanship were less mechanical on the other when contrasted with later aims and times.

If the unrest or revolt called "Futurism," or any other name, helps in restoring this natural freedom, it will have done a good service. But we must wait and see.

The oak leaves and acorns on the door hinges from St. Sebaldus' Church, Nuremberg, make a splendid piece of decoration. The door itself is painted vermilion, while the decorative forms and the beautiful lock are gilded. How these old craftsmen loved to decorate; how beautiful they made ordinary things; even their locks and hinges down to mere nail-heads are things of thought and beauty. We can read their lives when we look at the work of their hands and call to mind that art is nature seen through a temperament.

CHAPTER X

TO the modern decorator there is still a large field in the matter of floral forms unexplored. The old designers used but a small number of plants or flowers compared with the vast quantity in nature left untouched. Of course there are forms in Oriental decoration which may be recognised by those who are

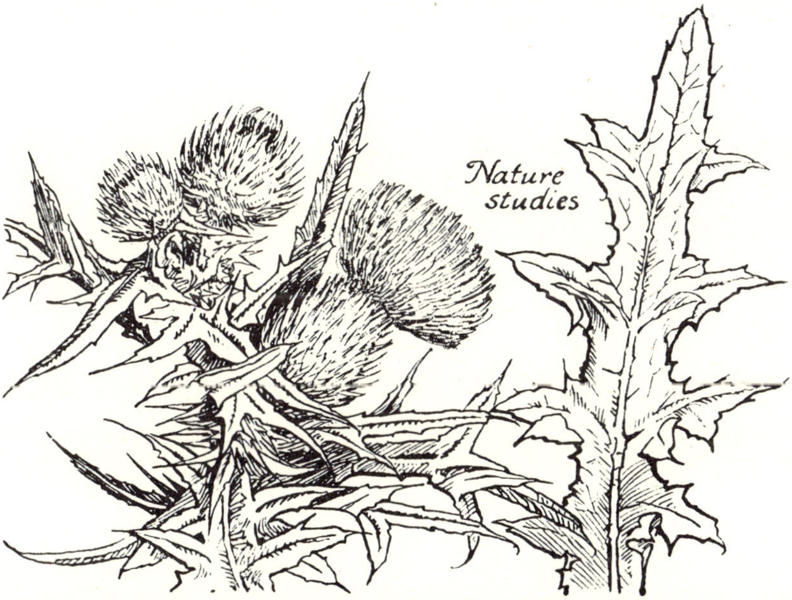

Thistle

acquainted with the flowers of India, Persia or China, and which add to the number, but as a rule a few favourites such as we have been reviewing have been used again and again. In this chapter two flowers are given which will serve to prove the point in question—the honeysuckle and the thistle. Both are beautiful plants in form and colour, both are full of interesting detail, but they have never been much used by designers. No doubt the farmer and the gardener

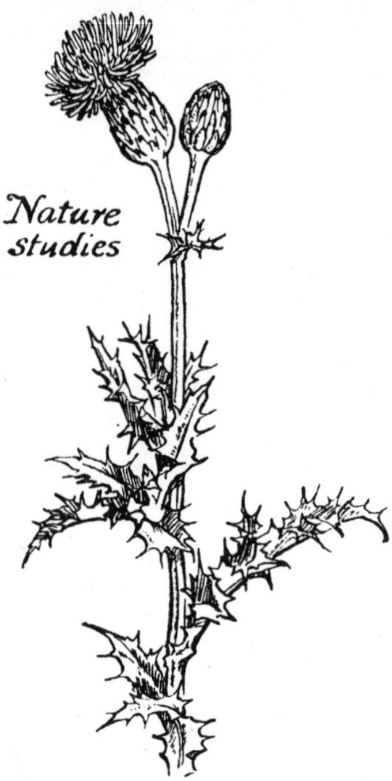

Thistle

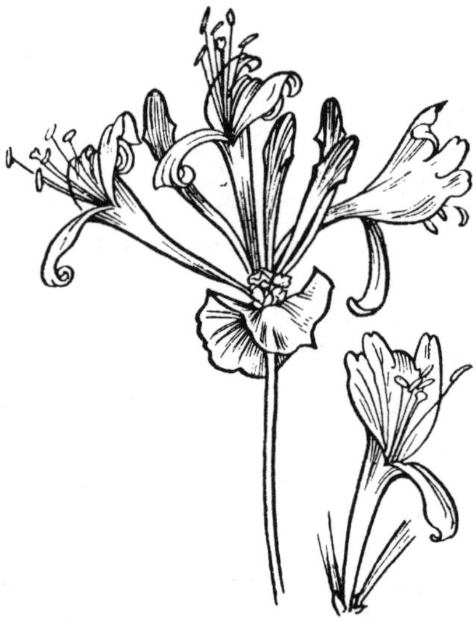

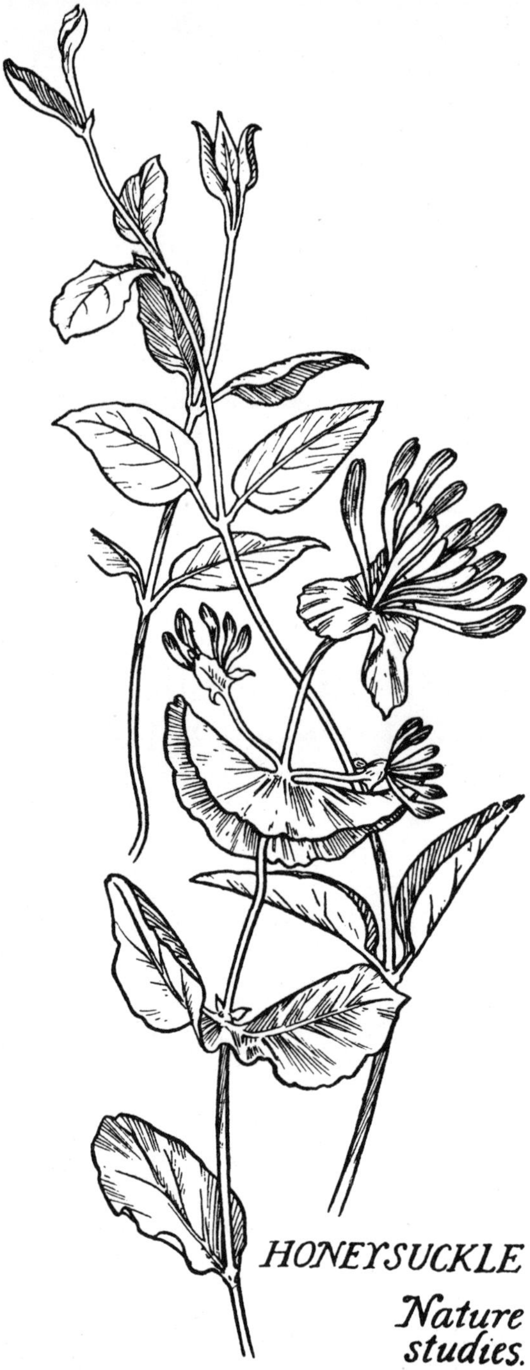

will be surprised at hearing the thistle referred to as a beautiful flower; probably they would argue that in this case beauty and utility were at variance with each other, and we should not be likely to find the cultivator of the soil buying a curtain or a wallpaper with a thistle pattern on it. I mention this merely to show that sentiment has played some part in the choice of floral forms in decoration, and as a reason why those flowers have been most employed which by association call to mind the garden and the pleasaunce; those which remind us of the freshness of spring, the fulness of summer, or the grateful coolness of shady wood. For all that, cases of exceptional appropriateness occur, and "Caledonia stern and wild" has a fitting emblem in the thistle of the uprightness and strength of the Scottish character. It was also sometimes used by the Gothic stone and wood

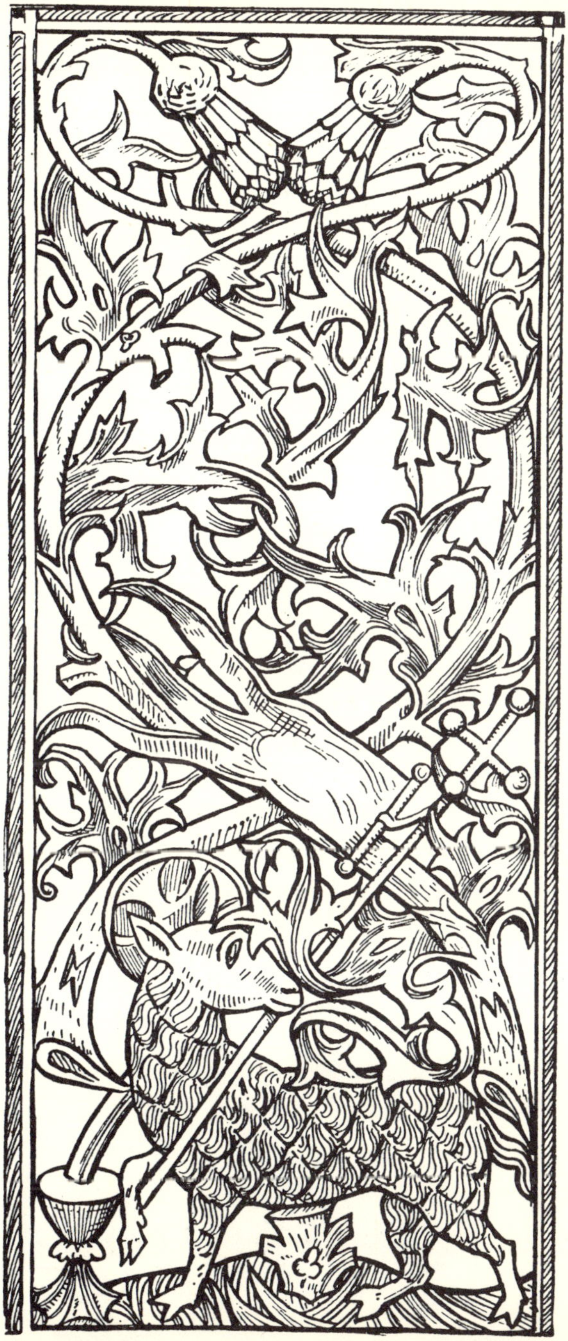

THISTLE. Oak panel—Eng., late 15*th cent.*

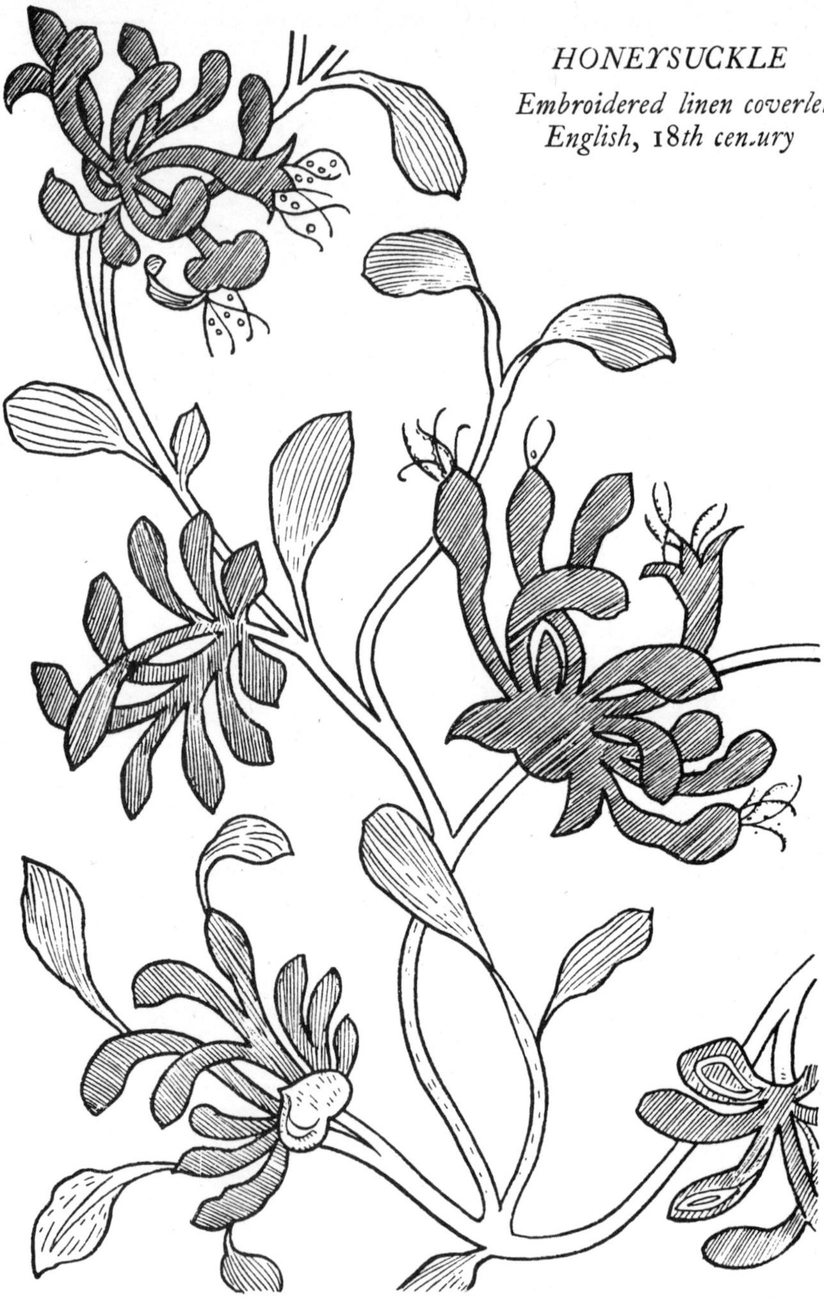

HONEYSUCKLE

Embroidered linen coverlet
English, 18th cen.ury

carvers, and with the vine it degenerated in the later periods to a conventional form of foliage without much reference to nature, and thereby lost its character as a vigorous decorative shape.

The example chosen in our illustrations, however, must be exempt from these base charges. Some designers may think it wrong to use curves for the main lines on which to place this plant in filling a space, claiming that it destroys the character of it; but granting that to be true to some extent, the specimen before us is so full of excellent work, so much use has been made of its various parts, that we waive a minor point in favour of the success of the whole. It is a masterly piece of woodcarving too. There is no background, the intervening spaces between the forms being cut away.

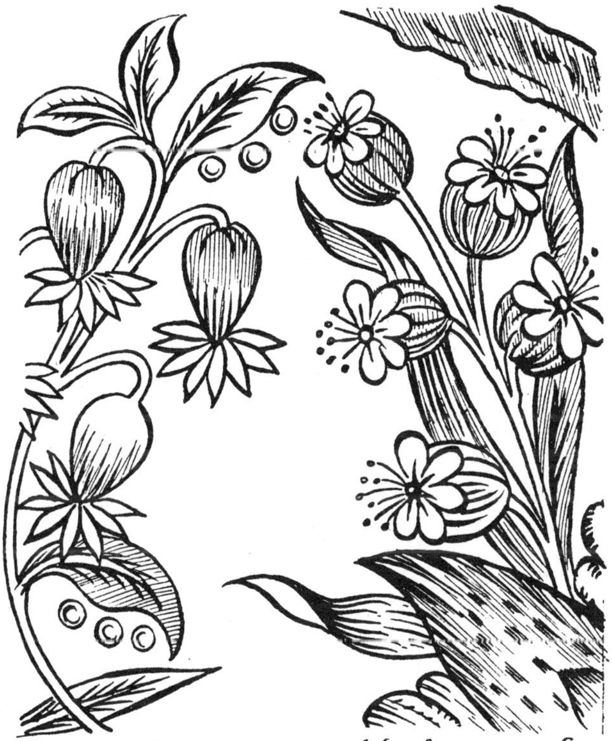

Campion on block-printed calico—Dutch or English—18th centy

Probably the stiffness and intractability of the thistle have gone against it as a useful flower to the decorator, and there is no doubt reason in the objection to its employment on curved lines.

But none of the faults found in regard to the thistle can be brought against the honeysuckle—a most lovely plant with a wonderfully beautiful flower, yet how little it has been used in design! There is a fine bold treatment of it in one of Morris's linen hangings. It appears in conjunction with large poppy flowers and leaves, running in and out and in between them with all the cunning expected of so great a master. Again, I know a very beautiful specimen designed and cut on wood by Charles Ricketts as a page-border in the lovely books issued some years ago by the Vale Press. In it, if the reader has a chance of seeing one of those models of fine printing, he will find all that beauty and refinement of design and delicacy of feeling which is never absent from this artist's work. There are one or two examples of the honeysuckle on plaster ceilings in old mansions, but they are only available in text-book reproductions, and my desire is to give all drawings in these chapters at first hand from the objects themselves. On p. 216 is one instance of its use in an eighteenth century embroidery, though it must be admitted it is a somewhat disappointing treatment of so beautiful a flower. More interesting decoration might have been made from its various features. Neither does the colour redeem it much, for the flowers are given merely in a flat red tint. The streaking of crimson and cream in the petals of the honeysuckle and the details of leaf and stamen could have been used with more effect, but the waving and winding character of the plant has been cleverly used, and as the illustration shows, it forms a running endless border round a central panel.

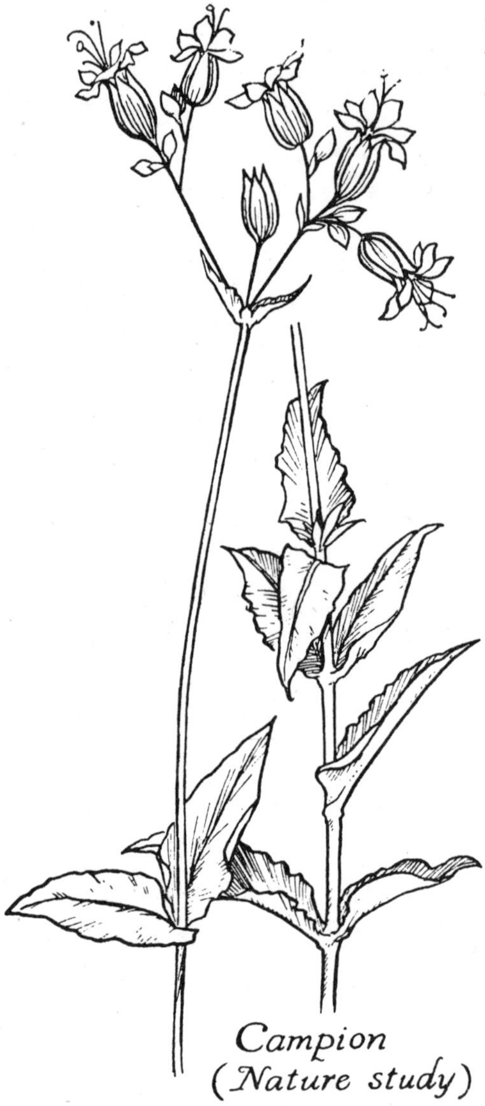

Campion (Nature study)

The campion in the piece of block-printed calico is also an instance of a flower seldom used in decoration. It appears in one of the eighteenth century patterns which are so largely influenced by Eastern designs that many of the main forms are directly copied from their flowers. That the English or Dutch designer should have inserted a common weed like the campion in the midst of Oriental shapes makes it somewhat of a curiosity in the use of floral form if nothing more.

The piece of oak and acorn patterning on the Dutch cheese press is a sturdy and vigorous bit of work in which the character of the leaf and fruit is given by a direct and straightforward technique. It is part of a long narrow panel cut on the lever of the press and is but a detail of a very elaborate and handsome piece of domestic furniture—a piece in which beauty and utility are most happily combined. Indeed, it is in Dutch domestic art that we see this combination at its best. There are no interiors so clean, so comfortable, so restful and beautiful in colour as the Dutch, and we can imagine this piece of rich dark oak in one of those essentially "living rooms" where the light plays on brass and copper pans, sconces and candlesticks or a brick hearth, flanked by blue and white tiles; an effect of beauty, utility, comfort and simplicity not often found elsewhere.

The porcelain plate of eighteenth century English design is yet another example of the influence of Eastern work in Western

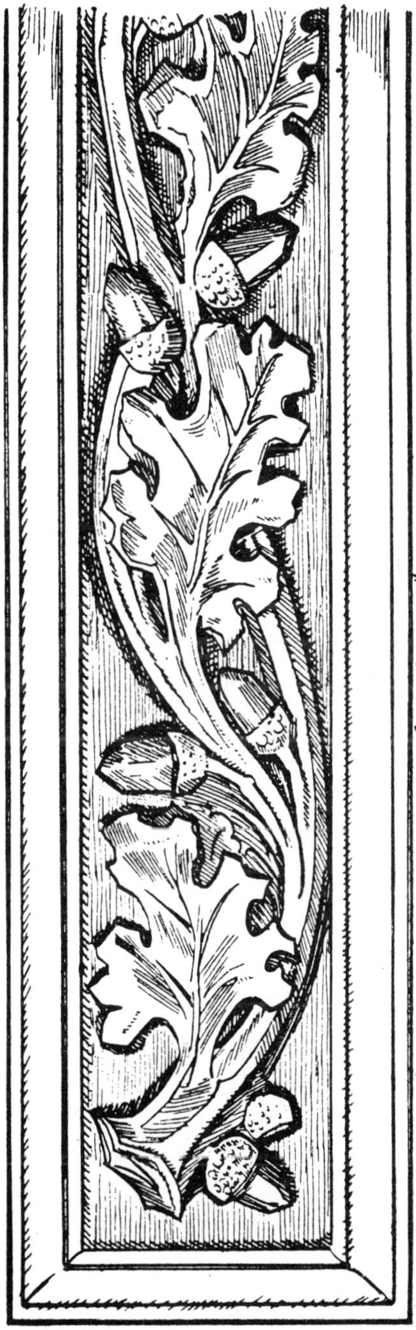

From a Dutch cheese press ~ carved oak ~ 17th cent.

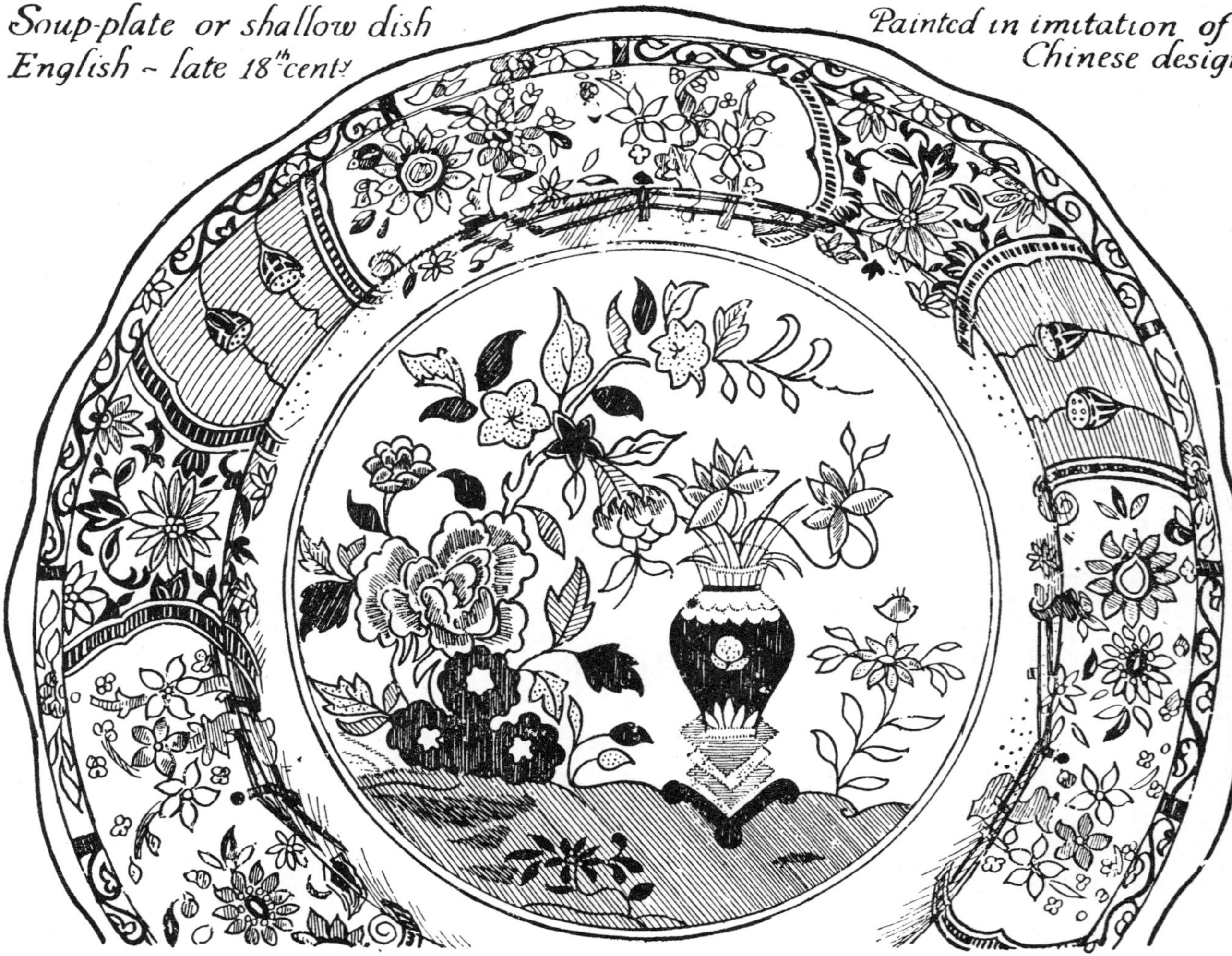

Soup-plate or shallow dish
English – late 18th centy

Painted in imitation of
Chinese designs

manufactures. The forms are direct and exact imitations—in fact, these articles were referred to by our grandfathers as "in the Chinese taste." The peony-tree will be noticed as the principal form, but I fear the other flowers have degenerated in the process of transfer from Chinese to English uses. The colour is mostly an orange red combined with a dark ultramarine blue—the latter represented by the darks in the illustration, though here and there touches of green occur and a small amount of gilt enhances the framing of the panelled spaces. Altogether there is in it a quaintness of design and a richness of colour and it is full of that eighteenth century admiration of Chinese work which dominated the English potters of that period. The ground is a tinted, not a raw, white.

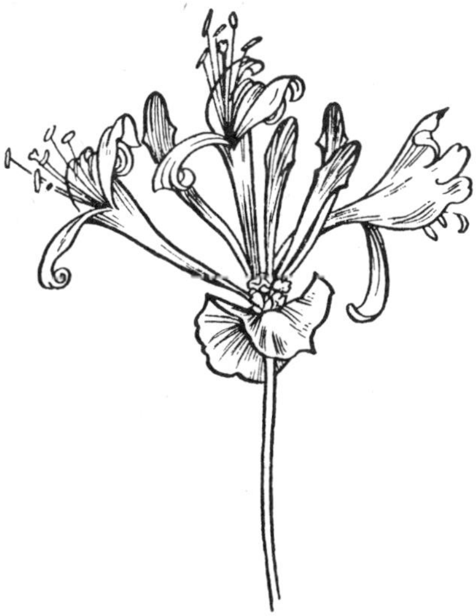

CHAPTER XI

IT has often been remarked that the art of primitive peoples is more decorative than the art of the more advanced, and for this there is a reason. When a new idea is started the main object is to realise that idea. and all available energy and artistic skill is bent towards that purpose. When it has been attained changes begin to take place and experiments are made, particularly in the method and manner of its expression. So we see on looking back that early efforts at decoration aim only, or mainly, at ornamenting the object, and as long as this result is obtained there is not a great deal of trouble expended on the means to that end, or it is, at any rate, considered as a secondary matter.

But afterwards, with the growth of skill, the means of expression become more and more an object of study, and the technical perfection which the craftsman obtains by constant practice brings about his undoing as a decorative artist. This has happened many times in the history of decorative art and it seems to be one aspect of that inevitable law of change which influences the course of all things.

As examples illustrating the truth of these remarks let us look at the two carved panels of the time of Louis XVI. which accompany this chapter. The technical skill exhibited in them is quite wonderful, particularly in the one containing the crown and ribbon.

But we feel that good design and effective decoration are quite secondary matters when compared with the display of technique in the carving. The arrangement of flower and leaf, ribbon and stem is too complex, a superficial imitation of the plant is preferred to that delight in pattern which the taste of a simpler age would have demanded. Moreover, as a further result of technical display the work itself gives evidence of a perverted taste, for the forms appear to be imitative of clay modelling rather than of wood carving. At the same time we cannot separate it from its period, and its style is part of the appropriate background to the figures of "*grande dame*" and high-heeled silken gallant or courtier strutting or minuetting before it. The second example is simpler and less showy, but it is only that the lily is well drawn which redeems it from the commonplace. Neither of these renderings of the lily can compare in dignity and simple decorative effect with those shown on the Assyrian bas-relief on page 178, Chapter VI., but in the latter case it was the expression of the idea which acted as the motive power behind the craftsman's hand; in the case of the French panels it was the cleverness of the carving which engaged most of his attention.

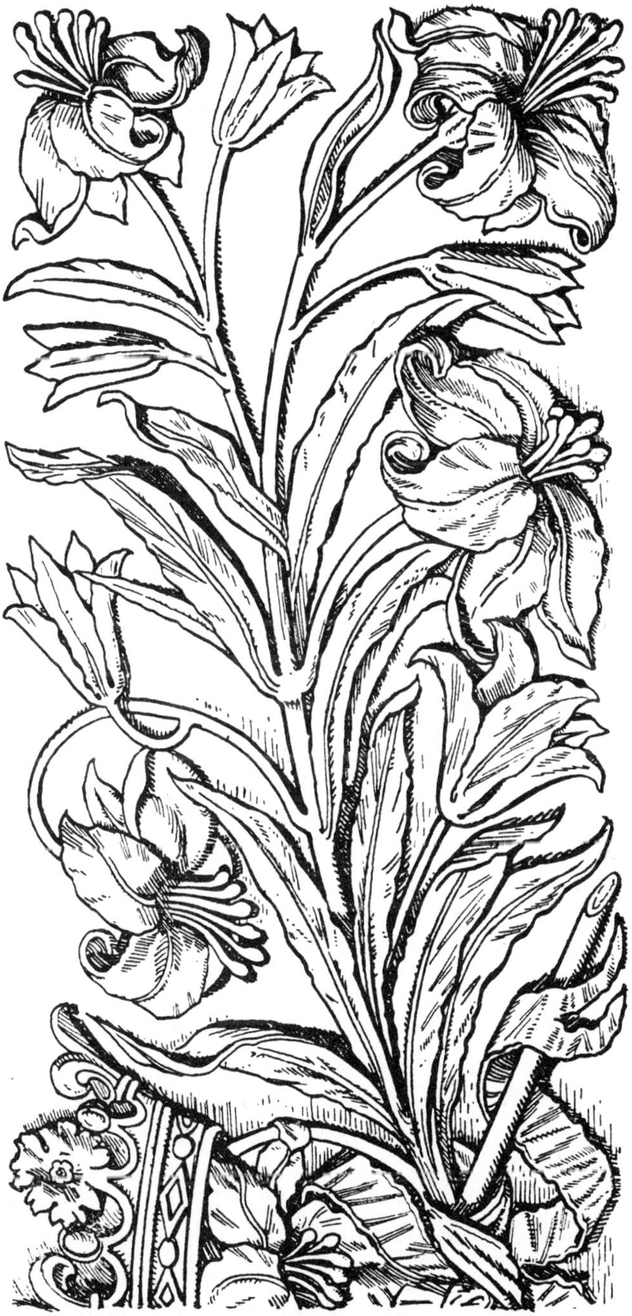

Oak panel - French - late 18th cent.y

The lily has not been very much used by designers, although it is surely one of the most beautiful of flowers. Most probably it is because it is so

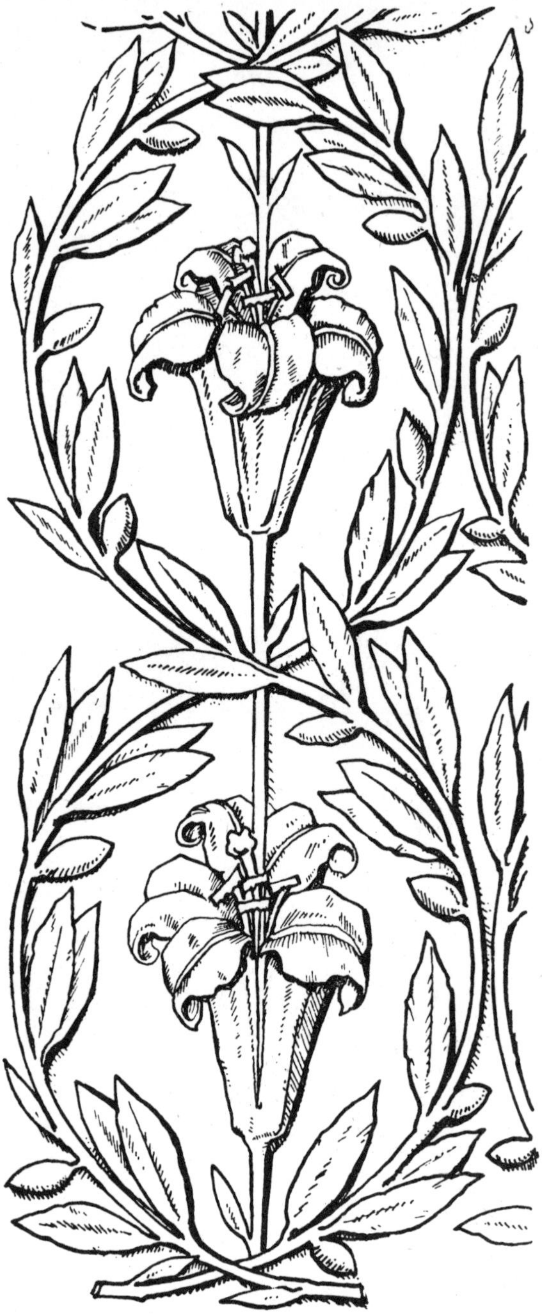

Oak panel—French, late 18th century

difficult to draw. Only those who have tried it can realise how six petals apparently simple in form can assume such exasperatingly difficult positions, but so it is, and each time the draughtsman attempts them new problems of foreshortened curves present themselves. The yellow lily in the Persian velvet is a very interesting rendering of the flower, and like all Persian decorative work it is most beautifully drawn. The Persian designers are masters in the art of knowing how much *nature* to put into their decoration. The Chinese and Japanese, marvellous plant draughtsmen, as no one can deny, often carry their work too far in the imitative spirit, producing flower pictures rather than true decorations.

I regret not being able to give more nature studies of the iris, but the plant drawings I have given are, after all, only supplementary to our main theme. The iris flowers in the Persian velvet and brocade are both beautifully drawn and varied in treatment. In the case of the velvet the colours are strong and rich, the crimson ground showing through the forms in some places—represented by the darks in the drawing, but for the sake of clearness no attempt has been made to give the tone of the ground work. The scheme of the brocade border is light and delicate in key. It is part of a dalmatic evidently woven in Persia for some Christian community, the whole garment being patterned all over with different flowers, rose, daffodil, iris, convolvulus and others, all in pale tones mingled with metal threads on a delicate buff ground.

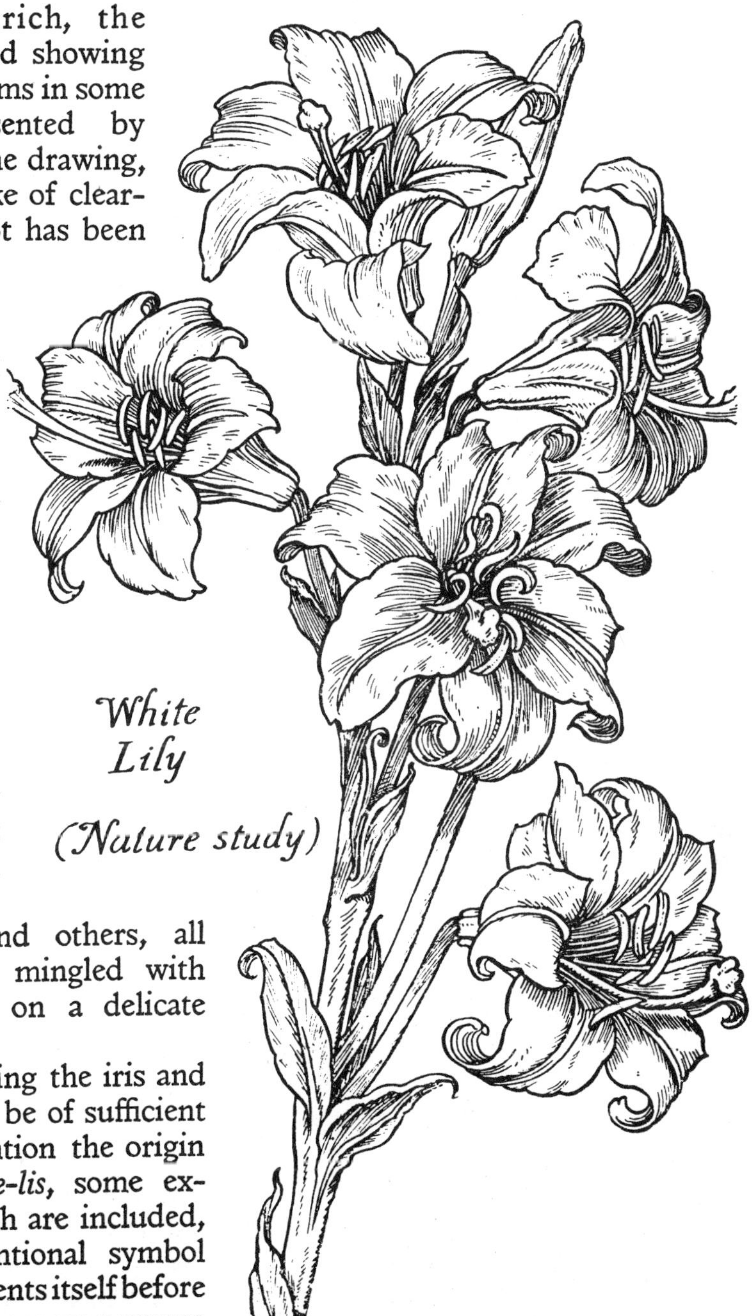

White Lily

(Nature study)

Before leaving the iris and the lily, it may be of sufficient interest to mention the origin of the *fleur-de-lis*, some examples of which are included, as this conventional symbol constantly presents itself before the decorator for some purpose

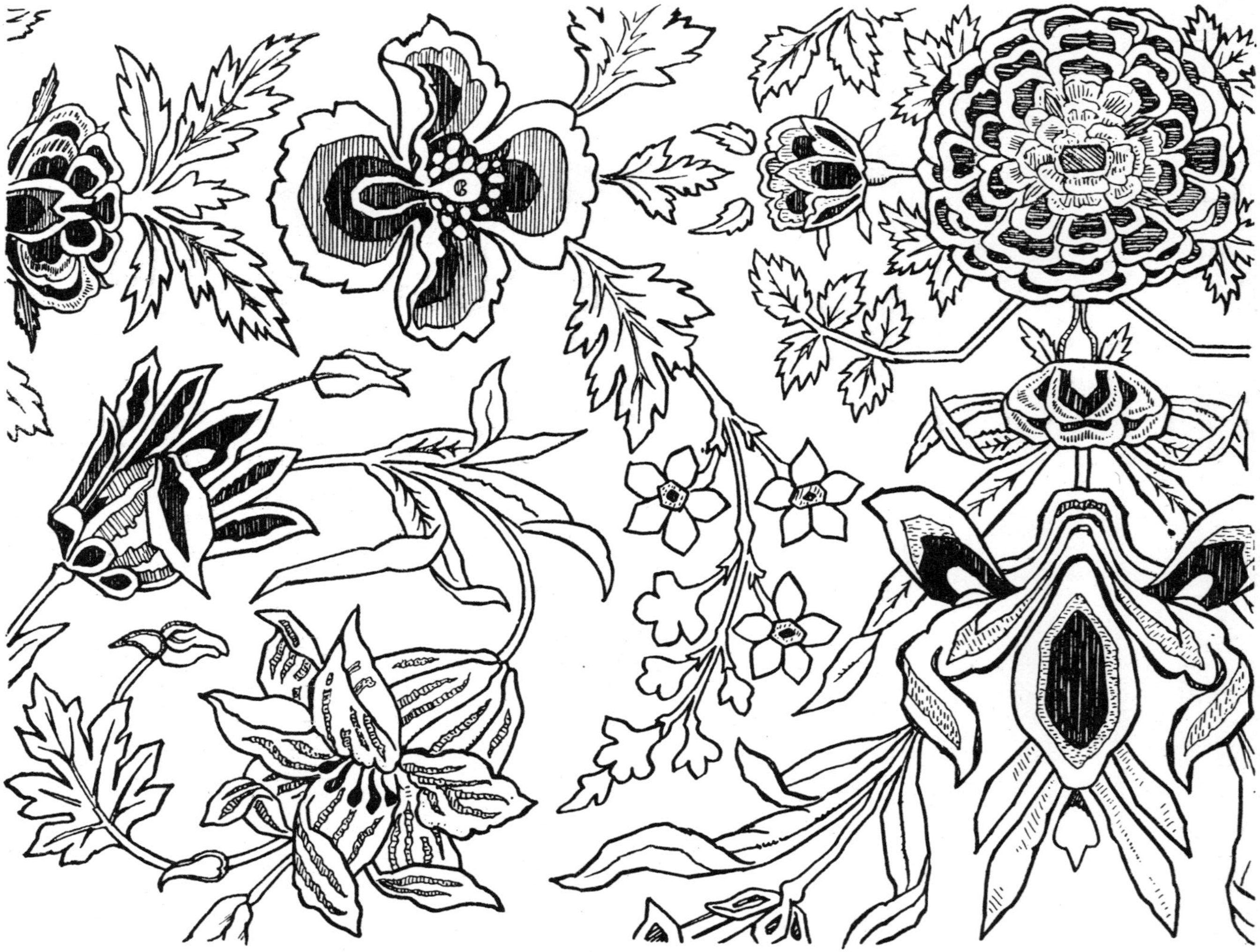

Silk velvet woven with pattern of roses, lilies, iris and narcissus on a crimson ground—Persian

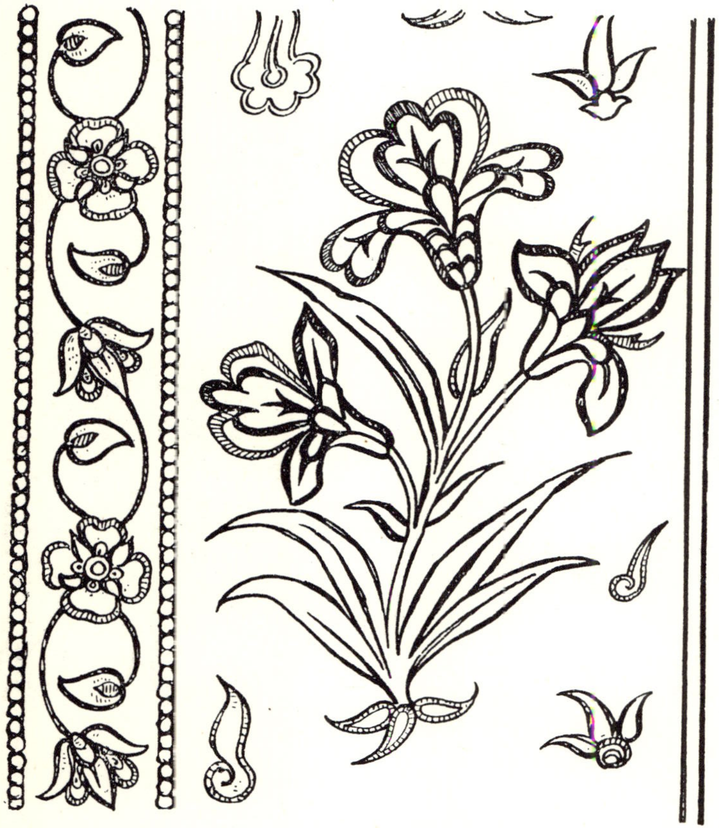

Persian Brocade, woven silks and silver and gilt thread, late 17th or early 18th century

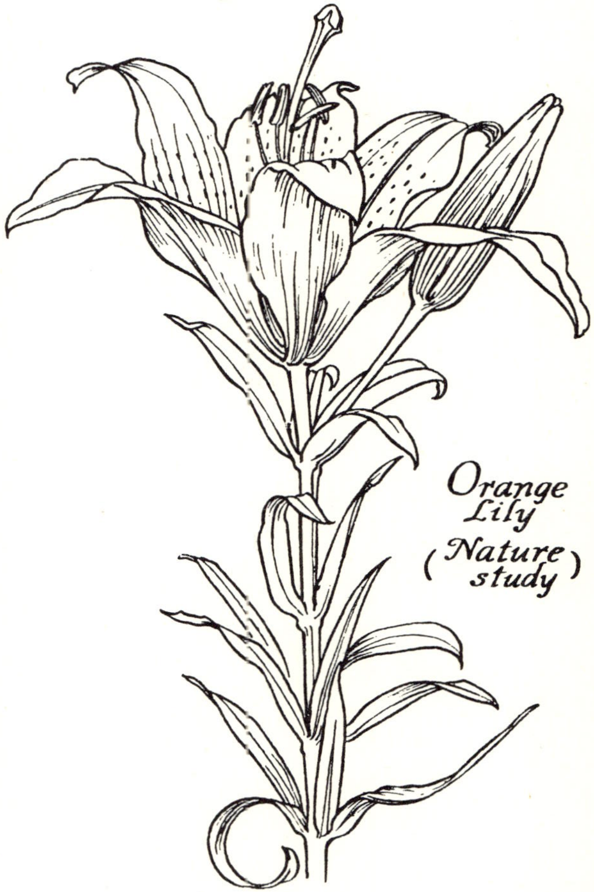

Orange Lily (Nature study)

or other. It requires careful planning and drawing to make it look well, and heralds, craftsmen and designers have expended an infinite amount of thought and invention on varying its treatment. In modern work it is often drawn in a commonplace and mechanical way, but reference to the old forms ought to supply us with fresh inspiration.

Whether this heraldic form was derived from the lily or the iris is a matter of dispute which will probably never be settled. Heraldic

Some forms of the Fleur-de-lis

glossaries give the same form to the "lilies of France" as they give to the lily on any other shield. The flower was often borne as an emblem of purity or of the Blessed Virgin, and nearly every "Annunciation" by the old masters contains a lily as a symbol or accessory; yet ancient heralds say that the Franks of old had a custom at the proclamation of a king to elevate him on a shield or target and place in his hand a reed or flag (iris) in blossom instead of a sceptre. This is a plausible explanation and seems as satisfactory as any, seeing that neither French nor English dictionaries are very clear in their definitions of *fleur-de-lis* or *flower-de-luce*.

I have ventured to describe the forms on the Old French kneading trough as wallflowers, as they have such close resemblance to them; the fact that they possess six petals instead of four does not count for much, as we have seen again and again that the old craftsmen were not slavishly particular where botanical accuracy was concerned, and in spite of deviations from nature the wallflower, I think, has inspired the decoration on these two very graceful panels. I wish that my space allowed of a drawing of the whole, as it is a very beautiful piece of furniture. The oblong trough stands on turned legs, the two panels acting (one directly underneath the trough, and the other near the feet) like chair rungs for strengthening purposes. It is another

Wallflower ~
Two carved wood panels on a Kneading trough-French 18th cent.

remnant from the time when even simple homes were beautiful and common things of domestic use were carefully and strongly made, and moreover lovingly decorated.

Portion of Altar frontal— brocade ground with columbines appliqué— Arms of Valencia

Spanish—15th cent.y

In the Spanish altar frontal design I am glad to present a much more beautiful specimen of the columbine than the one given in a previous chapter. One cannot complain in this instance that this charming flower has not received a worthy treatment. The design, which is beautiful both in mass and line, is repeated three times across the altar front. The colour scheme consists of a pale grey-blue for the ornament on a faded rose for the ground. The coat of arms in the centre is alternately gold and red, the ground tint serving for the latter, prominence being secured by the very decorative effect of quilting. The device of the interlacing stems, too, helps to add richness to the centre-piece and also affords a good basis from which to grow the ornament. The three repeats are not all alike, but are varied in detail. Mechanical repetition was never a fault of the old work, and except in printed or woven repeats, where it is unavoidable, it is a lazy way of decorating anything. Perhaps I am telling more than "a twice-told tale" when I mention that the name of the columbine is derived from the Latin word *columba*, which means a dove.

This design shows the resemblance very clearly, especially in the upper row where the flowers are seen hanging down from their stems. The likeness to a group of doves with half-opened wings putting their heads together at once explains how the flower received its name.

Spanish embroideries are generally very rich in colour and distinguished in design, and this one shares these good qualities in no small degree.

CHAPTER XII

WITH this chapter we come to the end of our journey, and the magic carpet upon which we have travelled must soon be folded up and put away. But before we return homewards, we must take notice of a few flower forms which we have not yet discussed. A beautiful but somewhat uncommon flower is the

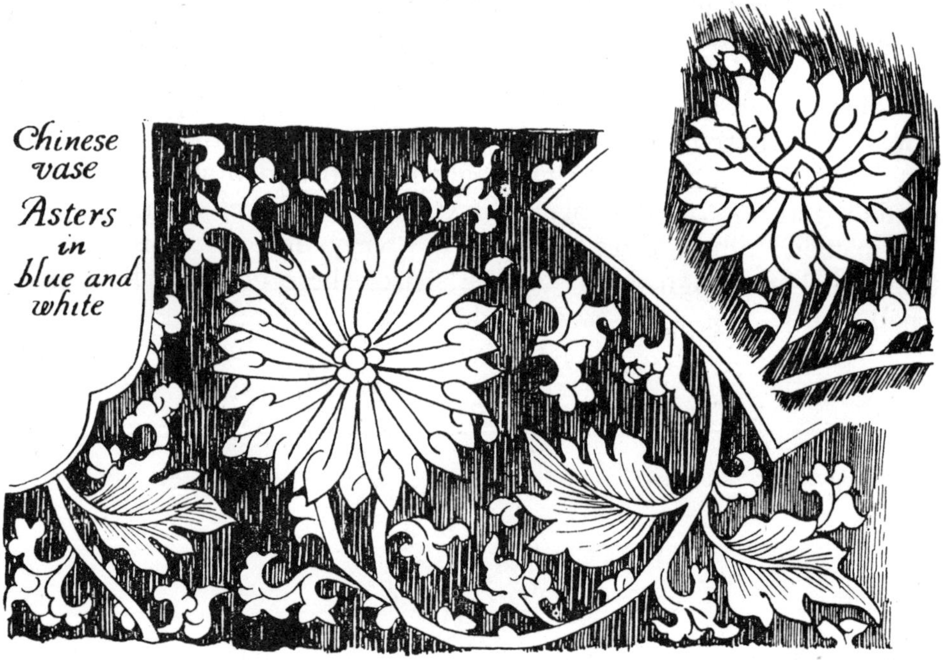

Chinese vase Asters in blue and white

magnolia, and in the drawing of a portion of a Chinese vase we have a good specimen of it in regard to both design and draughtsmanship. The characteristics of Chinese and Japanese art form a mixture of conventional and naturalistic treatment which is almost peculiar to themselves. Their sense of design is quite different from that of Western nations, and, admirable though it is, it never blends satisfactorily with the latter.

This may be accounted for by the fact that all our Western decoration rises from an architectural basis. It has grown out of the process of decorating architectural construction, and the structural side of

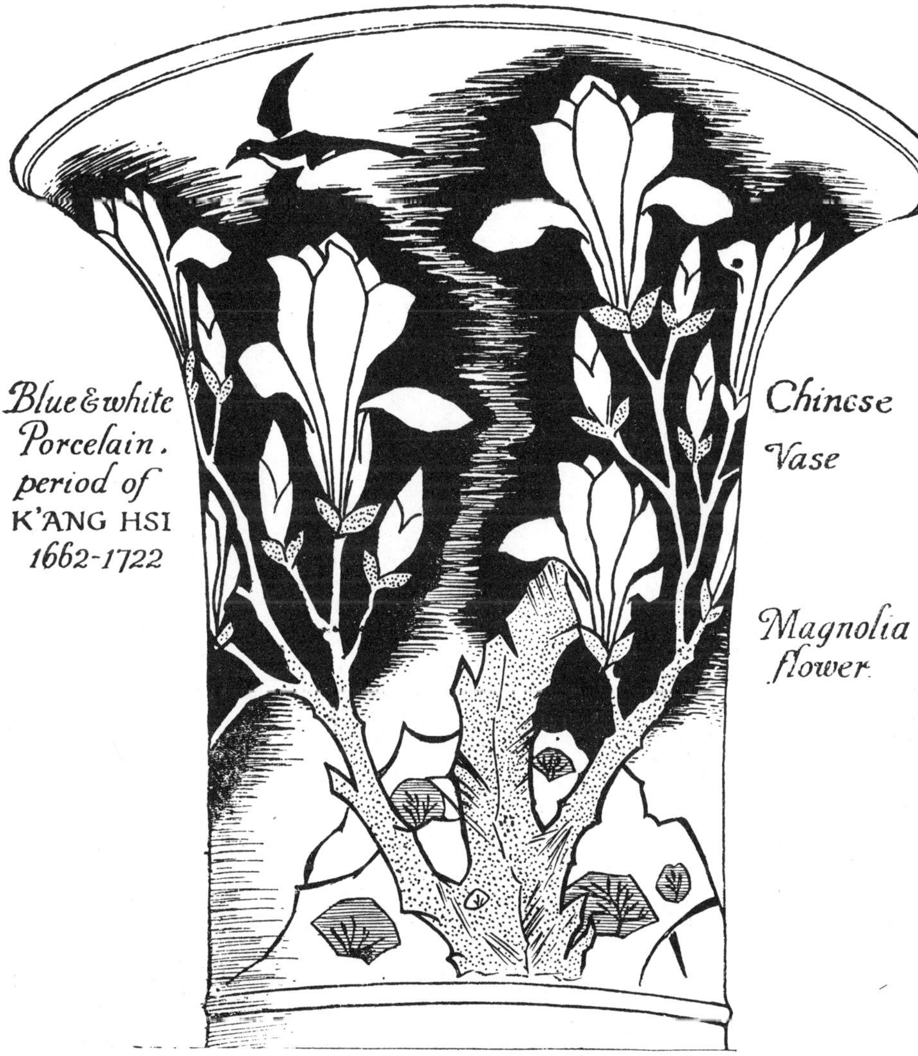

architecture is a much more important element in Western work than in Chinese or Japanese. In using the word Western, the Mahommedan buildings of Persia and India are included in this sense. The architecture of China and Japan is poor in itself and their decorative design

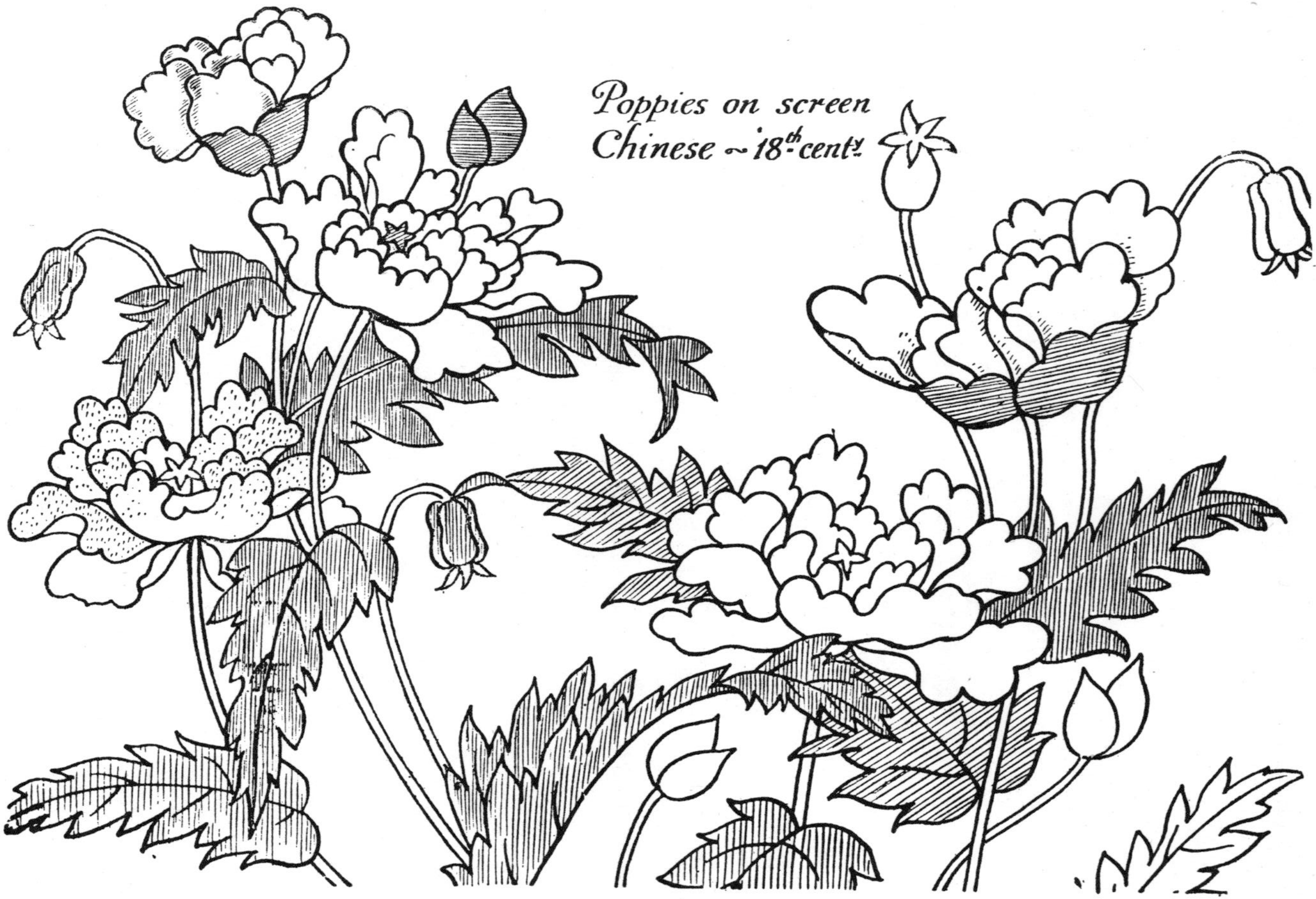

Poppies on screen
Chinese ~ 18th cent.y

is less dependent upon it and can exist more easily apart from it than is the case in other styles.

With the exception of the large temples their buildings are wooden shells of no great permanence; not so with the structures built by Western peoples, theirs being made of stone and brick are of a much more permanent character, and therefore the incentive to decorate the building itself and to make all the furniture and subsidiary portions harmonise with the structural features has always existed. When

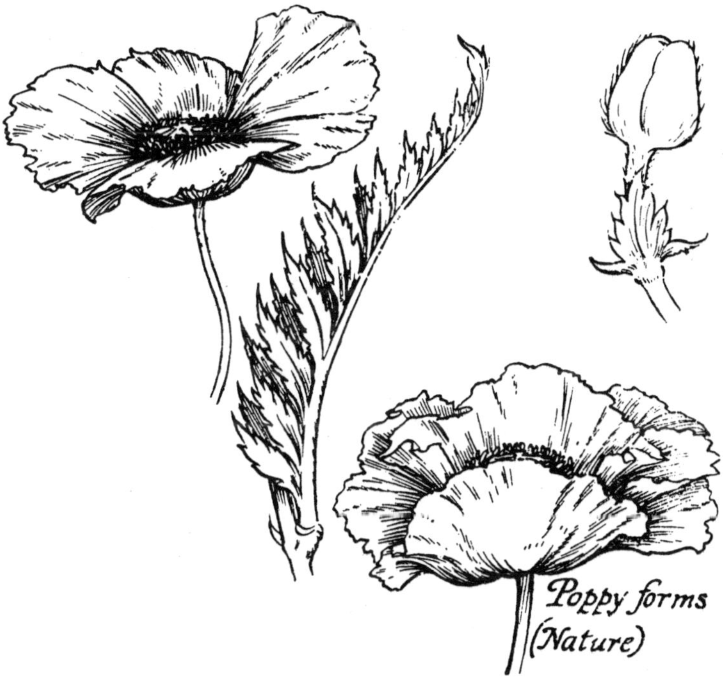

Poppy forms (Nature)

we consider that a Japanese house can be taken to pieces like unfolding or folding a set of screens, the intimate connection between architecture and decoration in our part of the world can be more readily understood.

We ought, therefore, to judge Chinese and Japanese decoration from a different standpoint from our own, and the fact that we have to do so is only another proof that our styles and theirs do not harmonise very successfully with each other.

For all this we need find no difficulty in admiring the dexterous drawing, the beautiful line and effective brushwork and spacing which

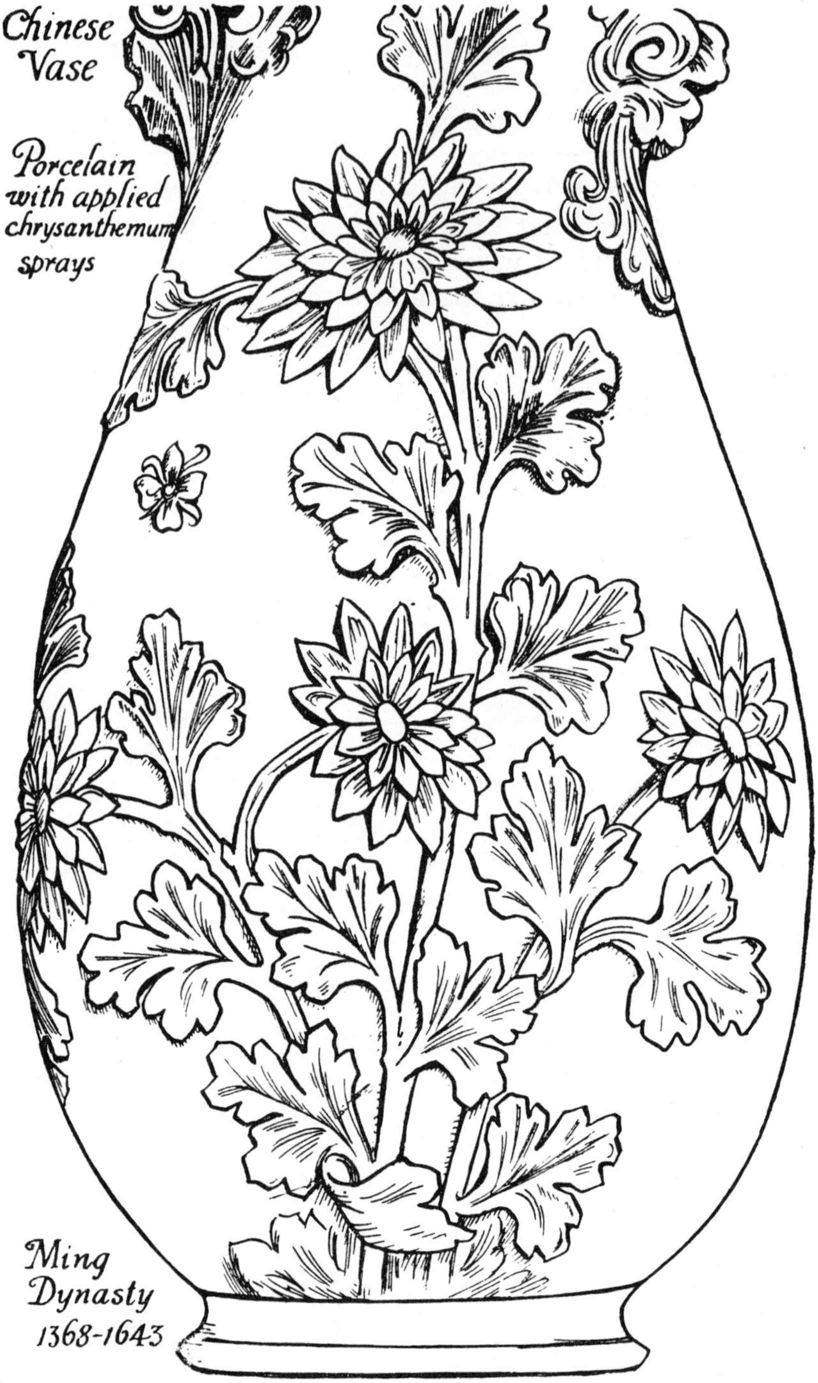

Chinese Vase

Porcelain with applied chrysanthemum sprays

Ming Dynasty 1368-1643

nearly always flow from the brain and fingers of the Chinese artist. In technical skill, too, they are the most perfect of craftsmen. They seem to attain a mastery over every process they employ, which is as scientific as it is artistic. Marco Polo, the Venetian traveller, in A.D. 1280 mentions Chinese pottery made for exportation. He also describes the care and foresight used in the preparation of the clay, saying that the Celestials piled it up in great heaps which were left exposed to the sun, wind and rain for periods of thirty or forty years. This beautiful blue and white ware, from which our specimens of magnolia and aster design in this chapter are taken, has always enjoyed great popularity among collectors in Europe. It was first brought to our part of the world by the Portuguese, then by the Dutch, who traded large quantities into Holland. Their Delft ware is closely imitative of the qualities of Chinese blue and white porcelain, but experts consider it a long way behind the latter in beauty of colour and surface. The French and English followed later, and their imports of this lovely pottery influenced the ceramic arts of both nations, especially our own eighteenth century productions, in no small degree.

Embroidery in silk and gold thread

Italian 17th cent.y Crown Imperial

It is said that the Chinese themselves compare the beautiful blue on their porcelain to the "blue of the sky after rain," and indeed this poetical and delicate compliment is fully justified. The "magnolia" and the "aster" designs may be compared together with advantage, one being decidedly naturalistic and the other extremely conventional —both qualities are often found side by side in Chinese decoration.

The poppies on the Chinese screen lean towards the naturalistic

SUNFLOWER

Iron Gates—
Italian, 17th century

plant drawing style, and with their delicate tints of pale flesh red in the flowers with mossy grey greens in the leaves on a black ground produce an unusual colour harmony. A few nature studies of the flower are given for comparison.

The Ming vase with chrysanthemum decoration represents another phase of Chinese ceramic art. In this piece the flower forms are modelled in relief and in the colouring more than one tint is used. The ground is a soft purple inclining to blue, while the leaves and flowers are mostly turquoise colour out of which peeps here and there a bit of pale buff softly gradated. The fragment of Italian embroidery is taken from one of those gorgeous ecclesiastical vestments which have been used for so many ages in the ceremonial of the Roman Church. Besides the flower shown in the illustration, the spaces are filled with iris, daffodil, tulip and other forms, but this is

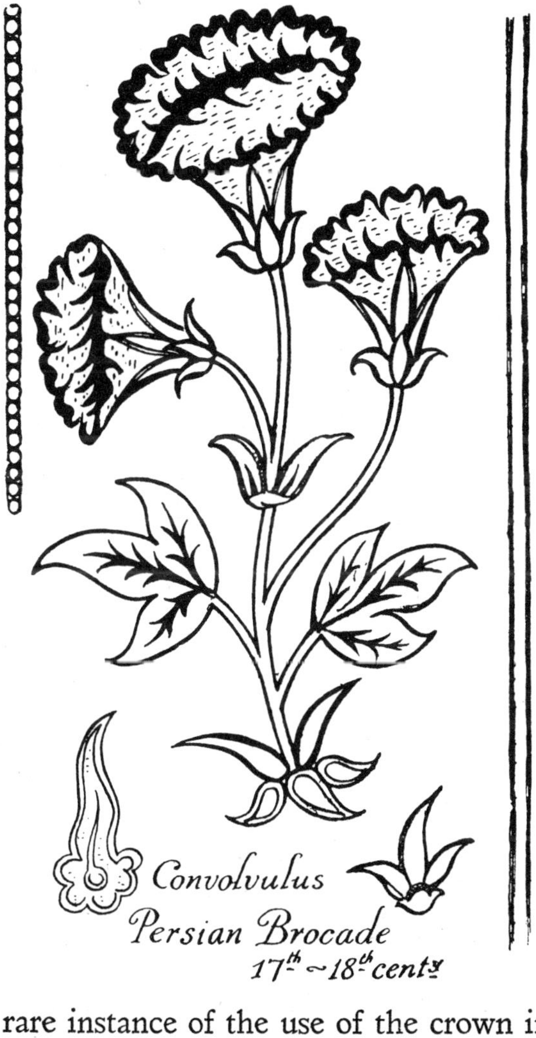

Convolvulus
Persian Brocade
17th–18th centy

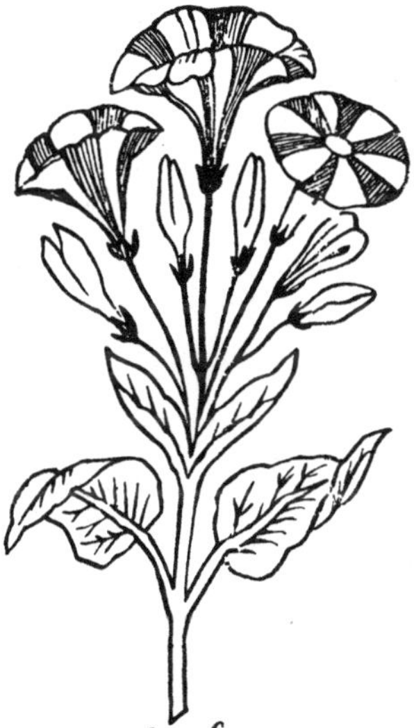

Convolvulus

a rare instance of the use of the crown imperial in decorative design. The conventional scrolls are mainly in gold thread, and the effect of the whole piece is as rich and resplendent as coloured silk and gold could make it.

The sunflower on the Italian iron gate is also an uncommon floral form in decoration. It is a fine shape and has such decorative qualities in arrangement of petals and seeds that it is strange to find it so little used in the past. The flowers and leaves in this example are gilded,

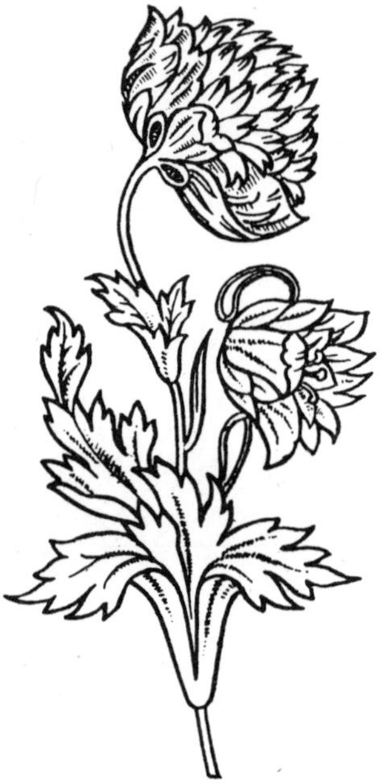

Persian Brocade
17*th*–18*th century*

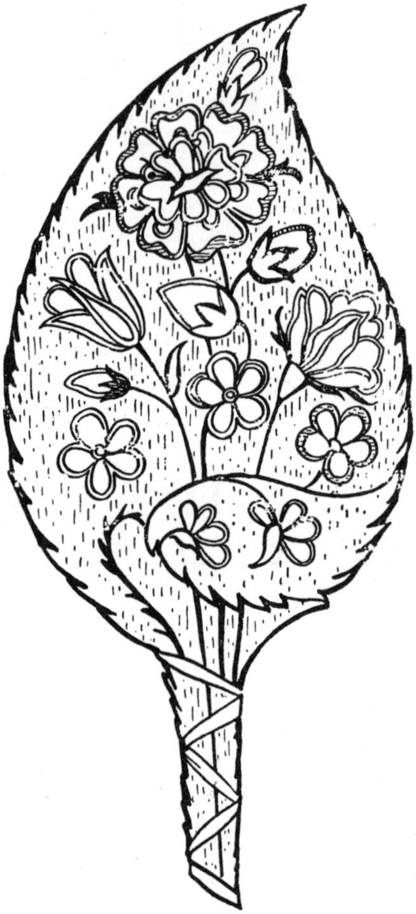

Detail—Persian Brocade—silk and metal thread—late 16*th century*

but the bars and scrolls remain black, making an agreeable contrast in colour and effect.

Two examples of the convolvulus from Persian brocades show that it is a flower which lends itself well to decorative effect, though very seldom used. The other two sprays I am unable to name, but they are very beautifully designed and drawn, and represent a side of Persian art less generally known than the carpets we are so well acquainted with. All these belong to the class of woven silk brocades, a material which gave the Persian artists a chance to show what they could do in delicacy of drawing and treatment. These three examples are all of them arranged in the original material as repeated sprays covering the surface an inch or two apart from each other. In grace and sweetness of feeling they would be hard to match in the arts of any other period or country, and I would that I could give in the illustrations the charm of the colour and surface of the material.

These small patterns were generally used on covers for cushions or small tablecloths, a square of brocade eighteen inches or two feet wide being first cut out and then a border added to it. The little borders are very happily designed, the Persian artists developing

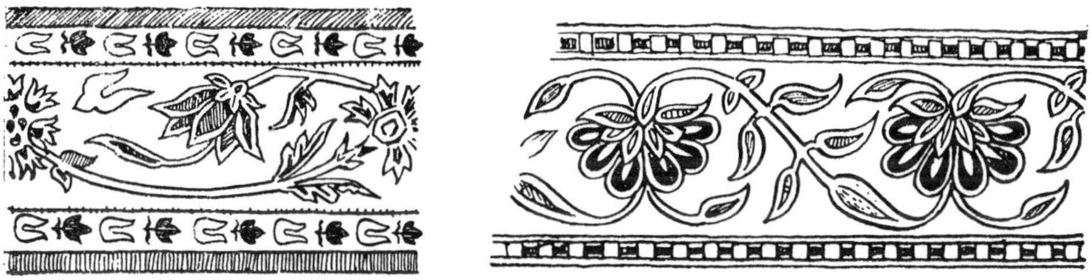

Persian brocade—17*th*–18*th century*

quite a distinct style in these alone. The fineness of the material in these silk brocades enabled them to do their best in beautiful plant drawing, yet they never forget to use their skill and knowledge "decoratively," and as decorative flower draughtsmen they are unsurpassed. (If I had a magic carpet of my own I think it would be a silken one and of Persian design.)

With the seventeenth century embroidered coverlet our journey ends and we are back in Old England again, though a century or two behind time. I have chosen to include it here because it contains the pansy, a flower we see very little of in decoration, though the reason why is hard to determine. This piece does not suffer from lack of variety; rose, pink, honeysuckle, pear and strawberry are to be found in it, while the mysterious bird of paradise, of a species unknown to naturalists, is perched on a conventional thistle, thus giving colour to the idea that he may be that fabled phœnix known beyond the Tweed as "Cock o' the North." Leaving this subtle point to individual

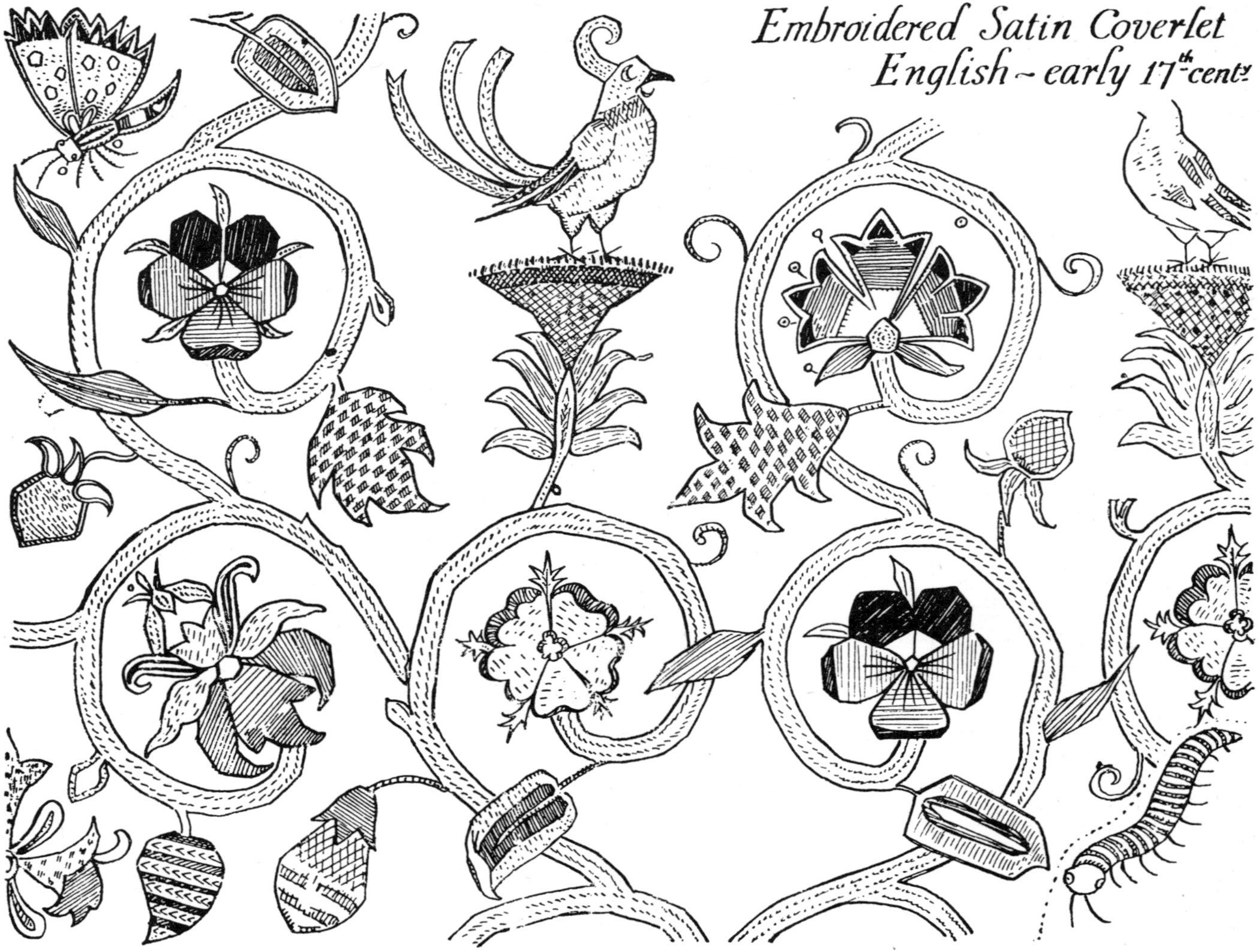

Embroidered Satin Coverlet
English – early 17th cent.

preferences, admitting at the same time that he makes a fine decorative item in the scheme, it will be noticed that butterflies and caterpillars also help to extend the range of interest. Some may object to their employment on a coverlet on the ground that they suggest bedfellows of a much more creepy nature, so here, again, "sentiment" has to be considered in conjunction with design. No one will deny, however, that they show considerable elaboration and invention in their rôle of decorative elements and parts of a harmonious *tout ensemble*.

Well, in closing this series of short chats on floral forms, I am bound to admit the difficulty of finding many more in the decoration of old times. Neither have I counted the number of flowers and plants we have passed in review, but it is quite obvious that in comparison with nature's infinite variety only a mere handful have been used. Surely this ought to encourage us, the heirs of all the ages, to help ourselves from the vast stores of material still left untouched, and if we do so by the guidance and aid of those splendid and worthy old artists and craftsmen whose work we have so much admired, we shall never really arrive at the end of floral forms in decoration.

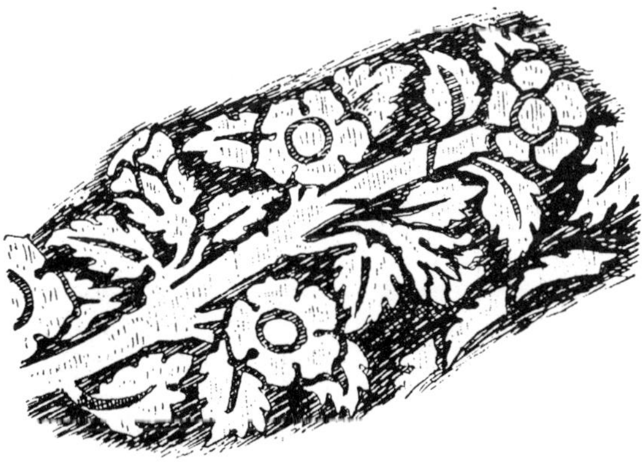

Chasuble—Florentine velvet, 15th century

INDEX

(Bold figures refer to illustrations, sometimes with text on same page; ordinary figures refer to text only.)

HERALDRY

FLORAL FORMS